Library Information Technology
AND
Networks

BOOKS IN LIBRARY AND INFORMATION SCIENCE

A Series of Monographs and Textbooks

1. Classified Library of Congress Subject Headings: Volume 1, Classified List, *edited by James G. Williams, Martha L. Manheimer, and Jay E. Daily*
2. Classified Library of Congress Subject Headings: Volume 2, Alphabetic List, *edited by James G. Williams, Martha L. Manheimer, and Jay E. Daily*
3. Organizing Nonprint Materials, *Jay E. Daily*
4. Computer-Based Chemical Information, *edited by Edward McC. Arnett and Allen Kent*
5. Style Manual: A Guide for the Preparation of Reports and Dissertations, *Martha L. Manheimer*
6. The Anatomy of Censorship, *Jay E. Daily*
7. Information Science: Search for Identity, *edited by Anthony Debons*
8. Resource Sharing in Libraries: Why · How · When · Next Action Steps, *edited by Allen Kent*
9. Reading the Russian Language: A Guide for Librarians and Other Professionals, *Rosalind Kent*
10. Statewide Computing Systems: Coordinating Academic Computer Planning, *edited by Charles Mosmann*
11. Using the Chemical Literature: A Practical Guide, *Henry M. Woodburn*
12. Cataloging and Classification: A Workbook, *Martha L. Manheimer*
13. Multi-media Indexes, Lists, and Review Sources: A Bibliographic Guide, *Thomas L. Hart, Mary Alice Hunt, and Blanche Woolls*
14. Document Retrieval Systems: Factors Affecting Search Time, *K. Leon Montgomery*
15. Library Automation Systems, *Stephen R. Salmon*
16. Black Literature Resources: Analysis and Organization, *Doris H. Clack*
17. Copyright–Information Technology–Public Policy: Part I–Copyright–Public Policies; Part II–Public Policies–Information Technology, *Nicholas Henry*
18. Crisis in Copyright, *William Z. Nasri*
19. Mental Health Information Systems: Design and Implementation, *David J. Kupfer, Michael S. Levine, and John A. Nelson*
20. Handbook of Library Regulations, *Marcy Murphy and Claude J. Johns, Jr.*
21. Library Resource Sharing, *Allen Kent and Thomas J. Galvin*
22. Computers in Newspaper Publishing: User-Oriented Systems, *Dineh Moghdam*
23. The On-Line Revolution in Libraries, *edited by Allen Kent and Thomas J. Galvin*
24. The Library as a Learning Service Center, *Patrick R. Penland and Aleyamma Mathai*
25. Using the Mathematical Literature: A Practical Guide, *Barbara Kirsch Schaefer*

26. Use of Library Materials: The University of Pittsburgh Study, *Allen Kent et al.*
27. The Structure and Governance of Library Networks, *edited by Allen Kent and Thomas J. Galvin*
28. The Development of Library Collections of Sound Recordings, *Frank W. Hoffmann*
29. Furnishing the Library Interior, *William S. Pierce*
30. Cataloging and Classification: A Workbook, Second Edition, Revised and Expanded, *Martha L. Manheimer*
31. Handbook of Computer-Aided Composition, *Arthus H. Phillips*
32. OCLC: Its Governance, Function, Financing, and Technology, *Albert F. Maruskin*
33. Scientific and Technical Information Resources, *Krishna Subramanyam*
34. An Author Index to Library of Congress Classification, Class P, Subclasses PN, PR, PS, PZ, General Literature, English and American Literature, Fiction in English, and Juvenile Belles Lettres, *Alan M. Greenberg*
35. Using the Biological Literature: A Practical Guide, *Elisabeth B. Davis*
36. An Introduction to Automated Literature Searching, *Elizabeth P. Hartner*
37. The Retrieval of Information in the Humanities and the Social Sciences: Problems as Aids to Learning, *edited by Thomas P. Slavens*
38. The Information Professional: Survey of an Emerging Field, *Anthony Debons, Donald W. King, Una Mansfield, and Donald L. Shirey*
39. Classified Library of Congress Subject Headings, Second Edition: Part A–Classified List; Part B–Alphabetic List, *edited by James G. Williams, Martha L. Manheimer, and Jay E. Daily*
40. Information Technology: Critical Choices for Library Decision-Makers, *edited by Allen Kent and Thomas J. Galvin*
41. Structure and Subject Interaction: Toward a Sociology of Knowledge in the Social Sciences, *Stephen Bulick*
42. World Librarianship: A Comparative Study, *Richard Krzys and Gaston Litton*
43. Guide to the Successful Thesis and Dissertation: Conception to Publication: A Handbook for Students and Faculty, *James E. Mauch and Jack W. Birch*
44. Physical Disability: An Annotated Literature Guide, *edited by Phyllis C. Self*
45. Effective Online Searching: A Basic Text, *Christine L. Borgman, Dineh Moghdam, and Patti K. Corbett*
46. Easy Access to DIALOG, ORBIT, and BRS, *Patricia J. Klingensmith and Elizabeth E. Duncan*
47. Subject and Information Analysis, *edited by Eleanor D. Dym*
48. Organizing Nonprint Materials: Second Edition, *Jay E. Daily*

49. An Introduction to Information Science, *Roger R. Flynn*
50. Designing Instruction for Library Users: A Practical Guide, *Marilla D. Svinicki and Barbara A. Schwartz*
51. Guide to the Successful Thesis and Dissertation: Conception to Publication: A Handbook for Students and Faculty, Second Edition, *James E. Mauch and Jack W. Birch*
52. The Retrieval of Information in the Humanities and the Social Sciences: Problems as Aids to Learning, Second Edition, *edited by Thomas P. Slavens*
53. Manheimer's Cataloging and Classification: A Workbook, Third Edition, Revised and Expanded, *Jerry D. Saye*
54. Electronic Printing and Publishing: The Document Processing Revolution, *Michael B. Spring*
55. Guide to the Successful Thesis and Dissertation: A Handbook for Students and Faculty, Third Edition, Revised and Expanded, *James E. Mauch and Jack W. Birch*
56. Library Information Technology and Networks, *Audrey N. Grosch*

ADDITIONAL VOLUMES IN PREPARATION

Library Information Technology and Networks

Audrey N. Grosch
University of Minnesota Libraries
Minneapolis, Minnesota

CRC Press
Taylor & Francis Group
Boca Raton London New York

CRC Press is an imprint of the
Taylor & Francis Group, an **informa** business

First published 1995 by Marcel Dekker

Published 2020 by CRC Press
Taylor & Francis Group
6000 Broken Sound Parkway NW, Suite 300
Boca Raton, FL 33487-2742

ISBN 13: 978-0-8247-8971-8 (hbk)

Visit the Taylor & Francis Web site at
http://www.taylorandfrancis.com

and the CRC Press Web site at
http://www.crcpress.com

Library of Congress Cataloging-in-Publication Data

Grosch, Audrey N.
Library information technology and networks / Audrey N. Grosch.
p. cm. — (Books in library and information science ; v. 56)
Includes bibliographical references and index.
ISBN 0-8247-8971-7
1. Libraries—United States—Data processing. 2. Library information networks—United States. I. Title. II. Series.
Z678.9.A4U64 1995
025'.00285—dc20 94-33628
CIP

To my loving husband, Charles, my AIS colleagues
and the faculty women of the University of Minnesota
who participated in the Rajendar Consent Decree.
I leave this as my last work in the field
in which I made my career.

PREFACE

This book started out as a revision of Stephen R. Salmon's *Library Automation Systems*. However, as work progressed, it became really a different book, one attempting to address current issues, with the past 25 years of historical background as a foundation.

The 1990's will be known as the decade of internetworking. The maturation of the integrated library automation system owes much to the development of the microcomputer, which has taken library automation along a very different path from when mainframe- and minicomputer-based systems prevailed. Bibliographic utilities and networks, particularly the Internet, have further shaped the use of information technology, especially since 1992. The 1990's have truly become the era of rapid cooperative and networking developments revolving around the Internet. Chapters 1–4 trace these important and ongoing developments.

Chapters 5–8 address frequently asked questions and the various stages of procuring and implementing systems in the library. They fill the need for a quick, single-source reference to give an overview of the various commercial system options available.

Just as it is useful to see where we are right now, it is interesting to see where we seem to be heading, especially since the whole concept of library automation now includes previously unimagined applications of new information technologies. Chapter 9 explores some of these likely trends.

This book should appeal to librarians, library and information science educators and institution administrators who need to have a broad continuing perspective of computer networking, database management and information delivery technologies, such as CD-ROM, as applied to library information services.

I want to thank the editors at Marcel Dekker, Inc., Henry Boehm specifically, for their patience and understanding over this long overdue work. Librarians Patricia Stark and Don Osier at the University of Minnesota Education and Psychology Library and Archivist Bruce H. Bruemmer of the Charles Babbage Institute Archives provided much valuable assistance during the preparation of this work. The staff of other university libraries—too numerous to mention—from time to time provided help and support as I spent time away from the office to complete the final drafts.

Audrey N. Grosch

CONTENTS

1

THE DECADE OF THE SEVENTIES

By a fiction as remarkable as any to be found in law, what has once been published, even though it be in the Russian language, is spoken of as "known", and it is often forgotten that the rediscovery in the library may be a more difficult and uncertain process than the first discovery in the laboratory.

— Lord Rayleigh, 1884

I. INTRODUCTION

This volume begins with a historical examination of automated library systems of the seventies, eighties and early nineties and the evolution of the functions that these systems were to provide. Stephen R. Salmon's *Library Automation Systems* (New York: Marcel Dekker, 1975) provides a classic reference to the prior historical periods, which are not within the scope of this volume.

Early library automation efforts were founded on the principle that library staff could improve their effectiveness and efficiency in serving their library users through application of current information technology. Prior to the seventies this meant the application of punched card–based systems using mechanical card-sorting and -tabulating equipment manufactured largely by IBM Corp. and represented by such devices as the IBM tabulating machines, which produced listings and could accumulate and total data in a specific set of columns on a punched card. These wire-board–programmed machines and tabulating systems were replaced by early stored-program computers such as the

IBM 1401/1410 systems. These early computers used punched cards for entry of programs and data, with magnetic tape a usual permanent storage form. Serial batch processing applications were used, as these systems had no interactive online capability, either through hardware or software in their operating systems. Their operating consoles in the computer room permitted computer operators to perform initial program loads of the operating system software and to do some job scheduling of the batch jobs as these facilities were added to basic operating system capabilities. From this basic premise that library automation should improve the operation and services of a library, it became evident through the experiences of libraries that some further principles emerged. These were:

1. Increasing the breadth of access to the libraries' collections and services since automation could provide portability to the library catalog
2. Improving the workflow in library technical processing together with improved book inventory control
3. Developing possible operating cost savings in one area to reallocate resources to other library service areas
4. Creating a more integrated functional perspective of managing a library to accommodate swings in funding and patron demand for new services
5. Using more standard bibliographic data, once early experiments showed the difficulty of developing systems without agreed-upon data definitions, as later embodied in the development of the MARC (Machine Readable Cataloging Record)
6. Fostering more interlibrary cooperative efforts designed to increase the breadth of a library's collection and its responsiveness to actual document delivery needs.

With the emergence of online interactive systems by the late seventies and the development of high-speed communications networks and the Internet by the late eighties, these early principles of library automation, while still valid, could be supplemented with additional new principles. These were:

1. Expanding the role of information technology beyond the traditional technical services and book inventory applications to encompass document imaging and full-text abstracting and indexing databases with broader and broader access by both librarians and users
2. Expanding the application of information technology to typical office automation functions made possible through desktop microcomputers
3. Extending the use of the desktop computer to the interactive device for delivery of bibliographic services via first local area network (LAN) connections and later wide area connections exemplified by the emergence of library catalogs and other electronic document collections on the Internet.

4. Viewing the library as an extended manager and provider of organized world knowledge independent of the physical format of the recorded knowledge, with increasing demands for electronically stored and accessed material making it necessary for libraries to develop strong, proactive institutional collaborative directions to develop these capabilities with vendors of automated library systems and institutional information technology infrastructures

As Lord Rayleigh observed, librarians have sought for years to improve their ability to provide information services. The development of the computer offered the promise of yet another, better technology to be applied to the information service enterprise. The decade of the sixties provided the opportunity for libraries to experiment with available batch processing computer technology. The decade of the seventies brought to light the following complexities:

1. The interrelationships between typical library computing applications
2. the need for more practical and affordable software and hardware
3. the need for standardization beyond that of the MARC format
4. the need for more generalized application software and improved ways to develop software to an operational and tested state
5. the need for collaborative development work, interlibrary cooperation and networking

If more widespread applications of data processing in the library and information center were to occur, these problem areas would require considerable attention from the profession.

The intent of this chapter is to review the trends, events and milestones in the seventies. This should provide a historical perspective from which to view current developments in computer applications to the library. I am concentrating on systems and not attempting to historically portray political or economic developments that may have played a lesser or greater role in nurturing the emergence of information technologies in particular settings. Without extensive risk taking and cost to develop library computer applications by a pioneering set of libraries, later commercial or cooperative network support might not have occurred when it did. Certainly, libraries through this period—and even to this day—could not justify their computer efforts on cost savings but rather had to justify them on planned service improvements to library users.

A. Major Trends

Library automation as a concept began with the task of applying first punched card equipment and later stored-program computer technology to improve library operations and management. Early work concentrated on such applications as printing catalog cards, creating book form catalogs, producing orders for purchasing and providing means to circulate materials from the collections. Most of these early systems were not visible to library users except when either using a library catalog or checking out materials.

With the coming of the seventies and improved mainframe computers such as the IBM 360/370 series, it became practical to think in terms of broader applications having increased functionality. Also, it became practical to move toward some online interactive capabilities within systems. The minicomputer facilitated this migration to interactive computing as these computers were initially built to serve real-time computing situations. As mainframe operating systems began to incorporate facilities for handling remote terminals, library systems designers began to use these facilities, first to upgrade existing batch systems and later to provide increasingly interactive input/output-based applications. Second-generation computers such as the IBM 1401, which was the mainstay of the sixties, really were not designed in their operating system software and device support for interactive processing, although several online experiments were carried out on these systems.

By 1975, with the advent of the minicomputer, the desirability and the necessity for library systems to be dynamic, real-time interactive systems was no longer conjecture. Interactive computing made it possible to seriously adopt the concept of a fully integrated multiple application system solution for performing library operations and services. The emergence of online bibliographic networks such as OCLC (Ohio College Library Center), UTLAS (University of Toronto Library Automation System), and RLG/RLIN (Research Libraries Group/Resrearch Libraries Information System), together with the pioneer work performed through individual institution systems such as Northwestern University's NOTIS and Stanford University's BALLOTS, the era of online systems for performing library applications was on its way to becoming the accepted and standard technology. Moreover, developments in interactive database searching through commercial vendors, such as SDC and BRS, fostered increased interest in bringing the same immediacy and power of information processing to the library's local information base.

By the mid to late 1970's, the emergence of vendor interest in developing software for performing library operations coupled with the lessening of research grant funding had made library administrators begin to think in terms of procuring and installing commercially available software rather than beginning their own development efforts. By the end of the decade, institutions that had done their own development increasingly began to examine alternatives for successor systems that would obviate the need for large in-house technical staff and the time and fiscal uncertainties connected with software development. Lower-cost hardware, e.g., the minicomputer, and increasingly intelligent peripherals, e.g., the microprocessor-based display terminal, and a sufficiently

IBM 360/50 mainframe computer.

IBM 1401 computer, a successful host for early automated library tasks. Shown with card reader/sorter and line printer.

large market base interested potential vendors to invest in software development for the library market. As Jesse Shera stated, "There are fashions, then, in librarianship as in clothes, and their virtues and idiosyncracies are debated with equal heat, and often with as little intelligence." (1)

Let us examine these automation fashions of the seventies in more detail through the major systems efforts that brought to light a basis of knowledge which permitted the evolution of systems designed to provide computer assistance for major library tasks.

B. Changing Attitudes in the Profession

In 1965, Paul Wasserman conducted a questionnaire-based study of library automation in which 50% of the respondents expressed concern with the need to introduce machine procedures but were unable to start any program because of a variety of reasons. The second group of respondents were either not convinced that applying computer technology was desirable or were decidedly of the opinion that computer technology would not improve libraries in any way. Only 20% of the respondents had taken any action at all to explore use of the data processing. (2)

Contrast this to the Library Automation Research and Consulting (LARC) survey, which showed 2,000 library automation projects in all types of libraries by 1968 and estimated that there were some 20,000 library automation projects under way in the world by 1973. (3)

Although this estimate might have been somewhat high, given that information about developments in many countries are difficult to determine, it is obvious that skepticism about applying computer technology decreased throughout the decade. Consequently, application of the computer to the library's operations and services became a question of the approach to take and the rationalization of the cost reductions and benefits to be obtained. Early in the period, it was still believed by many librarians that long term cost savings could result from computerization. In certain operations, such as cataloging, lower per-unit costs could be achieved by libraries using the OCLC system as OCLC's database grew in number and quality of records; however, computerization did not always yield true savings, as start-up and production costs of creating alternative forms of a public catalog on microfilm or in printed book form were not always lower than the cost of maintaining a catalog in card form, particularly for the small to medium-size library.

The emphasis on the development of individual institution systems focussed on the broad application areas, but within the context of a future goal of an integrated multifunctional system. Since the necessity for data standardization had emerged, but much standardization work still remained on both bibliographic and operational forms of data, it was both difficult and impractical to achieve any greater degree of system integration at a more rapid rate than was actually realized during the seventies. Although some institutions were conceiving of library automation systems as multiple application subsystems where there is an integration of both database and system functions, the reality was that institutions were concentrating their efforts on developing distinct operational applications, e.g., acquisitions, cataloging, serials management and circulation. In contrast to the previous decade, these were viewed in a somewhat broader light, in that more subfunctions or directly related printed output products were conceived. Throughout the 1970's, library automation was still viewed primarily as the application of the computer to the operational tasks necessary to provide the information services offered by the library. Only occasionally did there emerge the concept of library automation as the application of electronic technologies to office operations, services and knowledge systems themselves.

Perhaps the single most significant occurrence that fostered library cooperation and also pushed the Library of Congress ultimately to take a serious interest in leading the library networking initiatives a few years later was the amendment of the OCLC Articles of Incorporation on May 17, 1972 which permitted nonacademic libraries in Ohio to join OCLC. ("OCLC" originally stood for Ohio College Library Center; it now stands for Online Computer Library Center.) This opened the door to widening the infant OCLC online system to cooperative agreements with five regional library networks outside of Ohio: Pittsburgh Regional Library Center (PRLC), Union Library Catalog of Pennsylvania (ULC), Five Associated University Libraries (FAUL), New England Library Information Network (NELINET) and Cooperative College Library Center (CCLC). By 1975, OCLC had grown to over 500 participating libraries. By the end of the decade over 2,000 academic, research, public and special libraries were members.

With the establishment of the National Commission on Libraries and Information Science (NCLIS) in 1970, the movement to wield a national-level coordinated network of library resources began. On April 17–20, 1974 the National Science Foundation and Council on Library Resources jointly sponsored the Conference on National Bibliographic Control. This conference grew into the Advisory Group on National Bibliographic Control, which formed a number of working parties to address major issues on formats and authorities. The Library of Congress, in 1976, created the Network Development Office (NDO), with Henriette Avram as its chief. This truly signaled that Library of Congress was prepared to take a leadership role in applying networking technology to build a more cohesive library services program. Leading lights of networking were invited to the Library of Congress later in 1976. This group became known as the Network Advisory Group (NAG). NAG recommended the creation of a technical task force to design the network architecture. After some 12 months, Librarian of Congress Daniel J. Boorstin created the Network Advisory Committee (NAC) from the informal NAG group plus new members. This group in turn formed the Network Technical Architecture Group (NTAG) which worked with the Network Development Office (NDO), Council on Library Resources (CLR) and National Commission on Libraries and Information Sciences (NCLIS) to create a system of national-level network planning.

Meanwhile, in 1975, NCLIS had appointed the Task Force on a National Periodicals System, which worked with Vernon E. Palmour in a staff capacity. They issued a study that proposed a three level network where individual libraries, state and regional networks composed level one, where user requests would first arrive at the local library and be passed to these networks as appropriate. (4) Level two constituted the National Periodicals Center and level three would be the Library of Congress and certain specified backup collections. The Library of Congress would coordinate access to strong collections that would act in a backup role, while the National Periodicals Center would establish comprehensive collections except for agriculture and medicine. Obviously, such a plan required suitable interactive computer support and serials databases for performing item location and request-switching tasks. A following study fleshed out the National Periodicals Center. (5) Since the plan for such a center generated considerable discussion over alternatives, NCLIS requested Arthur D. Little, Inc., to perform a techno-economic analysis of three alternatives to providing access to retrospective serials holdings. (6)

II. SERIALS SYSTEMS

The pioneering system at the University of California, San Diego, became the pattern for the batch and early online systems developed in the early seventies. (7) Washington University School of Medicine Library's PHILSOM system, in its role as a system for a network of medical libraries, had the most far-reaching impact since the number of libraries involved would serve to test the functionality of the system to a degree that could not be found in a system used by a single library. Millard Johnson, a key developer of PHILSOM, in a paper presented at the LARC Institute on Automated Serials Systems in 1973, pointed out that he expected the current PHILSOM II batch system to be virtually obsolete by 1976. (8) His design strategy for Philsom III was predicated on a minicomputer as host. (9)

At the University of Minnesota Bio-Medical Library, considerable investigation and development was undertaken to again improve on batch mode serials management. The system developed there, which remained in operation until the mid-seventies, used a more involved manner of predicting expected arrivals in an attempt to better the check-in and claiming function. (10,11) This system was replaced by an interactive online serials system that did not incorporate any arrival prediction as the first application component to its grant-funded minicomputer development system. However, the conceptual work on prediction and on handling serials holdings statements was to serve as a basis for other investigators developing techniques for later serials systems. (12,13)

Another significant batch serial system was the New York State Library (NYSL) system, described by Pan. (14) Although Laval University in Quebec had used online technology in its system, record access was limited and required looking up an identification number in a printout in order to bring up the correct serial record. There was little experience in developing online systems generally, and more specifically for serials. The seminal development for online serials appeared in the mid-1970's when the University of California, Los Angeles, redesigned its batch-mode serials system into the first significant online interactive system in the United States.

The check-in list approach used in the University of Minnesota Bio-Medical Library batch mode serials system was adopted by NYSL. The prediction for arrival was the expected due date plus a lag factor determined through experience with the particular publication in which the lag factor equalled the date of receipt minus the publication date on the piece divided by the number of receipts. For example, suppose that the following issues of a title were received:

Date of receipt	Publication date	Lag
January 15, 1973	January 1, 1973	14
April 6, 1973	April 1, 1973	5
July 13, 1973	July 1, 1973	12
October 1, 1973	October 1, 1973	0
	Total	31

Divide 31 by 4 and the result is 7.75. With rounding this produces a lag factor of 8 for a specific title.

Although the NYSL system was primarily a periodicals control system rather than a bibliographic system, the data conversion for 10,000 active titles took some 41.5 person years of effort. However, similar levels of effort had been expended by many libraries that had produced union list printouts, using brief bibliographic data and summary holdings data up to this period. The report by Pan shows the richness of this system in the generation of output, including handling cross-references, claim forms and a KWIC index to the serials collection.

The UCLA Bio-Medical Library interactive online serials management system was developed under support from a National Library of Medicine (NLM) grant. It was the initial system in the United States to provide interactive data entry, updating and retrieval functions—the Laval University system was only partially interactive. Since NLM had begun its own efforts to develop a serials database in its SERLINE online database, wherein medical library holding symbols were included, it was logical that NLM support corollary efforts in computer applications in serials. SERLINE's goal was not to be a serials management system, but rather to be the information source to support interlibrary lending among its Regional Medical Library Network.

The UCLA Biomedical Library interactive serials management system was built on the former batch system and used an alphabetic sequential file. Programmed in PL/1 and operating on an IBM host computer, it provided online data entry via a visual display terminal, thereby replacing punched card input. It also provided a virtually simultaneous updating of the records and indexes in the files. Various access listings were produced by the system, but later in the project, library users could enter searches on a visual display terminal. As a result of this rapid file updating, users received the most current location and holdings information possible. Using IBM 2260 terminals, a general search program provided for access by one or more title words, subject, language, country, serial number and an assignable search code. (15,16,17) The relative success of this system pointed the way toward interactive systems, using MARC-compatible data formats and encompassing a wide variety of features necessary to the functioning of the serials department of a library. While UCLA's system provided considerable sophistication for serial arrival prediction, Northwestern's NOTIS system took the opposite, Kardex-like approach, providing operator-supplied action dates to alert for an issue claim or an expected arrival. (18)

Two other development paths emerged in the seventies with respect to serials automation. With the development and publication of the MARC serials format in preliminary edition in 1970 and first edition in 1974, considerable interest was being expressed by numerous libraries in developing as large a MARC serials database as was possible. The purpose of this database would be to supply records for individual institution serials records conversion and for production of various union lists. Up through the early seventies, union lists of serials were modelled largely on Gregory's Union List of Serials with brief bibliographic data and summary or open-ended holdings information. Moreover, library locations were usually institution-level locations and not specific at the physical collection level. Consequently, such tools, although simplifying somewhat the interlibrary loan function, were not the best tools that might have been produced, given the computer technology available. Local and regional networks providing document delivery services needed as specific holdings and location data as possible.

For example, at the University of Minnesota Libraries, the MINITEX network and the University Libraries were both interested in developing a union list of serials that would contain enriched bibliographic, holdings and location information. Moreover, the conception of this union list would be to eventually include MINITEX member libraries and possibly other libraries in adjoining states that were not being served by other networks. Thus, jointly sponsored, the Minnesota Union List of Serials (MULS) started in development in 1971, with a batch-processed suite of COBOL programs that implemented the MARC serials format as it had been defined in its preliminary edition, with a few local enhancements that were only later added in Addendum No. 1 to the serials format, such as the use of an indicator for filing omission in 1xx or 2xx main-entry variable fields. However, the subject heading tags 6xx were omitted.

The finished product was produced as a photocomposed and bound catalog, using a vendor's Harris Fototronic CRT composition system and IBM 370/145 computer system for processing the MULS MARC magnetic tape into the photocomposition driver tape. The full MARC character set and considerable typographic variation produced a finished product of excellent readability. The Preliminary edition contained 37,289 titles and 22,000 cross-references which were linked to their parent records to avoid blind cross-references. By 1973, the MULS file included the Minneapolis Public Library, ten Minnesota State Agency Libraries, the Minnesota Historical Society Library and eight private college libraries in Minnesota. (19) A new system programmed in PL/1 on an IBM 370 system that used data compression algorithms and an improved file structure, but still a batch system was used to produce several subsequent editions until the data was loaded into the OCLC system. Although MULS departed from MARC in a few respects, such as not using the indicators except for the filing omit and not incorporating any subject headings, the task of reconciling superimposed and de-superimposed main entries and permitting both forms to coexist created usable data, at least until the Library of Congress could provide a large volume of full serials MARC records. The serials MARC record service of the Library of Congress; however, at the time of completion of the Preliminary edition of MULS had produced a file of only approximately 2,000 records.

Consequently, the University of Minnesota, along with other libraries in states actively creating union lists, such as Florida and Indiana, was concerned with the rate of serials MARC record production. In late 1972, I was visited by Richard Anable of York University Libraries, who was engaged in a joint study with the National Library of Canada regarding the problems associated with machine-readable serials files. During that visit the idea of assembling a wider group of interested librarians over the problems of building MARC machine-readable serials records was developed. Anable went on to coordinate this idea and at the American Library Association conference in Las Vegas on June 26, 1973 an informal gathering of interested parties took place. (20) The meeting had been scheduled and publicized through informal means. It was felt that some 10 institutions might share this concern since it was known that the then current union list projects under way involved such a number of institutions. However, 25 people representing 20 institutions on the national (United States and Canada), regional and local levels attended.

This group felt that something should be done about the lack of communication among generators of machine-readable serials files, the incompatibilities of the various formats, their bibliographic data integrity and format and the confusion about existing and proposed bibliographic description standards. The group did not wish to duplicate any work being carried out by other ALA committees but sensed that none of these groups was looking at the overall picture. At this meeting it was decided that the group would constitute itself as the "Ad Hoc Discussion Group on Serials Data Bases" and schedule some further meetings. Cynthia Pugsley of the University of Waterloo, Richard Anable of York University and Jay Cunningham of the University of California University-wide Library Automation Program drafted a position paper. This paper was circulated the following month to the meeting attendees along with the minutes of the discussion. A steering committee was arbitrarily selected with representatives from the Council on Library Resources, Northwestern University, the State University of New York (SUNY), the Canadian Union Catalogue Taskgroup and its Subgroup on the Serials Union List, the University of California, the Association of Research Libraries, the Joint Committee on the Union List of Serials, OCLC, National Serials Data Program, the Library of Congress, the National Library of Canada, Laval University, International Serials Data System/Canada, and an observer from the British Library.

The Council on Library Resources funded a meeting of this steering group on September 21, 1973 at York University. The group wanted to establish mechanisms to create a set of agreed-upon practices for converting and communicating serials data in machine-readable form for cooperatively converting a comprehensive retrospective bibliographic database of serials records. At that meeting, four subcommittees were appointed and the Holding Statement Notation Committee was charged with preparing the agreed-upon practices document and to report at the next Ad Hoc Discussion Group meeting scheduled for October 22 at the American Society for Information Science Annual meeting in Los Angeles. However, prior to that meeting three of the four subcommittees met briefly at the Library of Congress on October 10,and the Cooperative Conversion Subcommittee recommended that a proposal for a cooperative conversion project be prepared as soon as possible and that OCLC be the conversion vehicle for the project.

Thus was born the project called CONSER (Cooperative CONversion of SERials). It came to be the singular serials cooperative project. Its full impact was not felt until several years after its beginning when the database had undergone sufficient authentication by the Library of Congress, National Serials Data Program and the National Library of Canada and ISDS/Canada to provide authoritative bibliographic data to actually constitute the national retrospective serials database for the United States and Canada. The Group believed that the project should start out by building on a foundation of one or more existing serials databases.

The MULS database became the major initial candidate since it was the largest in MARC format. It also was the richest in the amount of bibliographic data. However, there was no perfect database for the objective since all had observed differing standards, forms of entry, holdings notations and variant machine record formats. In order to prepare librarians to think in large terms about the work facing such a cooperative undertaking, I prepared a paper for the Ad Hoc Discussion Group which proposed a regional serials program under the auspices of the National Serials Data Program. The paper also served to identify responsibilities of NSDP, national libraries, regional centers and local libraries in order to foster discussion of the overall problem of serials bibliographic resources. (21) The Council on Library Resources provided the funding for the CONSER project and assumed management of it. (22) The MULS database and LC MARC serials records constituted the first database, and then the Pittsburgh Regional Library Center file was added as were additional large union list databases. Loading of the MULS file at OCLC did not proceed without problems and much of the original tagging structure of notes and cross reference data was not preserved; as a result many initial CONSER participants and others seeing these records believed them not of very high quality. However, those who had seen the original MULS database knew that this was a case of a "much was lost in translation" situation. The decision to use MULS as the initial file had been arrived at quite carefully through the work described below.

Prior to the decision to use the MULS database as the initial file to be loaded on the OCLC system for the initiation of CONSER input by the nine libraries that agreed to contribute records, the National Serials Data Program sponsored an investigation of what would be involved in converting the MULS file to NSDP requirements. (23) This study showed that it would be possible to convert MULS to such a format and demonstrated the degree to which MULS met the MARC serials communications format,which differed in some respects from the internal MARC processing format used by NSDP.

By 1976 CONSER was in full operation at the Library of Congress. Some dozen libraries were participating. By the end of the decade there were over 200,000 serials records in the database. The CONSER Edition of the MARC Serials Editing Guide served as the input guide for the project. (24) Since the vehicle used to create the CONSER database was the OCLC system, there remained the problem of record distribution from the CONSER database. The Library of Congress had no mechanism in place for any timely systematic distribution of these records. In 1979 over half of them were available only through OCLC. In December 1979, a snapshot record dump of the CONSER file was delivered to the Library of Congress and this was made available for a fee. (25) In the minds of many librarians, this was a poor substitute for a systematic and regular distribution service, much needed owing to the strictures connected with OCLC's databases and their requirement that participants perform all of their cataloging on OCLC.

In examining the literature of the decade it appears that several hundred libraries initiated their own serials automation programs, many concentrating on producing locating lists of holdings, some concentrating on the more complex aspects of such systems as outlined here and others doing pieces of the serials management application such as binding control and slip printing, routing of periodicals, duplicating simple Kardex methods of check-in or keeping track of serials subscription expirations and orders. Typical of these systems was the work reported by Collins and West. (26) Richard DeGennaro very lucidly stated the case for the use of minicomputer technology to offer libraries a much-needed serials management system. Ideally he saw this serials management system implemented as a component to an integrated system. In the alternative he saw that even a discrete system would go far toward improving both library processing and user services involving serial publications. (27) Yet, at the same time, there were serials librarians who were urging caution in adopting computer-based systems for serials management. Their contention was that a well-managed manual system would produce equally reliable control over serials receipts. They maintained that the issues of control or size of file were not in themselves reason enough to use a computer-based system. (28) While there is truth to this view, sometimes the mere effort needed to reorganize for an automated system when coupled with a large active collection will create long-term improvements. This assumes that the institution is able to manage such an undertaking well.

Finally, another substantial development in serials management deserves our attention. This was the implementation of the serials subsystem of OCLC in late 1976. Although during its decade of life only a small number of OCLC member libraries actually implemented the subsystem, with the related CONSER activity hosted at OCLC, the subsystem assumed importance. It also served to point out many design weaknesses in a networked system. Where the PHILSOM system was a relatively successful network serials management system for its medical library members, the OCLC system was borne out of one of the common beliefs of the early seventies: that bibliographic utilities could provide a solution to all aspects of a local library's automation needs. Many library administrators of the period felt that the network approach was more desirable than library applications to be served through distributed systems using local mainframe or minicomputer hosts. However, more technically astute librarians and many systems specialists believed that implementing such network-based systems would place a transaction processing load of considerable magnitude on the already barely acceptable response time found in typical time-shared computer networks. Also, if the majority of members elected to participate, the individual files for the large numbers of OCLC members would cause a substantial increase in direct access storage devices and central computer system growth. The Fall 1978 issue of *The Serials Librarian* was devoted to reporting the experiences of two of the early serials subsystem users and of one library carefully weighing the issue of use of this subsystem. Central Michigan University and Kent State University implemented the subsystem, whereas the University of Illinois at Champaign/Urbana decided against implementing it, preferring instead to concentrate on the cataloging subsystem. Illinois was worried that response time and cost were a problem as well as the retrospective conversion magnitude for holdings and check-in subscription data. (29)

The above libraries that implemented the serials subsystem soon found that this application did not provide as optimal a solution as they had hoped. Record retrieval time remained a concern throughout the decade this subsystem operated. Peculiarities of handling multiple part issues, weeklies and other arrival prediction problems brought more check-in and claiming problems to the surface. No binding module was implemented and this posed a problem for some libraries. Inevitably, with the advent of the microcomputer in the early eighties, OCLC adopted a new philosophy to complement its emerging minicomputer-based system. This was to design and implement microcomputer-based solutions where the OCLC workstation would assume a distributed function, sharing the processing with the OCLC host system to download data to the microcomputer for use in the micro-based Enhancer software.

Finally, in 1988, OCLC announced the demise of its host serials subsystem and the migration to its OCLC SC350 serials management system for the OCLC workstation. This system was developed for OCLC by Meta Micro Library Systems, which earlier in the seventies developed an excellent serials management system using a Southwest Technical Products S100 bus microcomputer as the host system. Therefore, this firm had considerable experience successfully implementing technologically mature software for library applications using microcomputer technology. Had all OCLC members chosen to use the serials subsystem, OCLC's host systems probably would have had to experience growth barely possible for the technology of the time to support. Even then, the system would not have had the flexibility desirable for this application. This flexibility could be built in more easily in dedicated systems using mini- or microcomputer hosts. Blackwell's PERLINE was to demonstrate this very well in the early eighties.

The interest of vendors supplying computer-based solutions to library operations emerged by the middle of the seventies. Initially vendors concentrated on circulation applications using the newly emerging class of computers known as minicomputers. It was not until the early 1980's that commercially supported serials management systems emerged. Moreover, when one examines currently offered "integrated library systems," the serials automation application is still usually the least functional or sometimes missing major components such as bindery preparation. In some cases no serials management support is provided except for bibliographic and holdings data for the purposes of the online catalog.

It is hoped that this background covering the development progression in the serials area may help explain why most of our present vendor-based integrated systems still need improvement.

III. ACQUISITIONS SYSTEMS

During the early 1970's, numerous acquisitions systems were designed and installed, most of which were batch processed. These systems, for the most part, were designed to prepare purchase orders for materials or print claims as required through either some default time period controlled by the vendor specified or by an action date on the order. They also maintained a file of items on order, claimed, received, received and not yet cataloged or cancelled. Most also included a fund accounting module and used a vendor file to supply pertinent information for generating output for the vendor. Some systems also kept track of vendor performance, linking such information to the vendor file. Most of these systems had their initial record entry built at the time of order of the material. A few systems, such as the University of Minnesota Bio-Medical Library's acquisition system, initiated record input of items being considered for purchase, so as to alert staff to items already recommended or deemed suitable for the collections. The concept of the in-process list, borne in the systems design work done in the sixties at the University of Illinois, Chicago Circle Campus Library, was virtually universally adopted in these systems.

Typical of the batch mode acquisitions systems was Arizona State University Library's Library Acquisitions Information System (LAIS), which operated in batch mode on a UNIVAC 1110 and was written by Bruce Alper originally for Florida Atlantic University for an IBM 360/40 in COBOL. (30) Some 43 programs were involved in the LAIS system, with punched cards used as the input medium. Also characteristic of these systems was their use of abbreviated bibliographic information. Consequently, it was rare to find a batch-mode acquisitions system that integrated with an actual cataloging system, owing to both the brief records and non-MARC format-defined data elements or record structure.

The acquisitions realm also attracted early vendor interest in providing computer support to libraries. Baker and Taylor's BATAB (Baker and Taylor's Automated Buying System for Libraries) was the first vendor entry. (31) This suite of COBOL programs was in rather wide use in the early seventies by university, public, school and cooperative library systems. It provided batch computer support for selection lists, automatic purchase order production to any vendor, open order control and claiming, acquisitions fund accounting and various statistics. Historical acquisitions data reports also formed part of this system. The system was offered through an initial installation/training charge but did not involve any further license or usage charges, although Baker and Taylor continued to provide software support. BATAB produced paper order forms for all vendors except Baker and Taylor, whose orders were output to magnetic tape, thereby becoming the input to Baker and Taylor's own order management system. Such a magnetic tape system was the precursor to the machine readable transfer of orders now possible using the BISAC (Book Industry Standard Acquisitions) formats by some current integrated library systems.

One of the most sophisticated and early online acquisitions systems was developed at Oregon State University Library and called LOLITA. (32) This system used a Control Data computer as its host processor and provided interactive input and file updating so that in-process, item and fund status were always current. It also provided rather elaborate vendor statistics and a full set of reports of system activity.

Special libraries were active in developing online systems also. Notable among these was the Bell Laboratories BELLTIP system which provided, initially through a Honeywell 6000 mainframe and later through an IBM 370, an integrated acquisitions, fund accounting and cataloging system. (33) Implementation of this system also included conversion of the Bell Laboratories Libraries retrospective catalog records into a simplified MARC-based record. GE Terminet 30 teleprinter terminals were initially used for access through the Bell Laboratories Time Sharing System. This made it possible for all libraries in the network to be a part of the union catalog. It made obsolete the card catalogs at each site and generally improved the time to process orders and receive materials.

Automating acquisitions was similar to automating other nonlibrary order-processing applications and, in comparison to serials, was more easily accomplished in the individual institution. By the middle of the decade it was apparent that this function was a key component to an integrated library system and specifically to an integrated technical processing environment. This was demonstrated by the Washington Library Network, which by early in the decade had proceeded to incorporate an acquisitions function having a very high degree of functional richness into its services to its members. (34,35)

Similarly, Project BALLOTS (Bibliographic Automation of Large Library Operations Using Time Shared Systems) also was developing, in a parallel time frame, the most intricate and option laden integrated technical processing system for use by Stanford University Libraries. (36) The system incorporated acquisitions and a full cataloging system. BALLOTS also was significant in that its implementation, much like that of WLN depended upon the use of a database management system at its heart. WLN used ADABAS to implement its system while BALLOTS used a Stanford system developed on another project and known as SPIRES (Stanford Public Information Retrieval). Both of these systems also involved sizeable development teams and the use of new systems development methodologies just coming into vogue in the data processing field in the late sixties.

OCLC also placed into operation an acquisitions subsystem as part of its Technical Processing System so that libraries could initiate orders and claims. The system maintained in-process status on the record. Finally it would generate cataloging information to produce a catalog in final form, usually as a card catalog, but increasingly as a microfilm-based catalog from magnetic tape records of the individual institutions. These latter magnetic tape records continued to assume increasing importance to OCLC member libraries as these records would be the foundation of local library databases. These history tape records preserved the local customization and field data, which was not a part of the actual online record the OCLC libraries would see in searching the OCLC databases. The emerging Canadian network built around the University of Toronto Library Automation System (UTLAS), maintained online the actual customized record for each of its participating libraries in their own database. Later in the decade, with the founding of the Research Libraries Group and its selection of the BALLOTS software to form its Research Libraries Information Network (RLIN), this latter approach would also be employed but using a different record storage technique.

Increasingly through the decade, the impetus for automated services was being led by developments at the bibliographic utilities, most notably OCLC. However, as OCLC moved ahead with its own vision of shared network facilities as the manner in which libraries could lower their per-unit processing costs, library automation specialists began to see that the heavy communications and processor demands of such transaction processing systems would not be, in the long term, the most desirable way to apply the computer to such individual in-library processes as serials management, acquisitions, circulation or a public online catalog. It became increasingly clear that a mix of automation approaches would be needed to address the local demands for more responsive and comprehensive functional systems coupled with the regional and national needs to increase resource sharing, shared cataloging and interlibrary loan processing.

IV. CIRCULATION SYSTEMS

Circulation systems were one of the earliest examples of applying data-processing technology since the advent of the punched card. Typically, most automated circulation systems in the early decade were batch mode file updating systems, where the transaction recording for charging and discharging was performed online. Punched card and punched plastic badges were used to provide book and borrower data, which was written out to a magnetic tape. The Mohawk 4401C Data Input station which attached to a Mohawk 4406A controller for a Mohawk 4411 magnetic tape drive was one common system. Another common system was the IBM 357 Data Collection System. The resultant magnetic tapes of charges and discharges were processed by a mainframe computer overnight. Nightly listings of circulating items were produced for the next day's circulation desk use. Similarly, the host computer produced overdue notices, recall notices and bills for lost materials. The Health Sciences Library at the University of New Mexico used one such system. (37) A number of libraries by the mid-seventies had installed circulation systems using smaller computers such as the IBM System 7. The University of Pennsylvania was an example of such a system. (38) In the Pennsylvania system, which used punched card and badge reading terminals, the System 7 acted as an online data collection system. The System 7 then uploaded the daily transaction file to an IBM 370/168 host computer, where batch master file updating was performed. These programs were developed jointly with IBM and were available through IBM as Field Developed Programs.

A few libraries, such as the University of Michigan. were using the Singer System 10, one of the early vendor-supplied systems using a minicomputer with online data collection and limited interactive functionality. With the advent of some research projects using minicomputers which had commenced around 1972, it became increasingly demonstrated to commercial systems developers that there would be a market for circulation systems that would improve these batch mode, card/badge-driven systems typical of the sixties. In England, Plessey Systems, Ltd., had entered the market with a hand-held light pen scanning device able to read labels with codes printed as bars of varying widths, wherein the code was the white space between these bars. Using such a device would make unnecessary the punching of book cards or the placement of pockets in the books. It would also simplify and lower the cost of the patron identification badge or card.

The need for an improved data collection device for circulation automation was recognized as part of the University of Chicago Library's project to develop an integrated library system. It approached a commercial vendor to design an improved circulation terminal, but the vendor did not complete the design. Turning to its own institution's Enrico Fermi Institute electronics shop, the library had 25 of these terminals designed and built at a manufacturing cost of $1,794 each. This device was known as the JRL 1000 circulation terminal. It incorporated a hand-held light pen scanner, a 31-column alphanumeric printer and a custom interface to a visual display terminal and keyboard. (39) This terminal was later manufactured and used in several other commercially marketed systems. The JRL 1000's significance was to demonstrate that a better alternative could be found to speedier, lower cost and more reliable data collection for circulation systems then being designed as fully interactive, with real-time updating of files.

With the desire for an improved computer-based circulation system, the prospect of using the emerging new class of small, typically 16-bit-word-length computers, known as minicomputers, first was made practical by the introduction of the Digital Equipment Corp. PDP-11 series systems. CL Systems, Inc. (CLSI), which initially developed and sold a minicomputer-based acquisitions system using a computer from Nuclear Data, soon turned its attention to developing an online circulation system employing the early and later PDP-11 and VAX systems. Also, initial grant-sponsored research at the University of Minnesota Bio-Medical Library to develop an integrated interactive library system proved the feasibility of using this technology. (40,41)

Up to the mid-seventies, all library systems were hosted on mainframe computers. With the emergence of these lower cost computers, which lacked many of the operating system and critical development aids of the current mainframes, there was a degree of controversy as well as considerable risk in using this technology. Even though declining hardware costs made minicomputers increasingly affordable, it was not until about 1975 that suitable operating system software for interactive multiprogramming and multitasking operation became available. This was why early systems used proprietary operating system software closely linked to their applications. This lesson was learned from the University of Minnesota's early work on minicomputers.

Building on these experiences and the availability of the MUMPS operating environment and development facility, the Lister Hill Center of the National Library of Medicine carried out its own research effort to develop its Integrated Library System (ILS). This resulted in the core of a system implemented in the MUMPS language and operating environment on Data General minicomputers and first installed in the U.S. Army Library in the Pentagon to test its use in a real library setting. ILS implemented circulation and incorporated the earliest online interactive catalog-searching user interface, which Charles Goldstein called "the user cordial interface." (42) The software became available from the National Technical Information Service, but its initial commercial installations were handled by Online Systems, Inc. for a brief period, then by a new firm formed by Richard Dick called Avatar Systems, Inc. Today, OCLC's LS/2000 is the current version of what was the ILS system as modified

Digital Equipment Corp. VAX 11/780 superminicomputer.

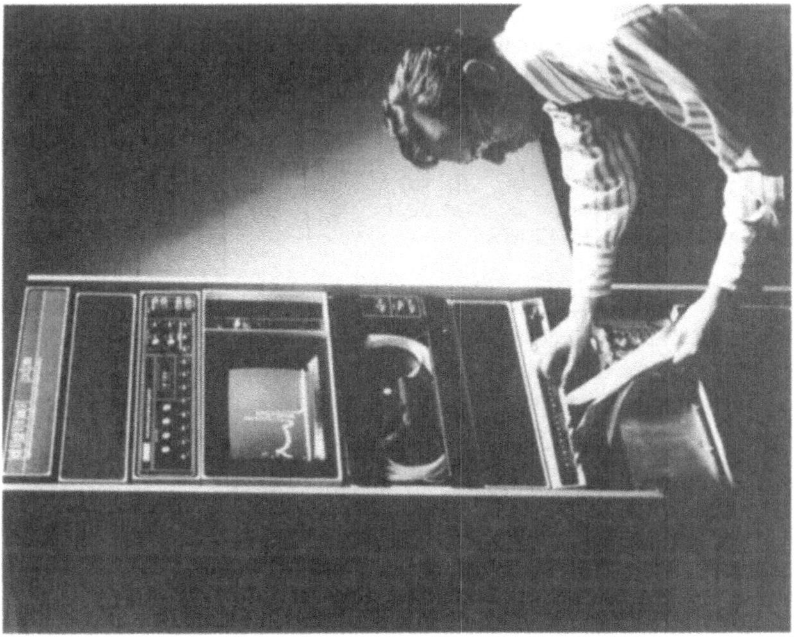

Digital Equipment Corp. PDP-11 series 16-bit minicomputer system.

by Avatar and by subsequent subcontract to Online Systems, Inc. to interface with the OCLC network system.

With the coming of the minicomputer, the emergence of commercial system vendors first produced practical circulation applications. (43–45) From 1977 to 1979 the number of these vendors doubled. CLSI, Inc., Systems Control, Inc., Gaylord Bros., and DataPhase, Inc., were the emerging vendors of this period. With the initiation of system development leadership on the part of the vendors, inevitably there were numerous opportunities for confusion between libraries' needs and what functions vendors were designing into their products.

In 1976, DeGennaro pointed out the progress made in applications during the eight years since his earlier paper. (46,47) He correctly forecast that the evolutionary approach to realizing a total automated solution would prove both the most viable and most popular. The vendor-based circulation systems were conceived largely as solutions employing a very narrow transaction processing view, without the incorporation of a full, multiple-use bibliographic database at their heart. Soon, the problems that this caused were evident and vendors began to redesign these systems to incorporate a MARC-based bibliographic database.

The emergence of vendor-based solutions also was responsible for the need for those in the profession to develop new skills related to writing a request for proposal and subsequently evaluating vendor responses. As a result, many workshops were held and continue to be held on procuring systems, systems evaluation and developing criteria for judging proposed systems. One of the typical early tutorials of this nature was held by the American Library Association's Library and Information Technology Association (LITA), reported in the literature by Brian Alley. (48)

V. CATALOGING SYSTEMS

With the development of the MARC II format for books having been initiated with the 1968 imprints received at the Library of Congress, non-MARC–compatible bibliographic systems developed in the sixties inevitably gave way to the development of new bibliographic systems using the fields and content designators employed in MARC II. With a degree of data standardization not previously possible, it became more realistic for system designers to consider developing more fully integrated systems, employing at their heart, a database able to accept MARC II records.

Opening the decade was the development of the Automated Book Catalog Subsystem at the New York Public Library (NYPL). (49) This system produced catalogs for the NYPL Research Libraries of a quality in typography never previously produced through a computer-based system. It was a significant and pioneering advance in developing the printed book format catalog as the replacement for the card catalog. Not only did this system implement MARC II, it also used the very latest computer-based photocomposition techniques to produce the final printed catalog. However, of even more importance was the implementation, for the first time, of an authority file linked to the bibliographic file and the use of a special heading called a "dual heading."

This authority file maintained all cross-reference structures and included names, series titles, uniform titles, conventional titles and topical subjects. The file also controlled all filing forms of the entry. It was to serve as the model for the authority subsystem implemented in the Washington Library Network software and ultimately for other future authority-driven cataloging systems. This "dual heading" brought together under a non-Library of Congress heading, items that the NYPL considered unique, by virtue of the nature of its collection. For example, for items having the Library of Congress subject heading "Elections — New York (City)," using the "dual heading" would allow these items to be sequenced under a subject heading indirectly regionalized to New York City, such as "New York (City) — Elections."

Implementing the NYPL system using batch-processing techniques required a series of computer programs to finally create the output magnetic tape designed to drive the photocomposer. The bibliographic file contained authority file control numbers for the author, title, added entry data and skeletonized MARC II data for the fixed fields and content designators not covered through the authority file. A bibliographic/authority linkage file used the unique authority file entry number and alphabetic sort key to link the bibliographic and authority file records together and maintain proper filing sequence for each record. These file system concepts also were later used in many other systems, including those which operated interactively. For example, the Washington Library Network system incorporated the linked authority file concept.

By the middle of the decade, several libraries had also obtained the NYPL software for this system and implemented their own book form catalogs. One of these libraries, the Hennepin County Public Library in Minnesota, which successfully implemented this system, later converted the output to COM microfilm and, in 1988, was still using this software to produce its catalog to accompany its automated online circulation system obtained from CLSI.

Although the actual future of the US MARC format in cataloging was destined to affect every U.S. library and ultimately libraries around the world, the opinion was expressed during this decade that the real future of MARC formats lay in the development of bibliographic networks to distribute these records. (50) With the cost of computing, particularly the emerging interactive form of computing, still relatively expensive, it was inevitable that the focus on developing cooperative networking automation solutions was still receiving the main emphasis. However, alternatives to the card catalog had already emerged. These were mainly computer-output-microfilm or microfilm output directly from photocomposition devices or created by stripping up individual page output from photocomposition devices to create microfiche instead of 16 mm, roll-type (spool-to-spool) microfilm. Roll microfilm and microfiche formats for catalogs were the main print form replacement for the card catalog.

The emergence of the Ohio College Library Center (OCLC) under its founding director, Frederick Kilgour, was a landmark event in the beginning of library networking that employed computer-based systems. As OCLC evolved and was able to change its charter to incorporate serving libraries beyond the state of Ohio, this provided the key impetus to developing cooperative cataloging databases, lowering the per-unit cost of cataloging and increasing the quality of the bibliographic record. OCLC carried these goals forward through the seventies to provide a firm operating philosophy, technically workable system and a positive cost/benefit ratio to its participating libraries. Without this firm foundation, OCLC's later rapid growth in the eighties and beyond would have been possibly more problematic. OCLC really got libraries thinking and actively planning state, regional or local cooperative efforts to utilize information technology for collection and service sharing. State networks or cooperative multi-type library networks might still have developed without the impetus provided by OCLC, but they may not have grown beyond document delivery services without the systems made possible by OCLC and automated library processes. When Minitex in Minnesota began in the late sixties, it was originally conceived as a document delivery/collection sharing network among Minnesota colleges, state agencies and the University of Minnesota. Soon, similar state or regional networks started, based largely on successful examples set by OCLC and Minitex.

In 1975, Kenneth Bierman received a grant from the Council on Library Resources to examine the current planning for replacement of card catalogs by libraries in the United States and Canada. (51) He found 34 libraries actively working on some form of replacement, with many others expressing interest in adopting another form of technology for producing their catalog. Interest in an online form of catalog was also increasing, although no large library actually had one implemented by 1974–1975. He issued some predictions for the future, which seemed reasonable at the time but which did not come to pass universally. He predicted that, "When a significant number of automated alternatives to card catalogs are implemented by large libraries, they will be done so cooperatively. The majority of large libraries will not have their own hardware/software systems and databases." (52) However, Bierman obviously did not foresee the impact of the development of lower cost, increasingly powerful computers designed for interactive transaction processing which were just emerging into respectability by the middle of the decade. These "minicomputers" made it possible for medium to larger size libraries to consider their own local library systems or for smaller libraries to consider a shared system in a local area.

Another prediction he made was

> As automated alternatives are implemented, the card catalogs will be first closed and then, within five to ten years, frozen and committed to microimage through photographic processes. Large libraries will have two catalogs at least for the next twenty-five years; a frozen retrospective catalog in card or microimage form and an open on-going catalog in machine readable form. (52)

While certainly this is already true for some libraries (and will be for others), increasingly, more and more libraries are actually doing full retrospective conversions. These are really necessitated with the implementation of integrated systems that automate both catalog and circulation to show the availability of materials. Even if a full MARC format record is not available, libraries are creating their own original cataloging record or accepting a record created by another library for the item which they may obtain from a bibliographic utility such as OCLC or from a retrospective conversion vendor such as Blackwell North America.

The Library of Congress MARC record production was critical to the success of fostering development of bibliographic systems in libraries, since standardized cataloging data able to be used by every library would create considerable savings in individual library labor costs. For the production of the actual MARC record at the Library of Congress, a technique called automatic format recognition had been pioneered, in which the computer could perform the field tagging and subfielding of tagged field data automatically, to minimize the amount of added work needed to produce a MARC record from the source cataloging worksheet. It was this technique which had considerable importance for the very large scale retrospective conversion project to be carried out for 800,000 University of California campus libraries records which would compose a union catalog for the University of California Libraries. The Institute of Library Research (ILR), Berkeley Campus, adopted this technique in a simplified form, which it called Original Format Recognition. (53) Using this technique, its costs to process bibliographic records for input to their union catalog were $1.00 per record, half that then being spent at the Library of Congress. Even though the record produced was simplified and not without quality control problems, the catalog ILR produced was a considerable improvement in access for library patrons.

As work proceeded on systems that employed computer technology to produce microfilm products, it became more evident that the improved technology of interactive online systems would provide a better alternative to the card catalog. With computer costs decreasing and software technology maturing, the early dreams of online systems envisioned at the beginning of the decade were now not only possible but actually affordable by a wider range of libraries. The realization of the degree of interrelatedness of library automation functions now turned systems designers toward seriously attempting to realize the integrated online system, with the system centerpiece being a catalog publicly accessible via a terminal.

It is natural that concern over improved terminal devices built momentum through the decade, since the entry of records using the full MARC roman character set posed problems both for keying and for lack of display on regular 96 character ASCII terminal devices. IBM had produced a print train assembly for its IBM 1403 N1 line printer, which implemented all but a few of the ALA MARC character set displayable codes. Use of this device in diacritical overprint mode where each line would be struck twice, slowed a 1200-line-per-minute device to about 250 lines per minute when striking lines using diacriticals or special characters found only once on the print chain assembly. However, this was the only device capable in the early-to-mid-seventies of giving such printed output.

For MARC record input, the Library of Congress had first used IBM MTST electronic tape typewriters for batch processing. With interactive terminal development, the Library of Congress had a pressing need for an interactive CRT terminal system that would display and allow more single-key entry for the character set. By 1972, OCLC also had decided to abandon its first terminal, the Spirascope LTE, for its new OCLC Model 100, being manufactured by Beehive. These were being delivered in quantity by the fall of 1973. The Library of Congress commissioned FourPhase, Inc., to develop a clustered terminal employing the IBM 2260 protocol, using a minicomputer as the cluster controller. For those inclined toward reading a complete history of terminal development, Malinconico presents a full treatment. (54)

With early vendor interest in the mid-seventies beginning with circulation systems and the pioneering mainframe-based projects such as Stanford's BALLOTS, Washington Library Network's acquisitions and cataloging network system, the University of Chicago Library's system, the Integrated Library System (ILS) of the Lister Hill Center for Biomedical Communications of the National Library of Medicine and Northwestern University Library's NOTIS project, the late seventies brought increased vendor interest in developing integrated solutions around their respective circulation system offerings. Also, new vendors began entering the market. Librarians began to see the early fruits of practical vendor-based systems borne of competition, while the trend toward local library software development decreased through the decade as these vendor-based solutions multiplied.

VI. TOWARD THE INTERACTIVE, INTEGRATED LIBRARY SYSTEM

Aside from network development projects such as OCLC, the work at Stanford University Library to develop its BALLOTS system was certainly one of the most widely reported and well-funded efforts to build an integrated technical processing and online searchable database that occurred during the decade. Initially, as did the WLN system, BALLOTS used mnemonic tagged input screens to perform data entry. One of the singular innovations that BALLOTS pioneered was the use of block mode terminals which incorporated its own built-in programs via a microprocessor and software in "firmware." (55)

BALLOTS was not only a costly system to develop, even though it used the SPIRES software as its data management platform, but it also was a costly system to operate, even for a library as large as Stanford. Costs during November, 1974 were $34,255 for the month. (55) Clearly, it was not surprising that BALLOTS' system planners were beginning to examine the factors necessary to turn BALLOTS into a system able to support multiple libraries in a network. The future for a system with such high operating costs would restrict its continued and long-term use if such costs were to continue indefinitely for a single library. With the use of the SPIRES software at its foundation, BALLOTS was also one of the pioneering systems in the use of a database management facility. This permitted very complex searching and manipulation of system output. By the end of the decade, the BALLOTS software became the basis for the Research Libraries Group, Inc., Research Libraries Information Network (RLG/RLIN). Thus the major economic goal of an expensive operational system made affordable through shared use was realized.

The University of Chicago Library Data Management System (LDMS) was also conceived as a multifunctional integrated system using a database management system at its core. (56) This system was designed as a fully functional integrated materials processing and public services system. LDMS continued to be developed through the seventies and is still supported and in use.

Northwestern University Library's NOTIS system, begun as an interactive circulation system, by the end of the decade had grown to incorporate acquisitions, including the check-in of serial receipts, cataloging and interactive searching of the database through CRT terminals. NOTIS was developed by the team of Velma Veneziano and James Aagaard, with these two doing all the design and programming, whereas other projects of the period such as the BALLOTS software, WLN system and the University of Chicago System were developed by much larger teams of individuals. One design goal of NOTIS was to provide a very cost affordable system, still functionally rich enough to provide for the needs of the Northwestern University Library. The goal was to allow operation on either smaller dedicated IBM mainframes or on a relatively small dedicated partition on a shared mainframe. By the end of the decade other libraries were showing considerable interest in NOTIS. Arrangements for its replication had been made with several institutions as the eighties dawned. By the last few years of the seventies, it was clear that libraries not previously engaging in any of their own systems development were really ready to acquire commercially available systems. Although initially these were mainly circulation systems, most of these libraries also envisioned their need eventually to evolve to an online, interactive and integrated system.

Through the late sixties and early seventies IBM had developed several experimental library systems which had been installed in their Los Gatos facility corporate library. However, none of these were made available commercially. IBM in what was then the Federal Republic of Germany had entered into a development contract for an integrated library system with the University of Dortmund. This system became known as DOBIS (Dortmunder Bibliotheks Informatisches Systeme). It consisted of an online cataloging system and search facility. Under another development contract, the Catholic University of Leuven, Belgium, jointly developed acquisitions, circulation, various batch product programs and background processing, which was called LIBIS (Leuvens Integraal Bibliotheek Systeem). DOBIS was based on the German MAB1 bibliographic format. LIBIS was based essentially on BNB MARC. IBM negotiated the right to market LIBIS as a companion product to the DOBIS software. By the end of the decade, the University of Pretoria, Union of South Africa, the University of Perugia, Italy and the College Bibliocentre in Scarborough, Canada, had leased and installed the DOBIS/LIBIS software. (57)

By the early 1980's there were several versions of this system due to the modifications made by the institutions that licensed the software. The customized version of major significance was installed at the National Library of Canada (NLC). After NLC had evaluated seven systems for acquisition and modification to suit its needs, DOBIS was chosen. NLC had licensed DOBIS directly from University of Dortmund along with distribution rights in Canada. It had purchased eight person-months of development time for DOBIS to make it MARC format compatible and add multilibrary and bilingual database/ terminal dialog features. This resulted in a new prototype version, which was then evaluated from June through December, 1976 for necessary functional changes to serve the NLC. (58) Also, the system was modified to support MARC character set diacriticals, and functional specifications for Boolean searching were defined. With this background, IBM began to actively promote the DOBIS/LIBIS original version system in the United States.

Another significant system, initially designed as an integrated system, was the previously introduced University of Chicago Library Data Management System (LDMS). (59) Supported with substantial federal grant funds, this system was designed to support full MARC record selection and processing, including ordering, receiving, gift and blanket order processing, cataloging, binding and labelling. A circulation module also was developed using the specially designed JRL 1000 circulation terminals. A resource file composed of Library of Congress MARC tape records was used to derive copy cataloging records for the database. In its initial design, the database was structured for a single institution. By the late seventies, work was under way on a major modification, called the Quadraplanar Data Structure. This would allow multiple institutions to share the database and system, with each preserving its own record specific content. As in the case of the Stanford BALLOTS system, here was another large IBM 370 mainframe-based system which would benefit from more reasonable operating costs if the software could serve multiple institutions. The University of Chicago system pioneered quite a few techniques for handling large, complex bibliographic databases, among them the Quadraplanar Data Structure, multiple levels of bibliographic display and the use of commercial access and data management facilities as the access and file handling basis to the system. System access was built around Informatics, Inc.'s INTERCOMM. File management services were provided by IFAM, a product from Computer Corporation of America.

It was clear that the emphasis was shifting from library-developed systems to those developed and supported by commercial vendors by the mid-to-late seventies. Although, some in the profession believe that this shift occurred because of the numerous inadequate or failed attempts at system development and the increasing lack of large grant funding for library-conducted research, I believe that these reasons were only small contributing factors in this shift.

Rather, the management of many libraries recognized that, with the increasing complexity of development, more risk exposure resulted. It was risky enough to try to adapt procedures and install a system purchased from the outside. By ceasing to consider developing custom systems, the risk exposure was minimized, while in many cases the operational compromises necessary to adopt a more generalized system actually served to improve library operations by weeding out some of the homegrown procedural complexities. Moreover, as these systems became multifunctional integrated systems involving fully interactive computing systems, the need for considerably more experienced and specialized technical personnel for such development was recognized. Only a few large libraries had these resources and the necessary management expertise to continue an in-house effort to attract the necessary technical staff and provide them with career paths equal to that found in other organizations' systems departments. Generally, in the data-processing field, the use of software packages procured under a license, sometimes modified, but essentially supported by the software vendor with new releases and bug fixes, was becoming accepted. However, the major difference in these nonlibrary systems computing centers was that some internal development of systems was still carried out, whereas the library most typically believed that it could eventually procure its total solution through the vendor. The libraries felt they would not need to use any other means to develop added functionality since the vendor eventually would provide this. Also, these minicomputer-based systems were designed to be run as "turnkey systems" by library personnel who were not data-processing professionals.

VII. BIBLIOGRAPHIC DATA CONCERNS

Clearly, the question of bibliographic data is at the very heart of library systems. The record format and rules for cataloging remain a central issue for the profession. Despite the opinions of such cataloging luminaries as Seymour Lubetsky, (60) who felt that the adoption of ISBD, with its repetition of the author's name before and after the title and with its esoteric punctuation, would confuse the user, the profession continues to embrace such standards, even displaying this punctuation on the screens of some current public access catalogs. This is why the emergence of the national bibliographic utilities such as OCLC and RLIN were so increasingly important by the end of the decade. Their databases of both MARC records originated by the Library of Congress and original cataloging contributed by member libraries would enable large-scale reuse of more standardized bibliographic data. This assumed some mechanism for assuring that a minimally acceptable level of quality control would be maintained. In the early seventies it was generally accepted that the storage of very large databases in direct access stores would be an experimental activity as far as the library was concerned. (61) The passage of but several years brought increasingly to the range of possibilities a complete library catalog in machine-readable format available for interactive search,no matter how large the library.

The ability to reuse these network-accessible records and widen the prospect of already finding a matching record through increasing both the numbers of participants and the retrospective conversion of significant pre-1968 books, the growing CONSER database of MARC serials records and the emergence of MARC formats for other types of materials—all served to make individual library retrospective conversion projects more viable and fiscally attractive. Also, grant funding from both private and public agencies for retrospective conversion projects enabled the addition of many thousands of records to the RLG/RLIN database and to the other networks. With the adoption of AACR II, libraries began to consider in earnest that their card catalogs were rapidly reaching the end of a long but useful life. Large libraries such as Cornell University, mounted studies of their catalog's futures. (62)

Cornell's task force recommended closing the current card catalog when AACR II was adopted in their library, essentially what the Library of Congress announced it was going to do. The task force then recommended a new online interactive union catalog be substituted as one component of a new automated system. It was proposed that this system be developed using distributed minicomputer technology. Similarly, other libraries felt the pressure to adopt a "closing of the card catalog" posture in preparation for the adoption of AACR II. Perceiving a panacea, more and more libraries nationwide felt that adopting AACR II was a singularly good justification for embarking on a new form of catalog.

However, many libraries had already built up large numbers of machine-readable records that were in the pre-AACR II and pre-ISBD format. What was to be done about this problem? If a library began a new form of catalog, it would be natural to produce that catalog using all of the library's available MARC records from OCLC or a commercial catalog vendor. There-fore, the rush to close the card catalog in practice did not turn out to be a necessity to justify implementing a new form of catalog. Of course, the smaller the catalog, the easier it would be for the necessary heading changes or guide cards to be inserted to convert a card catalog to AACR II form. ISBD punctuation was not a necessity to add to previous records since even such cataloging experts as Seymour Lubetsky believed that ISBD was introducing a level of redundancy in the record that was not needed, and he continues to believe that ISBD was an error in judgement now obsolete in the online catalog.

Conversion of these heading changes for AACR II was automatically realized with computer assistance using conversion programs that flipped the corporate author heading forms and performed other necessary cleanup work on the OCLC, RLIN, WLN and UTLAS databases. Similarly commercial catalog vendors did the same on their own databases. Therefore, machine-readable database-generated catalogs, whether microformat or online interactive, would have their headings conform to the new rules if the library obtained its records from an established source such as the bibliographic utilities. By the decade's end, the prospect of full retrospective conversion became more and more realistic as conversion prices were coming down, thanks to new techniques and large record bases from which to select premachine-readable records. William Axford made it clear at the Associated Colleges of the Midwest Conference on Management Issues in Automated Cataloging, held in Chicago in 1977. He said, "We must quit playing around with the computer and consummate quickly what is now called a 'meaningful relationship.'" (63)

Along with the concern over the catalog, consciousness was being raised over other material formats and improved access. The Association for Educational Communications and Technology (AECT) and the National Commission on Libraries and Information Science funded Project Media Base to investigate the feasibility of improving and recommending better means to access audiovisual materials. Their hypothesis was that all components existed to implement a national network for audiovisual materials based on the MARC format, Library of Congress subject headings, a standard set of cataloging rules and input from a variety of sources and systems. They recommended adoption of AACR II and MARC. Also, they recommended continuing an inventory of computerized systems for these resources and that a study be mounted to determine how local databases could be merged to form a union database of audiovisual materials. (64)

VIII. FORMAT STANDARDIZATION CONCERNS

The need for format standardization is problematic, since today in the United States alone we have USMARC emanating from the Library of Congress, OCLC MARC and RLIN MARC, not to mention that there are possibly other variant MARC formats originating from different vendor systems. Each of the world's developed countries also has devised its own customized MARC or MARC-like format. Although most of these conform to the International Standards Organization Standard 2709, which covers the physical format of a bibliographic data record on magnetic tape, the content designators, character sets and encoded data may vary considerably from USMARC. Therefore, further standardization is needed if bibliographic data sharing worldwide is to be made more practical. The literature of the decade is filled with papers discussing various national formats and possible international formats. The International Federation of Library Associations (IFLA) Working Group on Content Designators has continued to work on the assumption that there would be a "SuperMarc." (65) Avram reported on work to create international standards for the interchange of machine-readable bibliographic records. (66) Today, planning is underway at the Library of Congress to merge the individual MARC formats into one global format by the mid-1990's.

IX. COMPUTER-TO-COMPUTER APPLICATION PROTOCOL DEVELOPMENT CONCERNS

The need to make available on a timely basis bibliographic records and authority file data and eventually to build interlibrary loan systems able to reach thousands of libraries has made increasingly apparent that peer type computer-to-computer networks will eventually emerge to serve as the national bibliographic network and that such networks will form the future international networks as political, legal, proprietary, and transborder data flow issues are resolved. Work has proceeded since the mid-seventies on developing a series of application-level protocols, using the Open Systems Interconnection (OSI) Reference Model as the system interconnection architecture basis. The initial protocol definition work was carried out by a National Commission for Libraries and Information Science and National Bureau of Standards joint task force, which defined an initial version of a protocol for library and information science applications. (67) Since that time, considerable work on protocol development has proceeded, but the actual implementation of these peer computer connections has involved significant costly development to bring us to the current point, where Library of Congress, OCLC and RLIN interconnections permit the Library of Congresss to send authority data to these other bibliographic utilities computer to computer.

X. THE WIDENING VIEW OF LIBRARY SYSTEMS

The minicomputer, while promising a certain freedom from the strictures imposed from large data processing service-oriented systems, required the library to build a suitable, although smaller scale, computer facility and provide its own operations staff for typical turnkey systems or its own local programming staff for systems developed in-house in the library. With the power of distributed systems being oriented to the interactive computing environment and the seventies mainframes moving more slowly from the batch environment, the attraction of these lower cost minicomputer-based systems was assured. Also, the majority of libraries could be served by the evolving capacity of these minicomputer systems.

While this trend was evident, it was also apparent that, with the widening interest in the online public access catalog as the realistic replacement for microformat or card catalogs, larger numbers of terminals and wider distribution of these terminals was desirable. Moreover, as a library's parent institution invested in improved systems, there came the installation of institution-based systems such as office automation applications, accounting, payroll, and other functions where the library system could benefit from access and the institution staff could benefit also via remote access to the library's system from existing terminals. In 1981 MicroNet, Inc., demonstrated of the office of the future in Washington, D.C. (68) Just as the trend toward fully distributed systems was flourishing, it was apparent that these systems, with the technology existing then, would not support network access across large institutions. Consequently, academic libraries such as the University of California System Wide Union Catalog were mainframe implementations that would provide the necessary system throughput to serve a geographically dispersed access network. There no longer was a clear choice of whether to implement a library system employing in-library minicomputers, to place these in an institution's data-processing center or to adopt a mainframe-based solution, such as is possible today. With present networking products, a library's system computer, independent of its physical location, can be incorporated into a network of computers in an institution. Therefore, the issue of where to place the library's system offers many more alternatives today.

XI. MICROCOMPUTER TECHNOLOGY DEVELOPMENTS

In what appears to be the first paper published on the potential of the microprocessor in library and information, P. W. Williams in 1979 foresaw the initial application of microprocessors in sophisticated intelligent CRT display devices. An example was the RLG/RLIN network terminals and the desktop microcomputer systems that were later used to perform typical small-library applications, such as circulation, card printing, and order printing and tracking. (69) Also in 1979, Hines and Winkel reported on their work with the Children's Media Data Bank at the University of North Carolina. (70) They employed a SOL-20 65-kB RAM memory microcomputer manufactured by Processor Technology to generate back-of-the-book indexes. Their IBM mainframe indexing programs were translated from the SNOBOL/SPITBOL language to the BASIC language for the SOL-20. Of course, until the introduction of the IBM PC in 1981, use of microcomputers in libraries was limited but nonetheless appeared to be a powerful technology that would complement library systems in a variety of interesting ways.

Milford Public Library reported what appears to be the first coin-operated microcomputer for library patron use in October 1979. (71) Present library microcomputer applications for the smaller library are treated well by Lundeen. (72) In 1980, the National Science Foundation sponsored an experiment at Menlo Park Public Library called Computertown USA! which established the usefulness of microcomputers for public use, particularly for children and young adults. (73)

Several of the more notable early microcomputer applications in a library setting were:

1. The use of a Terak 8510/a micro as the front end to the Dartmouth College Library experimental online catalog. This catalog was implemented on the BRS, Inc., search service's mainframe under its BRS Search software, for which Terak provided, through its Pascal-implemented programs a more hospitable user/system command interface.
2. The use of an Intel MDS Micro with 64-kB RAM and the ISIS II operating system at Oberlin College as the transaction logging unit as

a fallback when their host Sigma 9 processor was out of service. The Intel also multiplexed six terminals to the host and identified terminal location, assigned loan periods for major borrower categories and handled check digit and bar code concatenation for transmission to the host. This demonstrated the desirability of using a micro as a fallback support device.

3. The use of a Micromation multiple Z-80 microprocessor system running CP/M, with four concurrent users possible through the four Z-80 microprocessors. This system at the Medical Sciences Library at Texas A&M also included a 25-MB Winchester disk drive, used ACT V-A display terminals hard wired, both a DecWriter III and Diablo for draft and letter-quality print and Ventel 300/1200 Baud and Bell 2112A modems. Software included a word processor, forms generator, communications program, COBOL, FORTRAN, PL-1, Pascal, C-BASIC and various utilities. The library invested $35,000 to support four simultaneous users. That may sound like a high cost, but this represented a very advanced system for the period. (In 1994, for the almost $9,000 per user this represents, one can purchase three Intel 80486 microprocessor systems from Compaq, IBM or other manufacturers with 120 times the speed throughput of the fastest Z-80 of the early 1980's).

XII. INTERACTIVE SYSTEMS USER INTERFACE DESIGN

As the decade of the 1970's drew to a close, it became more important to focus on issues of the design of user interfaces, since the potential for opening library systems to access by the library user demanded more ease of use. The complexities of Boolean searching, sets, and cryptic commands requiring exact formula-like statements for searching would preclude all but the most computer-literate user from actually searching the library's online catalog. Moreover, users of early interactive systems longed for simpler, more understandable screen displays and commands that would act in a uniform and consistent manner. Alternatively, menu-driven tutorial interfaces, which afforded more help to users, seemed to be preferred over command-based systems.

With the move from teletype-like terminals operating in character mode, early interactive systems were line oriented and command driven. With the coming of block-mode display terminals, the input/output to the terminal could be structured along the concept of the display area of the CRT screen—usually 24 lines, each 80 characters wide. Early systems which were moved to that format, in some cases, kept an appearance of earlier 80-column batch printer output. However, block-mode terminals made possible the use of menu-driven approaches. With direct cursor addressing, it was possible to define a specific command area on a screen and by moving the cursor to that area, strike the enter or return key and execute that command. With intelligent microprocessor-equipped terminals, it was possible to send only data itself back and forth to the system and retain field labels in protected screen areas during repetitive data entry or inquiry operations.

The last display technology development that appeared at the close of the seventies was the touchscreen display terminal. Several companies made these devices. One type of touchscreen device allowed any point on the screen to be touched and the coordinates sensed by a program using sensors around the screen. Another type used a sandwich glass and conductive layer technology, which divided the screen into a fixed number of areas that could be sensed by touch. This latter type of terminal was first incorporated into a library system by CLSI, with its Touch Screen Online Public Access Catalog unit. (74) Evanston (Illinois) Public Library was the first library to use these touchscreen terminals. Although the technology was intriguing, these terminals consumed considerably more processor resources and experienced slower response times. Also, sometimes the system would not correctly interpret touches. Another drawback was their expense. However, some patrons, particularly both the younger and more elderly library users who were not as accustomed to keyboards really appreciated the touchscreen units. This appeared to be a technology with some promise, at least to serve certain specific users of libraries, but still not a well-developed and proven user interface technique. Would that prove different with more time? The answer was no.

XIII. FOREIGN LIBRARY AUTOMATION AND INFORMATION RETRIEVAL

It is easy for those who have not visited other countries to believe that U.S. libraries have always been in the forefront of library and information technology. Although many countries were unable to proceed as rapidly as the major nations of the world, almost every country was watching developments in the United States and Europe with serious interest. National efforts to explore data-processing technology applications to information systems problems was proceeding quite apace with our own efforts in the major European countries, in our northern neighbor, Canada, and in such countries as Australia.

Developments abroad were influenced by the USMARC record development and the speed at which a country's own national formats emerged. The kinds and sizes of computers available, fiscal resources and the availability of skilled development staff were other factors. Another major influence affecting automation development, particularly in the area of specific applications work, was the differing character of operation and services provided by many foreign libraries. For example, many European libraries maintain closed stacks and a selected smaller number of privileged users whereas U.S. libraries have generally maintained open stacks and permitted both general library access and charging privileges to a larger and more diverse clientele.

Languages, too, were of influence in the development of library computing. Countries where Roman alphabet languages prevailed were in a better position to apply computing to database problems involving their vernacular language or foreign languages that could be represented by the Roman alphabet as used in English. In the seventies there were few commercially available, let alone widely used, devices that allowed input of vernacular forms of Chinese, Japanese or Korean, while even for languages that used non-Roman alphabets such as Thai, Arabic, Hebrew and Cyrillic languages there were few terminal devices on which these could be input or displayed in vernacular form. Therefore, most library databases that included these records handled them in a transliterated form. The printed book catalog produced by the New York Public Library for Hebrew works was the first such printed catalog done in the United States using photocomposition output. Early library automation systems in countries such as Japan initially focussed on databases for foreign works mainly in English until their vernacular input capabilities emerged toward the end of the decade. With this brief view of some of the factors influencing systems development, let us examine the progress in various regions of the world during the seventies.

A. Asia and the Pacific Basin

By 1976, the state of the art in Japan involved large university and public libraries and the National Diet Library. However, unlike the United States, Canada, or Europe, the Japanese lacked any central body assuming leadership. Development efforts were performed largely in isolation. No national plan for library automation existed and no cooperative mechanisms were growing to provide a substitute for the sort of national planning that was occurring in the United States. Systems were in place in Japanese libraries which handled acquisitions and cataloging, including catalog production in both card and book form, with most of this work funded by the Ministry of Education, Culture and Science in the National University Libraries. The intricacy and high cost of developing Japanese character processing had also presented a formidable problem. (75,76)

Since virtually all of the work in Japan in this period is reported in the Japanese language, few Americans would have been able to assess their progress unless privileged to read Japanese, visit the country or talk to Japanese visiting the United States Because I do not read Japanese, I have used personal contacts through this period to assess the situation. By the end of the decade, several dozen batch-mode systems had been installed and were operational. These were internally developed custom systems supported by their respective institutions. Several libraries were considering moving to interactive systems by 1979. While Japanese-built computers were not as powerful as U.S. systems at that time, they were well designed and highly reliable, sometimes compatible with IBM mainframes, but in most cases using unique proprietary architectures. With the excellent communications systems being developed in Japan, it could be forecast that in the near future excellent interactive retrieval systems would be on a par with those of the United States or Europe.

Margaret Fung has reported the history and status of library automation developments in Taiwan, the Republic of China. From 1975 to 1980, six database systems were under development using Perkin Elmer 3220 and Wang 2200 MVP minicomputers. Five institutions had developed eight applications using English. The IBM 370/135 was the dominant mainframe computer in use, but one institution was using a Digital equipment Corp. PDP-11/34. Serials control, catalog card production, acquisitions and building of bibliographic databases were typical applications. Ching-chen Su developed Taiwan's first integrated system at National Taiwan Normal University in 1975. Input for Chinese character processing was through a special Chinese keyboard developed by Professor Te-Yao Chiang and Wang Laboratories of the United States This explains the popularity of the Wang minicomputers. (77)

It is unclear from the literature what the level of computer usage was in the People's Republic of China during the seventies, but through inquiries and through several visits to the People's Republic in late 1979 and 1983, I was privileged to be involved in the planning for several of their agencies' information system efforts. Few library automation systems existed. Little native software development had taken place. Under UNESCO support, several agencies were planning their installation of either the ISIS software on small IBM 43xx series processors of which there were a dozen in Beijing in 1979. The Institute for Scientific and Technical Information (ISTIC) was one such organization. By 1983 ISTIC had installed its system and was in a production stage. In the early 1980's several agencies and universities installed the MINISIS software on Hewlett-Packard HP-3000 minicomputers, and many more were planning such installations. Very little cooperative information exchange was occurring between these agencies even though they were using the same software packages on similarly configured hardware. Such a lack of cooperative sharing was an impediment to more rapid progress.

Most Chinese computer usage involved small computers manufactured in Eastern bloc countries such as the Soviet Union or Poland. Some Western European systems were available. The U.S. computer presence opened with small IBM 4331 and 4341 systems and with some Hewlett-Packard and Digital Equipment systems. Software, though, was directed at generalized information storage and retrieval applications, in both batch and somewhat limited interactive mode. The opening of China to friendly relations with the United States meant that a further computerization was possible through both importation of technology and strengthening of educational opportunities for their students, with considerable progress despite the lack of funds and amenities in many facilities for computer installations to be easily maintained. Also, even though systems were interactive, this did not mean that an individual user could access the system from his or her own office. With air conditioning a scarce resource, it was most common to keep under climate control only a central computer terminal room and perhaps a nearby room for computer users.

Throughout other parts of Asia, numerous systems for indexing, information retrieval, serials control and catalog card production have been reported in the literature. These systems were all batch processed, but a few used line editors and CRT terminals for data entry. One reported system, a serials system developed on an IBM 360/44 at the Physical Research Laboratory in Abmedabad, India, used a terminal for interactive searching of the serial file by title or subject. (78) Although a file of only 560 current journals was processed under this system, its features matched many systems developed for special libraries, federal agencies and universities in the United States in the seventies.

Moving to the southern part of the Pacific Basin, it is clear that Australia has played a significant regional role in library automation development. Some of these directions parallel Great Britain, where regional bibliographic utilities were well established. In Australia, the state libraries exerted leadership in their states very early, with the Australia National Library concentrating mainly on MARC format development and record services. AUS MARC, its bibliographic format, was patterned more closely on the British BNB MARC; however, several Australian systems were processing mixtures of USMARC, BNB MARC and AUS MARC, since retrospective conversion or current cataloging for microfiche-based catalogs had been provided by American or British vendors.

When I was active in research in minicomputer-based library automation systems from 1972 to 1978, it was with great interest that I watched the Australian system developments parallel our own. For example, the University of New South Wales in Sydney had under development a minicomputer-based circulation system using Data General equipment, while several other institutions were using Digital Equipment Corp. PDP-11 series systems such as we were using at the University of Minnesota at that time. With the AUS MARC record service fully operational on March 1, 1974, US MARC and BNB MARC records became available to any Australian library. Several years later CAN MARC was added. Planning for the conversion of the Australian

National Bibliography was well under way. Just emerging were a few vendor-developed systems, initially from British companies such as the Automated Library Systems, Ltd. (ALS) circulation system installed in 1975 at the City of Stirling Library. These were as much the exception as were the early vendor-developed systems such as CLSI in the United States with its initial entry of the LIBS 100 circulation system.

In 1979, it was my privilege to be invited to participate as keynote speaker in the first conference in Australia devoted to use of minicomputer technology in bibliographic applications. (79) This conference, which was attended by almost 500 professionals, featured a program reporting on the history and development of minicomputer systems and applications showing the state of the art in the United States and Australia.

Australia, like several other countries, was unhampered by a "mainframe mentality or prejudice," whereas in the United States most data-processing individuals who were designing systems on mainframes did not feel there was much prospect for using minicomputers, owing to several conditions that complicated such developments. Lack of higher level language facilities and good real-time multitasking and multiprogramming operating systems were initial minicomputer problems. By the mid-1970's there were much improved operating environments and several higher level language platforms available. For example, Digital Equipment Corp. had introduced RSTS and its compiled BASIC. The MUMPS system, including its own language and operating system, was also offered through several sources. Toward the end of the decade the Pick operating system also became available on several hardware offerings. Australian library automation was characterized by emergence of several networks offering automated cataloging support and libraries actively developing their own systems on both mini- and mainframe computers. In an almost parallel fashion, vendor- developed systems began to emerge. In Australia this first occurred through importation, with Plessey and CLSI joining ALS in the Australian market. By decade's end, the Australian firm Almagamated Wireless Australasia (AWA) had started to market a system that it initially licensed from URICA Library Systems in South Africa and subsequently enhanced and marketed throughout the Pacific Basin. AWA began to exert market leadership in that area much like the Canadian firm GEAC did in Europe and the United States, and the U.S. company CLSI did in England. Thus, the end of the decade saw a worldwide market taking shape for vendor-developed library systems, while custom systems development by individual libraries in Australia became more infrequent.

B. Continental Europe

Most of the Western European countries were developing their own computer industries during the seventies, even though computer hardware imported from abroad was installed in universities, research establishments, government and industry. In France, Bull had developed mid-range systems and entered into a partnership with Honeywell Information Systems, of which ultimately in 1988 Bull took full control. Olivetti in Italy was emerging as a leading supplier of minicomputer systems and ultimately would supply AT&T microcomputers to be sold in the United States under the AT&T name. In West Germany, Siemens, Nixdorf and several other companies were developing families of large mainframe and minicomputer systems. Nokia Mikko of Finland was building a system that looked surprisingly like the Digital Equipment Corp. PDP-11 and Phillips in the Netherlands were also doing the same. Swedish Saab computers were to be found throughout Scandinavia, while in Eastern Europe, the communist bloc countries had mainly Russian, Czech and Polish computers. A budding terminal and peripheral industry was being developed in Bulgaria and Yugoslavia to provide input/output devices for these Eastern bloc systems. Many of these Eastern bloc systems were virtual copies of U.S. system architectures, but implemented using circuitry considered technologically obsolete by U.S. or Western European standards. Eastern bloc computers were estimated to be from five to eight years behind comparable developments in the West. Batch processing, much of the input through punched paper tape, was the norm, with small, discrete applications.

1. Eastern Bloc Developments

The State Public Scientific and Technical Library in Moscow began an ambitious automation program in 1969 and by 1977 had an integrated library system partially implemented, mainly as a batch system. It was developed with a project team of 150, showing that such a project team was gargantuan when contrasted with the largest of library system development projects in the United States such as at Stanford (BALLOTS) or the University of Chicago, which involved from a dozen to perhaps 30 individuals at a time. However, person power alone does not guarantee a successfully developed and maintained system, for the Soviets learned over an eight-year period that a team of librarians working with these system developers was really necessary to test the practicality of the system. (80) Much of the Soviet work may actually have resulted in either poor solutions to the wrong problem or impractical solutions to largely correctly defined problems since the system developers did not seem to want to involve the actual users of the system in determining its requirements or features. Moreover, it is well known that one does not necessarily produce the best software by assigning more and more programmers to a project. Careful determination of requirements and then external and internal systems designs must be accomplished before programs can be constructed and tested. Apparently, from the descriptions of this Soviet project, this procedure was not followed.

Ryabov, in 1975, reported that automation of individual libraries was inefficient but that network automation was otherwise impossible. This was exactly the opposite tack taken in the United States, where networks as typified by OCLC became the initial library automation strategy for so many libraries rather than systems developed in-house. With the scarcity of computers and the Soviets' lack of advanced technology as well as a less well developed communications system and a greater need to maintain secrecy, Soviet systems developed without much cooperation among libraries. Ryabov also reported that the planning of a new computer center for the Lenin Library was under way so that a new reader service system could be developed. Ryabov also reported that computers were no longer expected to replace card catalogs, since in large libraries a card catalog would provide basic, cheap and convenient information retrieval. Even printed, computer-produced catalogs were considered in an auxiliary role and online searches limited to the most important requests. (81) Such forecasting points out the lack of computer capacity and input/output devices for their systems.

By the mid-seventies the Slovak National Library of Matica Slovenska, the University of Bratislava Library and State Scientific Library at Kosice were developing systems in Czechoslovakia using the Tesla RPP 1968 computers. These were batch systems for cataloging and indexing. (82)

To summarize Eastern bloc developments, there apparently was work under way on machine-readable bibliographic formats, but only the largest and mainly scientific libraries were affected through use of batch-mode computing. No online bibliographic networks such as were found in the United States, Canada, Europe or Australia existed. Even though some highly centralized planning was undertaken, systems were the product of individual libraries, with little subsequent sharing of results. Even though considerable numbers of indexers were producing such important reference works as "Referativny Zhurnal," no online database searching industry was forming, although limited experimental online systems were to be encountered by 1978.

2. *Western Bloc Developments*

With less secrecy and better developed telecommunications between agencies in the West, Western European countries were active in developing library computer applications, with considerable emphasis on information retrieval systems. West Germany's efforts were concentrated in universities and state libraries, with some large special libraries such as Siemens AG developing systems. The Siemens effort was a technical processing system that was batch mode and incorporated a mechanized subscription acquisition system called SIMABON (Siemens Mechanized Subscription Acquisition System). This system ordered, routed, checked-in and claimed 30,000 subscriptions to some 3,500 titles, routing these to approximately 5,000 employees in the company.

German cataloging rules differed from the Anglo-American and the German bibliographic format called MAB1, and they employed a data element organization and structure different from our USMARC. Similarly, the East German format was modelled on the MAB1 format rather than on the ISO 2709 magnetic tape interchange format for bibliographic data on which USMARC is based. A symposium which discussed the development of the MAB1 format and German and English cataloging rules were the prelude to adoption of the MAB1 format for production of the Deutsche Bibliographie. (83)

The seventies saw the interest in the minicomputer grow with development of increasingly integrated library applications. As the minicomputer focus changed from 16-bit-word-length systems to those using 32-bit-word-length architectures, significantly larger complements of terminals could be served along with more complex applications. In articles typical of this period discussing the advantages and disadvantages of this technology, Wessel pointed out that improvements in storage capacity and better operating system software would improve the prospects for documentation systems using this class of computer. (84)

The most well known system developed in West Germany was the previously mentioned system known as DOBIS, developed by Caryl and A. Stratton McAllister of IBM. (85) Earlier Ehlert had presented a technical description in German of the DOBIS database structure and certain technical features as diacritical handling. (86) DOBIS was the major interactive library system developed on a mainframe by a U.S. computer company's German subsidiary working jointly with the University of Dortmund. Cataloging, file maintenance and searching of the bibliographic database were the interactive components to DOBIS. PL/1 language was used for the program for operation under CICS (Customer Information Control System), an IBM teleprocessing executive for IBM mainframe systems.

With the adoption of DOBIS at the Catholic University of Leuven, Belgium, further joint work between IBM and the Catholic University produced LIBIS (Leuvens Integraal Bibliotheek Systeem). This module provided acquisitions, circulation and many background processing batch programs. Originally, DOBIS was compatible with the MAB1 format, while LIBIS was modified to be compatible with the MARC format. IBM promoted the system throughout the world, with reasonable license fees for the software. Various installations were made in European libraries such as the University of Perugia (Italy), and in South Africa at the University of Pretoria (Union of South Africa). Perhaps the most well known installation was at the National Library of Canada, where the system was heavily customized so that multiple library holdings and the Canadian MARC format could be supported. (87) Moving to the Scandinavian countries, the Royal Institute of Technology in Stockholm was a distinguished leader in systems development, having started computer applications in 1967. Their cataloging system, LIBRIS, used the Swedish version of AACR II and Dewey Decimal classification. This system also pioneered the use of minicomputers and distributed processing in a network system with intelligent terminals. (88) Initially, the first LIBRIS system did not employ a MARC format. With the conversion to LIBRIS III, which used the Incoterm SPD 10/20 intelligent terminals, the MARC format was adopted. These Incoterm workstations emulated Alfascope 3500 units and incorporated a floppy disk and microprocessor. This system used a program within the terminal to store records on the floppy and later print them out on an attached printer. Also, one could catalog offline, storing the records to the floppy for later transmission to the LIBRIS host computer. When searching, it was possible to capture records selectively to floppy disk for printing and subsequent offline modification. Such an approach to record input and processing was more advanced than that being used at that time in the major U.S. bibliographic utility, OCLC. Also, LIBRIS certainly made more economical use of online connect time than a system such as OCLC, which required totally interactive input/output over a dedicated synchronous communications line. LIBRIS was a precursor to the microcomputer-based distributed processing now done in the U.S. and Canadian networks using products like OCLC's MicroEnhancer software for cataloging, interlibrary loans, serials management or acquisitions. LIBRIS did have its startup problems, with few machine-readable records online initially. This resulted in a high percentage of original cataloging on the part of its member libraries. However, once BNB/MARC and SWE/MARC files were loaded on a more timely basis, more and more matching records resulted. Today LIBRIS is a mature and functional network system accessed by many Scandinavian libraries.

In Denmark, academic and public libraries had a very fractious relationship over systems development. Consequently, the public libraries proceeded to develop their FAUST system using BNB/MARC format as the standard. However, the Danish research libraries proceeded to base their system plans on USMARC. FAUST was a batch system, and although there was much concern by Danish librarians that the system would threaten their livelihoods, in reality FAUST did not deliver the products and services that the public libraries wanted. FAUST's developers tried to justify their system and its continued development through cost savings and improved control of collections. (89) After much debate, FAUST came to an end in 1977. Debate renewed and another attempt at designing a new system was reported by Boje. (90) Perhaps a good parallel in U.S. history was the attempt to operate a centralized technical services organization having its own system called ANYLTS in New York, which was to have processed all items for member libraries in New York State but which quietly ceased after it failed to deliver expected cost savings or service improvements.

Bibliographic format development was proceeding through the work of the IFLA Working Group on Content Designators. In 1977, it published the Universal MARC (UNIMARC) format, which was designed to be an international exchange format. (91) Each nation would develop software to translate its national MARC or MARC-like format to UNIMARC for distribution and would in turn need only to produce a program that would translate UNIMARC to its own native MARC format. Unlike USMARC or similar formats, UNIMARC was structured into functional blocks of data that were not organized in parallel to the printed catalog card. As a computer-processing format, UNIMARC made very rational sense, but as a practical tool, it did not succeed as an exchange format since many countries had already developed software that enabled them to read and directly convert the major native MARC formats.

One would believe that in a small country such as Switzerland, considerable interlibrary cooperation over system development would occur. However, this was not the case. The French-speaking, western part of the country felt more closely related to developments in France, such as the University of Grenoble's MONOCLE bibliographic format development. Switzerland's most notable system, SIBIL (Système Intégré pour les Bibliothèques Universitaires de Lausanne), used the Canton of Lausanne's IBM 370 computer for an online, interactive, integrated system serving both the university and cantonal libraries. SIBIL was exported to France, where the Ecole Polytechnique in Paris adopted the system. By the beginning of the eighties, Cantonal libraries in Basel and Fribourg were also installing SIBIL.

Meanwhile in the German-speaking cantons, there was a closer relationship to libraries in southwest Germany. The Zentralbibliothek Zurich and the ETH-Bibliothek Zurich developed automated cataloging systems with limited online search access and updated using batch input. Microfiche catalogs were produced and both these libraries were planning to install online interactive systems as technology improved and software could be developed. The Universitatsbibliothek Konstanz was planning to join a new online cataloging system being developed for the German Federal State of Baden-Wurttemburg. Meanwhile, by 1980, the National Library in Bern was still showing no interest in library automation. It was not taking a leadership role and was still using manual methods for compiling the Swiss National Bibliography. Because of cantonal bias, the considerable technical achievement of SIBIL was not acknowledged for its technical merit, even though its state of advancement was beyond that of most of the individual library systems found in the eastern cantons or southwestern Germany. (92)

C. Great Britain and Canada

The literature of library technology contains hundreds of articles in the seventies recording development of library systems in Great Britain and Canada. To do justice to these would require a separate historical volume for each country. Therefore, we can mention here only a few system developments which will give the reader a flavor for the situation much as we have done in the above discussions of other foreign systems.

The University of Southampton Library was the first British library to automate circulation using an offline data collection system. Numerous university and public libraries developed circulation systems. Many of these used 80-column punched cards for input of book identification data and punched plastic badges for patron identification and data entry. By the latter third of the decade, Plessey Ltd., had brought out the Plessey Light Pen Library System, which used bar-coded labels to identify both book and borrower. There were obvious advantages to this since books no longer required book pockets and borrower identification cards could be more cheaply. Thus, the Plessey device started the commercial development of our present bar code, which remains at the heart of all modern library circulation applications as well as retailing, inventory control and shipping.

BNB MARC, cataloging networks and applications development were largely custom software projects of universities. Newcastle-upon-Tyne produced a very nice serials catalog. The Birmingham Libraries Co-operative Mechanization Project (BLCMP) was a leading example of a regional network as was the Scottish Libraries Co-operative Automation Project (SCOLCAP). Much work concentrated on cataloging systems with COM catalogs as the major product. The London and South Eastern Library Region (LASER), through grant funding, conceived of an operational network system to serve its members which would involve linking local library systems to LASER. (93) This plan called for implementing DOBIS but also keeping the British Library's Library Software Package as a contingency if DOBIS proved unsuccessful. The need for online, interactive systems, particularly acquisitions and cataloging was recognized; however, LASER still believed that circulation was distinct and severable as a function. By the close of the decade, the purchase of commercially developed systems assumed as significant an importance as in the United States. But unlike some of the smaller European countries a native infrastructure of both foreign and British companies was becoming active in the marketplace. The October 1979 issue of *Program* was devoted to tenders and contract negotiations. (94) Christopher William John Wilson edited a directory of operational library computer applications which provides a good overview of the state of some 150 libraries' computerization efforts. (95)

Canadian MARC format development proceeded in parallel to USMARC, providing for bilingual Canadian needs and other national variations. The National Library of Canada built its automated system, as previously mentioned, through a heavily customized version of DOBIS. This was a very risky undertaking and many Canadian librarians expressed doubts over the desirability of this undertaking. The modifications to handle the CAN MARC record were extreme. Much automation activity was centered in the provincial universities or other academic libraries. Most extensive of these developments was the University of Toronto Library Automated System (UTLAS), which became the de facto national Canadian network, much as OCLC became the de facto U.S. network. Like OCLC's system, UTLAS was based initially on Xerox Sigma computers, which were later phased out and replaced by the Tandem Computer system, a fault-tolerant redundant computer architecture designed for online transaction processing applications. The University of Toronto eventually administered UTLAS as a separate agency and finally sold it to the International Thompson organization. Later renamed Utlas, the system offers services that have appealed to U.S. libraries, and it now markets these services in the United States, with some customers using online network cataloging and interlibrary loan applications and others doing COM catalogs and retrospective conversion.

Examination of systems literature shows that much of the work done in Canadian university libraries closely paralleled the state of the art in the United States. (96) Guelph University's CODOC, a batch mode document indexing system, was used by both Canadian and U.S. libraries. Networking was also developing in a similar fashion. The Ontario union catalog project, UNICAT/TELECAT, involved libraries of six Quebec universities, seven Ontario universities, one provincial government and one federal government agency and one publisher. These organizations cataloged 231,374 titles from May 1975 to April 1976 using the UTLAS system. (97) This project showed that successful cooperative retrospective conversion and current cataloging could be done bilingually using the CATSS (Cataloging Support System) of UTLAS. Such a project led the way to forging a strong Canadian network, having its own distinctive features.

A Canadian company, GEAC Computers, Ltd., which initially built a line of minicomputers known as the GEAC 6000 and 8000 for the financial industry, entered the library system market with its circulation system jointly developed and installed at Guelph University. GEAC expanded marketing of its system, initially designed for circulation and followed by an online interactive catalog, to the United States and Europe. The GEAC Library Information System was not a well-integrated system but a collection of separate applications requiring separately tied terminals defined to the system. This meant that a very large library, needing over 80 terminals connected to a specific module such as the online catalog, would have had to replicate its database onto two networked systems and install terminals on both systems. This would later prove to be a major impediment as would the lack of module integration in the system. Another Canadian company, Universal Library Systems, had earlier sold its Digital Equipment Corp. computer-based circulation system called ULYSIS to several American customers.

The foreign systems suppliers now are active in markets throughout the world as are some American companies. Most of the current foreign software is compatible with American computer systems such as Digital Equipment minicomputers or systems that can run the UNIX or Pick operating systems. Transportability of software is becoming a greater issue as systems become more complex and integrated. It should be noted that the MUMPS language used in some early minicomputer-based library systems has dropped from the picture as an automated library system language.

XIV. CONCLUSION

By the close of the seventies, it was apparent that library automation was taking on a much broader perspective to include the user and to incorporate bibliographic networks. The provision of local in-library systems designed not only for use by librarians but increasingly for the library user as well and the view of the library's system as one integral to the broader parent institution's whole information systems environment were emerging by the end of the decade. In academic libraries, institutions began to view the provision of library systems as an integral part of educational computing. With an increase in computer vendors' abilities to provide system-level software to permit linking diverse systems, the potential for having users normally connected to one system access other systems via a gateway device and some standard network protocol schemes started to be realized. With the concurrent surge of end-user interest in online searching of remote databases, one could forecast that in the early part of the 1980's it would be possible to use the library system both as a host for other databases and also as a gateway to reach other database suppliers' services by using commercial packet switching networks. And, as the worldwide connectivity of the Internet began to emerge by 1992, it was inevitable that the library online catalogs would be an ever more visible scholarly resource available to researchers across the earth. It became clear that library automation was increasingly becoming practical, affordable and virtually a necessity for all types and sizes of libraries. With the lowest cost minicomputer systems still costing over $100,000, thousands of smaller libraries still awaited solutions to their bibliographic needs, even though many medium- to larger size libraries of all types could now afford systems. With more availability of machine readable cataloging for retrospective conversion from both bibliographic utilities and commercial vendors, some lowering of unit costs was occurring, which was making retrospective conversion increasingly attractive. Smaller libraries, such as those in primary and secondary schools, were the least impacted by automation developments of the sixties and seventies. Only a few school systems were using OCLC or had district level central computer applications operating. Usually these central computer applications were batch-processed materials orders or some form of catalog product. (98) With the advent of the full flourishing of the microcomputer in the early eighties, these smaller libraries would be able to examine computer-assisted alternatives to their manual systems and services. Also, the notion of decreasing operational costs through the use of computers finally proved itself largely invalid. Provision of more timely and improved service to the library user was the real reason to use computer and communications technology. Bibliographic utilities such as OCLC and the emerging Research Libraries Group/RLIN system legitimized the use of computers to improve library services. Local and regional network development was fostered by the success of the Ohio College network and the Minitex network in Minnesota. These early cooperative organizations saw the benefit that union catalog databases would have to their collection sharing and document delivery services.

By the eighties many of these concerns would be addressed and even faster progress in the use of technology would occur. Library automation was no longer met with the skepticism of the early seventies, even though librarians were still having difficult times receiving all of the system enhancements and benefits that vendors promised or that were planned for their systems developed in-house. Moreover, since some vendors had dozens of systems in place and CLSI had around 400 systems installed by 1980, system users began to form user groups and feel some comfort in their shared needs. However, the willingness to be pioneer spirits also seemed to vanish from many previously pioneering libraries.

The decade of the eighties would bring systems technology and new electronic forms of access to smaller libraries through the microcomputer. A more global view of functionality of automated library systems would emerge. Communications and linking of users to library systems remotely with gateways to arrays of locally available databases were becoming a brighter possibility. Finally, library automation and application of the computer to bibliographic activities would become a natural phenomenon since parent organizations also were evolving to a more global information systems strategy.

REFERENCES

1. Shera, Jesse H. *Documentation and the Organization of Knowledge*. London: Crosby Lockwood, 1966. p. 84.
2. Wasserman, Paul. *The Librarian and the Machine, Observations on the Application of Machines in Administration of College and University Libraries*. Detroit: Gale, 1965.
3. Patrinostro, Frank. Library Automation—The Last Ten Years. In: *Proceedings of the LARC Institute on Automation of Libraries in School Systems, September 27–28,*

1973, California State Polytechnic University, Pomona, CA. Edited by H. William Axford. Tempe, AZ: LARC Association, 1974. p. 7-10.
4. Effective Access to the Periodical Literature: A National Program. *Task Force on a National Periodicals System*. Washington, DC: National Commission on Libraries and Information Science, April 1977. 92 pp.
5. *National Periodical Center Technical Development Plan*. Washington, DC: Council on Library Resources, 1978.
6. Arthur D. Little, Inc. *A Comparative Evaluation of Alternative Systems for the Provision of Effective Access to the Periodical Literature: A Report to the National Commission on Libraries and Information Science*. Washington, DC: National Commission on Libraries and Information Science, October 1979.
7. Bosseau, Don. University of California, San Diego Serials System. In: *Computerized Serials Systems Series, Vol. 1. No. 2*. Tempe, AZ: LARC Association, 1973.
8. Johnson, Millard. The PHILSOM Network: Maintenance and Design. In: *Proceedings of the LARC Institute on Automated Serials Systems, St. Louis, MO, May 24-25, 1973*. p. 65-69. See also the related papers by Priscilla Mayden "The Problems of Entering a Computerized Serials Network or the Validity of Murphy's Law" p. 43-49; Virginia Feagler "The PHILSOM Network: The Coordinator's Viewpoint" p. 51-57; Neil Falvey "The PHILSOM Network: A Programmer/Analyst's View" p. 59-63; Dean Schmidt "The PHILSOM Network: A User Library Viewpoint" p. 71-75.
9. Johnson, Millard F. A Design for a Mini-computer Based Serials Control Network. *Special Libraries 67*(8): 386-390 (August 1976).
10. Grosch, Audrey N. University of Minnesota Bio-Medical Library Serials System. *Special Libraries 60*(7): 349-360 (July 1969).
11. Strom, Karen D. Software Design for Bio-Medical Library Serials Control System. In: *American Society for Information Science, Conference, 1968, Columbus, OH. Proceedings, Vol. 5: Information Transfer*. New York: Greenwood Press, 1968. p. 267-275.
12. Grosch, Audrey N. Serial Arrival Prediction Coding. *Information Processing and Management 12*(2): 141-146 (1976).
13. Grosch, Audrey N. Theory and Design of Serials Holding Statements in Computer-Based Serials Systems. *The Serials Librarian 1*(4): 341-352 (1977).
14. Pan, Elizabeth. *New York State Library Automated Serials Control System*. Albany, NY: University of the State of New York, The State Education Department, The New York State Library, 1974.
15. Fayollat, James. Online Serials Control System in a Large Bio-Medical Library: Part I. Description of the System. *Journal of the American Society for Information Science 23*: 318-322 (September 1972).
16. Fayollat, James. Online Serials Control System in a Large Bio-Medical Library: Part II. Evaluation of Retrieval Features. *Journal of the American Society for Information Science 23*: 353-358 (November 1972).
17. Fayollat, James. Online Serials Control System in a Large Bio-Medical Library: Part III. Comparison of Online and Batch Operations and Cost Analysis. *Journal of the American Society for Information Science 24*: 80-86 (March 1973).

18. Willmering, William J. On-line Centralized Serials Control. *The Serials Librarian 1*(3): 243-249 (Spring 1977).
19. Grosch, Audrey N. The Minnesota Union List of Serials. *Journal of Library Automation 6*(3): 167-181 (September 1973).
20. Anable, Richard. The Ad Hoc Discussion Group on Serials Data Bases: Its History, Current Position and Future. *Journal of Library Automation 6*(4): 207-214 (December 1973).
21. Grosch, Audrey N. A Regional Serials Program Under National Serials Data Program Auspices: Discussion Paper Prepared for Ad Hoc Serials Discussion Group. *Journal of Library Automation 6*(4): 201-206 (December 1973).
22. Anable, Richard. CONSER: An Update. *Journal of Library Automation 8*(1): 26-30 (March 1975).
23. Grosch, Audrey N. Conversion of the Minnesota Union List of Serials (MULS) to National Serials Data Program (NSDP) Requirements: A Proposal. Final Report. Submitted to the National Serials Data Program, Library of Congress. Minneapolis, MN: University of Minnesota Libraries, December 1973. 52 pp. (ERIC ED 088429).
24. Library of Congress. MARC Development Office. *MARC Serials Editing Guide, CONSER Edition*. Prepared by Phyllis A. Bruns and Mary E. Sauer. Washington, DC: Library of Congress, 1975.
25. Veneziano, Velma. Library Automation: Data for Processing and Processing for Data. In: *Annual Review of Information Science and Technology, Vol. 15, 1980*. White Plains, NY: Knowledge Industry Publications, Inc. for the American Society for Information Science, 1980. Chapter 4, p. 109-145.
26. Collins, Kenneth Alan. Data Management Systems, Part. I. A Model Approach to Automating Small Library Files. *Special Libraries 66*(3): 121-125 (March 1975); and Collins, Kenneth Alan and William W. West, Part II. Journal Routing—An Example of Library Applications. *Special Libraries 66*(4): 205-211 (April 1975).
27. DeGennaro, Richard. Wanted: A Minicomputer Serials Control System. *Library Journal 102*(8): 878-879 (April 15, 1977).
28. Paul, Hubert. Serials Processing: Manual vs. Automation. *Library Resources and Technical Services 21*(4): 345-353 (Fall 1977).
29. *The Serials Librarian 3(*1) (Fall 1978). Articles: Nancy Melin Buckeye "The OCLC Serials Subsystem: Implementation/implications at Central Michigan University" p. 31-32; Harry H. Kamers "OCLC's Serials Control Subsystem, a Case Study" p. 43-55; James F. Corey. "OCLC and serials Processing: a State of Transition at the University of Illinois" p. 57-67.
30. Alper, Bruce. An Automated Library Acquisition System. In: *Proceedings of the LARC Institute on Acquisitions Systems and Subsystems, May 25-26, 1972, Lake Geneva, WI*. Edited by H. William Axford. Tempe, AZ: LARC Association, 1973. p. 23-83.
31. Olsen, Lloyd. Baker and Taylor's Automated Buying System for Libraries (BATAB). In: *Proceedings of the LARC Institute on Acquisitions Systems and Subsystems, May 25-26, 1972, Lake Geneva, WI*. Edited by H. William Axford. Tempe, AZ: LARC Association, 1973. p. 85-101.
32. Auld, Larry and Robert Baker. LOLITA: An Online Book Order and Fund Accounting System. In: *Clinic on Library Applications of Data Processing, 9th,*

Urbana, IL., April 30-May 3, 1972. Proceedings: Applications of Online Computers to Library Problems. Edited by F. Wilfred Lancaster. Urbana, IL: University of Illinois Graduate School of Library Science, 1972. p. 29-53.

33. Sipfle, W. K. Bell Laboratories Book Acquisition, Accounting and Cataloging System (BELLTIP). Murray Hill, NJ: Bell Telephone Laboratories, November 1975. Available from the author, Bell Telephone Laboratories, Murray Hill, NJ 07974.
34. Woods, Richard. The Washington Library Computer Network. *Online Review 3*(3): 297-330 (September 1979).
35. Reed, Mary Jane Pobst. The Washington Library Network's Computerized Bibliographic System. *Journal of Library Automation 8*(3): 174-199 (September 1975).
36. Stanford University's BALLOTS System. Project BALLOTS and Stanford University Libraries. *Journal of Library Automation 8*(1): 31-50 (March 1975).
37. Almy, Robert. A Computer Assisted Circulation Section. In: *LARC Series on Automated Activities in Health Sciences Libraries 1*(4): 30-41 (1976).
38. Kershner, Lois M. Management Aspects of the Use of the IBM System 7 in Circulation Control. In: *Clinic on Library Applications of Data Processing, 11th, Urbana, IL, April 28-May 1, 1974. Proceedings: Applications of Minicomputers to Library and Related Problems.* Edited by F. Wilfred Lancaster. Urbana, IL: University of Illinois Graduate School of Library Science, 1975. p. 43-53.
39. McGee, Rob. The University of Chicago Library's JRL 1000 Circulation Terminal and Bar Coded Labels. *Journal of Library Automation 8*(1): 5-25 (March 1975).
40. Denny, Bob. System Design and Hardware for an Integrated Library Data Management System. In: *LARC Series on Automated Activities in Health Sciences Libraries 1*(2): 24-29 (1975).
41. Grosch, Audrey N. Minicomputer—Characteristics, Economics and Selection for an Integrated Library Management System. In: *Clinic on Library Applications of Data Processing, 11th, Urbana, IL, April 28-May 1, 1974. Proceedings: Applications of Minicomputers to Library and Related Problems.* Edited by F. Wilfred Lancaster. Urbana, IL: University of Illinois Graduate School of Library Science, 1975. p. 158-169.
42. Goldstein, Charles M.; Elizabeth A. Payne and Richard S. Dick. *The Integrated Library System (ILS): System Overview.* Bethesda, MD: U.S. Dept. of Health and Human Services, Public Health Services, National Institutes of Health, 1981. (Lister Hill Technical Report TR 81-05) (PB 188,039).
43. *Buying New Technology.* Edited by Karl Nyren. New York: Library Journal, 1978. (LJ Special Report No. 4).
44. Boss, Richard W. Circulation Systems: The Options. *Library Technology Reports 15*(1): 7-105 (January/February 1979).
45. Scholz, William H. Computer-based Circulation Systems—A Current Review and Evaluation. *Library Technology Reports 13*(3): 231-325 (May 1977).
46. DeGennaro, Richard. Library Automation: Changing Patterns and New Directions. *Library Journal 101*: 75-183 (January 1, 1976).
47. DeGennaro, Richard. The Development and Administration of Automated Systems in Academic Libraries. *Journal of Library Automation 1*(1): 75-91 (1968).

48. Alley, Brian. Spec Writing for Librarians: The Second LITA Tutorial. *Technicalities 1*(3): 6 (February 1981).
49. Malinconico, S.; Michael and James A. Rizzolo. The New York Public Library Automated Book Catalog Subsystem. *Journal of Library Automation 6*(1): 3-36 (March 1973).
50. Torkington, Roy B. MARC and its Application to Library Automation. In: *Advances in Librarianship, Vol. 4.* Edited by Melvin J. Voight. New York and London: Academic Press, 1974. p. 2-33.
51. Bierman, Kenneth John. *Automated Alternatives to Card Catalogs for Large Libraries: The Current State of Planning and Implementation: Final Report of a Council on Library Resources Fellowship Project.* Washington, DC: Council on Library Resources, 1975.
52. Ibid., p. 32.
53. Butler, Brett. Automatic Format Recognition of MARC Bibliographic Elements: A Review and Projection. *Journal of Library Automation 7*(1): 27-42 (March 1974).
54. Malinconico, S. Michael. Bibliographic Terminals, Development Status—United States—1977. *Libri 28*(2): 87-106 (June 1978).
55. Stanford University's BALLOTS System. Project BALLOTS and Stanford University Libraries. *Journal of Library Automation 8*(1): 31-50 (March 1975).
56. Payne, Charles T. The University of Chicago Library Data Management System. In: *Clinic on Library Applications of Data Processing, 11th, Urbana, IL., April 28-May 1, 1974. Proceedings: Applications of Minicomputers to Library and Related Problems.* Edited by F. Wilfred Lancaster. Urbana, IL: University of Illinois Graduate School of Library Science, 1975. p. 105-119.
57. McAllister, Caryl and A. Stratton McAllister. DOBIS/LIBIS: An Integrated, Online Library Management System. *Journal of Library Automation 12*(4): 300-313 (December 1979).
58. Newman, William L. et al. DOBIS: The Canadian Government Version. *Canadian Library Journal 36*(4): 181-194 (August 1979).
59. Payne, Charles; Rob McGee, Helen F. Schmierer and Howard S. Harris. The University of Chicago Library Data Management System. *Library Quarterly 47*(1): 1-22 (January 1977).
60. *The Nature and Future of the Catalog: Proceedings of the ALA's Information Science and Automation Division's 1975 and 1977 Institutes on the Catalog.* Edited by Maurice J. Freedman and S. Michael Malinconico. Phoenix, AZ: Oryx Press, 1979. p. 10-11.
61. Hayes, Robert M. and Joseph Becker. *Handbook of Data Processing for Libraries. 2nd ed.* Los Angeles, CA: Melville Publishing Co., 1974. p. 23.
62. Cornell University Libraries. *Task Force on the Future of the Cornell University Libraries Card Catalogs. Report no. 1: Recommendations and Future Agenda.* Ithaca, NY: Cornell University Libraries, 1977.
63. ACM Conference on Management Issues in Automated Cataloging, 1977, Chicago. *Requiem for the Card Catalog: Management Issues in Automated Cataloging; Papers.* Edited by Daniel Gore, Joseph Kimborough and Peter Spyers-Duran. Westport, CT: Greenwood Press, 1979. p. 179.
64. Project Media Base. *Problems of Bibliographic Access to Non-print Materials: Final*

Report. Washington, DC: National Commission on Libraries and Information Science, 1979.
65. Avram, Henriette D. and Lucia J. Rather. Principles of Format Design. *Journal of Library Automation 7*(3): 161-167 (September 1974).
66. Avram, Henriette D. International Standards for the Interchange of Bibliographic Records in Machine Readable Form. *Library Resources and Technical Services 20*(1): 25-35 (Winter 1976).
67. NCLIS/NBS Task Force on Computer Network Protocol. *A Computer Network Protocol for Library and Information Science Applications*. Washington, DC: National Commission on Libraries and Information Science, Government Printing Office, 1977.
68. Landau, Robert M. The Impact of Office Automation on Libraries. *Special Libraries 72*(2): 122-126 (April 1981).
69. Williams, P. W. The Potential of the Microprocessor in Library and Information Work. *Aslib Proceedings 31*(4): 202-209 (April 1979).
70. Hines, Theodore C. and Lois Winkel. Microcomputer-aided Production of Indexes. *The Indexer 11*(4): 198-201 (October 1979).
71. Zabinski, Toby and Michael P. Zabinsky. A Coin Operated Computer in a Public Library. *Library Journal 104*(18): 2174-2175 (October 15, 1979).
72. Lundeen, Gerald. The Role of Microcomputers in Libraries. *Wilson Library Bulletin 55*(3): 178-185 (November 1980).
73. Zamora, Ramon. Computertown USA! Using Personal Computers in a Public Library. School Library Journal 27(8): 28-31 (April 1981).
74. Plotnick, Art. CLSI: the Hatvany Hot Touch. *American Libraries 12*(1): 16-17 (January 1981).
75. Hosono, Kimio. The Characteristics of Library Automation in Japan. [In Japanese]. *Library and Information Science 14*: 211-227 (1976).
76. Asano, Jiro. Progress in Library Automation in National University Libraries in Japan; Around the Activities of Working Group on University Library Automation. [In Japanese] *Library and Information Science 15*: 97-105 (1977).
77. Fung, Margaret C. Library Automation in the Republic of China. *Journal of Library and Information Science (USA/Taiwan) 6*(1): 1-16 (April 1980).
78. Kulkorni, D. R.; R. R. Bhorucha and U. A. Ghiya. The Periodical Management System. Abmedabad, India: Physical Research Laboratory, 1980. (PB 82-116518).
79. *National Conference on Library and Bibliographic Applications of Minicomputers, Sydney, N.S.W., Australia, August 22-24, 1979. Proceedings*. Edited by Michael R. Middleton. Kensington, N.S.W.: Unisearch, 1979.
80. Orosz, Gabor. Az Autonotizalas a moszknai Allami Nyilvanos Tudomanyos—Muszaki Konyvtarban. (Mechanization in the State Public Scientific and Technical Library in Moscow). *Tudom. Musz Tojek 24*(1): 9-13 (January 1977).
81. Ryabov, A. B. Automatizatsiya Bibliotechno-bibliograficheskihk protessov—Odna iz vazheiskikh form povysheniya effektivnosti raboty bibliotek. (Automation of Library Bibliographical Processes—One of the Most Important Ways of Increasing the Efficiency of Library Work). *Sovetskoe Bibliotekovedenie 5*: 107-116 (1975).
82. Gabor, Frantisek. Perspektiny uplatnovania novey techniky v. knizniciach. (Prospect of New Technology in Libraries). *Cititel 29*(7-8): 264-267 (July-August 1980).
83. *Neuere, Formate fuer Verarbeitung und Austausch Bibliographischen Daten: Bericht*

eines Symposiums, veranstaltet von der Arbeitsstelle fuer Bibliotekstechnik am 30 April 1974. Pullach bei Munchen: Verlag Dokumentation, 1975.

84. Wessel, Andrew E. Einsatz von Minicomputern in der Dokumentation—Perspekti-nen und Probleme. (The Use of Minicomputers in Documentation: Perspective and Problems) *Nachrichten der Dokumentation 28*(3): 99-104 (June 1977).
85. McAllister, Caryl and A. Stratton McAllister. DOBIS/LIBIS: An Integrated Online Library Management System. *Journal of Library Automation 12*(4): 300-313 (December 1979).
86. Ehlert, Peter. Die Datenorganisation in Dortmunder On-line Bibliothekssystem DOBIS. (Data Organization in the Dortmund On-line Library system DOBIS). *Mitteilungsblatt (Verband der Bibliotheken des Landes Nordrhein-westfalen) 25*(4): 351-363 (December 1975).
87. Newman, William L. et al. DOBIS: The Canadian Government Version. *Canadian Library Journal 36*(4): 181-194 (August 1979).
88. Kungl. tekniska Logskolan. Biblioteket. *Library Services in Transition: A Presentation of Current Activities at the Royal Institute of Technology Library.* Edited by Stephen Schwartz, Gunnar Carlsson and Gudmund Froberg. Stockholm: The Library, 1978.
89. Bibliotekarforbundets FAUST-Udvalg. FAUST Committee of the Librarian's Union. Ny faseopdeling for EDB-awendebi i bibliotekerne? (Should there be a new division of the phases of computerization in libraries?) *Bibliotek 70*(7): 159-160 (1977).
90. Boje, Kirsten. Den nye biblioteksdataaftale—FAUST om igen. (The New Agreement on Library data—FAUST all Over Again). *Bibliotek 70*(16): 441-443 (1978).
91. IFLA Working Group on Content Designators. *UNIMARC: Universal MARC Format.* London: IFLA International Office for the UBC, 1977.
92. French, Thomas. *Automated Systems in Swiss Libraries and in Two Libraries in Southwest Germany and Development of Reader Services.* Birmingham, Eng.: University of Birmingham, 1982. (British Library R & D Report 5780).
93. Ashford, John; Ross Bourne and Jean Plaister. *London and South Eastern Library Region. Co-operative in Library Automation: the COLA Project: report of a Research Project Undertaken by LASER and Supported by a Grant from the British Library Research and Development Department During the Period November 1974 to March 1975.* London: LASER, 1975. (OSTI Report No. 5225).
94. Papers from Aslib Computer Information Group Seminar "Negotiating for a Computer," March 13, 1979. *Program 13*(4): 158-185 (October 1979).
95. *Directory of Operational Computer Applications in United Kingdom Libraries and Information Units. 2nd ed.* Edited by Christopher William John Wilson. London: Aslib, 1977. (Aslib Computer Applications Group, Acquisitions, Cataloging and Circulation Working Party).
96. Ready, William Bernard and Tom Drynan. *Library Automation: A View from Ontario.* Halifax: Dalhousie University, University Libraries, School of Library Science, 1977. (Occasional Paper No. 14).
97. Stierwalt, Ralph E. UNICAT/TELECAT: A Report on the Development of a Union Catalogue in Ontario. *Ontario Library Review 60*(3): 180-185 (September 1976).
98. Twaddle, Dan R. School Media Services and Automation. *School Media Quarterly 7*(4): 257-268, 273-276 (Summer 1979).

2

NEW DIRECTIONS FOR LIBRARY SYSTEMS
1980's PROGRESS

"Would you tell me please, which way I ought to go from here?" asked Alice.
"That depends on where you want to get to," answered the Cheshire Cat."
— *Alice in Wonderland,* Lewis Carroll

I. INTRODUCTION

Although it is somewhat artificial to approach the recent historical foundations of library automation by an examination of significant trends and developments by decade, it is nonetheless a convenient one since it appears that computing technology takes a major shift approximately every five years. Since computing technology encompasses many subtechnologies whose 5-year growth spurts are not necessarily in synchrony, the impression is that progress is gradual and more continuous when the whole field is examined. But when the subdisciplines and more specialized parts of the field are examined, for example microcomputing, one can cite numerous examples of this 5-year design and production cycle for introducing experimental technology as a marketable product. With the adoption of marketplace systems and the move away from locally developed software, library experimentation has been constrained by what a specific vendor's systems will allow and/or how much beta site (prerelease) testing a library may be willing to experience, working with the vendor on further product enhancements.

With the beginning of the 1980's, it was evident that computer and communications technology was making possible a number of trends in library and information services. As with Alice, librarians were busy determining where they should go from their present situation. There was some controversy as to where libraries should want to get to, something that is inevitable in every profession. Where librarians in the seventies tried to stress costs vs. benefits in justifying their inevitable use of newer technologies, by the end of the decade it was clear that their real justification for use of new computing and communications technologies was to make possible broader access and services to their clientele and to broaden the clientele base as well. In the eighties, this view was nicely summed up by Richard Boss when he stated, "In 1983, however, the consensus among those who have studied the costs and benefits of installing computer systems remained that improved services are a more compelling reason to automate than are possible reductions in costs." (1)

The major trends in the seventies continued to evolve, and when these were coupled with advances in data processing technology, some new and interesting directions in library and information science had clearly emerged by the end of the eighties. Let us now summarize these trends together with some examples of the major developments as reported in the literature of the decade.

1. With the continued trend toward installing vendor-developed automated systems technologies, it would become increasingly apparent that librarians at all levels would need to understand how to plan, evaluate, procure and install new technologies offered by vendors, including an assessment of the vendor's viability where continuing product support was a requirement.
2. If interlinked systems were ultimately to create a de facto multifaceted information environment for the library user and librarian, then increasing standardization efforts would be needed in data formats, transaction content, command language, communications protocols and distributed system functions. If library information systems were to increase functional processing at the workstation level rather than at the host computer or local area network application server level there would need to be standards in the workstation/host computer application program interface under specific systems architectures then being promulgated by the respective major computer manufacturers.
3. Lower cost and more powerful multiuser systems using such generic operating system environments as PICK and UNIX would bring smaller, yet manageable multiuser systems to the smaller library, but they would increasingly compete with microcomputer-based local area network solutions.
4. Individual more powerful microcomputer workstations would enable an increase in multitasking, particularly as host based systems moved

toward incorporation of the microcomputer as "scholar" workstation instead of merely using intelligent terminals, which are to some extent programmable for type of emulation or function key implementation but which do not have their own data storage capabilities.

5. With the increasing interest in library or scholar workstation development, our host-based library systems would eventually change from largely central host application processing to workstation-oriented environments, where most of the application functionality and user friendliness of the system would reside in the workstation, leaving the network-attached hosts to become fast and large database servers.
6. In the applications area, the development of the online public access catalog was the Cinderella of the decade, and this led to the rapid development of the user interface and renewed emphasis on information retrieval and authority control work.
7. New storage and access technologies such as CD-ROM, coupled with microcomputer and local area network technologies, would bring individual libraries to consider more creative ways to bring both publications and indexing tools to their users.
8. More vendors would adopt system development strategies that would make their systems less tied to specific hardware platforms and less dependent on customized nonindustry-standard hardware. Their strategy would also include generalized approaches to application solutions which would allow the specific library to customize the system to its needs upon installation.
9. The overall trend would be toward the ideal of an integrated multi-functional system. The incorporation of a powerful generalized database management and retrieval capability to permit new information in addition to the normal traditional library catalog information would prove to be a significant augmentation to the system. (2)
10. Library automation would no longer be viewed as merely systems to perform routine "housekeeping" tasks of use to library staff but rather as the total composite of technologies needed to bring to the library user the necessary access and services to answer real-world information needs and enable the library staff to be as responsive as possible to these needs.
11. Local area network (LAN) technology in server-type networks using very powerful server microcomputers, such as those manufactured by Tricord, Inc., would be capable of providing a host system for an integrated library system. Using over 40 gigabytes of storage and up to 250 terminals, LANs would again threaten the role of the supermini-computer and mainframe for integrated library systems.
12. Using the TCP/IP protocol, it would become a necessity for the online

catalogs of academic, public, and special libraries to be connected and available for searching on the Internet and for direct public access by modem.

13. Libraries would make use of other commonly accepted information technology tools, e.g., document imaging, Ethernet LAN technology and software, Gopher client/server software, World Wide Web client/server software, electronic mail and listserv/news group discussions, to provide library services and better operational tools.

II. AUTOMATION AND SYSTEMS MANAGEMENT

With the prospect of increasingly critical application support being provided by more complex integrated vendor-developed systems, the cost and risk of adopting new technology changed from software development risk to assessment of the respective strengths and weaknesses of the various products and the viability of vendors in a generally undercapitalized segment of the computing industry. When this shift was coupled with a less than ideal understanding of the system procurement process, contract negotiation, and basic technologies involved, there was a fruitful area for the development of tailored consulting practices specializing as library automation consultants. Once a system was selected and installation began, a library would face added challenges as to how it trained its staff and managed the systems it was installing. In larger institutions, particularly universities and colleges, the use of campus data centers and facilities management contracts to provide the actual operations support became the trend, and in-library computing installations involving super-minicomputer or mainframe-type systems decreased. This has required librarians to become adept at cooperative interrelationships within their own institutions and at broadening their views to consider the institution's goals rather than just the library's goals. As with any solution of this sort, the library faces a tradeoff of what is best for the institution vs. what is best for the library, so that compromise is inevitable. No single approach can be prescribed for every library to follow.

Many books were published through the decade that were aimed at educating librarians and particularly library managers on the basics of choosing systems and various new technologies. One of the best of these, by Joseph Mathews, was published in 1980. (3) Toohill, during the same period, made an important contribution on writing specifications for library systems and handling their installation. (4) Five prominent library automation consultants—Richard Boss, Rob McGee, Susan Baerg Epstein, Joseph Mathews and James Rush—concluded that the single mistake most often made by libraries in implementing systems is a lack of planning, followed by naive contracts with unrealistic implementation schedules and lack of definition of the vendor's and library's responsibilities. (5) In my own experiences over 25 years of systems consulting, this is an opinion with which I am wholeheartedly in agreement!

Noted facilities consultants Elaine and Aaron Cohen addressed the need for proper library building and interior design in their guidebook. (6) Cline and Sinott examined some case studies of larger libraries and their administrative changes due to automation and concluded that it was not clear who should manage large library resources—librarians or managers from other sectors such as computing. (7) Toward the end of the decade, the conceptualization of the Chief Information Officer (CIO) emerged. While there were a few isolated cases of major library directors in universities assuming this role, notably Patricia Battin at Columbia University, the position was usually occupied by another senior academic administrator, often from the computing sector. Similarly, in business and industry, the CIO's role came out of the broadening of the management information systems function, with a senior executive from the management information systems (MIS) area of the company often appointed. Now, in the mid-nineties the CIO position has been accepted by both business and academe, albeit with a differing span of authority within varying institutional cultures.

Corbin wrote an excellent book for any library planning on installing its own minicomputer-based system. (8) Often utilized as a resource for writing library system specifications were the *Library Systems Evaluation Guide* volumes by James E. Rush Associates, Inc. (9) These provide a sound foundation on which a specific library can develop its own requirements.

Finally, it appeared that some individuals in the profession showed their concern over the working conditions and facilities where staff needed to use automated systems. Cortez and Kazlauskas addressed these workplace design factors very well in Chapter 4 of their book. (10) To update the previously mentioned works dealing with library automation proposals and contracts, Cortez published a very thorough work with many examples from actual library procurements. (11) Since many staff who work with automated systems are library technicians, Tracy's was a timely book directed specifically at non-librarian library staff involved in technical processing or circulation. (12) It gave considerable attention to the details of both OCLC and RLG/RLIN systems operation. Many other authors also contributed works dealing with management of automation.

Numerous variations on essentially two themes for large library systems management were to be found in the literature. The first approach relied on an in-library systems unit or department and was more prevalent among libraries that had a long history of use of innovative technology, had their own data-processing staff and, in some cases, had in-library host computers. This might be known as the centralized management model. Both data processing and library professionals usually made up these staffs. Their working relationship with the library was very much the same as that of the MIS function in either their parent institution or in commercial sector. These units usually assumed responsibility for database administration, automated systems operation, troubleshooting, vendor liaison, short- and long-term planning and staff education, and training. They worked in concert with other appropriate library departments and individuals.

The second approach relied on the existing library administrative structure to administer library systems, usually via a library system administrator who had responsibility for contact with the vendor and the institution's computing facilities and coordination of such activities as database administration, education and training, and other in-library functions with existing library departments. This might be characterized as the distributed management model. It usually meant that librarians rather than computing professionals, even those with a library background, were most heavily involved in the system. While there would be some administrator, such as the head of technical or public services acting as the head of systems, responsibility was fragmented and distributed to lower level units. With this distributed responsibility, there could be more difficulty determining just what the actual technology-related expenditures really were in the library systems program, whereas with a responsible unit and centralized budget one could know precisely where the money was really going. Also, this distributed model made accountability more of a problem and made overall systems planning a more difficult matter, with much more coordination necessary among units. With such shared staff there could be numerous problems such as finding the time for the ongoing development of training materials and holding classes as each new system release was installed. This distributed responsibility approach worked best if the staff and management involved were very astute and experienced in both data processing and library needs. Also, such an administrative arrangement did not obviate the need for some specialized staff with full-time responsibilities for various aspects of the library's system.

The training example above is only one such area where an MIS-centered approach may be more effective but is not taken. It appears that the distributed responsibility administrative method is usually found in institutions where there has not been much positive experience with leading-edge technology. In fact, in many such cases, the public institution elects *not* to be on the leading edge of technology when it can adopt proven, vendor-supplied marketplace technology as it becomes available, as funds permit and as sister institutions all adopt the technology. Unfortunately, in some cases, institutions have not always adopted the optimal administrative approaches for their institutional circumstances. Properly handled, either of these methods can be made to work, but to work successfully, they depend on very well equipped personnel.

It seems strange that some librarians and library administrators still believe that a large library can get along fine without a full-time systems unit whose major task is training and support. Would you believe that any banking or insurance company, whose business is now quite tied to the online interactive computer as a major tool, would conceive of operating its enterprise without some form of information systems unit to oversee this aspect of its business? Why is it that many large libraries do not feel similarly disposed? I would postulate that this is because a number of library administrators do not see the problem within the library profession as the whole cloth of educating librarians in both information science and information technology. In fact, we are moving closer and closer to an inevitable merger of computing and libraries but one in which, at the present, the computing and MIS professions still have the edge because of superior technical knowledge of computing, communications and various integrated digital services bringing together data, voice and video.

Certainly, these two themes for management of information technology will continue to be used through the nineties and probably beyond. However successful each approach may be in its given circumstances, it is clear that unless a considerable growth in technical knowledge of the information systems environment takes place on the part of library management and staff, the rest of the nineties will not bring very many situations where library administrators become their institution's CIO, as these individuals generally do not yet have the base of technical program managerial experience found in the MIS and computing sectors, even though they are far better equipped in understanding the organization and retrieval of information. Furthermore, the current dependence on vendor-developed software solutions—even though such a trend is evident in other application areas—does not lend itself to as much innovation as usually results from properly managed custom systems development. Vendors attempt to implement functionality in as simple a manner as possible that will be accepted by the target market for the system, with as little development and maintenance cost as possible. Also, vendors have not provided all of the functionality that libraries demand, so that other system solutions need to be developed—even if interim solutions—to overcome some of these deficiencies.

An example of deficient functionality within a common subset application is found in the NOTIS library system, which allows the operator to enter an action date to trigger examination of a serial record for non-receipt of the next issue but which requires the operator to fill in the date on each check-in. The system does not predict the next issue to arrive with correct volume/issue/date labels. However, the CL Systems, Inc. (CLSI) serials system, which originated as Blackwell's PERLINE serials management system, allows the actual prediction of a serial issue's arrival and its proper volume and issue identifiers as do several other systems such as Faxon's LINX or OCLC's SC-350 Serials Management System. NOTIS customers who would like a bindery subsystem will need to provide some alternative solution as NOTIS user surveys have not placed this high on their development agenda. An example of one library's solution to this NOTIS deficiency is the Bindery Preparation system developed at the University of Minnesota Libraries using the DataEase database management system software on a Novell v.3.11 LAN. This is a typical application that a library doing binding would need to develop to provide capabilities not present in the NOTIS system.

With an increasing dependence on information technologies and on issues of software and hardware compatibilities and network-based systems solutions, there will be a a need to adopt much more dynamic library management structures for these new technologies. The trend in larger libraries is likely to swing again toward in-library units with responsibility for library-wide systems planning, user education and training, workstation and network support, and in-library computing facilities management or liaison with contracted institution facilities management and with software and hardware vendors. Library staff may rotate into such a unit on a specific need basis, with a core professional staff for continuing coordination. This is the pattern now prevalent in technology-based private enterprises, and if past patterns continue to emerge in academe and government, these institutions will continue to adopt techniques and approaches pioneered in the private sector.

III. USMARC DEVELOPMENTS AND STANDARDIZATION

The Library of Congress continued to develop the USMARC (United States Machine Readable Cataloging) formats in concert with the American Library Association's MARBI (Machine Readable Bibliographic Input) Committee reviewing, recommending and approving changes needed by the library community. In 1981, an extension to the Books format was published for technical reports. (13) It provided special tags such as Tag 088, Standard Technical Report Number; Tag 214, Augmented Title to cover enriched titles for title keyword indexing systems; Tag 302, Page Count; Tag 513, Type of Report and Period Covered Note; Tag 536, Funding Information Report—Contract/Grant Number and specific linking entries. A new subfield, $2, was provided for source of subject term in Tags 6xx. In Topical Subject Heading Tag 650, the first indicator was implemented to show whether the term was a primary or secondary one. Several other changes were also included to adapt the Books format for technical reports. Although at this time probably no one was thinking in terms of the eventual integration of all of the MARC formats, this modified format extension demonstrated that MARC format extension was entirely practical and feasible.

In 1981, the USMARC Authority Format was issued. (14) This format has profound implications for all library catalogs, as determining this format would make possible the long-awaited distribution of Library of Congress Authority data to the bibliographic utilities, ultimately via direct computer links through the Linked Systems Project. This format also drew attention to the need for authority control in computer-based catalogs. The early emerging online public catalogs of the time lacked authority control. This fact, coupled with findings of studies of catalog users and their need for good cross-referencing structures, pointed developers in a new, key direction.

Work was proceeding on the USMARC format for holdings and locations. This format would provide much-needed standardization in this data as this format included both bibliographic and physical holdings data. (15) SOLINET developed the initial implementation of this format and developed machine-independent functional algorithms, or pseudocode, that could be used by system developers in programming their systems to accommodate the holdings and locations format. Harvard University and Virginia Polytechnic University have used this pseudocode in their systems, the former system being a heavily customized form of NOTIS and the latter the VTLS system. (16)

Another USMARC format was the AMC (Archives and Manuscripts) format which was put to use in the Research Libraries Group, Inc., Research Libraries Information Network (RLG/RLIN), where noted archives were participating in initial use of the format. The Society of American Archivists (SAA) published a volume incorporating AMC format updates through number 10, SAA's data elements dictionary and a sample AMC data preparation form which was adapted from one designed by the Gallaudet College Archives. (17) Anyone wishing to gain an understanding of the USMARC formats should read the works by Walt Crawford. (18,19). He points out that the seven current USMARC formats are moving toward integration into one format. This is a significant factor for library systems developers and for all those in libraries that use USMARC format-based products. While this integration will simplify the continuing maintenance and updating of the format to meet new needs, it will necessitate most vendor and private systems to make major design revisions. Some systems may accommodate this integration more easily than others. But, most importantly, format integration will mean a continuing commitment to educating library staff about these changes and their effect on library databases. Moreover, every new software release will necessitate further education for library staff.

The major national standards program affecting libraries is that of the National Information Standards Organization (NISO), which formerly was known as Committee Z39. For example, one of the early standards published was Z39.2 "Bibliographic Information Interchange," which specifies the physical data structure underlying USMARC. Some 60 standards affecting information sciences have been published by NISO as American national standards. A dozen more standards are under development. Some of the key standards that specifically affect automated library systems are:

Z39.9 International Standard Serial Numbering
Z39.11 System for the Romanization of Japanese (as well as similar standards for Arabic; Slavic Cyrillic; Hebrew; Lao, Khmer and Pali; Armenian)
Z39.23 Standard Technical Report Number (STRN)
Z39.43 Standard Address Number for the Publishing Industry
Z39.44 Serials Holdings Statements
Z39.45 Claims for Missing Issues of Serials
Z39.47 Extended Latin Alphabet Coded Character Set for Bibliographic Use (ANSEL)
Z39.49 Computerized Book Ordering
Z39.50 Information Retrieval Service Definition and Protocol
Z39.55 Computerized Serials Orders, Claims, Etc.
Z39.57 Holdings Statement for Non-Serial Items
Z39.58 Common Command Language for Online Interactive Information Retrieval
Z39.59 Electronic Manuscript Preparation and Markup
Z39.63 Interlibrary Loan Data Elements
Z39.64 East Asian Character Code for Bibliographic Use

NISO, through its subcommittees and member organizations, is currently working on some other standards that will have significance to library systems designers. The Z39.50 Implementors Group was working on a version 3 draft as of July, 1993. Some 65 attendees were at the meeting of the group July 7–9, 1993 in St. Louis, MO. By October, 1993 an 8th draft was circulating. Some new standards in various stages of creation and adoption are:

Z39.69 Patron Record Data Elements
Z39.70 Format for Circulation Transactions
Z39.71 Holding Statements for Bibliographic Items
Z39.72 Format for Submission of Data for Multi-media CD-ROM Mastering (SCAE)

NISO's activity continues to increase as has its membership. The American National Standards Institute (ANSI), of which NISO is our member body, is the clearinghouse for all of America's voluntary standards bodies, with some 8000 ANSI and 7000 ISO (International Standards Organization) standards as well as national standards for 90 national standardizing bodies of other countries.

Another standards body that affects library automation systems is the Institute of Electrical and Electronics Engineers (IEEE), which has developed many computer and telecommunication standards. For example, IEEE 802.1, when completed, will detail how the other 802.x standards mentioned later relate to one another and to the International Standards Organization Open System Interconnection Reference Model (ISO/OSI). In the field of library and information science, the Linked Systems Project (LSP) has espoused the above OSI model as its standard for peer-to-peer computer systems linkage of the Library of Congress, OCLC, RLG/RLIN and WLN systems. In the actual implementation of LSP, however, the network is not in strict OSI compliance since such compliance also depends on numerous software products from various computer manufacturers which need to be brought into compliance with OSI. IEEE 802.2 Logical Link Control (LLC) Standard defines this specific sublayer and is positioned above the remaining 802.x specifications. IEEE 802.3 CSMA/CD Standard defines the carrier sense multiple access with collision detection access method, IEEE 802.4 Token Bus Standard defines the token-passing bus access method protocol, while IEEE 802.5 Token Ring Standard defines the token-ring access method protocol. Work is also underway to define IEEE 802.6 Metropolitan-Area Network (MAN) Standard, which will define media-access-control (MAC) sublayer and physical-layer definitions for a metropolitan-area network using broadband transmission methods. Competing schemes for 100-MB Ethernet over twisted pair wire are receiving considerable attention. This may result in an accepted standard as early as 1995–1996.

We may all expect that further standardization in all aspects influencing creation and operation of library computer systems will be the norm for the foreseeable future.

IV. IN PURSUIT OF THE INTEGRATED SYSTEM

With the surge in minicomputer-based systems being offered by the end of the seventies, the ideal of the integrated library system appeared to be attainable by some point in the eighties. All useful and successful systems are dynamic and never stop evolving; they improve as they are enhanced or as software bugs are fixed. These systems inevitably must respond to the library market's perceived needs or else they would not have new and continuing customers. The systems and their vendors working in concert with their customer libraries have intertwined destinies, governed by both what technology makes possible to develop in software and what the customer libraries can find useful and productive for their operations.

The traditional integrated library system (as opposed to nonintegrated system) was one in which interactive input and file updating occurred using a common database to perform the major functions of acquisitions, including fund accounting support; cataloging and database/authority maintenance; serials management and circulation. Added to that, with the coming of the eighties, was the provision of a directly patron searchable system, one that would act as the library's catalog itself, instead of producing serial magnetic tape output to create a catalog in microfilm or microfiche form. Probably the single most desired function of the integrated library system—the online public access catalog (OPAC)—was the ultimate product of technical processing subsystems, as it finally ushered in a new era of interactive library systems. I prefer to call these OPAC subsystems, and their related subsystems for any search operation, the interactive catalog-searching facility (ICSF) of the integrated system since it should also be a key facility when considering performance of all other library business functions. ICSF will provide the means to incorporate many other databases into the searchable offerings of the library, including full-text, numeric, physical properties, photographic, and abstracting and indexing information files.

With the early eighties, the reality of operating library systems was that none of the systems actually had the facility to serve all of the above functional areas in the library. Although more functional areas are now supported by the typical system, there still is no fully functional integrated library system providing support to every conceivable operation performed in a library. Most early systems grew out of the circulation application, were enhanced to use a MARC-compatible bibliographic database and were then revised to provide a direct interactive search access. Then, some other functions such as acquisitions were offered, but many of these systems of the early eighties did not actually offer a total cataloging support environment and did not have authority-based databases. Their databases were loaded by libraries performing and maintaining their cataloging on one or another bibliographic utility—usually OCLC. The resultant utility magnetic tape records were preprocessed and loaded into the local system. This tape loading started to change the volume of the bibliographic utilities' major batch-produced products—catalog cards and microfilm-based catalogs. One can certainly see an eventual demise to the card and microfilm based catalog. The ICSF either in an online integrated library system or as a microcomputer-driven CD-ROM facility will replace these earlier catalog forms.

With evermore powerful and low cost computing, it was inevitable that the functions of cataloging itself also would not need to be done on a large central host system but would most desirably be done on the local library system with links to the bibliographic utility for resource bibliographic record sharing and authority information. In other words, through the decade it became apparent that the networks' major role would become their union catalog, and locational and switching capability to facilitate actual document delivery via interlibrary loan and secondarily as a raw MARC record supplier. Their heretofore major activity as a provider of catalog cards would diminish with time.

In 1980 there were some 300–400 automated library systems in operation in the United States and from an examination of the literature and some direct experience in a number of foreign settings, I would surmise that a similar number of systems existed in the developed countries of the world. With the lowering of hardware costs and the extension of the range and number of terminals that could be served cost effectively on both the low and high end of these systems, the rate of new systems installation accelerated rapidly throughout the decade. Richard Boss estimated in 1985 that there were over 1,000 automated library systems installed in the United States and that of these some 80% installed between 1975 and 1985 were vendor supplied. (20) In 1994, various market estimates made from U.S. vendors' statements of systems they have sold, show over 10,000 minicomputer-based systems. With the advent of microcomputer systems bringing to the smaller library the benefits of online processing, another, vaster market has developed. This microcomputer market can be judged by various claims of numbers of microcomputer library software packages sold. By 1994 these amounted to over 50,000 from U.S. developers. Extrapolated worldwide, it might be safe to guess that these numbers could be doubled or even tripled.

Each year since the early eighties, *Library Journal* has published a review of the automated systems marketplace during the March–April period. Each of these articles has been written by a noted consultant on automated systems procurement. A steady increase in the number of systems installed has occurred in these multiuser supermini- to mainframe-hosted systems. In the April 1988 article Bridge and Walton reported that 302 systems were installed in 1987, which represented a growth of 56% over the previous year. (21) CLSI was the vendor on the fastest track, with 309 systems installed. GEAC's second place was deemed somewhat shaky due to gains by OCLC and Dynix as well as signs of technological obsolescence in their GEAC 8000 system and slowing U.S. sales. In academic libraries installations, Dynix installed 23 new sites and NOTIS installed 18 as did Carlyle. The very large system marketplace was firmly NOTIS installations. Dynix and Inlex started to sell to public school system libraries. Public libraries also chose Dynix in 31 cases, CLSI in 17 cases, Inlex in 8 cases.

In the following year's article in April 1989, these same authors noted 360 systems installed, which was a 16% increase over the previous year. (22) The market has grown and matured with some flattening. In a number of customer sites, the systems obtained were second or third systems replacing a former version or another vendor's system that had outlived its usefulness. CLSI, Advanced Libraries and Information, Dynix and Sobeco all tried to develop smaller scale and lower cost systems, but this smaller-system market was tapped with limited success. CLSI lost market share, falling from a 22% share to a 19% share with 331 total installations. Dynix, with 206 systems installed, eclipsed GEAC which who dropped to third place, with 154 total systems. Worldwide IBM, with its DOBIS/LEUVEN system, had 152 installations for fourth place, although its U.S. installations numbered few. At the end of 1992 IBM announced it was no longer licensing and supporting DOBIS/LEUVEN.

OCLC had 134 sites and NOTIS had 119 sites. Innovative Interfaces had 114 systems installed, Data Research Associates had 101 sites and Virginia Tech's VTLS claimed 102 sites. Each other vendor had well under 100 sites, several with so few sites and such little new sales that their viability would be questionable.

NOTIS established its dominance of the academic market, particularly the larger ARL libraries. Dynix continued its strong growth with its 1988 sales capturing 21% of the year's market share, with 77 installations in 1988, while worldwide IBM's DOBIS captured a 9% share, with 34 installations. NOTIS installed 30 systems for the second-place share of the U.S. market. Sobeco installed 32 systems, a major increase in its customer base. GEAC continued to loose ground and had only 8 installations in 1988. Another promising player to watch for large systems is Eyring Library Systems, which changed its name to CARL Systems, Inc. CARL also took over the former UTLAS T/50 Tandem sites and all but two of these had converted over to CARL software as of late 1993.

By 1992 Bridge stated that the major vendors he surveyed for the *Library Journal* Spring Market assessment had installed 6,459 systems, with 3,663 in the United States (23) However, with microcomputer LAN systems and smaller UNIX or proprietary operating system alternatives, there has been some confusion in the smaller system area as to the actual number of systems installed. In 1993, Bridge split his survey into two parts, the first dealing with the minicomputer or host-based systems and the second concentrating on the microcomputer/LAN system. (24,25) The worldwide figures grew to 8,789 systems in this 1993 survey.

The 1990 survey, reflecting 1989 sales, saw vendors focussing on software sales as opposed to turnkey solutions involving both hardware and software. (26) There was a slight flattening of the market, which could be expected as more systems were second or third systems replacing old systems, and fewer were systems sold to first-time automated system purchasers. A record 395 systems were installed worldwide by the U.S. and Canadian companies. Certainly, when European and Pacific Basin countries are examined, one can find additional installations of minicomputer level and mainframe systems to add to that total.

Another noticeable trend is the migration of systems to new hardware platforms. For example, the Dynix system, which is PICK Operating System based, now will operate on Hewlett-Packard 9000 and other UNIX-based systems since PICK can now run under UNIX. This provides libraries with a range of added software for a better automation solution to which they can aspire.

CLSI and Data Research Associates have made considerable progress in the U.S. market. Sirsi's UNICORN system in 1989 posted annual installations about equal to that of CLSI, the "elder statesperson." UNICORN is a UNIX- based product, giving good portability and a wide range of system such as the excellent NCR Tower series systems on which to base the system. INLEX increased its domestic system dominance while VTLS and INLEX competed equally world-wide for Hewlett-Packard-based solutions. However, these two systems face considerable competition from the Hewlett-Packard-based MINISIS and the IBM mainframe-based ISIS which are available to third-world countries essentially free of software cost. Although not really an integrated library system, the MINISIS/ISIS product is a powerful database and text management facility able to handle vernacular Asian languages and is often put to the task of performing functions found in the integrated library system product.

In Chapters 6-8, I will examine all of these systems in some detail, but it is safe to conclude that the era of the integrated system was firmly here by the end of the eighties. The need to complement these systems through the use of microcomputers, LANs and other media formats was also firmly established. Most integrated systems were still not completely up to every library's expectations, and there were still major enhancements that vendors had promised customers but had not yet delivered. Despite these shortcomings, a new level of systems maturity and functionality was present in most of the more successful systems. Integration had been broadened considerably beyond the application areas deemed critical to an integrated library system of the early decade.

What about the future of the nonintegrated system? In truth, in the multi-user and multitasking system environment, these systems also largely grew beyond their individual applications. As a typical case, one can examine the Innovative Interfaces system which originally provided a serials management system to a library. Next, an acquisitions system was offered, and a public access catalog as well as circulation followed. Certain systems, such as Carlyle, which did not offer specific functions such as acquisitions support or serials management, built links to systems that offered these functions. Carlyle offered links to Innovative Interfaces for serials and acquisitions functions. This data could then be provided from the serials or acquisitions system to the online catalog system so that users could know the items on order or in process or the serials issues received.

Whether libraries chose to automate through several specific application function systems or through an "integrated" system missing one or more specific library functions, the end result has been that libraries have come to provide interactive computing support for as many of these tasks as thought practical or affordable. Whether specific application oriented or integrated, these interactive systems have been able to incorporate data needed for public service into an interactive catalog-searching facility. The evolution of library systems has resulted in functional integration and data sharing, but the view of what is practical and affordable remains a constantly moving target.

Would you have thought 25 years ago that you would do all of your writing using today's microcomputer-based word processors, given the cumbersomeness of those 1960's mainframe or minicomputer line editors or text formatters? Would you go back to using a 1970 model typewriter for writing everything? Even if there was argument over the better approach, the result inevitably has been to move toward an integrated multifunctional system. With the mid-nineties upon us, it has been impossible for a vendor to offer merely a single-function product, as the competition has essentially matured to the point that all vendors now offer a suite of major automated library system functions in their products, with successful vendors offering continual feature enhancement, albeit certainly more slowly than many customers would wish.

V. ONLINE PUBLIC ACCESS CATALOG AND RETROSPECTIVE CONVERSION

User-searchable interactive catalogs appeared initially as interactive computer applications and then as CD-ROM products generated from a database of the library's cataloged holdings. The online catalog offers the advantages of linking directly to the other automated system modules so that availability status of the item and items in process can be included in the catalog. In this form it can be updated either in real time or some form of deferred queue batch processing, which enables the database and its indexes to appear always up to date. The CD-ROM form suffers from the same problem of batch production as the microfilm format, usually being produced only quarterly or at some other frequency deemed acceptable from a cost and currency policy. However, with additions made on a magnetic disk and software that searches these additions transparently, the CD-ROM catalog can appear completely up to date. In the online form, with the inclusion of other source bibliographic indexing data, the catalog can now be expanded to include periodical articles, documents or other materials heretofore indexed only by either periodical abstracting and indexing services in either hardcopy or online form. For example, many medical libraries now offer at least a partial set of MEDLARS indexing data to their users, through an in-house online access to that database, either as part of a library's online catalog or as a corollary database available through the same computer terminals but driven by special search software and possibly on another networked host computer.

The CD-ROM form of interactive catalog searching facility currently offers an attractive replacement for microfiche- or microfilm-format catalogs, with the same limitations as to the frequency of updating (normally quarterly). The absence of any availability status directly in the CD-ROM database certainly would not be a limitation to the use of this format, particularly for libraries with manual circulation systems. Libraries with automated circulation systems can probably generate a daily status list if their circulation is low, or provide a means through a public terminal to allow patrons to check availability themselves without staff assistance. However, unlike microfilm catalogs, the CD-ROM database can be searched through very powerful search engines, which essentially replicate most searching possible on large online searching systems and online computer-based library catalogs. The best prospect for these CD-ROM catalogs is to couple them with writable optical storage or standard Winchester technology magnetic hard disk storage and load the current bibliographic records to these systems, running the CD-ROM through a network of workstations. This enables a CD-ROM catalog to have the same currency as an online computer-based catalog. Also, attaching this network via a gateway to the library's system where circulation is performed and then downloading the status information to a writable storage medium on the CD-ROM network offers some fast updating and economy-of-scale possibilities for the next few years. This would lower the cost of interactive multifunction systems even further than their current base cost of around $50,000 for hardware plus software licenses, etc.

Tacoma Public Library has developed such a CD-ROM catalog interface to its circulation system operating on a Tandem computer. It is a search engine that can have its databases on either the Tandem host or the workstation. (27,28) The user interface is at the workstation. Ameritech acquired this system, called Alice-B, in 1991 but has not offered it as a product. Although this alternative appears promising for the near term, the cost of conventional mass storage is still decreasing. Given that presently 2.1-gigabyte, 3.5-inch form factor hard disks are available for individual workstation and network attachment for around $2,100 each, where current LAN technology can provide around 80 gigabytes online on a server, the average-size library will easily be served through this LAN-based, microcomputer-actuated approach.

Therefore, the present vendors supplying library automation systems using proprietary operating systems and large mini- or mainframe computers should have cause for concern, as it will be easier for the vendors using generic operating system environments, such as the UNIX family, PICK systems or MS-DOS, to move toward offering LAN-based, server-implemented solutions to replace minicomputer–host-based systems. This will lower costs somewhat on the smaller system and ease growth problems for rapidly expanding systems. Systems with a common user interface for both public and staff access, together with considerable functional modularization and parameterization, will be easier to re-engineer for a distributed function system using workstation and server power within the LAN, rather than present host power and limited intelligence in the workstation terminal. Systems with as much hardware independence as possible will also be easier to port to LAN-based servers.

User-interactive interfaces have moved toward some form of graphical user interface (GUI) in the microcomputer- and LAN-based systems, usually Microsoft Windows 3.1, although several other competing GUIs are available. Windows 3.1 has achieved common acceptance as the successor to MS-DOS character-based interfaces. Vendors moved further away from hardware-specific implementation and have adopted newer development approaches such as Object Oriented Programming Systems (OOPS). Library systems remaining on minicomputer hosts will need to move toward whatever user interface standard is promoted by their minicomputer supplier; for example, Hewlett-Packard's New Wave or Digital Equipment's ALL-IN-ONE or X-Windows under UNIX.

As we continue into the nineties, the direct interactive catalog searching facility found in the online catalog is still in its developmental stages as to the best techniques for the user interface, index structures and searching features to be provided, not to mention specific features to be provided through authority control. By 1994 many vendors featured Windows 3.1 interfaces and client software. More alternatives to bibliographic conversion have made it more practical for libraries to consider either full or substantial retrospective records conversion and this should accelerate the move to either form of interactive catalog search facility.

Library networks such as OCLC provided impetus to retrospective conversion by developing lower cost systems and providing discounted usage rates for using and contributing records in a reconversion (RECON) project. The Association of Research Libraries sponsored a coordinated RECON project in which ARL member libraries retrospectively converted original cataloged materials to add to the intellectual content of machine readable-records. As both bibliographic utilities and private vendor databases continue to grow, libraries starting RECON projects can plan to achieve higher hit rates and lower total costs for their conversion projects.

A. Progress in Public Access to Online Catalogs

In 1981, Maurice J. Freedman pointed out:

> The ISBD is probably of usefulness to national libraries, and conceivably to some of the large research libraries. It performed a valuable service by prescribing a standard sequence of descriptive elements. However, the value of the prescribed punctuation and Latin and other abbreviations required by ISBD, especially for public and school libraries, is totally unconvincing. In addition, the necessary repetition of the author statement when it is identical to the main entry violates any principle of reason or economy. (29)

He used this example to show that current cataloging practice does not always serve the user of the catalog. He felt that closing the card catalog (i.e., stopping all entries, additions, and corrections to a catalog and then beginning a totally new catalog without reference to the old catalog) should be viewed as an opportunity to truly open the catalog to the user. Eventually these improvements were to occur. This progress toward simplification and comprehension has just started, following the progress of the eighties.

In 1982, the Council on Library Resources (CLR) provided the beginning of research support in the area of online catalogs when it funded the Study of Online Catalogs with OCLC and four other organizations. This culminated in a series of study reports published by OCLC and several other books based on data from these studies. (30,31,33)

In the Summer of 1980, CLR sponsored a working meeting at Dartmouth College between OCLC and RLG for the work on developments, issues and priorities for online public access to library bibliographic databases. (32) It was recommended that CLR support research into the online catalog. From that meeting CLR called for study proposals and received five proposals from the following organizations: J. Mathews & Associates, Inc.; Library of Congress; OCLC; RLG; and University of California Division of Library Automation's Library Research and Analysis Group. These groups participated in the study funded by CLR. Also related to this study, CLR held a conference at the Aspen Institute which had 27 key library administrators and computer systems experts who discussed the online catalog. (33) Their recommendations can be summarized as follows:

1. Library administrators need to be aware of ongoing developments as libraries adopt the online catalog and they will have mounting pressure to provide what their colleagues are providing in sister institutions. The catalog will grow faster than foreseen, require more terminals than imagined and increase use of other library services, so system selection must keep this growth in mind.
2. Library systems designers should review existing systems before developing new systems and avoid the "not invented here" syndrome, with subject access well developed. Thesaurus and cross-referencing capabilities, Boolean searching, and a clean and simple user interface should be provided, with a database structure that can withstand continuing rapid growth.
3. CLR should continue to support OPAC research and communication, and monitor Z39 (NISO) standards, subject access improvement and technology impact analysis. CLR proposed a DATAPRO-like survey of existing OPAC systems in current use.

In 1876 Charles Cutter set the rules under which our current catalogs have been operating for more than a century when he wrote, "The catalog 1) should enable a person to find a book of which either the author or title or subject is known, 2) show what the library has by a given author on a given subject in a

given kind of literature, and 3) assist in the choice of a book as to its edition bibliographically or as to its character, literary or topical." (34)
To more contemporary library experts it was becoming clear that the merger of the library catalog with the technology of interactive computing represented in online information retrieval systems would be the ultimate direction that the user accessible online catalog should take. If this was to actually occur, an increasing attention to the user/system interface would be needed since the many factors involved in searching in information retrieval systems require the search service vendor to have a good deal of training and pre-understanding of the indexing and treatment of the database.

What results did the CLR study produce? Of the many conclusions drawn from the voluminous data procured, the most significant were:

1. Online catalog users were most often frequent library users but were not necessarily users of other computers and in academic institutions were most likely to be male, 20–34 years old and highly educated.
2. Online catalog nonusers were less frequent library users and also less frequent users of other forms of catalog, evenly split between male and female, sightly older and reporting nonuse because of no training in 45% of the cases and no time to take training in 40%. Also 30% of these users reported that they did not know there was an online catalog. Fear of computers was not an important nonuse reason, and nonusers were favorable toward the online catalog and said they were likely to use it in future.
3. One-third of users reported learning to use OPAC without assistance and felt they do not need help. First-time users were more likely to ask for help.
4. Response time was important, and one-third of users were dissatisfied with their system's response time.
5. Users wanted to retain control of their search to expand or narrow the search at any time.
6. From 37 to 62% of users reported doing subject searching, and only 41% reported searching for a known item.
7. Menu-based systems seemed to have more response time problems than command-based systems, and users perceived menu-based systems as less flexible. For Boolean searching, menu-based systems seemed to have a slight advantage. (30)

From the above, it was relatively easy to see that one of the significant areas that needed work was the user interface and the ergonomic situation of the access points themselves with respect to the online catalog. With users voicing concern over number of terminals in some 50% of the libraries involved in the CLR study, it was clear that libraries rarely, if ever, could actually determine the appropriate number of terminals that would be needed by library users within the library, despite algorithmic studies designed to predict the probable number of terminals to install. These studies merely offer a starting point, while actual practice judged by the level of user access complaints or observation of user queuing ultimately determines a satisfactory number of terminals.

By the mid-eighties, it was clear that numerous areas for improvement in the online catalog existed. Menu-based interfaces produced less user error and made Boolean searching easier but increasing or decreasing retrieval results and changing search direction were much harder. Also, a menu interface presented more burden on the host computer. Here is a perfect example of how a distributed system with menu and user interface handled in the workstation (client/server architecture) could free up the host computer to perform the actual search if search statement parsing and translation from the user interface were done in the workstation. With menu generation in the workstation, one could also offer a broader series of menus and options for broadening and narrowing the search. Moreover, with the user interface in the workstation, new graphically based interfaces using mouse, trackball or other pointing devices could give the online catalog a user interface common to many Macintosh and Microsoft Windows microcomputer programs.

This would create a seamless user interface common to both microcomputer, LAN or mainframe applications operating in a distributed mode. Two early conceptualizations of this common interface were Hewlett-Packard's New Wave and IBM's System Application Architecture Application Program Interface with the OS/2 Presentation Manager. Current directions have vendors providing Microsoft Windows, UNIX X Window and Macintosh client programs.

Since the command/menu dichotomy as well as the GUI approach represents another design dilemma for the system designer, the answer may lie in the use of highly powerful workstations and the relegation of any host computer to be essentially a large file server, possibly even a specialized database machine that will perform searches and file updates but that will leave the actual processing and formatting of input/output and user interface generation to the workstation. With the coming of the Intel Pentium or the competing Motorola/IBM/Apple PowerPC microprocessor to the desktop in personal workstations, this approach will look increasingly attractive to designers as the second half of the nineties begins. With microcomputer applications moving more and more toward the GUI, this trend has influenced mini- and mainframe computer application interfaces.

Some other trends were clear as a result of the online catalog becoming the preferred form of library access tool. There was increasing cooperation in libraries between public services and technical services personnel as the catalog suddenly made visible all sorts of inconsistencies that were largely hidden in card catalogs. Obviously, humans can overlook many nuances on a printed card when filing, whereas the computer still cannot until someone develops truly an "expert system" that can mimic such human behavior. The computer can approximate library filing if the appropriate algorithm is programmed. However, humans can foresee and handle all sorts of exceptional cases that would necessitate a complexity of programming that would be of questionable worth. One can easily see the effect of this if systems are examined as to their ordering of index entries, for example, a call number index.

Another trend that accelerated through the eighties was the desirability to convert card format records to machine-readable form to include them in the online catalog. At the beginning of the decade, such a prospect for very large libraries seemed unaffordable and only slightly more affordable for medium-size collections, since the magnitude of the conversion effort itself and the host computer mass storage devices and power needed for such large databases was not yet affordable by all of these very large to medium-scale libraries. Small libraries were just beginning to look at automation largely because, until the eighties, there were no attractively priced systems in the marketplace. With the increasing penetration of the market to the smaller library by the latter eighties, development quickened for numerous retrospective conversion options designed for smaller libraries and particularly for libraries employing microcomputer-based systems.

B. Retrospective Conversion (RECON)

In the early 1980's the ideal for most libraries was a complete retrospective conversion of their collections for inclusion in their online catalog. It had to remain an ideal because for most larger libraries, which had not converted all of their holdings to machine-readable form for bibliographic inclusion in even their own computer-output/microfilm catalogs, and so they maintained two forms of catalog—card and microfilm. While brief item data may have been converted for inclusion in a circulation system, this data was insufficient on its own to form the basis of bibliographic data for an online catalog searchable through a variety of conventional single-entry index terms or combinations of keywords or subjects. Relatively few libraries, these being usually smaller libraries, had performed a complete retrospective MARC format-compatible catalog conversion.

The Library of Congress RECON Pilot Project had demonstrated the high cost of centralized large-scale conversion. The Library's lack of funds made this retrospective conversion cease. Lack of funds also terminated the Cooperative MARC (COMARC) proposal wherein a cooperative building of a national database would take place. It was clear by the early 1980's that only through a wide use of existing machine-readable records—both USMARC and contributed cataloging records comprising OCLC, RLG, WLN, UTLAS systems or private catalog vendor databases such as Blackwell-North America or Marcive, that any large-scale conversions would be affordable.

In the spring of 1983, an RLG library survey found 6 libraries planning full RECON, involving some 5.4 million titles, while 16 planned a selective RECON. This survey forecast that by 1990 all ARL libraries would have converted retrospectively virtually their complete holdings. (35) Of course, although quite a number of libraries in the ARL were converting records at a speedy rate and all were doing some record conversion, there were relatively few of these large libraries that had completely converted their catalogs by 1990. The University of Minnesota Libraries did accomplish this conversion before 1990 and by 1994 had converted many previously uncataloged formats to achieve an ever-growing number of works in its online catalog. This library is the 16th largest of the Association of Research Library member libraries.

What finally made retrospective conversion more practical was the growing base of records already converted and the increase in vendor competition for RECON work. Also, new products, such as the CD-ROM-based Bibliofile MARC database, made it possible for smaller libraries to perform conversions, even for small microcomputer-based automated systems. Conversions involved monographic and serial records for the most part and other material formats to a lesser degree. The source of records, amount of local data to be added such as holdings and locations, name/subject authority checks, and type of output tape processing necessary or merging and de-duping of tapes from bibliographic utility cataloging—all of these would affect the cost in service fees for the conversion. Added to this were the costs for staff to capture the initial data for computer matching in some form, and for keying records for which no copy matched. Also, libraries were absorbing the costs of the inevitable checking to assure that vendor work was meeting standards for accuracy and completeness. Various articles in the literature and direct consulting experience show that at the beginning of the decade these costs ranged from $.65 to $2.80.. These costs varied depending on the many factors above and the individual vendor involved. By the nineties, improved technology resulted in maintaining and even lowering these costs, despite some increase in labor costs.

One major type of library—the public school libraries—was not being well served through existing USMARC records or member input records in such networks as OCLC, because the format of materials in their collections included many items not yet cataloged as USMARC records—even at the end of the decade. This is one of the reasons that relatively few public schools joined networks such as OCLC. The coming of the microcomputer and the product developed by Hank Epstein's Information Transform Industries, called MitiNET MARC, which used a MARC fiche file and member input from Wisconsin public schools as the starter database, were to transform retrospective conversion for these school libraries and eventually for other smaller libraries.

Although publication costs escalated through the 1980's, by the end of the decade competition in RECON had made it so that one could purchase records at lower hit rate costs and receive volume-based prices for the other services usually performed for preparing these records for use in an installed system. On the average, libraries were able to perform all of their RECON work for somewhere between $.75 and $1.75 depending upon their hit rates and the degree of other services performed. Some 25 companies or network organizations were acting as major conversion vendors, while dozens of smaller companies were offering more limited conversions using such sources as Bibliofile to capture and edit records and produce USMARC record output, usually to floppy disk for loading into microcomputer-based systems. These smaller companies appeared to charge low fees but some of them were not well set up to perform these services, and so some risk was inherent in these low-cost conversions. Rates under $.30 per record were sometimes encountered from these companies. Since I have examined numerous ways to obtain USMARC records and perform enhancements to them for local data inclusion, I have not been able to determine how any vendor in 1989 who charged under $.30 per record and included entry of local call number/location/copy data could make a profit.

The cost and ultimate success of any RECON project depends on both human and procedural factors. It is clear that all libraries eventually will need to develop a plan for conversion if they have not already done so. RECON is critical to the success of a library's total automation program. With the online catalog a major service benefit to library users, the key reason that RECON is now so important is that it cannot be considered as a separate issue from the installation of any integrated library system.

First, a carefully laid out conversion plan is necessary, even for the small library. This plan sets the standards for the conversion, the actual work and whose responsibility it is to perform each task—a vendor, the library staff, special personnel hired for the project, etc. It also provides the desired schedule, how problems are to be resolved, what records and how many will be converted, how data will be captured for matching to a bibliographic database and whether authority work is to be performed or special programs are needed to load the data to the library's system and any customization needed for this aspect of the conversion. A customer contact person should be named with whom the vendor(s) for each stage can discuss how to handle any matters that appear during the conversion and how they should be resolved.

Once it has a plan, but prior to developing an actual request for proposal (RFP) for all or part of the conversion work, the library should examine any prospective vendors and their conversion alternatives. Once the possible vendors that can meet the basic criteria of method, quality, timeliness and cost are determined, they should receive the RFP so that they can provide formal proposals for the library to consider. The library should evaluate vendors based on their ability to meet the library's conversion plan and in terms of the above criteria. The library can use prior customers of a vendor as references to assure that vendor claims are valid and based on fact rather than on merely some sales pitch designed to get the library signed on as a customer while the vendor determines how the work should be done—usually with considerable delays.

An excellent example of one library's retrospective conversion plan and manual was that done by the University of Rochester Library. (37) It left very little to the imagination and although it is from a relatively large library, it is indicative of the sort of document that even the smaller library will ultimately need to develop. Libraries searching for possible RECON vendors should begin by examining the Library Technology Report by Judy McQueen and Richard W. Boss. (38) This report goes over in some depth these vendors' database content, standards, authority control, tape processing and other services. The literature is full of interesting case studies from libraries over their RECON work. Reading several of these can be helpful to point out where problems may be encountered or where more effective ways may be developed to handle the work.

C. User Interface and Screen Displays

User interface and screen displays were a facet of the online catalog that received considerable study and attention as both are key factors in the development of this form of catalog. Another key factor was the search and retrieval facilities, i.e., indexing approaches used in the catalog: the more powerful, the more advanced the product. However, the advantage of power could be offset by a poor user interface and a screen display lacking clear bibliographic displays. I believe what Pauline Cochrane has stated: "Search strategy may be the real key to improvements in information retrieval quality. If it is, we need to study user behavior." (39)

NISO Subcommittee G had been working on an ANSI standard for a common command language for use in interactive information retrieval. In 1992, Z39.58 Common Command Language for Online Interactive Information Retrieval became a NISO standard. It specifies 19 nonproprietary command terms. It is clear that the distinctions between online catalog searching and information retrieval database searching are blurring as these databases become accessible by library users through common search engines. Therefore, the online catalog has to incorporate the search power of the retrieval systems, while the retrieval systems must incorporate the user friendliness of the online catalogs. The GUI will provide the future key to this design problem, and it is hoped that current progress will continue to accelerate. Basic research in command language and screen displays initially was founded initially on the work sponsored by the Council on Library Resources. (40) In chapter 4 of this report, Joseph Mathews reported on studies he conducted on screen displays. He found that online catalog users prefer displays with labelled fields rather than merely replications of a catalog card on the screen. These labels were preferred in their all-capitalized form. How much data is shown on a screen is also critical to user satisfaction and understanding. Ideally the user should not have to view multiple screens to receive the bibliographic data necessary to determine the validity of the record produced in a search.

In another study, funded by the J. Paul Getty Trust, RLG studied screen designs for a workstation-based patron access system to the RLIN network system. (41) The major researcher was Walt Crawford. He developed a Bibliographic Display Testbed Program (RBDISP) under this project to test user responses to RLIN screens. His findings in summary were:

1. Brief displays, either labelled or cardlike, can provide up to seven lines for holdings for 90% of RLIN records.
2. Medium-level displays (without notes fields) will provide three lines for holdings for 90% of RLIN records.
3. Complete cardlike displays can provide only minimal holdings on the first screen in most cases while labelled displays require at least two screens for minimal holdings.
4. Most systems should provide for a Brief, Medium, Full and MARC-tagged display.
5. AMC format records present special display problems because of their length.
6. Specific tagged fields should be included in the Brief, Medium, and Full displays.

This work is a firm foundation for online catalog system designers to examine as they consider screen display design and system tradeoffs. Although, for reasons of system economy in transmission, RLIN displays in a cardlike format might be preferred, Mathews supported the use of labelled displays in the online catalog, with screen design based on three screen segments with multiple-line, short- and full-record displays. (42) I prefer labelled displays because of their ease of examination and the ability to postprocess screen images captured to disk from an interactive search session.

The advent of the CD-ROM catalog has accelerated the importance of the user interface and the search flexibility of the online catalog, as today's microcomputer systems stress a more graphical interface than current host computer systems. Linda Bills and Linda Helgerson have examined the issues surrounding designing and procuring a CD-ROM–based catalog in a series of articles in *Library Hi-Tech*. (43,44,45) Their conclusion on the CD-ROM user interface was that, except for special libraries, very large collections or catalogs mediated by librarians, it is doubtful that full Boolean capabilities are worth the confusion they invite, at least with any of the interfaces available at this time. As the 1980's came to a close, many of the ARL libraries and even more of the smaller ACRL libraries had completed or nearly completed substantial retrospective conversion of their catalogs. However, given that many of the ARL libraries have vast specialized collections of documents, manuscripts or nonbook or serial forms of materials that may not have been cataloged previously, there still remains considerable very specialized original cataloging work to be done if each of these libraries is to actually achieve the ultimate goal of having its online catalog be the key access tool to its full collections. The previously mentioned ARL RECON project helped, but certainly it is only a beginning. The Council on Library Resources provided many libraries with RECON conversion grants through the eighties and continues to fund some projects of this nature in the nineties.

By 1989 academic institutions connected to the Internet network could access, via the Telnet TCP/IP supporting software, many online catalogs in such diverse institutions as the Colorado Alliance for Research Libraries (CARL), the University of Illinois, the University of Minnesota, the Research Libraries Group (RLG/RLIN) and some 40 other institutions. All of these, except RLG/RLIN, are free to anyone with an Internet access at one's institution and the Internet address of the system one wishes to reach. There is an Internet conference called the Public Access Computer Systems Forum (PACS-L@UHUPVM1) which is moderated through Lehigh University. This conference of librarians is concerned with library automation issues and problems, including the catalog and related matters. By 1994, over a thousand institutions worldwide had their library catalogs on the Internet. If this growth rate is maintained there will be over twice that number by the beginning of 1995. Thus, millions of bibliographic and holdings records actually within the institution's own database are accessible by Internet connected institution libraries without accessing OCLC for a holdings code. It is easy to see that this is only a first step to widely accessing libraries' catalogs directly via public Internet account providers, and this trend is bound to influence the way bibliographic databases are used and what services these utilities will have to provide in order to survive and prosper. Of course, accessing these Internet-connected systems points out very dramatically that there is a need for a common command language or easier-to-use interfaces, since online catalogs and database providers use many different programs that require the user to know their specific command structure. (46)

D. Online Catalog Access and the User Interface

With the trends in microcomputer user interfaces moving increasing toward graphically based user interfaces such as represented in Microsoft Windows version 3.1, Apple Macintosh, and in even more powerful workstations as the Sun using the X-Windows GUI standard under UNIX, there are likely to be more graphical interfaces for mainframe- and minicomputer-based systems. This trend brings with it the problem of increasing initial costs since the hardware required to run this form of software is more expensive. Does easier usage increase productivity or lessen system support costs sufficiently to offset the higher initial outlay? What about those of us who feel comfortable with command-based systems? Are we soon to be viewed as using an obsolete approach to systems?

As Walt Crawford pointed out, it is difficult to reconcile ease of learning vs. speed and flexibility of use. (47) The tradeoff over a standard program interface is that it does simplify ease of learning, but this is bound to come at the expense of some longer term convenience, power and flexibility. Is a mouse really more fun and easier to use? Obviously, the manufacturers of competing pointing devices such as the newer trackballs, trackball keyboards or stationary mice believe their tools are better. Shouldn't we be working on a uniform graphical user interface standard for library and information retrieval systems according to respective host computer platform? Will Microsoft Windows' new GUI in its Chicago product in Beta test become the new standard for automated library system client software on the Intel chip systems?

The current use of graphically based user interfaces is accelerating in the microcomputer- and LAN-based systems. This provides a distinct advantage as many of these systems incorporate menu-driven and graphical interfaces already. The systems with the greatest difficulty in such implementation will be the mainframe-hosted systems, particularly NOTIS, given their dual-user interfaces—the LUIS public catalog mode and the NOTIS staff mode—both command based and neither requiring use of host-generated graphics or microcomputers or terminals with graphics capabilities. NOTIS's new AIX (UNIX) -based Horizon system is its solution, with little further effort to be expended on enhancements to its MVS IBM mainframe software. Larger library systems will be new client/server designs, involving newer hardware platforms using the PowerPC processor, such as IBM's R/6000 or competing processors such as Digital Equipment Corp.'s Alpha.

Microcomputer-based library systems will be dramatically affected by the direction their development platform takes and by the cost of microcomputer hardware. For example, with the present price of good SVGA display adapters below $300, it would not be wise for an MS-DOS- or Windows-based software developer to write to any other standard. Even RLG/RLIN is going to provide its new CJK software using standard SVGA video instead of using such custom displays as the Wyse 700. For $500–600 a fully digital 15" monitor provides resolutions up to 1280 x 1024 pixels. Similarly, in the $900–1800 range fully digital 17" monitors can be used on some user stations, such as those compliant to the Americans With Disabilities Act computer provisions. Such developments in addition to the perception of customer needs will affect the direction in which microcomputer-based systems move. Now that multi-processor systems as the Compaq SystemPro have been brought to market, there will be an even more valid reason for many libraries that might have sought a superminicomputer-based solution to examine a LAN- or smaller UNIX-based system. There is no question that most of these systems are easier to use for both staff and library users, independent of whether they use a graphical or menu/command-driven interface.

In the end, user preference will be a factor in interface decisions, but there is no denying that present user preferences have made the GUI type the winner. By the late 1990's we can expect to see virtually all of the present automated library systems that survive the marketplace using GUI interfaces as the last mainframe systems are retired.

VI. NEAR-TERM ISSUES IN LIBRARY AUTOMATION

There are three most critical issues that libraries presently face. First, is the interconnection of several host systems within an institution to bring a variety of computer support to its libraries in addition to that directly provided by the automated library system or by other software that might run on the library system computer. Such connections would provide institutional and worldwide electronic mail and teleconferencing, various scheduling and calendar functions, file storage and transmission across its own or to remote institutions and access to a variety of other database services via such gateways as provided through the IBM Information Network (IIN) commonly used at IBM host computer sites as well as Internet, Usenet or other networks. Much of this is now working and in place. However, the ease of use and user satisfaction in many of these approaches is not as high as it could be due to both user interface variations and perceived performance failings in these products. A user must learn still to use Gopher, World-Wide Web clients such as Mosaic or Cello, Telnet VT-100 or TN3270 terminal emulation, news readers such as Trumpet and possibly other client software to access Internet resources.

The second near-term issue which, for the library user, will be far more important, is the online access to abstracting and indexing databases as a direct adjunct to the online catalog. These might use networked CD-ROM or host computer access. I predict that because of the cost the immediate future will see networked CD-ROM products. This will bring the serials literature in a much more directly accessible manner to the library user, without the constant expense of online searches via the search service suppliers or via personal accounts with such services as BRS AFTER DARK. Even if the libraries must charge for access to these databases, these charges will not have to cover telecommunications packet network expenses since the local library workstations or dial-up facilities would be used. As the library system vendors are still evolving host database access with file preloading processing or related services, it may be hazardous to forecast the total effect that this will have on how libraries provide services to their users. The intermediary role that staff still largely play will increasingly become more the role of teacher of information skills.

As the cost of computer systems continues to decease and their power and storage increase, it is inevitable that increasingly libraries will want to locally mount not only subject databases but various locally developed files that are pertinent to the institution or locale that the library serves. With tools like the Gopher servers and low-cost CD-ROM authoring systems, libraries have affordable tools to provide these services.

The third issue is the the continual improvement in the provision of CD-ROM and newer interactive forms of optical storage products to the library user. Presently, CD-ROM devices are largely single user oriented, with networking possible with such vendors' products as Meridian, Opti-Net, Virtual Microsystems or LANtastic. Both server- and peer-based LANs support CD-ROM networking. Critical issues will be the improvement of CD-ROM software, of device access speed and of the ability to use the same network technology to bring CD-ROM access to all library workstations under larger networks without employing complex and slowly performing gateways or bridges between several different network vendors' products. With present incompatibilities among certain CD-ROM networking products, it will take time for these incompatibilities to be rectified by the various vendors. The wide acceptance of the Microsoft CD-ROM (MSCDEX) extensions to MS-DOS enable a CD-ROM disk to be accessed as another logical storage volume, but one that is larger than the MS-DOS 3.x version 32-MB limit. A common manner of addressing CD-ROM is needed if network developers are to invest in these larger scale access solutions. Currently MSCDEX represents that first step in the present microcomputer-dominated environment. The summer of 1994 has brought the first widely available quadspeed CD-ROM drives. This speed increase will help CD-ROM network users and may make shadowing of the CD-ROM on magnetic storage less necessary for larger networks.

The larger question facing libraries will be whether to make their investments in database access mainly in software and files on their systems running their online catalog, or to move to a CD-ROM–based file environment running within a LAN solution. Also, the issue of whether libraries should run a CD-ROM public catalog or use an integrated library system for that function has not been fully resolved. Convenience, responsiveness, currentness of information, linking of availability status to a CD-ROM product (as invented in the Tacoma Public Library Alice-B system) and ultimately real costs versus benefits will play together to determine which approach will be right for any single library system.

Now let us complete our overview of the decade by examining some of the developments abroad.

VII. FOREIGN DEVELOPMENTS

A. The Americas

Many of the activities and trends above also apply to library automation systems in other developed countries of the world—certainly to Canada, where Canadian provincial university libraries have had active library automation programs. The GEAC Library System, developed out of initial work on software for the GEAC 8000 computer, performed at the University of Guelph Library. The National Library of Canada implemented a heavily modified version of IBM's DOBIS software, while the University of Quebec developed the system now being offered commercially by the Sobeco Group, called Multi-LIS. Also, Brandon University's Digital Equipment Corp. VAX-based system has been offered through a commercial venture and has been installed by some Canadian libraries, mainly public libraries.

Similar concerns in Canada over networking and the development of peer-to-peer computer networks have prompted the establishment of the Task Group on Computer/Communications Protocols and work on OSI compliant protocols. The Canadian iNET Gateway trial, which included participation of a half dozen libraries, proved that the concept of the distributed peer-to-peer network was feasible and that host systems running different library automation software could transfer records and access one another. Readers who would like to follow these developments should consult the Canadian Network Papers (No.1 (1980)-to date) published by the National Library of Canada.

Canada's bibliographic utility UTLAS, Inc. (renamed Utlas in 1986), has grown in its system scope and reach and is now being used in Japan and in other foreign libraries. With UTLAS's acquisition of the Tandem-based software from the now defunct DataPhase, Inc., it had transformed this software into a more reliable and practical system called the T/50 Series. Prior to the T/50 acquisition, UTLAS had converted its host system to Tandem and in that respect has a system base that will be similar to OCLC's when OCLC finally completes its move from its antique Sigma application processors to its fully Tandem-based system. However, UTLAS relinquished its T/50 user base to

CARL Systems, Inc. Apparently continuing as a library automation system vendor was not to be one of UTLAS's roles as a bibliographic utility.

When we leave the United States and Canada, we find countries less developed and less able to provide a commercial infrastructure that provides software and systems to libraries such as is the case in North America, Europe, Australia and several other developed regions.

When I visited some public library branches in Mexico in the early 1980's, I did not see any evidence of computer use. This is still largely the situation today. The National University of Mexico is operating a system called LIBERUNAM, which by 1987 had a database of 300,000 bibliographic records. The National Library of Mexico is using the MINISIS system running on a Hewlett-Packard HP-3000 computer to produce the Bibliografía Mexicana. The National Science Council (CONACYT) provides an online search node for Mexican Libraries, with some Mexican databases operational on their own computers. These are ARIES, the research activities in libraries of the National University, 19 state universities and the National Polytechnic University; SIE-BANXICO, the Bank of Mexico's economic performance indicators; and UNAM/JURE, the legislative actions in Mexico. Another 18 databases were under development in 1987. (48)

Some work has also been under way since the early 1980's on a system at the Universidad Nacional Autónoma de México, which purports to be one of the most advanced in Latin America. However, from the literature it appears that little has been published about this system. It appears to be an IBM host computer-based system as are NOTIS and DOBIS/Leuven. By 1994, Mexico's major universities were to have Internet connections in place, with some online catalogs accessible.

In South America, Brazil is the most highly developed country as far as use of computers. However, there is relatively low priority for applying them to libraries. In 1983, McCarthy found only 40 automated libraries in a country having 15,000 libraries. These were systems developed in-house, almost all still batch processed using punched cards as the data entry medium. These institutions claimed not to have been influenced by what other libraries had done. The automated libraries were in high-priority fields, such as agriculture and nuclear energy, with close links to the Brazilian Federal government, where centralized state control is traditional. In 1983 there were no libraries using bar-coded labels for data collection in a circulation system. Instead, the preferred application was to produce printed book or COM catalogs. Some 65% of these automated systems were implemented using IBM mainframe systems, with Burroughs systems the second most prevalent host. The only system imported from abroad was the IPEN—Institute for Nuclear Energy and Nuclear Research Library which had imported the system running in Ispra, Italy, at Euratom. (49,50) Although in 1990 Brazilian libraries were able to secure and use some microcomputer equipment, automation remains a low priority and there is no evidence of significant national development of standards or policies that would foster cooperative progress.

The only other South American project of significance is the Biblioteca Nacional y de Servicios de Bibliotecas Venezuela installation of the NOTIS software as part of this library's project to locate in U.S. libraries and acquire items of national bibliography that they do not hold. The decision to automate this procurement was the foundation of a project to automate the National Library of Venezuela. With the help of Henriette Avram as a consultant, they choose to use the NOTIS-3 software. This was the first of what would become over 100 NOTIS systems operating outside of Northwestern University. James Aagard, one of the major developers of NOTIS, provided special Spanish language support. (51)

B. Australia

Library automation in Australia is heavily influenced by individual institutional needs, with relatively weak influences from the National Library, centered mainly in their Australian Bibliographic Network (ABN) service. By 1980 ABN offered individual libraries access to some 6.5 million bibliographic records and 9 million holding statements. Some 900 libraries use one or more of its services. The Western Library Network software operating on an IBM 3081k mainframe is accessible via AUSTPAC, a packet-switched network, using any asynchronous terminal or microcomputer. ABN can also be accessed via a dedicated data service line using synchronous SNA protocol and IBM 3270 terminals or 3270 terminal emulation software. Special gateways from other Australian computer networks such as CSIRONet also provide a means for clients to reach ABN. As of late 1989, the Interlibrary Loan function of the WLN software was in a pilot project test.

There is much interest in the peer-to-peer linking of library systems. The work going on in the United States and Canada using the Open Systems Interconnection (OSI) Reference Model is being closely monitored. An X.400 interface to the ABN Interlibrary Loan subsystem was being investigated. The Canadian draft application layer protocols for Interlibrary Loan were suggested as the standard to be adopted. The National Library of Australia had established a Working Group on Library Systems Interconnection in late 1986. This group continues to push for adoption of this network approach, but its request for a feasibility study to be funded for AUS $30,000 over a 6-month period which was made in Summer 1989, had not thus far been funded in 1990. With ABN on an IBM host, the IBM announcement of OSI/CS (OSI/Communications Subsystems) for MVS and VS operating systems versions, which were released in May, 1990, offer some promise for ABN since this product is supportive of OSI layers 3-6. Ilanet, which is the interlibrary loan (ILL) subsystem of the State Library of New South Wales, operates on Digital's VAX system. With X.400 gateway software installed on the ABN IBM and Ilanet VAX, an appropriate interface at the ILL application level would be needed. X.400-mail could be used to transfer requests and responses between the systems. Another option might be to implement the SNA LU 6.2 Advanced Program-to-Program Communication available for both of these systems. Finally, commercial support for TCP/IP protocols by IBM and Digital Equipment Corp. make system interconnection an easier matter.

CLANN (College Libraries Activities Network) and CAVAL (Cooperative Action by Victorian Academic Libraries) are other active networks that wish to benefit from the OSI potential and certain services provided through ABN. Nonetheless, Australian libraries have major problems of fragmentation of library data and resources.

Within individual libraries in Australia, the trend accelerated to move away from privately developed systems to a number of vendor-supplied solutions. One of the early U.S. vendors was CLSI, with its LIBS 100 system. The firm representing CL Systems, Inc. (now GEAC, Inc.) is LIBRAMATICS, which has developed an interface for the system to the ABN. The Royal Melbourne Institute of Technology Library is one user of this system. Also, Amalgamated Wireless Australasia has invested in significant upgrades to the URICA software. It had originally secured the Pacific Basin marketing rights for URICA from the original developers, URICA Pty. Ltd., in the Union of South Africa. URICA also links to ABN. It runs under the PICK Operating system on McDonnell Douglas MicroData computers and is sold by McDonnell Douglas Automation Company in Europe and England. It can operate also on UniVerse, a version of UNIX that supports PICK BASIC and a dbms.

IBM's DOBIS has been installed at the Northern Territory Libraries. The University of New England in New South Wales installed the Virginia Tech Library System (VTLS) in 1984. Some locally developed systems were still in operation at the end of the eighties. For example, the Queensland Parliamentary Library's printed catalog production system, called AIRS, was still operating on an IBM System 32, written in RPG II. Some microcomputer-based systems were being developed, e.g., the Sydney College of Arts Apple II circulation system, called LOTHLORIEN. (52)

Of all of the systems installed through vendors, the AWA URICA system is one of the most well conceived. The searching facilities provide rapid access to bibliographic and copy holdings records, which have made the online public catalog function very well implemented. Complex indexing structures involving three levels of indexes provide both string searching and keyword searching. The database is fully authority controlled and the system handles acquisitions, serials management, cataloging and circulation. (53) Figure 1 shows the organization of the main files of URICA. This system is noted here because

```
ISBN/Pub    Publishers     ISBN's     ISSN's    LC Card No.   Dewey

  IPAF   --    PAF          IAF        ISAF        CAF          DAF
               :-----------:---------:----------:-----------:
                                     :
 Subject Keywords   LC Subjects:     :     :-Authors--Surnames-lst 4

 SHAF.KEY        --  SHAF          :     :     :  AAF     AAF.KEY
AAf.SURN
                                   :     :     :
                                   :-MAIN-:
                                   :     :     :
Title Keyword -----  Titles  ----:     :     :-Corp. Auth.  Corp. Auth.
TAF.KEY              TAF           :     :     : CAF          Keyword
                                   :     :     :               CAF.KEY
                                   : HOLD :
                                   :     :     :
Series Keywords ---  Series  ----:     :     :-Mono. Orders -- Completed
SAF.KEY              SAF                 :     : Requests         Orders
                                  COPIES :                        Archive
                                         :     :-Serials Orders
                                         :     : Ser. Data
                                         :     :
                                         :     :
                                         :     :-General Data
                                         :       GAF
Borrower Names -- Borrower ID's          :
Inverted          Borrower       --LOANS
Borrower                           ON-LOAN
```

Figure 1 The URICA system database and its indexes.

it was one of the earliest minicomputer-based systems that provided considerably more varied searching access than was typical of most of the competing systems worldwide.

C. Europe

1. Great Britain

By the eighties, automation in Britain was also following a similar course, increasingly toward adoption of vendor-based systems for performing routine library activities. GEAC of Canada had very early established a customer base in England to compete against such companies as Plessy and Automated Library Systems, Ltd., England was also the birthplace of a tradition of development of information retrieval software which formed the basis for quite a few cataloging systems. The United Kingdom Atomic Energy Agency's Harwell Laboratory Library and its STATUS information retrieval software had been the basis of dozens of systems due to its portability to different computer systems, from ICL mainframes to Prime minicomputers. The TRACS (Transport and Road Abstracting and Cataloguing System) produced at the Transport and Road Research Laboratory had a 120,000-article database using 200 MB of disk storage as reported in 1982. (54) At that time, however, STATUS in its mainframe version lacked any validation and recovery features to reestablish its database to its prefailed state, whereas the minicomputer version running on the Prime system included this advance. STATUS and its major competitors, ASSASSIN and CAIRS all share in the worldwide retrieval software market together with such U.S.-originated systems as BRS SEARCH, ORBIT, INQUIRE, and IBM's German developed STAIRS. Following the coming of the microcomputer as a practical tool (by 1983) and with the stabilization of software development around the MS-DOS IBM-compatible architecture, most of these British and American systems had microbased versions by 1989. Now, given that one can use multiple 2.1-gigabyte drives and fast 66-MHz servers under LAN software such as Novell Netware, these microversion retrieval packages can easily process and perform retrieval services that in the early 1980's could be done only on mainframe or super-minicomputer systems.

The Scottish Libraries Cooperative Automation Project (SCOLCAP) has been performing COM catalog generation and acquisitions services for its member libraries. By 1983, SCOLCAP had a database of some 600,000 UK MARC, USMARC and Extra-Marc material, with a dedicated line to the British Library's Blaise computer. South-Western Academic Libraries Cooperative Automation Project (SWALCAP), headquartered at the University of Bristol, has been self-sufficient since 1979, with some 20 members. Its local minicomputer is linked to the University of Bristol system used by SWALCAP. Online cataloging has been performed since 1978. The Birmingham Libraries Cooperative Mechanization Project (BLCMP) developed its CIRCO circulation system using Telepen bar code readers and a Data General Eclipse minicomputer. By 1983 eight libraries, mainly in polytechnic universities, had installed this system. In 1994 BLCMP, with its BLS integrated system, is another major vendor of automated library systems to British customers.

Librarians in Great Britain also wanted to achieve an integrated approach to applying the computer to library operations, but their systems remained focussed largely on individual applications such as catalog production or circulation until the latter eighties, when it clearly became practical to use more integrated software from a number of commercial vendors. Acceptance of well-integrated microcomputer-based systems, such as IME's TinLIB, coupled with today's powerful microcomputers and LANs make possible the use of interactive computing for a wider range of libraries than did the minicomputer-based systems. However, use of this newer technology, while less costly, still has required a larger investment to install than was originally thought, according to Leggate and Dyer, who reported on an experimental system. (55) Using a package called BookshelF from a software firm called Logical Choice, which ran on an Altos 586-40 system under the PICK and OASIS operating systems, a library budgeted at £250,000 could expect a base of 25–35% of its annual budget to get up and running. The library's original estimate of some £15,000 proved insufficient, with £50,000–75,000 the correct cost range. This experimental installation of BookshelF has yielded useful cost data.

More and more libraries are moving from locally developed in-house systems to commercially supplied software. Brunel University Library illustrated a typical case reported in the literature. (56) Its experience was moving from a locally developed circulation system to BLCMP's CIRCO and then to BLCMP's BLS, an integrated library system. Brunel's in-house software was all card driven and batch processed on the University's ICL 1903A mainframe. In 1981, the University dropped the ICL system and went to a Hewlett-Packard HP-3000/33 for administrative computing, while the library stayed on the new Honeywell Level 68 DPS/Multics system. The move to the BLCMP CIRCO software involved converting a short-title file from the Honeywell system, with a large number of these titles having ISBNs to ease later upgrading to a full Marc record. Bar coding was done using non-pre-linked or "dumb" bar codes as opposed to the "smart" barcodes. Then the ADD BOOK function of CIRCO was used to properly link the item to its proper record. CIRCO was installed on a Data General S/120 minicomputer having 512 kB RAM, 147 MB disk storage and 15 circulation terminals in the two campus library sites. In 1987, Brunel upgraded to a 32-bit Data General MV7800 series processor and added an online public catalog.

By 1989, the British market for automated library systems was very competitive, with some dozen minicomputer vendors and 17 microcomputer systems available. Pressure from foreign systems illustrates that the software market is truly an international one. Microcomputer development made this internationalization much more visible, with systems using design techniques that would make it much easier to develop vernacular language or multilingual support. Manson summarizes this market for microcomputer systems for libraries very well in an article in *Program*. (57) By 1994 there were 43 vendors active in the British market, with BLCMP leading in installations in the polytechnic universities and LIBERTAS in the University Libraries. Public libraries most often chose Galaxy. GEAC and Urica were also very close in installations. The most prevalent smaller system on UNIX was IME's TinLIB.

While most libraries are moving forward to adopt commercial software solutions, there are still some libraries doing their own systems, representing some innovative aspects. Scott Polar Research Institute uses an online catalog that originated at the Sedgewick Museum at Cambridge and is supported by the Cambridge University Computing Service. It is called MUSCAT and is written in BCPL language with great portability across various computer systems currently implemented on six different host systems. (58) The system uses a technique called probabilistic retrieval, with Boolean searching and relevance feedback. The National Library of Medicine's CITE is probably the most familiar production example of this approach of some familiarity to U.S. information professionals. The Irish Meteorological Service Library has produced its own system for cataloging and online catalog searching and circulation involving a relatively small collection on a Digital Equipment Corp. DEC 20-50 in Fortran 77. It was developed by one part-time analyst in 1983 and subsequently rewritten but was less costly to implement than currently available minicomputer-based systems. (59) At that point it was not really practical for this library to think in terms of a microcomputer solution, but given its situation and need, today's solution would probably be found in using one or another of the available microcomputer-based systems. Also, the University of Lancaster Library was implementing its own system design using a PICK operating system–based approach. It incorporated such techniques as split-screen editing of MARC records. Acquisitions was operational in April, 1987 with full-fund accounting. A single analyst wrote the acquisitions application in three months; the next priority was to work on cataloging and the online public catalog. The scale and direction of development were dictated by very limited funding and a desire to remain independent of any single supplier. (60,61)

Now, well into the last decade of this century, British librarians are turning their attention to information systems developments that parallel those in the United States. For example, almost all university library online catalogs are now available via the JANET network and the Internet as are U.S. systems through the Internet network. Hypertext and Expert Systems are also receiving attention through reports in the literature. CD-ROM has elicited as much attention and concern over similar problems of its introduction and use as in the United States To come to this conclusion, one need only examine the special issue of *Program 23*(4) in October, 1989, which was devoted totally to CD-ROM. British libraries are moving as rapidly as funds will permit to adopt new information technologies and are watching developments elsewhere.

2. Scandinavian Countries

In Sweden, the BUMS and LIBRIS networks continued to expand from their beginnings of the previous decade, despite an economic climate which was less than ideal. By 1987, the BUMS system was serving public libraries in 78 municipalities, by 1987, with 156 libraries using automated circulation. Their title database was one million records; however, the microfiche catalog, with 997 libraries participating, was still the major form of public library user catalog. The most common system for local libraries remains CLSI, since the Swedish Library Service, which is responsible for running BUMS, is also the country's agent for CLSI. The CLSI system uses the BUMS bar-coded labels.

Stockholm University had installed GEAC, and the Swedish LIBRIS was serving the other academic libraries. The Royal Library, Stockholm, continues to operate LIBRIS for the Swedish research libraries, which by 1982 had started to discuss development of standardized protocols for interlinking their systems. In 1983 the University of Oslo, University of Bergen Libraries and Norsk Dokumentdata were testing a link of their three computer systems using the UNINETT packet-switched network. This test was successful and demonstrated the need for standardized linked systems protocols. By 1986, Oslo University was using UBO:BOK, a DEC System 10–based cataloging system, and numerous other academic libraries were using the BIBSYS Univac 1100–based system. Under the BIBNETT project, an OSI application level protocol (Layer 7) was developed to transmit MARC format bibliographic records. Holm reported in some detail on the BIBNETT project. (62) Other participants in this experiment were users of Mico-PolyDOC, an MS-DOS based information retrieval system, who were to search both UBO:BOK and BIBSYS computers' databases with record transfer also to the microcomputers. Until a disk drive failure occurred in the network node system, this test worked well. (62) Paralleling the Swedish BUMS, the Norwegian Library Supply Service offers BIBBI.

In Iceland, library automation has been considered a central planning issue revolving around the establishment of the Committee for Automation in Icelandic Libraries (CAIL) in 1981. This committee did complete an ICEMARC format by 1985. In 1982, CAIL had proposed that two separate databases of bibliographic data be built. The Icelandic National Bibliography would comprise one of these while foreign acquisitions and imprints would comprise the other. The University of Iceland Computer Centre and the University Library were to be the site for this work. However, by 1984, CAIL proposed that a single database would be preferable, with the project to be undertaken cooperatively by the City Library of Reykjavik, the University Library and the National Library of Iceland. In 1986, a program to process ICEMARC records on microcomputer and print catalog cards was available. That same year DOBIS/LIBIS was tested at the State and Municipal Data Processing Centre (SMDPC), with the idea of acquiring one system to serve all of these libraries. However, the University Library was not satisfied with the testing results of DOBIS and wanted to test other systems for comparison. The SMDPC currently was running DOBIS/LIBIS, with the City of Reykjavik and the the National Medical Library, using it on a test basis.

Meanwhile, in 1988, other vendors were invited to demonstrate systems. These were VTLS, CLSI, LIBERTAS and INLEX. All but CLSI demonstrated their systems in January–February, 1988, with the Norwegian ND-BIB system demonstrating in July 1988. The consensus was that DOBIS/LIBIS was a better system. With all the disagreement over which system to choose, CAIL abandoned the idea of a national union catalog database in April 1988. (63) The governing structure of the Board of the Library Databank and its parent dissolved. The Minister of Culture and Education then appointed another committee on July 28, 1988 to promote interlibrary cooperation in the hope that a union catalog would be one of the outcomes. The government planned the merger of the National Library and the University Library into one new building under construction, with Saztec receiving the contract for retrospective conversion. A new system was to be chosen by the time the new library building would be occupied. In late 1988, CLSI and the Norwegian BIBLIOFIL systems were demonstrated. (64)

Finland had developed FINNMARC and had developed local cooperative library systems in both public and academic libraries. Finnish public libraries were using a system for circulation operated in the Helsinki City Data Centre on an IBM 3031. This system used online data collection via OCR-B font labels on books with ISBN codes but was a batch updated system. However, unlike their neighbors, Finnish libraries moved more quickly to decentralized systems and were quicker to acquire library automation systems developed commercially in foreign countries instead of investing in centralized systems such as BUMS or LIBRIS. VTLS has a large share of the Finnish market as of 1994.

In Denmark there is a hotbed of automation, with 19 large academic library sites online and available through the Internet, whereas just nine years earlier, in 1986, there were only two systems vendors. SAMKAT, which is very similar to the Swedish LIBRIS, serves Danish research libraries. ALEPH, sold by ICL in Europe, and BIBDATA, from Nord Partners, appear to have most of the large library market.

3. *The Rest of Western Europe*

By 1982, the PICA network in the Netherlands had 100 terminals in 18 libraries and was forecasting adding another dozen member libraries the coming year. It was expected that the COM catalogs would start to be replaced by online public catalogs by 1984. Rotterdam City Library had installed a circulation and touchscreen-accessed online catalog system from the Automated Library Systems, Ltd., from Great Britain. A Systems Engineering Laboratories SEL 32/77 minicomputer, with 1.5 gigabytes of disk storage, housed the 100,000 full and 400,000 brief cataloging records for this library. By 1994, 100% of the Dutch national and university libraries had installed computer systems. Independent libraries were at least 80% automated. VUBIS and ADLIB lead in special library installations. ALS, LIBS/100, GEAC, LIBRA, SIAS and Buks had the academic and public market locked up. Today the libraries of the Netherlands have the highest level of installed systems in Europe.

There had been a long tradition of use of minicomputers in library systems in Belgium, with the pioneering work done by S. Micha Namenwirth on the VUBIS system. This system at the Free University of Brussels used a Digital Equipment PDP-11 minicomputer and MUMPS for one of the early public access catalogs in a European library. In a collaboration between the Technische Hogeschool in Eindhoven and the Eindhoven Public Library, a development team is now working on VUBIS II. The integrated system will ultimately be a multi-institution union catalog, with the public catalog to be developed first. Boolean searching is masked from the users through carefully constructed menus that allow the user to enter the search without using a structured query with Boolean operators. (65)

In France, the Bibliothèque Nationale (BN) started installing a GEAC system in April, 1986, loading 400,000 bibliographic records and 250,000 authority records. It also had written a conversion program to transform its INTERMARC format records into UNIMARC. Now, its exchange tape production for the Bibliographie de la France uses the UNIMARC format. (66)

The first fully operational online public catalog in France was implemented in the newly opened "La Médiathèque" at the Cité des Sciences, La Villette, Paris in 1983. A GEAC 8000 system provides the catalog and circulation support for this highly automated multimedia public library. A native French system called MEDICIS provides ordering, accounting and other in-process or business functions for this library. Over 300,000 volumes, includng 6,000 current journals and 300 computer programs, are accessible via this catalog. Even a special facility named after Louis Braille provides four workstations for the visually impaired, using Compaq 386 microcomputers with Edivox sound synthesizers, Braille typewriters and scanners. Acoustic and olfactory aids implemented through an indoor fountain, shrubs and flowers provides a guiding system in addition to a studded floor strip. (67)

Although the BN has made good progress in automating the national bibliography, up through the seventies the automation of French libraries was impeded by low funding levels, lack of staff resources and the need to build a higher computer literacy level among professional librarians.

In France, there has also been a strong tradition of resistance to library automation. However, the eighties seemed to bring a wave of change and library automation suddenly seemed to legitimize itself. This occurred more as French firms, such as G. Cam Co. (BRIGITTE), Matra Co. (TOBIAS), Opsys Co. (OPALS), Sagir Co. (GABY), Polyphot Co. (DIDEROT) and Intertechnique Co. (OASIS) entered the market. In addition, foreign systems, such as GEAC and Plessey, were quite active in the French market. The University of Montpellier installed the SIBIL system from the Bibliothèque Cantonale et Universitaire de Lausanne. The French universities are moving toward a decentralized system of databases and not toward a centralized system such as OCLC or RLG/RLIN. (68) By 1994, 75% of French libraries had installed systems. The three most prevalent systems are GEAC in the Bibliotheque Nationale and other national centers, MOBICAT in most University Libraries and OPSYS in public libraries.

An excellent report on the activities of Swiss libraries, particularly the university libraries of the Universitat Freiberg im Breisgau and the Universitat Konstanz, was written in 1982 by French. (69) In this report, French details the lack of cooperation among Swiss libraries and the lack of any interest in computerization or leadership in the National Library in Bern. In my visit to the National Library in 1974, I found that none of the individuals I met expressed the least interest in using computing for bibliographic purposes. The separation of the French- and German-speaking areas into noncooperating camps was all too apparent from the Eastern cantons' lack of interest in using the SIBIL system developed at Lausanne. SIBIL has been installed in the Ecole Polytechnique Paris, the University of Basel, the City and University Library of Bern and the Cantonal and University Library of Fribourg.

The Zentral Bibliothek Zurich, founded in 1629, acts as the City, Cantonal and University Library, with a collection of over 2 million items but a registered user population of just under 5,000. It is doubling its size every 20 years, which is similar to the growth of American university libraries. However, its small user population, while typical of European academic libraries, is not at all like American libraries. The University IBM 3033 is used for acquisitions processing via two IBM 3276 terminals and Inforex key-to-tape data capture equipment, recording transactions on magnetic tape. These tapes are processed thrice weekly. The ISBN or accession number can be used via the online terminals to query the acquisition file, but COM fiche, produced weekly, is the main access tool. The Zentral Bibliothek has also been working on a union list of serials. Since the Swiss cataloging rules have been undergoing revision, the library has decided to wait until these are revised and adopted before doing any automation of the manual card catalog. Those interested in a detailed view of this acquisitions system should consult Hofliger's account in German. (70)

The Eidgenossische Technische Hochschule, Zurich (ETH-Federal Institute of Technology), has a collection of three million items, largely in closed stacks. It has developed a paging and circulation system and appears to be the most progressive of the German Swiss libraries. Its PECOS catalog can be queried via Euronet Diane terminals by their fee-paying business users. Users need the "Bestellnummer" of the book in order for it to be paged. Once an item is paged by entering the Bestellnummer and user identification card in a library terminal, the user can pick up the volume at a special desk. Charging is self-service via terminals in the reader area. This first version of the system was called ELAS (Elektronische Ausleihkontroll-System) and began operation in 1976 on a Control Data mainframe using Olivetti TE300 terminals. A new system to replace this one was at the planning stage in 1982 and was to be implemented on an IBM host computer. It was to include an improved catalog searching function and issue/paging system. This is the system called ETHICS.

It will also incorporate a periodicals system to replace its present PECOS and staff-accessed UDC classified online catalog. By 1988 ETHICS, with over 500,000 titles in its database, was a well-running system serving ETH users, both in the library and remotely. It was put into operation in 1986 and continues to be improved, with very good user acceptance. (71) The system runs 135 terminals, and UDC searching is supported. The system runs on an IBM 4381 R14 dual processor with 15 gigabytes of mass storage under VM/CMS with VSE/SP, VTAM, and CICS. It uses the ADABAS software from Software AG as its foundation, as does the Western Library Network software in the United States.

As of 1985, Swiss libraries needed to do some serious catching up to their European neighbors in moving into interactive multifunctional integrated systems and adopting more commercially available solutions. Most future commercial systems will probably will be imported, as there has been little native Swiss commerical development of automated library systems. In the mid-eighties SIBIL appears to have been the only current native system with continued promise of replication. By the nineties, SIBIL had been replicated in numerous Swiss libraries and it had helped Swiss libraries catch up almost to the level of their sister institutions in neighboring countries.

Coming out of IBM in Germany, the DOBIS/LIBIS system started receiving attention in the literature. (72) On May 6–7, 1982, 26 of the 38 licensees of this system worldwide came together and formed a DOBIS/LIBIS users group at a meeting in Leuven, Belgium. Their second meeting was held in December 1982, in Paris. The group has met at least annually since then. Although, IBM has not had much success in marketing this system in the United States, the number of its sites installed abroad continued to grow until 1990. By 1989 some 70 sites had been installed. In 1993 IBM ceased support and development of this software worldwide. Many of these sites are using heavily customized versions of this software, such as at the National Library of Canada and other Canadian government sites.

McDonnell Douglas's URICA system continued to gain ground in installations in Great Britain, such as at the National Library of Wales, and at some other European sites, mainly in Germany. However, it was withdrawn from the U.S. market in which it had trouble competing with systems from more established vendors. IME's TinLib, based on its TinMan database software, was one of the most popular microcomputer-based systems throughout Europe. Conversely, IME's product is selling successfully to U.S. libraries. By the late 1980's much of the activity in European library automation was centered on the public access catalog and on linking of systems.

Another system from Germany providing advanced retrieval capabilities for that era was the MINDOK system. (73) MINDOK was developed in parts, the first providing text and data acquisition and the second providing indexing and retrieval. A third part, MINDOK III, provided the database management and retrieval module. It operated on Digital Equipment PDP-11 and VAX, MODCOMP and Siemens minicomputers. Pioneering microcomputer development took place on this system, as the initial MINDOK parts one and two had been developed using a Tandberg TDV 2114/2324 microcomputer with an Intel 8080 microprocessor. The operating system, called TOS, was proprietary to Tandberg. This microsoftware also operated on the Siemens 6-610 and 6-611 microcomputers using AM BOSS1. A CP/M implementation was underway in 1983. This was one of the earliest micro/host computer integrated systems. The most interesting facet of this development was that at that time no one in the United States was even beginning to investigate using this level of microcomputer and host system for full-scale retrieval systems or for any other serious retrieval applications that involved linking to a host computer.

In Germany DOBIS/LIBIS, ALS and URICA are popular systems as is Siemens' SISIS. BIS-LOK, a smaller version of BIS from DABIS, is popular in the former East German sites. In Italy, again DOBIS/LIBIS and ALEPH seem to be the prevalent large systems. SIBIL has also moved to Luxembourg where the National Library has installed it. The second automated library in that country is the Abbey of St. Maurice in Clervaux, which has installed VUBIS from the Netherlands and which is now a commercial system. In Portugal, the national Library has installed GEAC, and by 1993 52 other libraries were using the CDS/ISIS supplied by UNESCO. CDS/ISIS stands for Computerized Document System/Integrated Set of Information System. It is available on IBM mainframes, in a micro version from UNESCO and on HP/3000 minicomputers from Canada. In Spain, DOBIS/LIBIS, Sabini and ALEPH, Absys, PALS and VTLS are represented, with these latter two getting their first installations in 1992.

D. The Middle East, Africa, and Asia

1. *Israel*

In Israel there has been a strong tradition of minicomputers for development and operation of automated library management systems and for interactive information retrieval systems. Even the ALEPH (Automated Library Expandable Program) system of the Hebrew University of Jerusalem, operating in a bilingual Hebrew/English mode, was later ported to the Digital Equipment VAX from its original Control Data Cyber mainframe version. This enabled ALEPH to be an exportable system, affordable and operable in institutions that did not have Cyber systems.

In 1983, an important meeting brought together participants from many countries to the very first International Conference on the Application of Mini- and Micro-Computers in Information, Documentation, and Libraries, in Tel

Aviv. (74) This meeting showcased Israeli developments alongside British, French and particularly German systems. The National Center of Scientific and Technological Information, Tel Aviv, had jointly developed the DOMESTIC indexing and retrieval software with KTS-Informationssysteme, Munich. (75) The German version of this system operated on a Philips P857 minicomputer which was a minicomputer with architecture somewhat similar to the Digital Equipment PDP-11 series while the Israeli version was operating on a Digital Equipment Corp. PDP-11/70 minicomputer.

As one reflects over the early eighties, it is apparent that microcomputer and mass storage developments—for example, the availability of the PC/AT and the ability of UNIX-like operating systems to permit porting of minicomputer software to the microcomputer platform—accelerated the bringing to market of functionally rich retrieval software in the United States. Couple this with the increased capacity of mass storage and the commensurate cost reductions per megabyte and it is plain to see that by 1986 relatively larger retrieval applications could be implemented in settings not previously possible. In 1983, superminicomputer systems costing $500,000 could be equipped with mass storage of around 1 gigabyte. Today, one can procure a microcomputer system using a multiprocessor architecture, such as the Compaq SystemPRO, for around $20,000 and add in as much as 80 gigabytes of storage for less than $1,000 per gigabyte. Consequently, on local area networks, we are looking at multi-gigabyte servers at a fraction of the hardware cost of just a half decade ago. Similarly, application software for microcomputers and LANs is priced lower than for the minicomputer and mainframe markets.

One of the earliest Israeli systems involving development of an advanced database management system in an unusual application for the period was the Q.D.M.S. (Qualitative Data Management System), which operated on the PDP-11 under RSTS/E and RSX-11M or on VAX minicomputers under VMS. It consisted of an application generator, real-time file updating, intricate security levels, SDI profiles, a word processor and either fully automatic or selective indexing of free text. It also supported a full thesaurus and bilingual operation. (76) This system was in operation at the Beth Hatefutsoth Museum of the Jewish Diaspora. One of its interesting data management applications was to trace the occurrence of specific name forms throughout the world. Since this museum was an early pioneer in computer usage, this was an important place to visit when considering automated systems in Israel. A competing system, developed by Yael Management Automation, Ltd., of Ramat Gan, Israel, was Y-DOC, which also operated on Digital Equipment systems. (77)

Boys Town Jerusalem consists of a junior high, academic and technical high schools and the Institute of Practical Engineering, with 1200 students 12–20 years old. The Isaac L. Auerbach School of Computer Studies is one of its established programs. Some 30,000 grades are processed each trimester.

Students have written programs for this Boys Town system using BASIC for instructional software and COBOL for the school's management system. (78)

MAIMON (Management of Israeli Medical Libraries Online), using a PDP-11 system under Digital Standard MUMPS, was providing very low cost services for the Muriel and Philip Berman National Medical Library. (79) For a $120,000 initial investment, with $16,000 annual costs for operation, or $2,000 per terminal, this library had automated its circulation and provided an online public catalog with Boolean searching, order processing and serials management. Named after Maimonides, a Jewish philosopher (1135 A.D.–1204 A.D.), it seems a fitting name for a system in a medical library setting.

In what might be characterized as the closest thing to a network or a shared system, the University of Haifa Library, using a relatively small PDP-11/34, had been producing card sets, book form and COM form catalogs for several libraries. (80) It is interesting to note that in 1975, a MARC Israel system on a Control Data Corp. Cyber computer was a project of Ben Gurion, Bar-Ilan and Haifa Universities, three of the seven Israeli universities. However, the larger university libraries preferred manual cataloging and so a proposal to fund a MARC tape subscription nationally was turned down. Shared MARC services were stopped in 1980. The Haifa system produces the Index to Hebrew Periodicals, HOBITS (Haifa Online Bibliographic Text System), with some 20 different databases, ORICAT original cataloging system, and HEBCAT Hebrew cataloging system. Haifa now subscribes to USMARC tapes and provides an informal de facto cataloging network.

Many other interesting and pioneering systems were reported at the 1983 conference in Tel Aviv. Innovation in systems concepts probably was encouraged due to the relatively small-scale hardware affordable in Israel, compared with counterpart systems in the United States.

With Ralph Shoffner as a consultant, the University of Petroleum and Minerals in Saudi Arabia implemented the IBM DOBIS/LIBIS system on the University's IBM mainframe. It developed programs to convert USMARC records to DOBIS MARC structure and to support Arabic script processing. However, there remained both the serious need for added material formats for nonbook materials and a lack of any serials management module and interactive tutorial mode for end-user searching. (81)

2. *Africa*

DOBIS/LIBIS was one of the two most popular software products for library automation in the Union of South Africa; the URICA Library System, using MicroData Reality minicomputers, was second. This latter system was developed and sold by UNICOM Pty., Ltd. (82) The DOBIS/LIBIS system had been installed at the Universities of Natal, Durban, Pretoria, Witwatersrand, the Council for Scientific and Industrial Research, the State Library and the Human

Sciences Research Council as of 1985. URICA had seven systems at the Universities of Natal/Pietermaritzburg, Durban/Westville, Zululand, and The North; the Port Elizabeth Municipal Library; the Transvaal Education Media Service; and the Anglo-American Corporation. Public and provincial libraries were operating mainly mainframe cataloging and circulation systems using COM catalogs. The South African Post Office provided access to European and American Databases via SAPONET connections to international networks. Lodder and Borshoff reported on the development of SA MARC distribution services, with 17 libraries initially signing up for this service. (83,84) The American software from the Western Library Network was chosen and the system was modelled after both OCLC and WLN networks. By 1986, SABINET was fully active and its membership was growing.

With the reintegration of South Africa into the world community, the available options for South African Libraries can only expand. As the South African social scene becomes more settled this potential market will remain to be tapped by foreign and possibly new domestic vendors.

3. Asia

It is difficult to assess the state of library automation in Asian countries as little is published in English or non-Asian language publications. However, in most of these countries, there are active projects under way to implement automated library systems, some being commerical systems and some being developed locally from in-house software.

In 1982, a postal questionnaire on automation in Japanese public libraries revealed that most of their systems had been developed by domestic companies. Most were older systems using computer service bureaus and batch processing. Online interactive processing was starting to be more prevalent, particularly for circulation systems. (85) There were no network library systems reported; only connections between central and branch libraries or bookmobiles. With advances in vernacular Japanese character processing, library automation will be affected mainly by whether Japanese institutions place priority on using mainly domestically developed software or imported software which has been adapted to handle Japanese language processing.

In 1982, there was some rapid basic development in Taiwan of the Chinese Character Code for Information Interchange, Chinese MARC and a prototype online catalog. (86) Hong Kong Polytechnic University was using an RSTS/E-based system of its own design on a large PDP 11/70 system used for school administration to implement a library catalog system. (87) It used MARC records from Hong Kong University Library and short form records to produce an author/title/subject COM catalog using the full records and the short-form for an interactive online catalog. Its system also has an online circulation system and strong integration with its institution's student record and personnel system.

While the system was well conceived, it was hampered by lack of mass storage and the limitations of limited terminal support offered by the PDP-11/70 system. The system used a monitor program called Superman, which called the individual subsystems. These were, curiously enough, alphabetically referred to by human names, e.g., ALFRED, BOBBY, CHRIS, DICK, EDWARD and FRED or A= Subject Authority, B=Data Entry, C=Validation, D=Printing, E=File Maintenance and F=General Services. These in turn had similar submenus.

In the People's Republic of China, by 1982, there were some 300–400 people working on information retrieval systems, with one-half of these in Beijing. (88) There was very little cooperation among any Chinese agencies, with much "re-inventing of the wheel" occurring. This reflection is based on my visits to Beijing on two separate occasions, in 1981 and 1985, in which I did see some improvement in the application of computing, particularly with the installation of many MINISIS-based systems using Hewlett-Packard HP-3000 minicomputers and several ISIS systems operating on smaller models of the IBM 43xx series computers. Some STAIRS applications also were to be found in agencies having access to IBM systems. There were a few microcomputer-based systems by 1983 which used either imported microcomputers, such as PDP-11/23, Wang VS-80 and TRS-80, or Zilog Z-80 CP/M–based programs. Chinese microcomputers using the Zilog Z80A chip were to be found such as the BCM series and TP801. Lack of good Chinese character input and processing was hampering development along with problems of importing or domestically building hardware competitive with that available in the Western world.

By 1985, although the climate of interaction among agencies had improved only slightly, there was immense progress in computer applications. MS-DOS–based microcomputers, including some excellent domestically manufactured systems, such as the Great Wall systems, then using an Intel 80286 microprocessor, were available but expensive. These systems could handle over 10,000 Chinese characters in a Chinese character BIOS of Chinese design. (The Chinese wrote their own BIOS to replace the English version we sell on our micros. It can display >10,000 Chinese ideograph characters using a 16-bit format instead of our 8-bit format.) The Intel 8088 version was much more limited and handled around 5,000 characters. Although the first library computer had been installed in the National Library of China (NLC) in Beijing in 1975, few other libraries received any direct benefit as Chinese MARC services were not yet developed. (89) By 1984 a Hitachi M-1504 mainframe had been installed. This system is quite similar to the IBM 43xx series computers. The International Serials Data System (ISDS), payroll management and USMARC system were transferred to this new computer. An immense new complex of buildings for the library was built, with the new National

Bibliographic Center Computer System to be a major new service provider. In 1988, to help achieve these goals, NLC licensed the Western Library Network (WLN) software and contracted with CLSI for a circulation system to be linked to the WLN software. By 1991 these developments were encountering considerable interfacing difficulty and by 1993 it appeared that the NLC had abandoned this effort. The challenge for the National Library will be to provide services to the separately libraries scattered throughout the country, all of which have growing clientele who eagerly await better library services. It was both my pleasure and pain, in 1985, to see several thousand people lined up awaiting the opening of the main public library in Beijing. The building could only hold a fraction of those in line, so when people left, more were permitted to enter. I have never seen such a phenomenon in an American library, public or academic. China would need vast development of its libraries to realize library services comparable to those expected in Western countries. It would also require a new telephone system to use interactive information technologies. Hopefully, through some adoption of computer technology, the situation will gradually improve, although the government, since the 1989 demonstrations, has become increasingly repressive. Such repression is bound to affect China's ability to gain further foreign technology, particularly as the U.S. government remains sensitive to China's human rights record.

The National University of Singapore Library reported its experiences with the Hewlett-Packard HP-3000–based MINISIS software in a test from June, 1981 to March, 1982 where it tested MARC record conversion to MINISIS internal format and output again to MARC as well as the suitability of this software to form an integrated library system. The library expected full university support to continue MINISIS use, and its experience was generally positive, but the absence of indicators in the MINISIS records and ordered subfields makes producing a MARC format output tape difficult. Therefore, special programs will need to be developed for this purpose. It was hoped that several other problems with the database and its lack of integrated cross-reference structure would be solved through subsequent releases of the software. (90)

In India, library automation began in the late 1960's when some of the larger university libraries began developing their own systems. But some two-thirds of the systems that were initiated were later dropped. Consequently, instead of more and more institutions adopting automation, there has been a growing indifference to computerization among the professional librarians. In the late 1980's, Kumar reported that the situation was going from bad to worse. (91) The remaining systems tend to be primitive for this era, and the problem is aggravated by a social situation of vast manpower available and little motivation to adopt technology that might displace human workers. Despite microcomputers, the start-up costs are still beyond all but a few institutions, with rapid obsolescence of hardware a major problem. There also is a shrinking infrastructure of trained personnel, with most computer professionals emigrating abroad because of poor pay and poor computer facilities with which to work. Kumar recommends development of a national information policy and leadership from India's library schools but does not recommend adoption of the MARC format, development of a national bibliographic database or any network-based services.

VIII. CONCLUSION

While monumental progress was made in the 1980's in installing automated library systems in developed countries of the world, only very slow progress or really no progress was made in many developing countries. Developed countries also broadened their views of how technologies such as office automation, electronic mail, facsimile, peer-to-peer library networks, bibliographic utilities, locally mounted databases, CD-ROM products and remote online search services all should fit together to form an integrated, multifunctional system able to continue future growth using commercially developed solutions. Underdeveloped countries had limited access to technology and often were not able to employ it due to a lack of library personnel with sufficient computer expertise and a lack of any commercial software development and access to appropriate hardware and telecommunications. Increasingly, the software market became more global, but until underdeveloped countries represent a good market for systems, it is unlikely that foreign developers will make the necessary investments to handle such refinements as multilingual, Asian language, and other non-Roman alphabet processing or customization to the specifics of differing national practices in library operations and services.

One of the challenges of the 1990's awaiting libraries in the developed countries is to facilitate and help their sister libraries throughout the less developed countries. Libraries in the developed countries also will need large infusions of capital in order to continue to adopt new technology. The needed investment will depend on national and institutional program priorities and respective national economies. In the United States, federal initiatives to build a commercially operated replacement for the National Science Foundation–operated network backbone, i.e., the Internet, will provide a solid vehicle for accelerated and wider use of this network by libraries of all types. The decade of the eighties saw libraries in developed countries poised to benefit from increased collection sharing and services, while in underdeveloped countries only very limited progress has been made. It is these underdeveloped countries, being information poor, that really need all the improvements in information acquisition that they can get. But it may be a decade or more before they acquire all of the necessary technology.

REFERENCES

1. Boss, Richard W. *The Library Manager's Guide to Automation. 2nd ed.* White Plains, NY:Knowledge Industry Publications, Inc., 1984. p. 8.
2. Grosch, Audrey N. The Challenge of the Eighties—The Comprehensive Electronic Service System (CESS). *The Electronic Library 1*(2): 117-140 (April 1983).
3. Mathews, Joseph R. *Choosing an Automated Library System: A Planning Guide.* Chicago: American Library Association, 1980.
4. Toohill, Barbara G. *Guide to Library Automation.* Sponsor: U.S. Dept. of Health, Education and Welfare, Office of Libraries and Learning Resources. McLean, VA: Mitre Corp. Metrek Division, 1980.
5. Drabenstott, Jon. Automating Libraries: The Major Mistakes Librarians are Likely to Make. *Library Hi-Tech 3*(1):93-99 (1985).
6. Cohen, Elaine and Aaron Cohen. *Automation, Space Management and Productivity: A Guide for Libraries.* New York: R. R. Bowker Co., 1982.
7. Cline, Hugh F. and Loraine T. Sinnott. *The Electronic Library: The Impact of Automation on Academic Libraries.* Lexington, MA: Lexington Books, 1983.
8. Corbin, John Boyd. *Managing the Library Automation Project.* Phoenix, AZ: Oryx Press, 1985.
9. *Library Systems Evaluation Guide.* Powell, OH: James E. Rush Associates, Inc., 1983–1985. 8 volumes (1. Serials 2. Circulation 3. Public Service 4. Acquisitions 5. Management Services 6. Inter-Library Loan 7. Cataloging 8. System Integration).
10. Cortez, Edwin M. and Edward John Kazlauskas. Planning and Designing Information Systems: Human factors and the Human/Machine/Environment Interface. In: *Managing Information Systems and Technologies: A Basic Guide for Design, Selection, Evaluation and Use.* New York: Neal-Schuman, 1986. Chapter 4.
11. Cortez, Edwin M. *Proposals and Contracts for Library Automation: Guidelines for Preparing RFP's.* Studio City, CA: Pacific Information, Chicago: American Library Association, 1987.
12. Tracy, Joan I. *Library Automation for Library Technicians: An Introduction.* Metuchen, NJ: Scarecrow Press, 1986.
13. Library of Congress. *Summary of MARC Format Specifications for Technical Reports. Preliminary Edition.* Washington, DC: Library of Congress, 1981.
14. Library of Congress. Processing Division. *Authority, a MARC Format. 1st ed.* Washington, DC: Processing Services, Library of Congress, 1981.
15. *USMARC Format for Holdings and Locations.* Washington, DC: Network Development Office, Library of Congress, 1984–to date.
16. Sapp, Linda H. The USMARC Format for Holdings and Locations. *Drexel Library Quarterly 21*(1): 87-100 (Winter 1985).
17. Sahli, Nancy Ann. *MARC for Archives and Manuscripts: The AMC format.* Chicago: Society of American Archivists, 1985.

18. Crawford, Walt. *MARC for Library Use: Understanding the USMARC formats.* White Plains, NY: Knowledge Industry Publications, 1984.
19. Crawford, Walt. *MARC for Library Use: Understanding Integrated USMARC. Second Edition.* Boston: G.K. Hall & Co., 1989.
20. Boss, Richard. *Information Technologies and Space Planning for Libraries and Information Centers.* Boston: G. K. Hall, 1987.
21. Bridge, Frank R. and Robert A. Walton. Automated System Marketplace 1987: Maturity and Competition. *Library Journal 113* (6): 33-44 (April 1, 1988).
22. Bridge, Frank R. and Robert A. Walton. Automated System Marketplace 1988. Focussed on Fulfilling Commitments. *Library Journal 114 (6)*: 41-54 (April 1, 1989).
23. Bridge, Frank R. Automated System Marketplace 1992: Redefining the Market Itself. *Library Journal 117*(6): 58-75 (April 1, 1992).
24. Bridge, Frank R. Automated System Marketplace 1993. Part 1: Focus on Minicomputers. *Library Journal 118*(6): 52-64 (April 1, 1993).
25. Bridge, Frank R. Automated System Marketplace 1993. Part 2: Microcomputers. *Library Journal 118*(7): 50-55 (April 15, 1993).
26. Walton, Robert A. and Frank R. Bridge. Automated System Marketplace 1990. Focusing on Software Sales and Joint Ventures. *Library Journal 115*:55-66 (April 1, 1990).
27. Mischo, Lare. The Alice-B Information Retrieval (IR) System: A Locally Developed Library System at Tacoma Public Library. *Library Hi-Tech* 8(1) (Issue 29):7-20 (1990).
28. Mischo, Lare and Stuart Soffer. The Alice-B System at Tacoma Public Library. *Library Hi-Tech News 56*:1-5 (January 1989).
29. Freedman, Marice J. Opening a Library Catalog. In: *The Card Catalog, Current Issues: Readings and Selected Bibliography.* Edited by Cynthia C. Ryans. Metuchen, NJ: Scarecrow Press, 1981. pp. 51-58.
30. Using Online Catalogs: *A Nationwide Survey: A Report of a Study sponsored by the Council on Library Resources.* Edited by Joseph R. Mathews, Gary S. Lawrence and Douglas K. Ferguson. New York: Neal-Schuman, 1983. Note: this book integrates the four reports published by the OCLC Office of Research reporting the findings of the study.
31. *Online Catalogs, Online Conference: Converging Trends: Proceedings of a Library and Information Technology Association Pre-Conference Institute, June 23-24, 1983, Los Angeles.* Edited by Brian Aveney and Brett Butler. Chicago: American Library Association, 1984.
32. *Online Public Access to Library Bibliographic Databases: Developments, Issues and Priorities.* Council on Library Resources, OCLC and The Research Libraries Group, September 1980. ERIC Document ED195,275.
33. *Online Catalogs: Requirements, Characteristics and Costs: Report of a Conference Sponsored by the Council on Library Resources at the Aspen Institute, Wye Plantation, Queenstown, MD, December 14–16, 1982.* Compiled and Edited by Davis McCarn. Washington, DC: The Council, 1983.
34. Cutter, Charles A. *Rules for a Dictionary Catalog. 4th ed.* Washington, DC: U.S. Government Printing Office, 1904.

35. *The Impact of Online Catalogs.* Edited by Joseph R. Mathews. New York: Neal-Schuman Publishers, 1986.
36. Reed-Scott, Jutta. *Issues in Retrospective Conversion: Report of a Study Conducted for the Council on Library Resources.* Washington, DC: Bibliographic Service Development Program, Council on Library Resources, 1984.
37. Weber, Christine A. *Retrospective Conversion Manual.* Rochester, NY: University of Rochester Library, 1984.
38. McQueen, Judy and Richard W. Boss. Sources of Machine-Readable Cataloging and Retrospective Conversion. *Library Technology Reports 21*(6): 597-732 (November/December 1985).
39. Cochrane, Pauline A. *Redesign of Catalogs and Indexes for Improved Online Subject Access: Selected Papers of Pauline A. Cochrane.* Phoenix, AZ: Oryx Press, 1985. p. 77.
40. *Command Language and Screen Displays for Public Online Systems: Report of a Meeting Sponsored by the Council on Library Resources, March 29–30, 1984, Dublin, OH.* Compiled and edited by Paul Evan Peters. Washington, DC: Bibliographic Services Development Program, Council on Library Resources, 1985.
41. Crawford, Walt. *Bibliographic Displays in the Online Catalog.* White Plains, NY: Knowledge Industry Publications, Inc., 1986.
42. Mathews, Joseph R. Suggested Guidelines for Screen Layouts and Design of Online Catalogs. *Library Trends 35*(4): 555-570 (Spring 1987). (Issue devoted to the online catalog).
43. Bills, Linda G. and Linda W. Helgerson. CD-ROM Public Access Catalogs: Database Creation and Maintenance. *Library Hi Tech 6*(1) (Issue 21): 67-86 (1988).
44. Helgerson, Linda W. Acquiring a CD-ROM Public Access Catalog System. *Library Hi-Tech 5*(3) (Issue 19):49-75 (Fall 1987).
45. Bills, Linda G. and Linda W. Helgerson. User Interfaces for CD-ROM PACs. *Library Hi Tech 6*(2) (Issue 22): 73-115 (1988).
46. Hildreth, Charles R. Communicating with Online Catalogs and Other Retrieval Systems: The Need for a Standard Command Language. *Library Hi-Tech 4*(1): 7-11 (Spring 1986).
47. Crawford, Walt. Common Sense and User Interfaces: Issues Beyond the Keyboard. *Library Hi-Tech 6*(2): 7-16 (1988).
48. Johnson, Ian. Recent Developments in Library Automation in Mexico and Venezuela. *Program 21*(4): 379-381 (October 1987).
49. McCarthy, Cavan. Library Automation in Brazil: The State of the Art. *Program 17*(4): 233-240 (October 1983).
50. McCarthy, Cavan Michael. The Automation of Libraries and Bibliographic Information Systems in Brazil. Ph.D. Dissertation. Loughborough University of Technology, Department of Library and Information Studies, 1982. 323 pp.
51. McGuinn, Thomas P. The Automation of Technical Services in Venezuela's National Library: Aspects of a Transfer of Library Technology. *Library Resources and Technical Services 26*(2):170-176 (Apr/June 1982).
52. Blank, Karen L. Library Automation in Australia. *Library Hi-Tech 2*(3): 47-57 (1984).

53. Goodrum, Richard J. The AWA URICA System and TULIPS: Its Application at the University of Tasmania Library. *Program 18*(1): 46-65 (January 1984).
54. Mongar, P. E. STATUS Software: Application and Experience at the Transport and Road Research Laboratory. *Program 16*(3): 111-129 (July 1982).
55. Leggate, Peter and Hilary Dyer. *The Development of a Microcomputer Facility for Small Libraries.* London: British Library Research and Development Department, 1987. Chapter 5.
56. Thomas, David. Moving from Locally Written Systems to Turnkey Systems: The Story of Automation at Brunel University Library. *Program 22*(3): 209-221 (July 1988).
57. Manson, Pat. Integrated Automated Systems for Cataloguing, Circulation, and Acquisitions on Microcomputers: An Overview of Functions and Products on the UK Market. *Program 23*(1): 1-12 (January 1989).
58. Porter, Martin and Valarie Galpin. Relevance Feedback in a Public Access Catalogue for a Research Library: MUSCAT at the Scott Polar Research Institute. *Program 22*(1): 1-20 (January 1988).
59. Shields, Lisa. An In-house System for Cataloguing, Retrieval and Loans in the Irish Meteorological Service Library. *Program 22*(4): 337-354 (October 1988).
60. Harrison, Ken and David Summers. Development of an Automated Acquisitions System at the University of Lancaster Library. *Program 22*(2): 143-162 (April 1988).
61. Richardson, Jan S. A Library Computing Strategy for the Future: A Personal View from Lancaster University. *Program 21*(1): 49-55 (January 1987).
62. Holm, Liv A. *The BIBNETT Project: System-to-system Communication Using a Computer Network.* Steering Committee of BIBNETT. Oslo: Norsk Dokument-data, 1982.
63. Brisis, Katarzyna de. Test Run of a Network of Library and Information Systems. In: *Impact of New Information Technology on International Library Cooperation. Essen Symposium, 8 September - 11 September, 1986.* Edited by Ahmed H. Helal and Joachim W. Weiss. Essen, Universitatsbibliothek, 1987. (Publications of the Essen University Library, 9) pp. 122-136.
64. Julius dottir, Stefania. Plans for Co-Operative Automation in Icelandic Libraries. *Scandinavian Public Library Quarterly 22*(1): 21-26 (1989).
65. Alewaeters, Gerrit, S. Micha Namenwirth and Marc Verpoorten. Choices in the Design of the VUBIS (II) Online Public Access Module. In: *Local Library Systems: Essen Symposium, 24 September - 27 September 1984; Festschrift in honor of Frederick G. Kilgour to his 70th birthday.* Edited by Ahmed H. Helal and Joachim W. Weiss. Essen: Gesamthochschule-bibibliothek Essen, 1984. pp. 29-54.
66. Finelle, Françoise. Mise en place a la Bibliothèque Nationale Paris d'un système informatique. (Installation of a Computerized System at the Bibliothèque Nationale, Paris). *IFLA Journal 12*(4): 303-304 (1986).
67. Witt, Maria. The Online Public Access Catalogue at the Cite des Sciences Médiathèque in Paris. *The Electronic Library 8*(1):36-44 (February 1990).
68. Chauveinc, Marc. Library Automation. *Journal of Library History 19*(1): 103-123 (Winter 1984).

69. French, Thomas. *Automated Systems in Swiss Libraries and in Two Libraries in South-West Germany and Development of Reader Services.* Birmingham, England: University of Birmingham, University Library, 1982. (British Library R&D Report 5780).
70. Hofliger, Paul. Die Automatisierung in der Zentralbibliothek Zurich. *Nachrichten/ Nouvelles/Notizie 56*(1): 15-19 (February 1980).
71. Hug, Hannes and Rudolf Nothiger. ETHICS: an Online Public Access Catalogue at ETH-Bibliothek, Zurich. *Program 22*(2): 133-142 (April 1988).
72. McAllister, A.S and C. M. McAllister. A Design for an Online Bibliographic Database: the DOBIS/LIBIS database. *Information Processing and Management 17*: 27-38 (1981).
73. Dudek, J. et al. MINDOK—a Microcomputer-Based Text-Acquisition and Information Retrieval System. Ibid. pp. 71-78.
74. *International Conference on the Application of Mini- and Micro-Computers in Information, Documentation and Libraries, March 13–18, 1983, Tel Aviv, Israel. Proceedings of the International Conference.* Edited by Carl Keren and Linda Perlmutter. Amsterdam, New York: North-Holland, Sole Distributors for the U.S.A. and Canada, Elsevier Science Pub. Co., 1983. 801 pp.
75. Seydel, Dietrich. Structure, Functions and Operation of an Integrated Information and Documentation System on Minicomputer. Ibid.pp. 93-101.
76. Yakubovitz, Z. Q.D.M.S., A Qualitative Data Management System for PDP and VAX under RSTS/E, RSX or VMS. Ibid. pp. 63-69.
77. Beilis, Shai et al. Y-DOC: An Application Generator for Information Systems. Ibid. pp. 85-92.
78. Goldenberg, Naftali et al. Boys Town Jerusalem—A Mini-computer Managed Comprehensive School. Ibid. pp 87-92.
79. Avriel, Deborah. Cost Effectiveness and Ergonomics of a Library Dedicated Minicomputer System. Ibid. pp. 503-511.
80. Adler, Elhanan. A Minicomputer-Based Cataloging Network. Ibid. pp. 729-735.
81. Ashoor, Mohammed Saleh. Planning for Library Automation at the University of Petroleum and Minerals. *Journal of Information Science 5*(5): 193-198 (February 1983).
81. Ashoor, Mohammed Saleh. Planning for Library Automation at the University of Petroleum and Minerals. *Journal of Information Science 5*(5): 193-198 (February 1983).
82. Musiker, R. The New Technology in South African Libraries—An update to 1984. *South African Journal of Library and Information Science (Suid-Afrikaanse Tydskrif vir Bibliotheek) 53*(2): 68-71 (June 1985).
83. Lodder, Margaret. Short State of-the-Art Report on Computerization in South African Libraries, September 1981. *South African Journal for Librarianship and Information Science* (Suid-Afrikaanse Tydskrif vir Bibliotheek) 49(4): 191-199 (April 1982).
84. Borshoff, M.C. and A. J. Bergesen. A Tentative Tariff Structure for the South African Bibliographic Information Network (SABINET). *South African Journal for Librarianship and Information Science (Suid-Afrikaanse Tydskrif vir Bibliotheek) 49 (4)*: 200-209. (April 1982).

85. Tamura, Shunsaku and Hiromi Oba. Automation in Japanese Public Libraries: A Survey (in Japanese). *Annals of the Japan Society of Library Science 28*(3): 117-123 (September 1982).
86. Poon, Kee-Hoo and Wan-Kam Chan. In-House Library Catalogue System Using a Mini-computer. In: *International Conference on the Application of Mini- and Micro-Computers in Information, Documentation and Libraries, March 13–18, 1983, Tel Aviv, Israel. Proceedings of the International Conference.* Edited by Carl Keren and Linda Perlmutter. Amsterdam, New York: North-Holland, Sole Distributors for the U.S.A. and Canada, Elsevier Science Pub. Co., 1983. pp. 571-582.
87. Lee, Hwa-Wei. Recent Breakthroughs in Library Automation in Taiwan. *Journal of Educational Media Science 19*(2): 119-136 Winter 1982).
88. Jiang, Xiang-Dong and Liu Xiao-Quing. The Computer Applications in Some Libraries and Information Institutes in China. *Electronic Library 1*(4): 279-285 (October 1983).
89. Sun, Beixin. Automation Development at the National Library of China. *Library Resources and Technical Services 29*(4): 367-368 (October/December 1985).
90. Hochstadt, Peggy Wai Chee et al. Towards an Online Integrated System at the National University of Singapore Library. In: *FID Congress (41st: 1982: Hong Kong). The Challenge of Information Technology: Proceedings of the Forty-First FID Congress held in Hong Kong, 13–16 September 1982.* Edited by K. R. Brown. Amsterdam; New York: North-Holland Publishing Company, 1983. Sole Distributor for the U.S.A. and Canada, Elsevier Science Publishing Co., 1983. pp. 11-61.
91. Kumar, P. S. G. *Computerization of Indian Libraries.* Delhi: B. R. Corp. New Delhi: Distributed by D. K. Publisher's Distributors, 1987.

3

BIBLIOGRAPHIC UTILITIES AND COOPERATIVE PROGRAMS

It's not true; I do search by subject!

—James Billington

I. INTRODUCTION

In 1696, Most Reverend Thomas Bray, sent as Commissary for the Anglican Church to the British colonies in America, discovered no books! As a result, upon his return to England a few years later, he dedicated his life to getting books to the colonies. By 1731, at his death, some 39,000 volumes had been sent, but by 1740 they had all disappeared. This appeared to be not a very good beginning for literacy and education in this country. Another legacy that Reverend Bray left was his written works in which he espoused a network of libraries for the colonies which would foster education and enhance productivity of the colonizers. Thus, the concept of library networking might be somewhat older than most of us may have thought. The first actual cooperative librarianship in America can be traced to the founding of the American Library Association (ALA) in 1876 and other significant developments such as those made by Charles Ami Cutter and Melvil Dewey.

Establishment of the ALA focussed on cooperation among libraries and librarians, particularly to share resources and professional expertise. Similarly, when a small group of librarians who were in charge of specialized subject libraries joined John Cotton Dana at the July 1909, ALA Annual Meeting to found the Special Libraries Association (SLA), one of their goals was to foster cooperative endeavors to share specialized collections and subject field expertise.

Pushing libraries along cooperative paths has been further necessitated by the increase in: volume of publications, expenses involved in obtaining them, and new forms of publication. These latter require new expensive investments in technology such as CD-ROM and other computerized delivery forms competing for library budgets, almost all of which have not kept up with inflation. With the dramatic 100–400% in the price of printed scholarly journals over the last several years, the large research library has been particularly adversely affected at a time that it has had to fund these new technology expenditures. Since the early seventies, the development of bibliographic utilities, as an answer to the above pressures, has been shaped in large part by the following factors:

1. The development of the Machine Readable Cataloging Record (MARC) format and the MARC Record Magnetic Tape Subscription Service by the Library of Congress
2. The creation of a critical mass of users to afford development of mainframe computer applications since these applications had been premised mainly on batch processing
3. The promise of lowering cataloging and technical processing costs to stem the increase in per-unit processing costs in the face of increasingly tightened library budgets
4. The prospect that resulting savings could be reallocated to improve collections, services, and access
5. The increase in interdisciplinary research and scholarship and a clientele that has come to expect a broader and deeper collection resource at one location
6. The emergence of much improved communications through electronic communications networks, e.g., the Internet, and allied equipment to make possible online, real-time applications that could be location independent.

With improved communication came the ability to envision more complex and costly cooperative programs and services, particularly as libraries were able to develop standards that governed data communication, storage and retrieval among a diverse library community. Although it is thought that the rapid improvement in computing is what accelerated the development of the bibliographic utility, it was really the development of data communications networks and their underlying technologies that made the bibliographic utilities practical. Without these communications networks, the utilities would not have been able to deliver the online, interactive services that form the technological basis for their success.

This is why the decade of the nineties is continuing to be the decade of networking library and parent institutional systems into a vast and far-reaching web of knowledge and communications resources available to the librarian and library user. The eighties concentrated on distributing computing power to the user through the development of cheaper, more powerful central processors, making both individual personal computers and local area network (LAN) servers widely affordable. The eighties also brought the earliest forms of new systems design architectures for the individual library system as well as the bibliographic utility. This made possible combinations of central and distributed computing resources as well as LAN-based systems to provide broader application solutions than those provided merely by mainframe or host computer software. With the use of microcomputers also came a widening of the market for automated library systems and the broadening of tasks that would be computer-aided in the library, to the point that it is now inconceivable in developed countries that any library would not be able to have an interactive system to support both its technical and public services activities. In other words, the library system itself and the bibliographic utility have become ubiquitous, somewhat invisible to library users and quite taken for granted. A key ingredient making this possible was the emergence of standards, with the LC MARC record the initial significant bibliographic standard.

II. EMERGENCE OF MACHINE-READABLE CATALOGING STANDARDS

The complex and costly software designed to perform library functions, is dependent on vast volumes of data, much of which has taken varied natural language or encoded forms. Prior to the pilot test of the MARC record in 1968, individual library systems defined data elements in completely uncoordinated ways, making sharing of databases virtually impossible without extensive conversion programming. Even in that situation, data elements thought to be important to one library might not be deemed important to another. For example some libraries used only volume/issue labelling in their serials check-in, while other systems made little or no attempt at keeping track of volume/issue, rather depending only on issue date.

Henriette Avram (1) pointed out only two years after the MARC Pilot Project, in which a small number of libraries tested the MARC record by developing some software to process these records, that the dynamic characteristics of library bibliographic records were underestimated. She also pointed out the need for various character set and coding standards in addition to the problems of search key design. Even something seemingly as simple as abbreviating the country of publication resulted in many variant abbreviations for the same country. I have seen systems that used FR, FRA, FRAN and FRNC to stand for France. Thus, without agreement on a common set of bibliographic data elements and a common "physical envelope" as a beginning, there would not be a common shareable basis of bibliographic data and data structures to permit the design of widely used and more generalized computer-aided systems.

The physical envelope would be that provided by the International Standards Organization (ISO) 2709 magnetic tape communications format, with the application of this to bibliographic record data elements defined by the LC MARC record format. In 1991, the ISO began revising 2709 under its Subcommittee 4: Computer Applications in Information and Documentation of Technical Committee 46: Information and Documentation. This ISO standard is a key element along with the MARC record for establishing a firm foundation for system developers.

The initial MARC format defined the data elements and knowledge tags for books, i.e., monographic works. Further developments brought specific formats for other types of materials—serials, music scores, authorities, sound recordings, maps, archive records, films, holdings. By the mid-1980's the complexities of these formats was a major maintenance problem to every supplier of services and software based on these formats. Given the emergence of much lower cost storage and the usage of random access file techniques, it has become increasingly apparent that this multiplicity of formats is not desirable.

From the earliest days of MARC, I questioned the development of format-specific data records, given my experiences in designing numerous batch-mode systems for library technical processing, but it was much more difficult, without considerable experience in usage of the data, to design more generalized record formats encompassing a much broader class of data elements. It probably was necessary for the LC MARC formats to move through this evolution of separate formats so that in codifying the specifics of each format the commonalities would become clearer and enable a good rationalization for the design of a combined all-purpose MARC format for cataloging of any material likely to be found in a library. By 1970, when the MARC record service started, I was already thinking in terms of a generalized bibliographic database that would identify what an item was as to material type but involve a bibliographic record format that was not composed of separate record types as was MARC. Unfortunately, although some work defining such a system was done in

Minnesota, the plan put forth for a statewide library system was never funded or supported by those outside the University of Minnesota Libraries. (2) Certainly, other system designers were also thinking along these lines for new, as yet to be programmed systems.

Over more than the two decades since the introduction of MARC, the National Information Standards Organization (NISO), the successor to the American National Standards Institute Z39 Subcommittee, has promulgated numerous standards that affect bibliographic cooperative efforts. Two recently adopted standards are Z39.58 Common Command Language and its international counterpart ISO 8777. Another is Z39.67 Computer Software Description. Having such standards enables both software designers and users of the data produced by these systems to have widely applicable software and widely understood data content, in the correct MARC-tagged format, augmenting the standardized data element descriptions provided by LC MARC or member- contributed records.

It was clear from the MARC pilot project that one of the most sought after products was sets of catalog cards, as most libraries were dependent on a card form of catalog as relatively few libraries in the United States had moved to book-form or microfilm-based catalogs. Therefore, it was natural for libraries to look first at somehow realizing improvements in using this standardized cataloging data to generate cards for their catalogs in machine readable form. Then, with the progress in and declining cost of technology, the path of evolution for many libraries moved from microfilm/microfiche to CD-ROM and/or to in-house interactive online catalogs as part of an integrated library system. Later in this chapter we will examine the bibliographic utilities that resulted from cooperative efforts and the supply of MARC bibliographic data.

Along with understanding the importance of many standards developments in making possible today's bibliographic utilities and local library systems, it is important to know about, in a general sense, the major issues faced by libraries participating in cooperative endeavors and the major organizations that were created to formalize these cooperative relations.

III. LIBRARY COOPERATION ISSUES

There are a number of significant issues that libraries face and that also affect library cooperative ventures, particularly as these develop, grow in scope and mature in operation. Although this is not an exhaustive view of all of the myriad issues that have been faced in the hundreds of cooperative undertakings here and abroad, they will set the scene for examining each of the major bibliographic utilities in the United States and Canada. As these same organizations have served as examples for many other developed countries, we will not try to examine foreign bibliographic utility/network development here. Rather, an understanding of the basic elements of these cooperative ventures will make clearer where problems have surfaced and perhaps why the problems existed. One can study these problem areas to understand how a particular cooperative endeavor may have evolved to its present form, bearing in mind that local culture and circumstances have played a part in shaping it organizationally and politically.

A. Broadening Access to Materials

With the publishing explosion in the decades following World War II, even the largest and wealthiest libraries were no longer able to maintain self-sufficient, comprehensive collection levels in every subject. Libraries have exercised much more purchasing selectivity with respect to scholarly journals and monographic works. Thus, while library users of several decades ago deemed interlibrary loan a rare privilege, today's library users view it as a normal service to obtain virtually any sort of material. Consequently, many larger libraries, while always being net lenders, became overwhelmingly so. In some cases the impact of interlibrary borrowing on the collections of large libraries has been minimized by the more efficient sharing of materials among smaller libraries that have formed cooperative loan systems such as that initially provided by OCLC, Inc., and later by RLIN. However, the costs for providing these services continues to increase, which has necessitated various cost recovery policies and/or incentive measures by larger and smaller libraries.

Broadening access to materials via shared databases, such as those OCLC or RLIN provide, carries the risk of increased demand for these materials from users outside the parent institution. However, this risk is managed relatively well through improving acquisitions policies and focussing more on the scope of the collection. Thus, it is probable that in the future every library will naturally assume a role of extension for other libraries, with clusters of libraries developing their strengths and reputations along certain interdisciplinary lines, such as geopolitical areas, topical subject areas (as is now mostly the case), or the areas of science and technology.

There is no doubt that despite photocopy, facsimile, and electronic communication, the actual physical delivery of materials to a given user is still the area where much improvement can be made. We can order hot meals delivered to our home, with the surcharge for delivery not much above the cost of the meal in the restaurant. However, only library users in certain larger institutions have subsidized delivery of materials to their offices or are able to pay the costs associated with the use of private commercial information brokers obtaining these materials. Therefore, unless users actually physically go to the library, the bookmobile or travelling collection, there is no way for them to obtain the physical materials easily. However, the time will come when the level of service delivery that allows one to telephone for an airline ticket or make a booking by using one's personal computer to access the Official Airline Guide on CompuServe will be expected of the individual library. This means increasing dependence on cooperative access, more information-rich databases and distributed computing power. It also means that some reasonable funding mechanism must be put into place to make document delivery affordable to a broader population than merely those who can afford to pay the relatively high fees for this service.

B. Lowering the Per-Unit Cost of Cataloging

The cost of technical processing and the increase in numbers of items to be processed were the original impetus for early cooperative groups, some of which failed. However, there was one very notable success, which fostered the development of other similar cooperatives. This was the Ohio College Library Center (which would later be renamed the Online Computer Library Center), established in 1971, whose founding Director, Frederick Kilgour, proselytized at every instance how OCLC would enable libraries to lower their per-unit costs of cataloging. Although a result of library cooperatives, this lowering of per-unit costs came about through libraries being willing to make up-front investments in new equipment that would become obsolescent much more quickly than the type of equipment in use prior to the computer, i.e., mainly manual or electric typewriters. Also, they had to make further investments in on-going training of staff in online cataloging using the MARC formats. The libraries, meanwhile were already stretching their budgets to accommodate increased acquisitions and labor costs. In spite of these pressures, libraries viewed these cooperative developments over the long-term and continued to make these investments, even as developments in information technology would change the nature of what services should be offered centrally through these bibliographic utilities. The bibliographic utilities were also rapidly undergoing change. Their fiscal health from the late 1970's to the present continued largely to improve (particularly that of OCLC, Inc., and some regional networks such as WLN or SOLINET), although some bibliographic utilities and regional cooperatives experienced rather tenuous or break-even existence.

While, per-unit costs lowered initially, this incentive is no longer a major factor in justifying bibliographic utility use. The larger libraries have, in fact, stopped performing their cataloging on such systems as OCLC and RLG/RLIN (Research Libraries Group, Inc., Research Libraries Information Network), preferring to contribute their records via tape loading. The cost of processing on a local system now is offset by the benefit of having records immediately visible in the institution's own online catalog and other products typically produced by today's automated library systems. The broadening of access that accompanies reciprocal collection use, facilitated through OCLC or other union catalog databases and systems, has become the major factor in justifying continued cooperative bibliographic utility memberships. Further strengthening this view is RLG's aborted discussions of merger of its network and computer system with OCLC's and a strengthening of RLG's resolve to concentrate on cooperative acquisitions programs revolving around the collections' conspectus of its members and its own database.

C. Document Delivery

Except via their interlibrary loan subsystems, the bibliographic utilities, have pretty much left document delivery to the local or regional multitype library cooperatives, for example, MINITEX in Minnesota and the Dakotas and WILS in Wisconsin. MINITEX, headquartered at the University of Minnesota provides collection sharing and delivery of materials for over 130 libraries and colleges, universities and public libraries are the major groups served. It is agencies such as these that needed union lists of serials and shared catalogs to foster their collection sharing. Such was the beginning of the Minnesota Union List of Serials (MULS) in 1972, the first enriched MARC format-based, detailed holdings statement product of this genre. Photocomposed, bound with a buckram cover and later produced on microfiche, this publication featured the full MARC character set. It was an early example of high-quality modern phototypesetting from a computer-based file. Such a tool was critical to the mission of an agency such as MINITEX, and many other regional library networks developed similar databases. MULS was chosen to be the initial file converted at OCLC for the Conversion of Serials Project—which came to be widely known as CONSER and in which many libraries participated—to create a usable retrospective database of serials records. CONSER was a major reason that OCLC developed its union listing capabilities and further support for serials records in its system.

The actual provision of document delivery services is best done by local or regional agencies, where there is a tight-knit but manageably sized staff to provide this service. Such an organization can be more dynamic and better able to (1) respond quickly to changes in service needs, (2) minimize organizational overhead common to very large organizations, and (3) take advantage of newer technologies. However, a delivery service that might be provided better through a centralized bibliographic utility would include electronic publication-on-demand products, particularly more derivative distributable products from the utility's own database. For example, the Western Library Network (WLN) has produced a CD-ROM version of its database, with quarterly updates. (3) This makes it possible for libraries to search offline by author, title, subject,

ISBN, ISSN and keywords with scoping features to further define searches by library or groups of libraries, languages, format and publication date, with record downloading to local systems. This means that much work can be done without using interactive online network connections, further taxing centralized mainframe computer resources or incurring telecommunications costs. The online database search services pioneered ordering documents online. Dialog, RLIN and later CARL's Uncover service are examples.

D. Local Library Systems: Role of the Bibliographic Utility

In the early 1970's the bibliographic utilities were not much interested in encouraging libraries to install their own minicomputer-based library systems, except for performing circulation transaction support. RLG/RLIN talked about the possibility of acquiring a local library system product for its members but instead opted to mount centralized applications such as acquisitions, which would produce cash flow, something RLG desperately needed in its early years. Philosophically, it supported the concept of local library systems but never developed or acquired rights to market such a system. RLG did invest in creating its locally based Chinese, Japanese, Korean (CJK) support for the creation of full vernacular records for its online database.

In that same period, OCLC discouraged talk of local systems and the prospect of these somehow linking up to OCLC or other service providers' mainframes. However, member libraries were quite interested in OCLC providing a local system. It was not until 1980 that OCLC publicly showed any interest in providing a local library system. In the *OCLC Newsletter* No. 127 (February 6, 1980) it was stated, "The OCLC Board of Trustees at its meeting in Columbus on [December 14, 1979] reaffirmed OCLC's intention to implement an on-line circulation system and directed OCLC staff to develop an original-equipment manufacturer type of arrangement for a circulation system." (4) OCLC had just completed a survey and review of existing operational circulation systems suitable for integration with existing and planned OCLC library processes and products and had announced that the primary candidate for an original manufacturer (OEM) arrangement was GEAC Computer Corp., Ltd., of Canada. Thompson Little, OCLC's Associate Executive Director, stated that OCLC intended to reach a decision concerning GEAC by April 1, 1980. However, the May 20, 1980 issue of the *OCLC Newsletter* reported that "OCLC, Inc. has decided to reexamine its approach to providing an integrated circulation control system with existing and planned OCLC processes." As a result, OCLC and GEAC agreed to discontinue discussions over an OEM agreement. The uncertainty of current economic conditions was cited as a major factor. The performance or cost effectiveness of the GEAC system were not in any way related to this decision. (5)

At this same time OCLC and SOLINET were arguing about how many lines should be installed in the remote communications processor OCLC had installed in the SOLINET Atlanta office. OCLC wanted to connect only 12 of 25 lines to the SOLINET Burroughs computer, with the remaining lines routed directly to OCLC. (6) Although OCLC's publicly stated reason for this was communications reliability, the real reason was to make it more difficult for SOLINET to pursue its own local system development for its members while maintaining a gateway to OCLC via its own processor. Thus, while OCLC was pursuing its own course to provide its members a local library system, it clearly was trying to prevent any competition from others in this area.

Several months later, hidden on the last page of the July 7, 1980 *OCLC Newsletter*, was the news that the OCLC Board of Trustees wanted a priority effort to develop circulation in-house. (7) According to Dr. W. David Penniman, this would be a centralized system that would operate from Columbus, with some functions to be decentralized. Given that the technological development of minicomputer-based systems was already in its early commercially proven state—with successful systems from such vendors as CL Systems, Inc. (CLSI), Geac and Dataphase—such an announcement was tantamount to retrogression to early 1970's systems technology. Clearly, if we use OCLC as an example, there was considerable confusion over the direction to be taken regarding local systems and their interfaces with the bibliographic utilities.

Eighteen months later, OCLC announced its intention to market the Claremont College's Total Library System (TLS). An agreement was signed with Claremont, with OCLC President Rowland Brown explaining that "TLS was selected after careful screening of many alternatives because it offered the best combination of operationally-tested features and equipment at a price that libraries can afford." (8) It was now apparent to the change in top management at OCLC that circulation was a natural distributed application to clarify OCLC's direction with regard to current and future technology. At the ALA Midwinter Meeting in Denver, January 22–27, 1982, attenders saw the Claremont system demonstrated by appointment in OCLC's suite. However, in the OCLC booth, an internally developed local library system running on Tandem minicomputers was also demonstrated. Now, it appeared that there were two OCLC local library systems! What was really going on? By May, 1982 it was announced that OCLC would collaborate with the Five Colleges, Inc., cooperative, composed of Amherst, Hampshire, Mount Holyoke and Smith Colleges and the University of Massachusetts—Amherst, to develop, install and evaluate a local library system linking their libraries. OCLC's initial offering from its local library systems product line would be TLS. (9) As a postscript, Carpenter reported on the success of this installation—but not of TLS—at the Five Colleges. (10) It appeared that OCLC was attempting to unleash a stable of local library system products but was focussing on the TLS product.

News about the above system faded to the background, and 11 months later OCLC announced its agreement with Online Computer Systems, Inc., for joint development of a local library system to be supported and marketed by OCLC. (11,12) Online had entered the library automation market with its version of the Lister Hill-developed Integrated Library System (ILS). This meant another directional twist had occurred, with a MUMPS language approach constituting a new system, to be known as LS/2000. It would be demonstrated first at the upcoming ALA annual meeting in Los Angeles. This was the system that was installed at Five Colleges, Inc., to fulfill the 1982 agreement with OCLC.

Again, the library community saw another change of direction without any explanation of what was really occurring. Could the award winning TLS have been impossible to replicate in another setting? Could its performance, which had been a success at Claremont, have suffered within the larger setting of the Five Colleges? The literature does not reveal any public pronouncements addressing these questions. But, by November 1983, it was clear that the OCLC local library system would be a version of the ILS system. (13) And, in February, 1984, OCLC announced that the initial LS/2000 system was installed in Hampshire College as a first step in development of a system for the Five Colleges, Inc. (14) In that same issue of the *OCLC Newsletter*, it was announced that OCLC had acquired. (15,16) Avatar had also taken the ILS system and developed its own enhanced version which had been sold to 16 libraries. Avatar's Potomac, Maryland office became OCLC's Washington office. This Avatar version also was to be merged into LS/2000. Online Computer Systems would integrate the OCLC and Avatar versions to become one LS/2000 system. With all of the principals in the development of this system now involved, the system enjoyed enhanced credibility and found itself able to compete well in the widening local system market. Also, in this process, Online Computer Systems agreed to no longer market the version it had sold to several customers, although it would continue to support those systems.

The University of Kentucky became the first Association of Research Libraries member to acquire LS/2000 in June, 1984. By mid-1985 34 LS/2000 systems had been installed and these supported 45 libraries. In January, 1987, OCLC acquired the ALIS I and II software from DataPhase which was also MUMPS language based, and the OCLC Local Systems Division supported these users though it had no intention of marketing this software. This was a good development to assure some support for these MUMPS-based systems, since DataPhase was going out of business and had sold its Tandem-based ALIS III to Utlas, Inc. Since these ALIS MUMPS systems also used Data General minicomputers, these libraries, most of whom were OCLC members, would have decent future systems choices. By the fall of 1987, OCLC had sold 100 LS/2000 systems, with the 100th system being acquired by the Manchester, New Hampshire City Library. After six years of continued growth in system installations, OCLC decided to get out of the local systems business and signed an agreement with Ameritech Information Systems, Inc., a wholly owned subsidiary of Ameritech, to acquire the OCLC Local Systems Division. Ameritech also had another library automation product, called Discovery Place, a system developed at Tacoma Public Library. OCLC's local systems products, including LS/2000, ACQ350 and SC350 and the old ALIS I and II products, now called LS/2, would all be taken over and its staff would become Ameritech employees. (17)

As a postscript to the Claremont affair, it should be noted that Claremont Librarian, Patrick T. Barkey, had established the OCLC Western Service Center, and despite OCLC's rejection of the Claremont system, Mr. Barkey had continued in the Executive Directorship of the OCLC Pacific Coast Network (PACNET) until 1985 when he resigned to devote more time to planning the new $8 million addition to the Claremont Colleges Libraries. He continued to serve as a consultant to OCLC and in 1986 formed the OCLC Advisory Committee on College and University Libraries. Until his death on May 17, 1988, he continued to be an active OCLC supporter. Therefore, even though OCLC had rejected the system he inspired at Claremont, Mr. Barkey continued to productively serve OCLC and the library profession. By the 1990's Claremont had replaced its system with a commercial product.

Except for the Utlas, Inc., local system offering, no other bibliographic utilities made investments in this area comparable to OCLC. Utlas too finally left this market area to companies specializing in library automation systems. It is clear that the future will bring a shakedown in library automation systems, with the growth in power of microcomputers and local area networks further forcing minicomputer-based systems to become distributed client/server architecture systems. This will involve a large investment, and thus OCLC, which had an 8% market share at the time of its sale, practiced considerable foresight in moving away from being a local system vendor. Utlas, Inc., faced a similar situation since its Tandem-based local system had not gained any significant market share.

For the 1990's, the bibliographic utilities' major role in local systems will continue to be to facilitate record transfer and sharing, leaving local automation to the respective commercial firms now in the marketplace.

E. Cooperative Acquisitions

Much has been written about how the online databases of major libraries' holdings could be utilized for more cooperative acquisitions to spread the materials budgets of the libraries further. RLG member libraries have developed conspectus documents that describe in great detail collection policies and levels in the hope that this knowledge will make cooperative collection building more of a reality. Although more cooperative efforts are being undertaken, the once envisioned nirvana of ideal cooperative acquisitions has not been realized among RLG members or among other library consortia, for that matter.

An RLG cooperative endeavor designed to strengthen information sharing among art libraries was the development of the SCIPIO Art Sales Catalog Database on RLIN. The initial external design document was developed at the University of Minnesota Libraries in a collaborative undertaking with RLIN, just after the University of Minnesota joined RLIN in 1979. The project was then taken over at RLG headquarters and further developed under a Kress Foundation grant. One can search this database by auction house, collector, date of sale, keywords in title and several other means. (18) The Avery Architecture database of RLG is another successful specialized resource on its system.

It will depend on individual institutions, to what degree cooperative acquisitions programs succeed. Individual libraries must still determine their greatest areas of need to acquire materials for their own collections, and this determination is dependent on their own clientele's needs, first, and their wider obligations as a national resource, second. As societal needs are forcing libraries to change their collections to fit their parent institution's programs, and as the price of published documents continues to rise far faster than the rate of inflation, it is clear that some increase in cooperative acquisitions will be forced on libraries if they are to continue to serve all of their relevant subject areas. Ultimately, new forms of electronic journal publishing—including electronic text collections on the Internet and retrievability of individual articles—may supplant today's dependence on the scholarly journal subscription. This will further force libraries and software product developers to increase their use of electronic technologies to bring more and varied products to the information marketplace.

F. Copyright

The existing cooperative databases maintained by the bibliographic utilities, whether as a composite single database as in the OCLC system or as logically separated individual institution records accessible as in the Utlas, Inc., RLG/RLIN and WLN systems, are composed of both LC MARC records and original shared cataloging records created by member libraries. Therefore, logic dictates that these individual records should be usable by the respective member library in any local system it might implement and should be made available, through mutual agreement, to other institutions.

In February, 1983, OCLC managed to shock the whole library community by announcing that it had put its database under copyright: "Copyright will be one tool in a broad educational program being undertaken by OCLC and its members to ensure the integrity of the database as well as its appropriate and responsible use in keeping with the mutual rights and obligations of its members." (19) OCLC's counsel, David L. Hill, said this was nothing new, as the Library of Congress has a copyright on the National Union Catalog. This decision caused considerable controversy among the regional library network members of OCLC and, as a result, numerous contracts were left unsigned. By 1987, it was clear that OCLC had to pacify its members over the database copyright concerns. On November 16, 1987 the OCLC Board of Trustees adopted a new document, "Guidelines for the Use and Transfer of OCLC Derived Records," whose purpose was to clarify this relationship between OCLC and its member libraries. (20) Essentially, the OCLC copyright filing was as a compiler, and it was their rights as a compiler that were protected by copyright so as to prevent another entity from taking over the total database without incurring the costs of its production. With this guideline, all limitations on member libraries sharing their records were removed.

Meanwhile, UTLAS, Inc. (later to become Utlas) reaffirmed its members' ownership of their contributed or derived records, a pronouncement they much welcomed. (21) RLG/RLIN similarly reaffirmed the ownership of its members.

It would appear that copyright over these bibliographic databases will no longer be a significant issue for the future.

G. New, Experimental Directions

New endeavors must receive start-up funding. For the bibliographic utilities in the United States, this was usually provided by various foundation grants. With UTLAS, Inc. becoming a for-profit organization, it had to derive funds for new ventures from its generated revenues, whereas the nonprofit status of OCLC, RLG/RLIN and WLN made them more likely candidates for continued foundation support for their new ventures.

UTLAS, Inc., and CLSI, developer of the LIBS-100 library automation system, entered a joint marketing agreement in which UTLAS would market CLSI products and services in Canada, while CLSI would market UTLAS's network products in the United States. (22) Given CLSI's dominant share of the U.S. library automation market, this appeared to be a mutually beneficial agreement. With the acquisition of CLSI, Inc., by GEAC, this marketing relationship no longer appears to be in place.

Utlas's CD-CATSS, serials compact disk database, was announced in 1989. It will compete with Bibliofile from Library Corp., Gaylord's SuperCat and WLN's Laser-CAT products for retrospective conversion. Jasco tested and reviewed this product from its January 1989 Preview Edition on its editing, searching, display, printing and record transfer. (23) Its documentation needs corrections and inclusion of omissions, but his conclusion was that the product would compete well with the above CD-ROM databases.

WLN's Laser-CAT has proved to be a boon in reducing its members online connection costs. It also was attractive to smaller libraries as an economical catalog product. (24)

As might be expected, OCLC, with its ever-growing staff and fiscal resources, is the most active in initiating new programs and research activities that might result in new programs. Particularly OCLC is prone to such high-exposure experiments as Channel 2000 videotex where the Academic American Encyclopedia became the first online encyclopedia in a field test to 200 homes. Users were enthusiastic about having an encyclopedia accessible, but they found the interface cumbersome. (25) Videotex has fallen flat commercially in the United States, but these experiments did prove that some library services could be delivered in this manner if the medium of videotex ever becomes commercially viable. In early 1992 there were some signs that videotex might find a U.S. market as the regional Bell telephone operating companies were becoming interested. Cable television companies are positioning themselves to deliver computer-based services to the home and institutional markets; however, by 1994 no significant video text market had emerged.

Through various grants from such agencies as the Council on Library Resources, OCLC's research activities were very broad and resulted in some seminal work that would have considerable influence on the application of information technologies. OCLC's Office of Research completed a 17-month study of eight online catalogs under a Council grant. A three-volume report was issued which formed a solid basis for those developing online catalogs to use in designing features and operation. (26–28)

Another interesting research project was the study of the Dewey Decimal Classification (DDC) as an online browsing tool. With $55,000 from the Forest Press, publishers of DDC, $94,350 from the Council, and $137,511 from OCLC in contributed services, this study began on January 1, 1984 and was completed in September, 1985. Forest Press had recognized the need to investigate through a computer-assisted approach, the value of the DDC's hierarchical subject structure in searching and browsing. The research methodology comprised three phases. Phase 1 used expert opinion to arrive at a consensus about selection of DDC fields and text for subject access, browsing and display in a public access catalog. Phase 2 demonstrated the DDC as an online catalog searcher's tool by building the DDC into the experimental online catalog. Phase 3 involved library patrons and staff in a test of the tool's effectiveness. The Library of Congress, New York State Library, Public Library of Columbus and Franklin County and the University of Illinois also were participants. (29) OCLC published a report of the findings of this research and held an invitational conference January 27-28, 1986 at OCLC. The findings essentially pointed out that traditional searching by subject heading, title and keyword; searching by an enhanced subject keyword; and browsing displays of the DDC were all relatively equal in precision, i.e. relevance of items retrieved and search time. However, each method retrieved different relevant bibliographic items from the same database. (30) Although some European systems have incorporated Universal Decimal Classification (UDC) searching and browsing in their systems, it is yet to be seen whether such features based either on DDC or LC classification will be incorporated into an actual online catalog product in the United States.

With the growth of OCLC and the improved financial stability of networks such as the regional library cooperatives and the RLG/RLIN utility, there will be a continuing concern over developing new services and products for libraries.

H. Governance

By 1980, library networks and cooperatives were an accepted part of the library scene. As the networks increased in strength, their members showed increased interest in network governance, tending to become more bureaucratic and perceived as less sensitive to their members' needs. Still, the networks were supposed to be cooperative ventures, existing to serve their members' needs in terms of products, services and research undertaken. Thus, there has been a growing concern over assuring that members' views are able to influence network policy in an appropriate fashion.

Richard DeGennaro has pointed out that by 1984 there was a growing perception that OCLC was isolating itself from the mainstream of library cooperation and that it was becoming increasingly unresponsive to its member libraries. It was becoming too corporate, but it also could not return to its small, close-knit origins as an Ohio consortium of college libraries. However, it could not afford to forget these origins as it created a new approach to insuring that its members have a voice in its policy development. DeGennaro pointed out that what is good for OCLC is *usually* good for libraries, but what is good for libraries will *always* be good for OCLC. Thus OCLC would have to learn to listen to its friendly critics if it was to restore its members, beliefs that it is listening to their wishes. (31)

Toward that end, OCLC did restructure its governance, and its User's Council assumed a more prominent role in determining OCLC's directions. Having earlier overcome poor systems performance problems worsened by the complex, protracted move from Columbus to the new Dublin, Ohio facility, OCLC faced a large backlog of new members requesting terminal installations and an Ohio Supreme Court decision that OCLC was liable for property taxes on its Dublin facility. Despite these problems, OCLC committed some $40 million to capital expenditures for its new-generation system, while also making noises to Ohio officials that it would relocate if this tax decision was not reversed. With over $1 million due in back property taxes and with future annual real estate taxes expected to be $375,000, OCLC made the first of five installment payments in July, 1984. An appeal to the Ohio legislature to seek relief from real estate, personal property and sales taxes was made. On June 12, 1985 Ohio Governor Richard Celeste signed legislation exempting OCLC from personal property tax and sales tax. On February 18, 1985 an agreement was made with the Dublin Board of Education by which OCLC would make ongoing payments to support local schools and school library services. Three yearly installments for a total of $500,000 would be paid to the Dublin Board of Education together with annual payments of $100 per full-time OCLC employee, or about $74,000 in 1985. Starting in 1987 these payments would not be less than $75,000—unless the number of OCLC employees dropped below 100—nor more than $100,000. OCLC would pay real estate taxes, but in return it received the legislated exemption from personal property and sales taxes.

The regional networks, which acted as brokers for OCLC services, were getting increasingly fractious, particularly the Southeastern Library Network (SOLINET), which had chosen to implement its own regional system using WLN software, converted to a Burroughs mainframe. SOLINET members wanted their network to be more proactive in providing services such as authority control, local information access, a regional online catalog and a circulation database. SOLINET and OCLC in January, 1981 had signed an agreement to establish a mutual support corporation to jointly develop and deliver products that they had been producing separately. But seven months later, the OCLC board voted to dissolve this agreement, quoting a lack of funds to pursue a subject access capability enhancement. The issue over copyright of OCLC's database and the resultant cooling of relations among many of the regional networks resulted in OCLC's issuing the "Relationship Between OCLC and Networks: General Statement of Mutual Tenants, Commitments and Expectations," which was agreed to by OCLC and network service center directors on October 5, 1982. (32)

The Regional OCLC Network Directors Advisory Committee (RONDAC) was put in place to provide a vehicle for a stronger collaborative relationship between OCLC and regional affiliated networks. Together with the OCLC User's Council, there are now appropriate vehicles to assure member input into policy development and services.

With ever larger financial responsibilities connected with the responsible governance of the bibliographic utilities, it is necessary to have a broad range of expertise both from member libraries and from other sectors involved.

The inevitable pull and push among consortia of professional management, their members' interests and the diverse factions within their memberships will continue to be influenced by real-world developments, such as tightening of funding, political upheavals changing world trade and politics, and the impact of new information technologies. Bibliographic utilities and consortia will need to forge new cooperative links in an ever widening sphere of influence.

Those interested in further governance issues for networks and the implications for large research libraries should consult Susan K. Martin's doctoral dissertation. (33)

IV. OCLC

Our purpose here is not to give a comprehensive treatment of OCLC's history, activities and influence on library and information science. Rather it is to highlight recent significant developments and provide the reader with some references to enable further pursuit of OCLC's past activities. Key works to understanding OCLC's first decade are the volume by Kathleen Maciuszko (34), the history by Albert Maruskin (35) and Frederick Kilgour's collected papers. (36)

With this brief introduction to OCLC's past, let us examine some developments stemming from the very rapid growth of information technology in the 1980's that pushed OCLC to respond with new systems and services.

A. The Early Eighties: Half a Decade of Progress and Problems

In 1980, Dataphase Systems, Innovative Interfaces and Universal Library Systems all announced links from an OCLC terminal to their systems to permit importing of OCLC records into their local library systems. This now made these local library systems practical for a suite of integrated functions and not just the recording of circulation transactions using an abbreviated bibliographic database. This development, coupled with better software on lower cost hardware, hastened the move to local systems by OCLC member libraries.

OCLC launched host-based acquisitions and serials control systems. Although these systems did not perform all of the operations associated with these areas, numerous libraries did begin using them. With the interlibrary loan and cataloging subsystems, OCLC had some additional services of interest to its members. The OCLC Serials Control Users Group held its first meeting June 26, 1984 at the ALA Annual Meeting in Dallas. (37) EBSCO and Faxon, the two largest periodical subscription agencies, alleged that libraries were now claiming too quickly and were inundating them with paper which needed to be rekeyed to be put into their systems. This prompted OCLC to consider tape transmission of claims. However, until 1991, when Notis Systems, Inc. initiated the pilot test of Electronic Data Interchange (EDI), using its NOTIS software for sending claims to Faxon, the use of magnetic tape or electronic transmission of substantial amounts of data between vendors and automated library systems was not widespread. By the mid-1980's it was clear that with the microcomputer, there was a better way to service applications such as acquisitions and serials management. Also, fewer libraries than anticipated had opted to use these subsystems, and the potential transaction load in a system such as serials foreshadowed potential host computer response and loading problems with the aging Xerox Sigma 9 application processors.

With the move to the $25 million new facility in Dublin, Ohio came a host of systems problems, all of which were worked through eventually to improve system performance for member libraries. But in order to do this OCLC had to declare a 7-month moratorium on new terminal installations. The previously mentioned real estate liability judgment further served to divert OCLC's attention away from other, more productive areas. Difficulties with Ramtek Display Corp. over the new OCLC Model 110 had also resulted in a terminal that had lots of overheating problems. This dispute escalated into a lawsuit which eventually was settled out of court. Meanwhile, OCLC was forced to use the Beehive-manufactured Model 105 to reduce installation backlogs and then design a new terminal that would use the newly emerging microcomputer technology. In the first quarter of 1984, the OCLC M300, designed around a specially modified IBM PC, would signal a new potential direction for OCLC services.

For the research library members, the collaboration between OCLC and Asiagraphics to develop a Chinese/Japanese/Korean (CJK) terminal to compete with the RLG/RLIN unit from TransTech would make it possible, via software, to use a standard M300 to process vernacular records in these languages. Instead of the shape approach used by TransTech, the OCLC approach would use a phonetics technique to construct these characters.

While the seventies had brought OCLC growth and technical progress, the operational problems of the early eighties diverted OCLC from its mission to develop further user services. Having weathered these problems, OCLC still faced the second half of the decade with the challenge of developing a new application system to replace its aging Xerox system and to answer the need for (1) subject access to its database, (2) much improved searching and access for public service use and (3) more viable support over local systems. Moreover, the advance in microcomputing was opening up other new frontiers for communication and information technology, just being envisioned in the mid-1980's.

B. The Later Eighties: Phenomenal Growth and the Big Business of Networking the Nation's Libraries

By 1986 several microcomputer-based serials control systems had been introduced—among them, OCLC's SC350, developed for OCLC by Maurice

Leatherbury's MetaMicro Systems, Inc., and Faxon's MicroLinx, little sister to the Faxon Linx host system. This application is a natural for a distributed-system approach as locally operated systems can be more closely tailored to local needs. OCLC had decided to withdraw its mainframe-hosted Serials Control System, which by 1986 had 53 institutions using it. At that time, Sandy Folsom sent a questionnaire to these users. (38) Given the over 3,000 member libraries at the time, the Serials Control System on OCLC's host generated a small but dependent customer base. The respondents' comments divided the group about evenly divided into thirds—one third planning on using OCLC's SC350 micro product, one third moving to another automated system, and the final third not yet sure of what they would use. None of the libraries were planning to go to a manual Kardex-type system. With 45 of the institutions responding to the questionnaire, 23 admitted that a decision to drop the system would have a major impact on their libraries, 9 believed it would be moderate, 4 believed it would be minor and 3 did not answer.

Certainly, there were some viable options, among them the previously mentioned Faxon MicroLinx, and the just-released SC350 and several offerings that ran on minicomputers or non-MS-DOS microcomputers. Central Michigan University was a beta site for OCLC's SC350, and it also tested the Faxon product. (39) The MicroLinx, when introduced, did not have fund accounting, but this was a promised addition by Faxon. The SC350 had a fully integrated bindery module, fund accounting and subscription maintenance. Some bugs were encountered in the SC350 beta software, not unusual as one function of beta release testing is to discover bugs in a customer's normal operating situation. SC350 was superior to MicroLinx in binding, claims, invoice and fund accounting but was somewhat marred by poor execution, a less functional design and poorer check-in and maintenance capabilities than MicroLinx. Both systems suffered from a poor password-driven security module. Neither system offered a means of purging obsolete data or archiving the old data offline. Neither system was designed for—nor adequate for—public service and both lacked the documentation necessary for troubleshooting.

OCLC announced a deactivation date of July 1, 1987 of the host-based Serials Control System, which was later moved to January 1, 1988. By 1987, it was clear that users were understanding why OCLC was deactivating this subsystem as the user base was insufficient and the advance of technology had made a mainframe solution outmoded. The truth is that this subsystem was brought up exceedingly late, was already using an old technology and never met all of the needs that should be answered by a satisfactory serials management system. (40)

Another service was also discontinued by OCLC in 1988. This was the LINK electronic gateway to database vendors that made it possible for OCLC terminal users to search various online databases. Introduced in June, 1986, it saw usage decline in the face of microcomputers with modems and asynchronous communications software with direct packet-switched network connections available. When this service had started less than 35% of OCLC member libraries owned a microcomputer. The increase in CD-ROM versions of abstracting and indexing databases further eroded usage. Thus, LINK quietly dropped from the scene without controversy.

The host-based acquisitions system deactivation proposal met with considerable attack, particularly by federal libraries, 20 of which joined Barbara Pruett, Librarian at the International Trade Commission, in a letter of protest. Their complaint argued that the Gramm-Rudman-Hollings legislation would make it impossible for them to invest in new systems. (41) The introduction of the ACQ350 microcomputer-based acquisitions system provided a much-needed enhancement to users of the LS/2000 minicomputer-based local library system as well as to libraries that needed some acquisitions support whether or not they ever used the mainframe system. Finally, the move to the new OCLC system would make it possible to drop this subsystem.

Having used both the RLG/RLIN CJK terminal and the OCLC CJK terminal, the Asian Library of the University of Illinois has found that OCLC's CJK system is less expensive and that it can print a complete set of catalog cards on a Toshiba P351 printer. The second-generation RLG/RLIN system, using a standard Intel microprocessor rather than the Digital Equipment Corp. LSI 11/23 cpu, will be comparable in cost. Using the special keyboard on RLG/RLIN's system an average of 3.4 keystrokes is needed to record a Chinese character. Since the OCLC system uses a phonetic approach there is no extensive keyboard training as is required for the RLG/RLIN system. The OCLC system is geared to do catalog cards directly, whereas the RLG/RLIN system was not designed for this. (42)

By 1988, OCLC had over 8,000 libraries affiliated through the member consortia in the United States and in 25 foreign countries. This was quite a growth from 1971 when the original Ohio College Library Center comprised 54 Ohio libraries using 80 terminals. OCLC's computer architecture had grown immensely from the initial Xerox Sigma 9's to a system with a front-end (communications processors), a middle (application processors) and a back-end (database processors). Tandem TXP processors were used for the front and back ends, while 15 Sigma 9's were serving in the middle. This incredible installation comprised some 248 central processing units. Some 2,000 libraries access OCLC via dial access on the CompuServe Information Network, OCLC having switched to this network in late 1986. Where CompuServe is not available, Telenet and Tymnet would continue to be used since these do provide a gateway to the CompuServe network.

A $40 million capital expenditure over a three-year period beginning in 1986 was announced to redesign and reimplement the OCLC system, using a device-independent architecture, a client/server-type application architecture and new equipment. This project was named the Oxford Project, and as a first step toward its realization, OCLC installed a new telecommunications system component called the Advanced Communications Processor (ACP). The ACP network provides standard X.25 packet-switched protocol service, with control possible through several distributed switching centers and is an open-system architecture so that users will eventually be able to access other host systems as well as OCLC. By 1992, this new system was installed and was completely Tandem computer based, with considerable use of the latest software and hardware.

Through this period there was continuing concern over the quality of OCLC bibliographic records. A study by Sheila Intner found no statistical differences between matching pairs of records on OCLC and the supposedly more quality-preserving RLG/RLIN database. (43) Two hundred fifteen matched pairs of member-contributed cataloging from 1983 and later, for which no LC MARC or other "authoritative" record existed, formed the basis for this study. Only 39 of these records (22 from OCLC and 17 from RLIN) were found to be totally error free, but main entry errors, which would affect retrieval, were found to be insignificant. For practical considerations, one can say that these network databases are quite comparable in quality today. Also, OCLC made particular efforts to monitor quality and to establish its "Enhance Libraries," which routinely enhance records on the system.

Rowland Brown, OCLC's President, stated in 1988 that "The vision for OCLC is to remain pre-eminent in providing an international bibliographic database, and services based on that database, in electronic form, and during the next 10 years to go beyond bibliographic records and services, in providing expanded information services to libraries and other information users." The scope and content of the online catalog would expand as would OCLC's expansion in Europe and the Pacific. (44)

The OCLC database had reached 18 million records by mid-1988, with some 300 million location listings. Over 17 million interlibrary loan transactions had been handled by the ILL subsystem. OCLC's CAT CD450 compact disc cataloging system was in field test. This system would enable offline cataloging of the vast majority of titles, with the remainder to sent to the OCLC system online. This offline cataloging was designed to cut telecommunications costs associated with processing.

Many research initiatives were also undertaken, and typical of these was the collaboration of OCLC with Carnegie Mellon University in Project Mercury. This work demonstrates that a large-scale distributed library can be built with today's technology and provide a laboratory for studies in handling electronic information. It is a real library for computer science research. UNIX-based workstations connected to a network with servers, connected in turn to NSFNET, provide the platform for this work. Mercury uses the campus-wide Andrew network at Carnegie Mellon, which was developed in partnership with IBM.

The Search CD450 retrieval software for CD-ROM–based products saw version 3.0 in June, 1989 and 16 CD-ROM databases in agriculture, education, science/technology and general reference areas. This application also works with the new EPIC service for online reference searching, which was made available in 1990. The CAT450 system was enhanced by offering all records from the National Library of Medicine in a Medical Cataloging Collection CD-ROM.

The summer of 1989 saw a significant change in the third- and fourth-floor computer rooms at OCLC as 153 Tandem and 96 Tecstor disk drives, which had been used to hold the entire OCLC online catalog, were wheeled away. Replacing these were 11 Tandem XL80's, which equalled the capacity of the 249 old disk drives and were physically smaller. Twenty million records actually now take up less physical space than the 10 million records did some years ago. Each of these new drives provides about 7.2 gigabytes of storage in six square feet of floor space. It takes about 1 gigabyte to store 1.75 million bibliographic records in the OCLC system.

The end of 1989 saw OCLC making five proposals to the Library of Congress (LC). The first was to make the online catalog available to LC for its current cataloging at a reduced price over a multiyear period so that LC's per-record cost to catalog could be lowered from its present in-house system costs. Moreover, this would bring LC MARC records to OCLC members more quickly, further reducing original cataloging. The second proposal was to make the online system available to LC to reduce its cataloging backlog, particularly in sound recordings and monographs. The third proposal was to extend its catalog card production facilities to LC since the cost of producing them continued to rise and their volume was rapidly declining. OCLC believes that only a modest development effort on its part would be needed to accomplish this and provide economies of scale to both organizations. Since LC had discontinued the printing and distribution of CJK catalog cards, OCLC offered to assume responsibility for printing and distributing these. Finally, OCLC offered its retrospective conversion services to LC for long-term projects at very attractive prices.

Further hardware replacements for the launch of the new OCLC system were installed. Nineteen new Tandem VLX processors replaced 46 Tandem TNSII processors controlling the database access or back-end part of the system. Testing of the Tandem CSAP02 Central Systems Application Processor hardware, which will eventually replace the Sigma 9 application processors, was also proceeding well with the new system software.

C. The Nineties: What Will the Rest of This Decade Bring?

In preparation for their new communications system, OCLC chose Telenet Communications Corp. to install a new X.25 packet-switched telecommunications network, with ongoing work and migration of the first libraries having begun in the fall of 1990. This network will utilize fiber optic circuits provided by Sprint. Present dedicated leased lines now linked to Dublin will be relinked from libraries to OCLC equipment located in the nearest of 45 Telenet Public Data Network central offices throughout the United States. Also, the 1200 bits-per-second (bps) modems now at library sites will be replaced by 9600 bps modems. All 45 of these network-switching processors will accept OCLC terminal protocol, standard asynchronous protocol for dial-up and X.25 protocol. The switchover to the new telecommunications network was nothing short of herculean and came off on time and within budget. By September, 1991, 90% of the network was installed, and on November 26, 1991, the last connection to the old network was switched to the new network.

The beginning of 1990 brought the EPIC system and subject access to the OCLC database, after many years of experiments and development efforts. EPIC provides keyword and Boolean searching on a variety of databases in addition to the OCLC online catalog. This service was announced with a cost of $37 per connect-hour for OCLC members who contribute records to the database and $110 per connect hour to nonmembers. Per-record charges for display and print vary with the format selected. Telecommunications charges will vary with the method used. The NISO Z39.58 Common Command Language standard was chosen for the first version of this system's user interface. Within six months of its introduction, over 3,000 libraries had subscribed to EPIC. The ERIC database was added by summer, with a $19.80 per connect-hour charge for OCLC members. Five more databases followed, and EasyNet and Internet access to EPIC was available by year's end, as the subscriber base grew to 3,700 libraries. In early 1991, OCLC was also field testing an end-user EPIC, designed to appeal to students and library users for their direct searching. This was released as FirstSearch in late 1992 and was an instant success.

By 1993 over 41 million bibliographic records had been converted by OCLC member libraries through the OCLC Retrospective Conversion Division, which employs 170 staff working two shifts. Over 300,000 new records are added yearly to the OCLC database through the various reconversion (RECON) projects. RETROCON, MICROCON, MICROCON*PRO, TAPECON and Online Retrospective Conversion are their five conversion options. With RETROCON, libraries send their shelf lists to OCLC where they are converted according to the library's specifications by OCLC's experienced staff. With MICROCON, software for a microcomputer is provided to a library to load its search keys onto diskette, which is then returned to OCLC for machine matching to the OCLC database. Libraries receive single matches on magnetic tape. With MICROCON*PRO, the RETROCON and MICROCON services are combined, with resolution of multiple hits and original inputs. TAPECON services permit libraries to submit search keys on magnetic tape for searching against the OCLC database to have partial records upgraded to full LC MARC standard. Finally, at reduced rates, a library can use the online cataloging system itself to perform its own conversion.

Other good news destined to improve the availability of cataloging records was the announcement of a two-year pilot project in 1991 between LC and OCLC as a response to OCLC's earlier five proposals to LC. For this period, OCLC will waive its membership requirement and all standard charges for bibliographic searching, cataloging and training associated with LC's use of the OCLC system for backlog and current cataloging, a discount of an estimated $50,000 annually. Thus LC has moved ahead with the first two of OCLC's five proposals. At the end of two years, the project was to be evaluated and a more normal billing relationship between LC and OCLC was expected to result.

The previously mentioned Oxford Project, which was to develop an entirely new online system for OCLC's continuing support of the information community was making excellent progress. Its successor, to be called PRISM service, would soon be introduced, with member libraries moving over gradually to the new system. OCLC recognized the importance of local library systems in this effort and established the Local System Vendor Access Program (LSVAP). Vendors who joined were able to access the OCLC system, purchase OCLC software and hardware and receive OCLC documentation and support as well as access to PRISM in its field test in late 1990. CLSI, DRA, Dynix, GEAC, Innovative Interfaces, LS/2000, NOTIS, Unisys, Ulisys and VTLS are in one or more of the OCLC PRISM field test libraries, and these vendors are developing interfaces for the new OCLC system. November 12, 1990 was the date scheduled for the fully operational launch of PRISM. This date was met and the move of libraries to PRISM began, staged over an 18-month period. Nineteen libraries participated in the field test and their suggestions were incorporated into the first production version of PRISM. All of OCLC's old- system users were on PRISM by April, 1992, the scheduled date.

New terminal emulation software, called PASSPORT, provides connection to PRISM and virtually any other online database. PRISM allows access through menus and through the familiar OCLC commands, with users able to turn off the menu bar if they wish to use the commands. Help screens are available throughout the system. Searching is derived through search keys and numerical searches as in the former OCLC system, but two new twists have been provided. A combined search key feature lets the user combine any two search keys except the OCLC number with the Boolean "AND." A new Title Browse capability is most helpful for titles beginning with common words such as *Journal of* . . . . Catalogers now have a full-screen editor with cut and paste. Real-time validation of records is performed. Record export now works on the full record and not on the screen-by-screen basis.

OCLC and RLG finally agreed to implement an open systems interconnection that would utilize the Basic Reference Model, the Search and Retrieval Protocol Specification, and the Inter-Library Loan Protocol Specification on a direct computer-to-computer linkage to enable users of each system to engage in automated interlibrary loan with libraries supported by the other system. The collaboration of these two networks to develop standards began in 1987. OCLC's Linked Systems Project, which began in 1985 between LC, RLG and OCLC to distribute name authority records, has now been expanded to record contribution and intersystem searching of name authority data. OCLC linked systems locations were expanded to include 28 member libraries.

The OCLC ILL subsystem could now be used to request interlibrary loans (ILLs) from the National Library of Canada, whereas previously these could be sent only via conventional ILL means.

1991 marked the 20th anniversary of the founding of OCLC. The creation of the National Research Education Network, which will ultimately replace the Internet presently tying together numerous institutions across the United States and worldwide provided the basis for broader network access. Thus, the decade of the nineties has undoubtedly become the decade of virtually universal linking and access to network connected libraries and services. At one point, OCLC and Thomson Canada Limited had started discussing the possibility of OCLC acquiring Utlas, Inc. However, the parties could not reach a definitive agreement and they stopped these discussions quite amicably. Some formidable technical and contractual difficulties would have been involved to consolidate the Utlas and OCLC systems. Utlas, Inc., will continue as an OCLC regional member network, having gained that position in June 1990. The economic recession of the early 1990's finally forced OCLC to lay off 5% of its work force as a result of lower income from member libraries, which were being hit quite hard by the recession. OCLC also announced that a price increase of 5%, the first in three years, would have to be instituted at the beginning of 1992.

There is no question that, despite any real national information policy in the United States, OCLC has become the major U.S. and international switching center for access to library collections. Although such bibliographic utilities as RLG/RLIN and Utlas, Inc., in Canada continue to serve their members and cooperate with OCLC to varying extent, their smaller size will not permit them to engage in research and development to the extent as

OCLC. Some competition is healthy in the library networking field, but it is difficult to tell how much longer RLG, which represents a specialized network of research libraries, can continue operating its own online catalog system, particularly in the face of rising costs of telecommunications and of local integrated library systems that now enable member libraries to perform their cataloging locally and to rely on LC MARC databases and the network only for records not found in LC MARC. If the OCLC RONDAC and Users Advisory Council continue to be heard by OCLC management, there should be a rosy future for OCLC, even in recessionary economic times, since the major role of Inter-Library Loan system provider will become more important as will the comprehensiveness of OCLC's databases.

The directions set by OCLC's president, K. Wayne Smith, who assumed OCLC's helm in 1989, were to (1) focus on electronic text publishing, (2) improve the quality and extent of the OCLC database and the reach of OCLC services to libraries not using the shared cataloging system, (3) expand abroad and spin off OCLC's Local Systems Division to Ameritech Information Systems and (4) concentrate on software critical to electronic publishing and to OCLC's growing database through the acquisition of Information Dimensions, Inc., from Battelle Memorial Institute. Also assuming more importance was the preservation of library materials through the acquisition of the Mid-Atlantic Preservation Service, which, in 1994, changed its name to Preservation Resources Division of OCLC. The Forest Press acquisition also strengthens OCLC in classification activities. The publication of DDC 20 on CD-ROM in 1993 was a milestone achievement. GUIDON software provides the interface to the electronic text publications *Online Journal of Clinical Trials* and *Electronic Letters*. By December, 1992 all interlibrary loan system transactions had been moved to PRISM.

By January, 1994, 23 years after its founding, OCLC had grown to 17,540 participating libraries with 13,952 terminals. The database contained 29.7 million records and 509 million holdings location symbols. 48 million ILL transactions had been processed through OCLC's systems. Many OCLC services are now available through Internet connections. Three listservs are provided by OCLC, with two open to subscription by e-mail at listserv@oclc.org. These are TECH_BUL-L and FIRSTSEARCH-L for technical bulletins and FirstSearch documentation and helpful aids. Through DOC, OCLC members can order documentation and claim forms. Another activity that will strengthen the OCLC database is the conversion of 5 million titles being performed for the 46 Harvard libraries. This is one of the largest RECON projects ever. One could enumerate numerous other examples of projects undertaken, and OCLC's success seems to be improving all the time, despite increasing technological complexities and wider program availability. The staff of OCLC and its member libraries has much to be proud of.

V. RESEARCH LIBRARIES GROUP (RLG)/RESEARCH LIBRARIES INFORMATION NETWORK (RLIN)

The Research Libraries Group (RLG) is a consortium of research institutions that began collaborative programs and evolved their own computer system from the Stanford University-developed BALLOTS software. This network is called the Research Libraries Information Network (RLIN). During the 1970's, Stanford University, together with numerous supporting foundation grants—notably $348,000 awarded by the Council on Library Resources in 1975—invested major resources into this software development. What originally was conceived as a system for Stanford University broadened its objectives to being a multiple institution system for California, partly in response to the U.S. Department of Education-funded demonstration project undertaken by OCLC with 12 private California colleges. However, the development and operational expenses of BALLOTS showed that this system would have to be shared by a broad base of institutions in order to be affordable.

By 1975, the fledgling RLG consortium had determined that it needed to develop its own computer-based cataloging system, and it proceeded to investigate existing systems. Meanwhile, BALLOTS had made some progress in extending its system beyond Stanford University, signing up the Mid-Mississippi Regional Library on a pay-as-you-use hourly rate, with no membership fees or binding contracts for search-only access. Also, seven public libraries forming the Public Library Automation Network (PLAN) were using BALLOTS in line-by-line mode under a California State Library contract. In 1978, RLG chose to acquire the BALLOTS software, restructure the software development and support effort, and create the RLIN network.

A. Early Times

RLG's first major grant for the RLIN network was a Carnegie Corporation of New York grant to BALLOTS to support the development of what came to be known as the Linked Systems Project (LSP). This $197,200 grant would pay for development of a cooperative interactive online computer link with the BALLOTS, Columbia University and Library of Congress systems. LSP became the first remote online interconnection of different computers serving libraries. As is typical of such projects, this effort became much more complex and demanded more standardization than initially thought. Had it not been for this initial actual operational development, the interactive computer-linked technology and standards now in place and under development probably would have been later in coming.

BALLOTS was chosen to be RLG's system, with Yale University Columbia University and the New York Public Library (NYPL) casting affirmative votes and Harvard University voting opposed. (45) Although NYPL was considered to have the best cataloging system at the time, it had less ability to add acquisitions capability, which RLG required. Also, the NYPL system operated largely in batch mode. WLN really was not in contention as it had not been able to meet the proposal deadline, although its system could run both acquisitions and cataloging and it had shelf listing and serials modules under development. There was fear that Harvard's negative vote could have an adverse impact on RLG securing major funding from CLR or other sources. The target date for all RLG members to be up on the new system was December 31, 1981, as Stanford had agreed to fund BALLOTS for only one more year.

A month after the vote to adopt BALLOTS as RLG's system, Harvard quit RLG, leaving the three remaining RLG founding institutions—Columbia, Yale and NYPL—to broaden the consortium. Harvard's negative vote had resulted from the relative independence and differing financial, organizational and bibliographic systems in its 90 separate libraries. These rather disparate conditions forced Harvard to withdraw.

Despite losing this key player, RLG was able to attract two significant grants of $300,000 each from the Charles A. Dana and William & Flora Hewlett Foundations. Brigham Young University, Dartmouth College, University of Michigan, University of Pennsylvania, Princeton University, Rutgers University and several other universities joined RLG. The Cleveland Museum of Art, Art Institute of Chicago and Metropolitan Museum of Art had also joined. By 1979, RLG had moved its offices from Bramford, Connecticut, to Stanford, California, with Ed Shaw replacing RLG's founding president, James Skipper.

In 1980, CLR gave a further $318,317 to RLG to jointly develop a shared authority file between RLG and the Washington (now Western) Library Network (WLN). Each system would operate its own authority file, sharing data between them. Softening Harvard's earlier withdrawal from RLG, the Harvard Fine Arts Library was funded by the Andrew Mellon Foundation to rejoin RLG/RLIN.

B. Broadening Membership and Programs

With the rise of interest in RLG membership, OCLC had taken steps to discourage its members from joining or collaborating with RLIN. the interest was fed by the early development of commercially available local minicomputer-based library circulation systems and a trend building toward distributed systems approaches to library automation. This very trend made RLG/RLIN more appealing than OCLC to the University of Minnesota and was one factor in its decision to join RLG. Collaborative development of further RLIN subsystems also had attracted Minnesota to membership.

RLG had also begun cooperating with UTLAS, enabling RLIN members to use UTLAS's excellent system to produce page-form microfiche catalogs for member libraries. Some database and authority data sharing was also to take place.

Given that a number of RLG member libraries had significant vernacular collections in Asian languages—Chinese, Japanese and Korean—RLG wanted to pursue development of vernacular cataloging in these languages. Toward that end, in 1982, RLG entered into a contract with TransTech to create a modified version of its SINOTERM unit, which had been on the market since 1979. This system was used by Taiwan's Ministry of National Defense. The Library of Congress also wanted to use this terminal, which came to be known as RLIN's CJK Terminal. RLIN expected that some 10 other institutions would install it, for a total of 50 terminals on the system.

At the time of this large investment in the summer of 1982, RLG was experiencing both financial and technical difficulties. (46) Donald Kennedy, President of Stanford University, reported to Stanford's faculty senate that should RLG fail, its member libraries would confront a much larger financial disaster since 24 separate hulls make much more of a wave then one big ship going down. Adding to RLIN's operational woes was the fact that its IBM 3081 was seriously overloaded. This problem was compounded by the Stanford/RLIN shared computing environment, which involved a mix of computing tasks, all demanding the same resources. Moreover, a series of major defective mass storage devices had raised havoc with disk storage on the system, further degrading services. Stanford managed to lend RLG $300,000 for a dedicated computer since RLG, although it had gained some foundation support, continued to be chronically undercapitalized. Stanford wanted these problems cured by September, 1982 to keep RLG from falling into grave jeopardy. Ed Shaw resigned as president of RLG, returning to his role as Director of the Stanford Computer Center and Associate Provost for Information Systems.

Patricia Battin, on a six-month leave from Columbia University, was named as interim president of RLG to try to correct these problems. By the above deadline, she reported that RLG was back on track. She noted that publicity surrounding all of the technical and financial problems had overshadowed considerable progress behind the scenes to stabilize the new RLIN II system, to move it to its own dedicated IBM 3081 and to secure reliable hard-disk storage and reload the database. (47) Also, of critical importance to members' resource sharing, RLIN introduced its new interlibrary loan system, which was designed to inform potential borrowers within three days if a loan request could not be fulfilled—a turnaround competitive with OCLC's.

By the end of 1983, RLIN had managed to process some 4 million records representing the archival tapes of its member libraries' records prior to joining

RLG. This archive load project took over a year to complete and brought the RLIN database to 12 million records. Added to this were the University of Toronto East Asian collection records, numbering 89,000, and the U.S. Superintendent of Documents, National Library of Medicine and CONSER serials records.

The most notable achievement of RLIN during this period was the creation of the CJK terminal, which became available for $34,000 each to member libraries. They incorporated a Digital Equipment Corp. PDP-11 super-microcomputer, with an 8 inch Winchester disk to store all characters in a local dictionary. CJK characters are decomposed into 245 component parts on a special keyboard, which means that 3 to 4 strokes—with a maximum of 9 strokes per character—are needed to compose each one. The main unit serves as a printer and a cluster controller for one to four terminals. 14,000 Chinese characters, 51 Kana syllables for Japanese and 33 Hangul symbols for Korean plus the Roman alphabet are incorporated into this device. A dozen RLIN libraries have now installed this system, which took four years to develop and a total investment of $1.1 million.

By 1984, the long-delayed LSP Project to link the RLG, LC and WLN systems for the exchange of authority records was put into operation using what had been developed under the Open Systems Interconnection (OSI) 7-layer standard. (48) Layers 1-4 had standards that could be used, while a NISO drafting committee was still working on layers 5 and 6 and the just part relating to intersystem searching for layer 7. Consequently, LSP chose to use completed ISO and ANSI standards where available and drafts where standards were not as yet approved. The computer-to-computer scenario envisions a WLN user searching RLIN by using WLN commands and being shown WLN output displays, for a transparent connection. Authority records will be the first link put into operation, with the LC Name Authority Cooperative Project (NACO) undertaken as LC converts its 28 NACO libraries' worksheets. This work facilitated the creation of the Z39.50 Information Retrieval Application Service Definition and Protocol for Open Systems Interconnection, which is the present standard method for diverse systems to intercommunicate in the user's own interface. Now, many commercial systems use Z39.50, and its use is growing.

By 1987, RLIN was experiencing quite rapid growth in its database and member library transactions through the online system. Their host computer had required an upgrade every nine months through this period. Prior to becoming RLIN's system, BALLOTS had gone from its original IBM 360/67, through a 370/158, to a 370/168, then a shared IBM 3033-U, a dedicated 3033-N and the shared 3081-D. When RLIN took over, it moved to a dedicated IBM 3081-D and then soon upgraded to a 3081-K. Then, in 1984, it moved to an Amdahl 580 series system and through several more upgrades. It was during this time that RLIN became intrigued by Amdahl's experimental operating system, called MDF-II. Since the Amdahl systems were IBM compatible and could run multiple operating systems in different partitions, this enabled separate production and development partitions for MVS/XA and a third partition for MDF-II. However, it should be noted that several years later, Amdahl threw in the towel and ceased developing MDF-II. Instead Amdahl turned its attention to competing with IBM and with Hitachi, which as a mainframe clone maker was increasingly biting off a share of the IBM mainframe market.

The communications network serving RLIN member libraries was becoming increasingly costly to operate. Unlike OCLC, RLIN member libraries were scattered across the United States, meaning that fewer libraries could be connected to the same leased communications line. This made communications more expensive for RLIN-dedicated terminals than those serving OCLC, where many additional libraries could be multidropped to share a line. In 1989, RLIN proposed moving to a packet-switched network, and it selected Telematics International to provide this switching equipment. (49) Through this change, communications costs were expected to either remain stable or decrease. Response time improvements, simplification of network operations, increased reliability and expendability would be the added benefits. Moving away from the ADCCP polling environment to the X.25 packet standard would also benefit international links as ADCCP polling does not work well with satellite links. Replacing the previous Digital Equipment PDP-11 communications controllers were a series of AST 80286 microcomputers connected to the Amdahl 589 through a Network Systems Corp. Hyperbus. By 1990, the following year conversion to this new network was completed.

Late in 1989, Transtech completed development of a new CJK Terminal that no longer required a cluster controller. It was based on an Intel 80286–equipped AST microcomputer equipped with special software. A Microsoft Windows system is now under development by RLG and Transtech which will use standard SVGA video and a standard 101-key keyboard.

With the decade of the nineties being the era of networked, interconnected computer-based resources, the RLIN database became available via the Internet, as Stanford University's SUNet, part of the Bay Area Regional Network, was connected to NSFNet.

C. Current Directions

With most RLIN member libraries now performing cataloging and materials ordering on their local automated library systems, it is increasingly clear that RLIN's central system and services need to move away from technical processing support to collection development, sharing and union catalog locational functions. Thus, widely available searching that can be done by the individual scholar and not through intermediaries will become more important.

In 1991, RLIN began talks with OCLC over the possibility of OCLC's system providing access to RLIN's database and other member services. Had this materialized, RLG would not have had to maintain its own computer center and computer operations staff. However, these talks did not result in any further collaboration. Meanwhile, OCLC, with its new subscription reference system, EPIC, now available for subject searching, has overcome the last remaining obstacle to satisfying a wide range of public service needs in libraries. This offers some formidable competition to RLIN since one of the previous attractions to its system was its excellent subject searching.

It is becoming increasingly apparent that RLIN will have to offer some truly unique capabilities if it is to remain financially viable. Competition from OCLC, with its much greater access to development capital, will undoubtedly move the OCLC system along new paths more quickly.

RLIN is still trying to appeal to specialized libraries and to large research libraries, with some emphasis on collection development and preservation, specialized databases as well as resource sharing. Whether this emphasis will assure RLIN's success for the long-term future remains to be seen. The costs to operate its system and the patterns of usage have required considerable rethinking of usage charges. As these databases continue to grow their operational costs can be expected to rise at least slowly—despite new storage technologies—due simply to their greater size and complexity, which require additional database processing and backup/recovery resources.

By 1994, RLIN had its Z39.50 server in late stages of development, which when finished would enable RLIN member libraries to access RLIN using their home system's commands. The Eureka system, which was unveiled in January, 1994, provides a fully integrated gateway to RLIN's Cita-Del rapidly expanding citation and document delivery system. RLIN's ARIEL system for sending scanned document images over fax and requests via the Internet to member libraries has been very successful. Also, the Arabic script cataloging system was first used by the Library of Congress in 1991, and it has proven to be a good system. RLG/RLIN has managed to pull out of the quiet sea propelled by a strong wind of creative system and database efforts which have excellent appeal to its members. The latter half of the nineties should be a very strong period for this network.

VI. UNIVERSITY OF TORONTO LIBRARY AUTOMATION SYSTEM (UTLAS)

UTLAS, Inc., had its beginnings in the mid-1960's at the University of Toronto, where it started as one of Canada's most ambitious library data processing efforts. The university spun off UTLAS as a separate nonprofit corporation in 1971. This was similar to Northwestern University, which also "privatized" what had been an internally operated automation program with its NOTIS software. Toronto took similar measures to divest itself of its program, given that the expense of operating and enhancing it could be spread over numerous libraries.

While UTLAS, Inc., was created mainly as an automation system for the University of Toronto, it was recognized that the software could form the basis for a networked system. It should be noted that the interactive online system was hosted on the same Sigma 9-type computer that OCLC was using. More recently, it became a Tandem computer-hosted system. OCLC, too, had turned to Tandem as a front- and back-end computing solution, retaining until 1991 its string of Sigma 9 computers. Finally in 1991, with its new-generation PRISM software, OCLC retired its remaining Sigmas. UTLAS was certainly ahead of OCLC in modernizing its system hardware.

While UTLAS was growing through the seventies, it suffered from some typical growth pains that also were also plaguing U.S. networks. UTLAS customers liked the cataloging products and services produced, but these customers also wanted some significant improvements in online services and product deliveries. In 1981, a consultant's report made clear that a comprehensive system upgrade was required, and the University of Toronto approved a sizeable loan—$8.9 million (Can.)—for obtaining two additional Sigma 9 computers and signing a lease for a new UTLAS site that would bring together all staff and equipment under one roof. To improve system performance, a strategy of dual parallel systems and databases was designed, which was called Dual CATSS (Catalogue Support System). This system was actually put into operation several weeks ahead of schedule, on January 25, 1982.

In 1982, UTLAS retired its minicomputer-based LCMS (Library Collection Management System), which was one of the pioneering minicomputer-based circulation systems in Canada. An acquisitions subsystem had also been designed and tested in a pilot project in 1980, but it could not be implemented due to the hardware overloading problem. With Dual CATSS, this acquisitions module could then be operational.

Perhaps the most important developments for UTLAS during the early 1980's were its entry into the U.S. market and an agreement with the Maruzen Company of Japan, a dealer in imported publications in Japan. UTLAS management recognized very early the international nature of the bibliographic products and services market. The Rochester Institute of Technology (RIT) had contracted with UTLAS in 1980 for a COM catalog. This required UTLAS to process a file of 120,000 titles (built previously by a service bureau) and expect from RIT an anticipated 8,000 titles for annual cataloging. (50) The agreement, signed in 1981, to supply Maruzen with cataloging products was expected to produce $1 million (Can.) in revenue by 1984. (51) In 1983 UTLAS received a further $2 million (Can.) in Province of Ontario funds for system upgrades. (52) Also in that year, Maurice J. Freedman, Director of the Westchester (New York) County Library System chose UTLAS over OCLC because of its features and price advantage. By then, UTLAS had over 200 institutions, representing 1,800 individual member libraries.

With significant capital investments needed and the long-term future of UTLAS perhaps not best served as an independent not-for-profit university-controlled corporation, the University of Toronto began to make it known that UTLAS was available for acquisition. The International Thompson organization had just acquired Gale Research and was moving toward being a significant force in the information services sector. UTLAS had just concluded an agreement with DataPhase, Inc., to take over its Tandem computer-based library system, which was experiencing considerable difficulties at its Chicago Public Library site. UTLAS needed to provide a local library system for its customers. Since UTLAS's central system was being revamped to use Tandem, it seemed a natural route to acquire another company's product and to make it its own. Meanwhile, the University of Toronto sold UTLAS to the International Thompson firm, with the University of Toronto remaining a customer for current cataloging services and a circulation system.

In 1986, UTLAS, Inc., became Utlas International Canada and UTLAS International U.S., changing the acronym form of its name to Utlas. A marketing agreement with Innovative Interfaces to market its INNOVACQ system in Canada and the United States provided further depth to the UTLAS product line. UTLAS recognized that future systems would involve a distributed processing approach. This design approach was pioneered in the Tandem operating software on which its new CATSS II system was based. At this time UTLAS took steps to make clear that its members would own their own distinct databases on the UTLAS system and all rights to their data. UTLAS, unlike OCLC, never sought to copyright these databases. Therefore, there was no confrontation over database ownership as had resulted among OCLC and its members over the copyright issue.

UTLAS proceeded to remake the acquired ALIS III system from DataPhase into the UTLAS T/50 and salvage the several system sites that were inherited in the acquisition from DataPhase. However, T/50 was taken over by CARL Systems, Inc., which proceeded to upgrade all but two sites to the CARL system, which is the only remaining Tandem computer-based system commercially available. UTLAS also acquired the management of the Tandem effort and continued to maintain an office in Kansas City as well as establishing an office in Washington, D.C. By the end of 1986, the conversion to CATSS II on the Tandem system was completed and the Sigma computers were retired. (53) Utlas then adopted a cooperative approach to furthering its penetration of the U.S. market. For example, the AMIGOS network agreed to offer UTLAS authority control to its members and UTLAS, in turn, agreed to offer Canadian customers AMIGOS collection analysis service.

While Utlas had widened its international impact and gained further U.S. customers, it certainly is not a serious threat to OCLC's dominance as the world's leading bibliographic utility. However, in its market areas, it is particularly strong with customers in English and French and virtually all of the Foreign language cataloging market in Japan. In 1989, Chinese CATSS began in the National Central Library of Taiwan. Specific features of its system, for example, the Precis indexing system, are able to perform functions not offered by any U.S. bibliographic utility. The cataloging system is used by other Chinese speaking countries and has further strengthened Utlas as a major force in Asia for the support of bibliographic systems.

In the nineties Utlas is producing its CD-CATTS serials CD-ROM cataloging system and is having excellent success in its marketing. In February, 1993, Utlas, Inc., was purchased from the International Thompson organization by Information Services Management Corp. of Winnipeg. At that time, it had 2,500 libraries using its system. Since this acquisition, there has been little news reported in the trade press, but it is assumed that the present management and directions of Utlas, Inc., will be maintained.

OCLC had conducted some talks with Utlas in January and February, 1991 as to an acquisition of Utlas by OCLC, but these talks broke off on February 14, 1991. Utlas remains an OCLC regional network affiliate. By itself, Utlas will continue to appeal to a wide variety of libraries, particularly as its costs for services remain highly competitive with alternative utilities.

VII. REGIONAL AND LOCAL COOPERATIVE ORGANIZATIONS

Apart from the large bibliographic utilities, there are numerous regional, state and local networks or cooperatives which serve distinct needs of their members. These receive less attention in the national library press. For example, some of these operate shared automated library systems on their members' behalf, thus pooling resources to cut costs and increase sharing of collection resources. Some provide document delivery services. Others supply some unique service that they have developed, such as the previously mentioned AMIGOS collection analysis service. They provide training and support for OCLC services and broker database search services, obtaining lower rates for their members on bulk contracts. They also provide consulting expertise to members on a variety of library problems and produce collection-sharing tools such as Union Lists of Serials or Union catalog products. Finally, these local cooperatives provide a mechanism for libraries in a particular geographic area or of a particular type to come together to mutually work to improve their services, continue to educate their staffs about new information technologies and materials, and solve some common problems of daily operations.

A. Typical Programs

There are hundreds of networks and cooperatives flourishing today in the United States, not to mention throughout the rest of the developed world. For our purposes here, we will mention only a few programs that are typical or that have gained some attention for developing new products and services. These programs have set the pace for others to try to emulate.

The Western Library Network (WLN), which grew out of a Becker and Hayes, Inc., consulting report as the Washington Library Network, progressed from a state network to a regional network providing resource sharing and cataloging services. By 1976 this network had expanded its services into seventeen western states and British Columbia. The software for its computer system is a model of its type and has been installed by many foreign national libraries to provide the basis for their native MARC distribution services and union catalog facilities. Its software also has been converted to run on the SOLINET Burroughs mainframe for this regional network. Historically, WLN has had close ties first with the Stanford University BALLOTS project and later with the RLG/RLIN network. WLN, by 1982, had attained sufficient financial stability to hold its pricing over a sustained period. It was servicing libraries northward to Alaska, eastward to Montana and southward to Arizona. This growth, coupled with increased computing systems effectiveness, provided a firm foundation for further evolution within a stable organization. WLN pioneered CD-ROM catalog development. It also pioneered techniques to lower a library's host computing costs through use of its CD-ROM database and IBM PC-based terminals. Like OCLC, WLN also heavily modified this micro-computer approach to support its communications and the MARC character set display and input. By 1986, its interlibrary lending system was operating, with charges of $1.25 per request and a $.25 credit toward future borrowing for each item lent by a member. Its system also handled generation of copyright compliance data and gave status displays for each transaction. (54) By 1988, it was decided that WLN, having been managed by the Washington State Library, could best fulfill its broader mission as a private, not-for-profit corporation. (55) The Washington State Legislature passed special legislation in 1989 so that the final steps could be taken to give WLN its new incorporated status. In September, 1990, with the ratification of new articles of incorporation and bylaws by the WLN Interim Board of Directors and the Washington State Library Commission, this transition was completed. (56)

Table 1 OCLC-Affiliated Networks

AMIGOS Bibliographic Council, Dallas, Texas. Founded 1979. Tier 1. Texas, Oklahoma, New Mexico, Arkansas, Arizona, Mexico and members in Louisiana, Kansas and Nevada

BCR: Bibliographical Center for Research, Denver, Colorado. Founded 1935. Tier 1. Colorado, Idaho, Iowa, Kansas, Montana, Nevada, Utah and Wyoming

CAPCON, Washington, D.C. Founded 1974. Tier 1 for reference services; tier 2 for core and RECON services. Washington, D.C., Maryland and Virginia

FEDLINK: Federal Library and Information Center Committee, Washington, D.C. Founded 1977. Tier 1. Nationwide Federal government library network with members in Germany and Saudi Arabia

ILLINET/OCLC Services, Springfield, Illinois. Founded 1976. Tier 1. Illinois

INCOLSA: Indiana Cooperative Library Services Authority, Indianapolis, Indiana. Founded 1974. Tier 2. Indiana

MINITEX Library and Information Network, Minneapolis, Minnesota. Founded 1969. Tier 1. Minnesota, South Dakota, North Dakota

MLC: Michigan Library Consortium, Lansing, Michigan. Founded 1974. Tier 1. Michigan with automated reference services to libraries in Minnesota, Wisconsin, New York, Illinois, Missouri and Windsor, Canada

MLNC: Missouri Library Network Corporation, St. Louis, Missouri. Founded 1981. Tier 1. Missouri and general midwestern region

NEBASE: Nebraska Library Commission, Lincoln, Nebraska. Founded 1976. Tier 1. Nebraska

NELINET, Inc., Boston, Massachusetts. Founded 1979. Tier 2. Connecticut, Maine, Massachusetts, New Hampshire, Rhode Island and Vermont

OCLC Europe, Birmingham, England. Founded 1981. Branch of OCLC International Division. Europe, Middle East and Africa

OCLC/PACNET: OCLC Pacific Network, Rancho Cucamonga, California. Founded 1976. Tier 2. California, Oregon, Washington, Hawaii, Alaska, Idaho, Montana and Canada

OHIONET, Columbus, Ohio. Founded 1977. Tier 1. Ohio

PALINET and Union Library Catalog of Pennsylvania, Philadelphia, Pennsylvania. Founded 1936. Tier 1. Eastern Pennsylvania, New Jersey, Delaware, Maryland and Washington, D.C.

PRLC: Pittsburgh Regional Library Center, Pittsburgh, Pennsylvania. Founded 1967. Tier 1. Western Pennsylvania, West Virginia and Maryland

SOLINET: Southeastern Library Network, Atlanta, Georgia. Founded 1973. Tier 2. Alabama, Florida, Georgia, Kentucky, Louisiana, Mississippi, North Carolina, South Carolina, Tennessee, Virginia, Puerto Rico, and Virgin Islands

SUNY: State University of New York, Albany. Founded 1974. Tier 1. New York State

WILS: Wisconsin Interlibrary Services, Madison, Wisconsin. Founded 1972. Tier 2. Wisconsin

Utlas, Inc. Represents OCLC Services in Canada

Another type of network consists of those affiliated with OCLC. These are of two types. Tier 1 networks provide training and support for OCLC services, while tier 2 networks also provide marketing of OCLC services. Examples of Tier 1 affiliates are AMIGOS Bibliographic Council, Dallas, Texas; NELINET, Inc., Newton, Massachusetts; OHIONET, Columbus, Ohio; PALINET, Philadelphia, Pennsylvania; and MINITEX, Minneapolis, Minnesota. Examples of tier 2 affiliates are INCOLSA—Indiana Cooperative Library Services Authority, Indianapolis, Indiana—and SOLINET—Southeastern Library Network, Atlanta, Georgia. Table 1 shows OCLC-affiliated networks and the regions they cover.

Finally, there are local library cooperatives of many different types, which have been formed for differing purposes but mainly for resource and bibliographic systems sharing or cooperative service development. They may be libraries of a similar type, or libraries clustered in a geographic area, independent of type. They may provide one or more key services to make them viable in their local area. Local library cooperatives can respond to local needs and concerns, with their members providing the necessary governance and policy direction. This cooperative approach has fostered improved relations among libraries for the most part.

B. Reasons for Success

It is clear that the present success of cooperatives is due to their ability to fill needs that individual libraries could not fill themselves. For example, immense databases and online cataloging of the bibliographic utilities continue to meet the needs of libraries that cannot afford to mount their own resource LC MARC files as part of their local automated system. But, most importantly, these large databases enable interlibrary loan and collection sharing on a wide scale, not previously possible without any locational tools except the National Union Catalog. Provision of microform catalogs and now CD-ROM-based catalogs offer a cost-effective alternative to libraries that have not as yet obtained their own online catalogs or that wish to provide remote copies of their catalogs to populations that would not be able to access their systems interactively.

The local and regional cooperatives fulfill more immediate needs of their members for professional training and document delivery services in a local area. They can be more responsive to members' needs when maintained at a manageable scale, while still providing a large enough base to offer viable cooperative host computer-based solutions for their members.

C. Continued Viability

The trend is quite clear that by the end of the twentieth century a library of virtually any size will have an online system through which it will perform its daily operational tasks. Moreover, this system will be part of a vast international communications network, which will bring worldwide resources to even small libraries, once the National Research Education Network (NREN) is a reality. Presently, academic institutions and an increasing number of commercial organizations are able to use the resources provided through the Internet to access via the TCP/IP protocol numerous library online catalogs, digitized text databases, other file and program repositories and messaging services such as the Bitnet Listservs or the Usenet News Groups. SLIP (Serial Line Interface Protocol) server connections make home connection to the Internet by modem practical. In addition these connections provide electronic mail and file transfer. Since the necessary software to enable any of the current MS-DOS, Macintosh or UNIX-based workstations to perform terminal emulation and file transfer is in the public domain on TCP/IP based networks, wider usage is only a matter of time and development of a new expanded form of the Internet.

With the addition of the bibliographic utilities and the regional and local cooperatives to this network, the emphasis in the coming century will be on the refinement of these worldwide connections and the development of improved electronic data interchange among these systems, including new information services suppliers. Moreover, with the emphasis also moving toward local systems that can incorporate vastly improved online storage, the next decade will bring immense digitized collections of bibliographic items to the user's desktop, with specialized scholar's integrated desktop software designed to facilitate such wide access and intersystem sharing. As a present example of this direction, one need look only at the Virginia Tech INFOSTATION based on the NeXt UNIX system and its NeXtStep user interface.

The movement to a graphical user interface (GUI) will be necessitated by the move to the construction of systems using object-oriented techniques. This, in turn, will allow the user to build custom applications on the desktop using these same techniques, heretofore reserved for professional programmers. Since these techniques are dependent on a GUI and also on client/server application design, it will be necessary to develop a new set of intersystem standards that will move from the Common Command Language current standard level to one that will incorporate various GUI's on the major platforms to translate to some common object-based interchange medium. Currently X Windows serves this purpose in the UNIX world.

Therefore, the bibliographic utilities will have to move in new directions. One will be to bring in many smaller libraries as members to maintain some viability for the utilities' existing cataloging services as they gradually change their emphasis from cataloging services to being repositories of enhanced bibliographic, locational data and to providing digitized publications. Make no mistake, the electronic journal will be a significant publication and research medium for the archival scholarly press. It will be necessary for libraries to have access since individual scholars will also be travelling over the network for access. This will undoubtedly produce new reference service delivery problems for libraries. Libraries should take the lead in determining where these repositories should be located on the network. The repository role could belong to the bibliographic utilities. Increasingly, the bibliographic utilities will assume the switching center role for interlibrary loan and electronic document ordering while at the same time building their own collections of electronic publications and information services available on the worldwide network. Various private firms will continue to contract to provide some of these document delivery and database repository services as is now the case.

Local cooperatives will maintain their viability through continuing to serve their members' immediate daily document delivery needs, focussing on expanding their members' ability to use computer and communications technology and reaching out to their user communities to encourage more public involvement in computing and communications. One way to do this is for these library cooperatives to take the lead in community-level organization of such systems as those affiliated with the National Public Telecomputing Network, which has grown out of the Cleveland FreeNet, operated at Case Western Reserve University in Cleveland, Ohio. Such systems open some network access to anyone with a computer, modem and asynchronous communications software. And, ultimately, since libraries will be moving to provide more and more services via online connections, it is critical that library networks and cooperatives maintain some leadership in developing the user's abilities to access and capitalize on these systems if libraries are to continue receiving taxpayers' support.

VIII. CONCLUSION

Library cooperation and networks have made considerable progress during the last 25 years. We can expect that their continued development will focus increasingly on providing information technology-based solutions to their clientele. Issues forcing libraries to cooperate will not disappear; rather, the increased proliferation of publications, many in electronic form, will necessitate further cooperation and electronic outreach from libraries. We can expect that governance of these cooperatives will bring more member input into their direction and that more professional business management will increasingly be necessary to operate them. Although, one can see new, emerging roles for the current bibliographic utilities, one can also make the case for some consolidation in the United States. However, much of this will depend on both economic and political factors as the large libraries and their parent institutions review their continuing participatory arrangements in OCLC and RLIN. The rest of the decade should see increasing competition among bibliographic utilities to fill niche areas.

REFERENCES

1. Avram, Henriette D. Bibliographic and technical problems in implementing a national library network. *Library Trends 18*: 487-502 (April 1970).
2. Fusaro, Janice B. and Audrey N. Grosch. Minnesota's challenge for the seventies: planning and implementing a state-wide computer-aided library system. *Minnesota Libraries 23*: 84-88 (Autumn 1970).
3. WLN releases LaserCat. *Wilson Library Bulletin 61*: 10 (May 1987).
4. Board of Trustees reaffirms OCLC's intention to implement an online circulation system. *OCLC Newsletter 127*: 1 (February 6, 1980).
5. OCLC and Geac discontinue discussions on circulation control system. *OCLC Newsletter 129*: 2 (May 20, 1980).
6. OCLC and SOLINET at odds over processor. *Library Journal 105*: 2001-2002 (October 1, 1980).
7. Board of Trustees directs OCLC to develop circulation control system in-house within nine months. *OCLC Newsletter 130*: 4 (July 7, 1980).
8. OCLC will market Claremont system. *OCLC Newsletter 138*: 1 (November 1981).
9. Local library system Five Colleges, OCLC to collaborate. *OCLC Newsletter 141*: 1-2 (May 1982).
10. Carpenter, Gai. LS/2000 and Five Colleges, Inc.: The user's perspective. *Library HiTech* 2(2): 21-24 (1984).
11. OCLC accelerates local system development with agreement with Online Computer Systems. *OCLC Newsletter 146*: 1-2(April 1983).
12. OCLC and Online Computer Systems, Inc. to jointly develop NLM automation. *Library Journal 108*: 1081-1082 (June 1, 1983).
13. Lutz, Marilyn. ILS—The origin of LS/2000. *OCLC Newsletter 149*: 14-15 (November 1983).
14. First LS/2000 system up at Hampshire College. *OCLC Newsletter 150*: 1-2 (February 1984).
15. OCLC acquires Avatar Systems. *OCLC Newsletter 150*: 2 (February 1984).
16. OCLC acquires Avatar Systems. *Wilson Library Bulletin 58*: 393-394 (February 1984).
17. Ameritech Information Systems to purchase OCLC Local Systems Division. *OCLC Newsletter 184*: 4-5 (March/April 1990).
18. Brandehoff, S. E. RLG launches unique art sales catalog database. *American Libraries 13*: 266 (April 1982).
19. OCLC puts its database under copyright. *Wilson Library Bulletin 57*: 458 (February 1983).
20. Mason, Marilyn G. Copyright in context: The OCLC database. *Library Journal 113*: 31-34 (July 1988).

21. UTLAS states policy on record ownership. *Library Journal 110*: 23 (November 15, 1985).
22. CLSI and UTLAS, Inc. enter joint marketing venture. *Wilson Library Bulletin 58*: 538 (April 1984).
23. Jasco, P. CD-CATSS: UTLAS' serials compact disk database, a review and critique. *Serials Review 15*(4): 7-18, 58 (Winter 1989).
24. Zeigman, B. N. The Western Library Network: An evolving entity. *Library HiTech 6*(4): 109-111 (1988).
25. Bendig, Mack W. Encyclopedia online: Channel 2000 and the Academic American Encyclopedia. *Reference Services Review 10*(2): 25-26 (Summer 1982).
26. Current utilization of online catalogs: Transaction log analysis; final report to the Council on Library Resources. Vol. 1, by J. E. Tolle. OCLC Research Report OCLC/OPR/RR-83/2. 128 pp.
27. Online catalog use: Results of surveys and focus group interviews in several libraries; final report to the Council on Library Resources. Vol. 2, by K. Markey. OCLC Research Report OCLC/OPR/RR-83/3. 284 pp.
28. A Comprehensive study of online public access catalogs: An overview and application of findings; final report to the Council on Library Resources. Vol. 3, N. K. Kaske and N. P. Sanders. OCLC Research Report OCLC/OPR/RR-83/4. 102 pp.
29. CLR awards Forest Press, OCLC $94,350 for study of Dewey classification as online tool. *OCLC Newsletter 150*: 4 (February 1984).
30. Markey, Karen. *Use of Classification in Online Catalogs*. Dublin, OH: OCLC Office of Research, 1985. 500 pp.
31. DeGennaro, Richard. Will success spoil OCLC? *Library Journal 109*: 626 (April 1, 1984).
32. OCLC/Network relationship statement. *OCLC Newsletter 145*: 2-3 (February 1983).
33. Martin, Susan Katherine. *Governance issues for automated library networks: the impact of and implications for large research libraries*. University of California, Berkeley, 1983. 156 pp.
34. Maciuszko, Kathleen L. *OCLC, a Decade of Development, 1967–1977*. Foreword by Robert F. Cayton and Epilogue by Philip Schieber. Littleton, CO: Libraries Unlimited, 1984.
35. Maruskin, Albert F. *OCLC: Its Governance, Function, Financing, and Technology*. New York: Marcel Dekker, 1980.
36. Kilgour, Frederick G. *Collected Papers of Frederick G. Kilgour*. Compiled by Patricia A. Becker and Ann T. Dodson; edited by Lois L. Yoakam. Dublin, OH: OCLC Online Computer Library Center, 1984.
37. Davis, Susan. Report of the first meeting of the OCLC Serials Control User's Group, June 26, 1984. *Serials Review 10*(4): 96-98 (Winter 1984).
38. Folsom, Sandy L. The elimination of the OCLC Serials Control subsystem: A survey of reactions and plans. *Serials Review 12*: 43-47 (Spring 1986).
39. Riddick, John F. A tale of two tests; or SC350 and MicroLinx: a comparison. *Serials Review 12*(4): 37-54 (Winter 1986).
40. Diodato, Louise W. The deactivation of OCLC's Serials Control System. *Serials Librarian 12*(3/4): 21-27 (1987).

41. Librarians attack OCLC for abandoning systems. *Library Journal 111*: 21 (April 1, 1986).
42. Wei, K. T. and S. Noguchi. RLIN CJK versus OCLC CJK: The Illinois experience. *Library Resources and Technical Services 33*: 140-151 (April 1989).
43. Intner, Sheila. Much ado about nothing: OCLC and RLIN cataloging quality. *Library Journal 114*(2): 38-40 (February 1, 1989).
44. Brown, Rowland C. w. and S. Walbridge. OCLC: Current and future issues. *Library Hi-Tech 6*(4): 114-117 (1988).
45. Research Libraries Group goes for BALLOTS. *Library Journal 103*: 916-917 (May 1, 1978).
46. RLG in difficult straits. *Wilson Library Bulletin 56*: 731-732 (June 1982).
47. RLG network problems overcome claims Interim President Batten. *Library Journal 107*: 1928+ (October 15, 1982).
48. Denenberg, Ray and Sally H. McCallum. RLG/WLN/LC computers ready to "talk." *American Libraries 15*(6): 400, 402, 404 (June 1984).
49. Richards, D. and Carol Lerche. Evolution of the Research Libraries Information Network. *Library HiTech 7*(1): 29-36 (1989). Erratum *7*(2): 16 (1989).
50. First American contract to UTLAS (University of Toronto Library Automation System). *Wilson Library Bulletin 55*: 7 (September 1980).
51. Japanese firm buys $1 million in utlas products and services. *Library Journal 106*: 16-17 (January 1, 1981).
52. UTLAS receives $2 million in support. *Wilson Library Bulletin 57*: 733 (May 1983).
53. Feuer, Sam. Moving to the next generation system: a case history of a vendor's approach. *Library HiTech 8*(1): 57-63 (1990).
54. WLN launches online interlibrary loan system. *Library Journal 111*: 138 (September 1, 1986).
55. WLN seeks private non-profit status. *Wilson Library Bulletin 62*: 8 (April 1988).
56. WLN transition completed. *Wilson Library Bulletin 65*: 15 (September 1990).

4

NETWORKS, INTERNETWORKING AND STANDARDS

Usenet is like Tetris for people who still remember how to read.

—J. Heller

I. INTRODUCTION

Twenty years ago it seemed so much simpler to connect a remote terminal to its host computer. First, we used a physical twisted-pair wire, which ran from the terminal to some sort of an interface unit at the computer. We programmed the interface unit with a hardware driver that recognized and handled the code sets sent and received. Next, we could use an acoustic coupler to translate the terminal's digital signal to analog form and send it over telephone lines to the host computer. At the host computer, similar equipment, called a "modem," would transform this analog signal to digital and send it to that same sort of interface unit used in the direct-wire situation described above. The introduction of more affordable, higher speed modems meant the obsolescence of acoustic-coupled devices except for some remote laptop computer users who still need to overcome the lack of modular phone jacks in certain older buildings. Now, it is typical to see modems operating in the range of 9600 to 38,400 bits per second (bps). The advance of direct-wire connections from a nonstandard 4-wire to a fully compliant RS-232C connection brought standardized multiplexing units. These multiplexers, employing time or frequency division techniques, allow more than one terminal to share a physical line.

Today, we still use physical wire connections, albeit in more complex architectures that demand great amounts of software control. Our physical wires, in some cases, have changed to coaxial cable, fiber optic cable for backbone networks, or to newer cabling schemes like the IBM Premises Wiring product. Thick and thin coaxial-type cable is giving away to shielded or unshielded twisted pair again, so that sometimes existing telephone wiring can be used to implement our local area network (LAN). Current 10Base-T implements Ethernet over type 5 twisted-pair cable. When two or more LANs are coupled together through a bridge, router or gateway over a 5- to 20-square mile area, they are referred to as metropolitan area networks (MANs). These, in turn, when linked together across national and international boundaries form wide area networks (WANs). The interconnection of numerous MANs and WANs is called internetworking, with a small *i*. For such internetworking, it is desirable to have a high degree of interoperability so that a user is able to fully access resources as transparently as possible anywhere in the interconnected network.

In 1961, the first computer time-sharing operating system was developed at Massachusetts Institute of Technology. It was called CTSS (Compatible Time Sharing System). This development, together with M.I.T. Lincoln Laboratory's creation of the very first computer network for the U.S. Air Defense Command in the early 1950's, called SAGE (Semi-Automatic Ground Environment), were the pioneering efforts which made possible the evolution to current levels of networking.

Of major interest to information professionals and perhaps the most widely known of the WAN developments is the evolution of the Internet, spelled with a capital *I*. This computer network is now based on the NSFnet, operated by the National Science Foundation, which connects numerous other networks in the United States and links to foreign networks. Since it is critical that information professionals be able to use Internet resources, this chapter will provide some necessary background and information on resources accessible via the Internet.

One significant problem with the Internet is that access to it is largely from academic and governmental sites, with still relatively few commercial or business sites. Thus, while academic libraries and many public libraries are accessible via the Internet, many resources such as private special libraries in major corporations are not as yet able to offer their catalogs in a searchable state across the Internet. With the development of what was first proposed as the National Research Education Network (NREN) and now is popularly called the "information superhighway," commercial nodes should increase and more small public libraries will be brought into this loop. Meanwhile, individual citizens are also eager for Internet access. The Cleveland FreeNet, a member of the National Public Telecomputing Network (NPTN), offers public access to some Internet resources. Commercial suppliers such as The Well, CompuServe and Delphi and regional networks offer accounts for fees that average $30 per month for basic access.

The typical university library has access to both host-based resources and distributed computing sites via typical desktop computers or more powerful UNIX-based workstations. This composite of application support reaches beyond the capabilities of any single integrated library system itself. We will examine some basic local and wider area networking concepts to tie this interoperable environment together. The decade of the eighties saw the maturation of multifunctional library automation systems, the acquisition of microcomputers and local workgroup software, and the implementation of LANs in our libraries. The decade of the nineties has produced further fine tuning of these automated library systems, with increased emphasis on workstation-based distributed applications, i.e., client/server designs, and interconnectivity and interoperability of these systems through worldwide internetworking. First, let us examine the Internet.

II. THE INTERNET

The term "Internet" (CAPITALIZED) denotes the collection of networks that has evolved out of the Advanced Research Projects Agency (ARPA). This ARPA network uses the Transmission Control Protocol (TCP) and Internet Protocol (IP) for its architectural basis. The term "internet" (lower case) means any collection of networks that uses the TCP/IP protocol suite and is based on the Open Systems Interconnection (OSI) Reference Model.

A. History and Evolution

The present Internet began with the establishment of the ARPAnet, an experimental wide area network which connected host computers and terminal servers together. ARPA, which was to change its name to the Defense Advance Research Projects Agency (DARPA), started with host computers on the West Coast at the University of California, Santa Barbara; UCLA; Stanford Research Institute; Stanford University; University of Utah; System Development Corp.; and Rand Corp. being connected together and to host computers on the East Coast at Case Western Reserve University, Carnegie Mellon University, Massachusetts Institute of Technology Lincoln Laboratory, Harvard University and Bolt, Beranek and Newman (BBN). By 1983, this network had split into two networks: the Defense Data Network (DDN), or MILnet, and ARPAnet, which was being phased into the DARPA Internet. DDN had some 160 nodes in the United States, Europe and the Pacific. The DARPA Internet comprised mainly university and research institute participants.

Both of these networks pioneered the concept of a layered network architecture designed to simplify design, implementation and operation of large networks of diverse computing equipment. A specialized network called the NSFnet, operated by the National Science Foundation to link supercomputer sites, eventually assumed the ARPAnet traffic. In fact, in June, 1990, when ARPAnet officially shut down, no one but the network staff was even aware that the old network had been shut down for the final time, so smoothly switched was the traffic routing and flow.

Currently, the Internet encompasses over 2,218 distinct networks, according to the tables kept at the DDN Network Information Center. The Informational Sciences Institute (ISI) does much of the research, standardization and allocation work of the Internet. Information services for the Internet are provided largely by SRI, International. Each independent network connected to the Internet has its own operations center. For example, the ARPAnet was operated by BBN, under contract from DARPA. All of these interconnected networks use the TCP/IP protocols and incorporate layered architectures based on the OSI Reference Model.

Every major research network worldwide now has some sort of connection to the Internet. Accessing these resources for basic service requires use of three pieces of software on your microcomputer or host system. These are Telnet, TN3270 and FTP. Telnet software, allows a host-connected terminal or microcomputer on a LAN to emulate a Digital Equipment Corp. VT-100 family terminal, or in some cases another emulation, in order to log on to another network-attached computer. The TN3270 program provides similar services, except that the emulation is for IBM computers using the IBM 3270 emulation for IBM 3178/3278 terminal models. FTP is a program that implements the file transfer protocol, which allows a user to send or receive ASCII or binary-type files to or from a remote host, using commands that are relatively host independent and that support locating the appropriate file source or destination. Further services require Gopher client software to access these numerous Gopher information servers. Similarly, the World Wide Web (WWW), which uses Hypertext to provide information, requires a client such as Mosaic or Cello for Windows 3.1. Gopher servers worldwide are indexed through a service called Veronica. Similarly, Archie servers index major anonymous FTP file repositories on the Internet. WAIS is another locational service to find various Internet accessible resources. Gopher servers often provide a connection to these search servers, or they may be accessed directly.

Your connection to the Internet will be through one or more networks operating in your institution area. The major research networks, themselves sometimes collections of specific local or regional networks, are listed below:

ACSNET Australian Computer Science Network

AUSEANET Asian Countries Micro-electronics Project Network (Indonesia, Thailand, Malaysia, Singapore, Brunei and Philippines)

BITNET Because It's Time Network (Worldwide academic network)

CDNNET Canadian National Network

COSAC Communications SANS Connections Network

CNET Centre Nationale d'Etudes des Télécommunications (French research network)

CSNET Computer Science Network (United States, United Kingdom, France, Australia and other countries with academic computer science programs)

DFN Deutsche Forschung Netz (German National Research Network)

EARN European Academic Research Network (analogous to BITNET)

EUNET European UNIX Network

FUNET Finland UNIX Network

HEATNET Ireland Network

JANET Joint Academic Network in the United Kingdom

JUNET Japanese UNIX Network

MFENET Magnetic Fusion Energy Network (Nuclear Physics Research, United States and Japan)

NORDUNET Nordic Countries Network

NSFNET National Science Foundation Network

ROSE Research Open Systems for Europe (European Strategic Program for Information Technology (ESPRIT) R&D)

SDN South Korea System Development Network

SPAN Space Physics Analysis Network (NASA and ESA)

SUNET Swedish UNIX Network

UNINETT Norwegian UNIX Network

Usenet Largely UNIX network in the United States for NewsGroup article exchange

UUCPNET UNIX-to-UNIX Copy Network (over 10,000 systems)

Each of these networks has its own operations center. For example, Cornell University currently operates NSFNET on a temporary basis through its Network Information Service Center (NISC). Regional networks have similar monitoring agencies. If a problem occurs locally, the campus network liaison contacts the operator of the network that the campus uses. How is this mosaic governed? The internal network workings are defined in a set of documents called Request for Comments (RFCs). If you have an issue to bring before the Internet, you can write it up as an RFC, to be considered for formalization. Jon Postel (postel@isi.edu) is the RFC referee to whom any proposal is sent. He will electronically broadcast the RFC for comment by anyone who wishes to use Internet electronic mail.

These RFCs can be classified into five groups: required, suggested, directional, informational and obsolete. An example of a required RFC would be RFC-791, which defines the Internet Protocol (IP). Because it is required, it must be implemented on every connected host computer. Suggested RFCs such as RFC-793, Transmission Control Protocol, are generally implemented by network hosts, since they do impact on useability. Directional RFCs are ones that have been discussed and agreed upon but not widely applied. An example is RFC-937, the Post Office Protocol, which was not felt to be widely needed. However, if a site feels certain protocols are needed, then they should implement them according to the agreed upon RFC. Informational RFCs contain factual information about the Internet and its operation. For example RFC-990 tells how numbers are assigned for the numeric IP addresses for each host on the Internet. The last category, obsolete RFCs, is needed because RFCs which supersede earlier ones may not be completely understandable by themselves as they may not include the whole model, only the changes and their rationale.

Another part of the Internet that users should know is the Network Information Center (NIC). The facility is available to all Internet users. Network and telephone may be used to contact the NIC, with the most prevalent contact being electronic mail on the network. This is done by using the Telnet software facility to access nic.ddn.mil. Anonymous FTP is used to retrieve selected documents. For IP address and domain name assignments, one must contact the NIC electronically with a message to hostmaster@nic.ddn.mil.

The way most people keep up to date on network news is to subscribe to one or more mail reflectors. These are special electronic mailboxes which broadcast received messages to those subscribing addresses. The NIC provides a registration service for mail reflectors in the files netinfo:interest-groups-1.txt; netinfo:interest-groups-2.txt; and netinfo:interest-groups-3.txt.

How does all of this message traffic get to the appropriate destinations? It does so by using a standard unique IP address. The path to this address is controlled by routing schemes through gateways that pass on the message between connected networks comprised by the Internet. The IP address is allocated by the NIC above via an application template by e-mail to the above NIC address. These addresses take the form of four decimal numbers separated by periods. Each number is the value of an octet of 32 bits, e.g., 128.39.7.90. Addresses have different meanings for these octets, depending on the net organization, i.e. one net with lots of nodes or a hierarchical site of nets with fewer nodes each. Thus, there are Class A, B and C networks.

Class A networks have the first octet as a network address and the remaining three as a host address on that network. Class B networks use the first two octets as a network address and the last two as the host address. Class C addresses use three octets as the network address and one as the host. All Class A networks have now been assigned, so that any current applications must choose Class B or C. There is an infrequently encountered Class D for multi-cast-type networks that may seen more frequently in the future. Also, for purely experimental networks, there is a Class E experimental format.

Since these IP addresses are not very easily remembered by humans, a symbolic name register was set up at the NIC where the IP address was to be equated to a text form address such as "lambda." However, with the Internet expansion, a domain-based symbolic name in the form "sun.min.stk.edu" is more commonly used by users when sending messages or accessing remote computers. The root of this tree is the rightmost group of characters. In the example above, "edu" is the domain service educational institutions, "sun" is the actual computer's name and, within the subdomain method of allocation, "min" is a subdomain within the institution "stk." Root name servers are contacted by software on the user's machine, called a resolver, to determine who is responsible for these first-level domains. What root server to contact is an installation parameter. The resolver finds out who provides "edu" or another domain's services. Then, it contacts the "edu" or other domain name server, which supplies it with a list of addresses of servers for the subdomains, such as "stk" above. Next, the subdomain server similarly gives another portion, such as "min," until the final subdomain returns a list of addresses of interfaces on that host, e.g., "sun" in the above example.

With this background on the Internet, it is time to consider the utility of the Internet to libraries as well as some resources of interest to librarians and information specialists.

B. Utility to Libraries' Resources

The early developers' conception of the Internet was of a pathway between a few supercomputer sites connecting fewer than 100 systems across the United States. The growth of the Internet as a much wider utility really took off beginning in 1989. In just a few short years, the following benefits of Internet growth have been amply demonstrated:

Direct search access to the major research library catalogs in the developed world, with more additions each year

Ability of one institution to provide its clienteles access to a remote service provided by another information provider

Access to rapidly expanding numbers of scholarly journals in electronic form and electronic archive sites for collections of these electronic publications

Mail reflectors, or in the language of BITNET, Listserv's or Usenet's News Groups, devoted to hundreds of topics, allowing concerned com-munities to have continuing interactions that are rapid and dynamic compared with annual scholarly meetings, telephone conferencing or conventional mail

Data transfer among researchers that can be accomplished in minutes or hours instead of days or weeks,

Archive sites to serve as repositories for much public domain or shareware distributed software, accessible to Internet connected users just as microcomputer bulletin boards have made such resources available to the modem-equipped community

Worldwide electronic mail, including gateways between such disparate commercial services as MCI Mail or CompuServe

Ability of users to secure accounts on remote computers for specialized software or other resources, with a savings in telecommunications costs since each Internet connected site pays for the line charge to its regional network hub

We can look forward to the Internet's functions being taken over by the National Research Education Network (NREN), following the enabling legislation Congress passed on November 22, 1991. On that date a final compromise version of the High Performance Computer Act was sent to the White House. This act is now signed and forms the basis for President Bill Clinton's initiative on the National Information Infrastructure Act of 1993, which describes further initiatives to bring about the NREN. This legislation provides funding authority for two-thirds of the NREN to the National Science Foundation and the remainder to an interagency group under the White House Office of Science Technology Policy. Although George Bush signed this legislation when he was president, it is likely to be still several years before the beginnings of NREN are in place to provide expansion of services beyond the present Internet community—largely higher education, think tanks, high-technology industry and governmental sites. Groups such as the Coalition for Networked Information are taking an active voice in pushing for NREN and Internet expansion as well as providing more organized resource information for users.

C. TCP/IP Protocol Software

Internet-connected host computers provide Transmission Control Protocol (TCP) services to their users through the NCSA Telnet software. This program allows a user on one system to emulate a terminal on another system, usually a Digital Equipment Corp. VT-100 family terminal, although several other emulations are sometimes encountered. For systems that are either IBM or compatible mainframes, where IBM 3278 terminal emulation is the norm, the TN3270 software is used. Its services are similar to those of Telnet. UNIX-based computer systems provide these programs as part of the UNIX operating system facilities. Sun Computer pioneered UNIX as an operating system of choice for engineering and scientific workstations. Other competing workstation manufacturers such as Hewlett-Packard, IBM and NeXT Computer also use UNIX and provide this TCP protocol. The third piece of software used across the Internet is the File Transfer Protocol (FTP) program. This allows either sending or receiving an ASCII or binary-type file, independent of various proprietary file transfer schemes. It also allows access to whatever directory and subdirectory structure may be present on the host computer being accessed, using a common command set that frees the user from having to know the specifics of each system. Thus, one command, "cd," for example, allows a user to change to the proper directory to either find the file desired or to receive the file the user wishes to upload. This command means "Change Directory" and can be used independent of the type or brand of host computer connected to the Internet.

For the microcomputer user—either MS/PC-DOS or Macintosh—Telnet, TN3270 and FTP are available as public domain programs, usually supplied by campus computer centers but also downloadable by FTP from several Internet servers. If such systems are connected directly to a campus or institution-based backbone network having its own IP address registered with the DDN NIC, all of the systems connected will also have their own unique address within that network and will be able to access Internet resources without any host computer intervention. These LANs can be provided a numeric IP address and their own English alphabet domain name form. An Ethernet card is used in these microcomputers and the above software can be used in appropriate format for these systems. To complete such a connection it is also necessary to obtain the correct packet driver software for the Ethernet card. A numbre of these have been developed at Clarkson University and constitute the Clarkson Packet Driver distribution also available from sites distributing the NCSA Telnet software. These Clarkson drivers have now been taken over by Crynwyr and are being distributed as the Crynwyr drivers. Before connecting to your backbone network, be sure to check with your network administration as to what specific Ethernet cards perform best with your backbone and to obtain the correct Crynwyr packet driver for that card. For example, at the University of Minnesota, where connections to the campus Ethernet backbone are via the Etherjack/10Base-T connection, Western Digital (now SMC) Ethernet Cards (WD-8003 series) and their corresponding Crynwyr packet driver are preferred for performance on this form of Ethernet backbone. As an alternative, ODI type drivers can be used which enable both Novell ipx and TCP/IP to be used together. These ODI drivers are supplied by the Ethernet card manufacturers.

D. Resource Guides

When I started out several years ago to become familiar with Internet workings and resources, most information seemed to be passed by word of mouth. The staff of computer centers, while they may have had some RFC's tucked away, usually had little to offer in the way of helpful descriptions or addresses of archive sites or specific resources. Also, if you did not know the electronic mail address of your recipient you could not send that party mail electronically on the Internet. Unfortunately, this latter situation still presently holds true, although it is easier now to find out the IP address or the domain-based symbolic name for a given computer site. There are some valuable guides to various Internet resources that have been compiled, and these should become familiar to all who would use the Internet for more than electronic mail services. For Internet beginners, Brendan P. Kehoe has produced "Zen and the Art of the Internet: A Beginner's Guide to the Internet" (first edition January, 1992). This is available for Anonymous file transfer from various sites, but the author can be contacted at Widener University via the Internet, using the address brendan@cs.widener.edu.

1. Maasinfo

The mother of Internet guides is a collection of indexes by Robert Elton Maas. As of December 23, 1991, his indexes were in version 0.16. The first part of this collection is called "maasinfo.topindex." It contains addressing and accessing information to 52 resources, including files available only by Internet FTP or electronic mail daemon (a UNIX mail server used on the Internet). He does not include any files that are only available within Usenet News groups (the UNIX network's equivalent to Bitnet Listserv's, which provides a moderated conference area on a designated topic) or dial-up, modem-accessed bulletin boards. Maas has built this index with contributors of resources, who receive a waiver of a shareware payment in return for their contribution. Surprisingly, although resources in the hobby bulletin board networks like FidoNET or RBBSnet are not included, Maas is reachable for short messages over FidoNET, with the address ROBERT.MAAS@F212.N143.Z1.FIDONET.ORG or as rem@darkside.com. Typical of entries in this index is the following entry:

> "INTEREST.GROUPS (800K) -- The famous "List of Lists", every known open mailing list and digest on the Internet and Bitnet, in alphabetical order. (Mail to: interest-groups-request@nisc.sri.com to add or delete an entry to that list.) (Bad news from nisc@nisc.sri.com (Steven, for the SRI NISC): INTEREST.GROUPS is not updated with any great frequency at this time.)
>
> To: LISTSERV@NDSUVM1
>
> GET INTEREST PACKAGE (511K, old version?, split into eleven pieces)

To: mail-server@nisc.sri.com
Send netinfo/interest-groups (817K, split into 23 pieces)
FTP ftp.nisc.sri.com (192.33.33.22) netinfo/interest-groups (800K)
FTP noc.sura.net (192.80.214.100) nic/interest.groups (800K)
FTP csuvax1.csu.murdoch.edu.au (134.115.4.1) pub/library/listof.lists (800K)"

The above entry assumes the reader knows how to send electronic mail from his or her site on the Internet and how to use the FTP software to get files.

The second part to this index of indexes is maasinfo.docindex. This is a bibliography of online tutorials and other useful documents for the user to learn how to use many available Internet and BITNET resources. For example, one very useful document is the Inter-Network Mail Guide, which describes how to send electronic mail from one network to another, such as from Internet to CompuServe or MCI Mail, given that you know the local address of your recipient. To obtain this guide written by John J. Chen, you can send the e-mail message GET NETWORK GUIDE to LISTSERV@UNMVM. Or you may FTP to ftp.syr.edu (128.230.1.49) for networks/doc/ingmail.txt.

The third part is maasinfo.hownet. This briefly describes how to get started using various network services. The fourth part is called maasinfo. archie. It explains a file-finding database service called "Archie." If you know the file name, "Archie" will find the FTP site. Several other smaller files complete maasinfo, such as maasinfo.mactexed, which lists shareware and public domain text editors for the Apple Macintosh computers.

2. *Other Guides*

Another Internet resource tool is the NNSC Internet Tour, a Macintosh Hypercard stack. It is a rather general introduction but contains some valuable leads to data archive sites.

The mainly UNIX network called Usenet, which is one of the Internet-connected networks, has many news groups, since this is its purpose. These are similar to the BITNET Listserv or the Echo Conference in the FidoNET electronic bulletin board network. Each of these is devoted to a specific topic and has some sort of moderator that makes sure that relevant discussions are the norm. These Usenet news groups are listed in act.news.newusen, compiled by Gene Spafford (spaf@cs.purdue.edu), and it can be obtained via anonymous FTP to pit-manager.mit.edu (18.72.1.58) in the directory: pub/usenet/news.announce. newusers/list_of_active_newsgroups. Edward Vielnetti (emv@msen. com) has revised the Spafford list, and this is available by FTP from ftp.cs. toronto.edu (128.100.3.6) in pub/emv/news-archives/list_of_newsgroups. There are other lists of discussion or conferences on the Internet. For example, BITNET Listserv lists can be obtained by sending an e-mail message to either of two different sites. The first is to LISTSERV@DARTCMS1, with the message SEND LISTSERV LISTS, or via anonymous FTP to DARTCMS1.DARTMOUTH.EDU (129.170.16.19) in SIGLISTS/LISTSERV.LISTS. The second is to LISTSERV@NCSUVM, with the message LIST GLOBAL, or by anonymous FTP to utarlvm1.uta.edu (129.107.1.6) in directory bitnet/listserv.lists.

The "Directory of Scholarly Electronic Conferences" overlaps with the previous two lists. It is compiled by Diane K. Kovacs (dkovacs@kentvm.bitnet) and can be obtained by sending a message to LISTSERV@KENTVM or LISTSERV@BROWNVM or LISTSERV@UOTTAWA. The message to any of these sites should read:

GET ACADLIST README
GET ACADLIST INDEX
GET ACADLIST FILE1
GET ACADLIST FILE2
GET ACADLIST FILE3
GET ACADLIST FILE4
GET ACADLIST FILE5
GET ACADLIST FILE6

3. St. George and Barron Guides

For researchers and librarians, the ability to access remote library catalogs through Telnet or TN3270 connections makes possible a workable window to certain worldwide resources heretofore accessible only through a direct on-site visit. The first key to this resource class is Art St. George's "Internet-Accessible Library Catalogs and Databases." It is available from many sites via anonymous FTP. It also can be obtained by sending the e-mail message GET LIBRARY PACKAGE to LISTSERV@UNMVM. One ftp site is ariel.unm.edu (129.24.8.1) in directory library/internet.library.

The second key to this resource class is Billy Barron's catalog, which lists over 100 libraries. Quite good logon instructions and other information are this list's strong points, though there is some overlap with the St. George guide. Billy Barron may be reached at billy@unt.edu, and his list may be obtained by anonymous FTP to ftp.unt.edu (129.120.1.4) in directory library.libraries.txt. A companion BBS list can be obtained via the e-mail message GET INTERNET BBS sent to LISTSERV@TEMPLEVM.

4. Other Resource Guides

Dana Noonan is the author of a shorter and more concise list of library catalogs accessible via Telnet or TN3270. This list can be obtained by anonymous FTP to hydra.uwo.ca (129.100.2.13) in directory libsoft/internet_libraries.txt. In addition, Peter Scott is the creator of Hytelnet which is a Hypertext guide following the form of the Barron list. Peter Scott's address is aa375 @freenet.carleton.ca. Hytelnet lists Internet and Britain's JANET-connected libraries, campus-wide information systems and other database resources. To keep up to date, subscribe to the HYTEL-L listserv at hytel-l@kentm.kent.edu. Finally, three is Richard Duggan's CATALIST which is a Hypertext version of the Barron guide that runs under Microsoft Windows 3.1. Duggan may be reached at duggan@brahms.udel.edu. Anonymous FTP will obtain this list from zebra.acs.udel.edu (128.175.8.11) in the directory pub/library. The filenames are cat10.exe, fullcat.exe and readme.txt.

Since one of the basic activities you will want to perform on the Internet is file transfer through the FTP protocol, Jeff Linder (V5057U@vm.temple.edu) has created "File Transfer Protocol—Basic Primer." Obtain it by sending the e-mail message GET FTP PRIMER to LISTSERV@TEMPLEVM.

These are the major resource guides to the Internet that you will want to examine. Others can be located that describe specific services or sites. Many of these are rather dated as they have no fixed scheme for updating, so their authors update when they feel like it and not necessarily when there are a lot of accumulated changes. However, the guides mentioned here are kept at least reasonably current by their authors.

5. Other Internet Facilities

There are over 800 sites on the Internet that offer anonymous file transfer and serve as servers for distributing software programs, particularly programs in the public domain. Since over one million files exist, finding these can be difficult and often rather frustrating. McGill University programmers have created software for a server called Archie, which maintains catalogs of many of these sites and their files. It is updated monthly, so it is reasonably up to date. The best way to connect to an Archie server is by Telnet or Gopher, although command line and X-windows clients do exist for many systems and e-mail access can be done via FTP by mail servers such as BITFTP@PUCC for BITNET-only users. Some currently operating Archie servers are:

archie.ans.net	(New York)
archie.rutgers.edu	(New Jersey)
archie.sura.net	(Maryland)
archie.unl.edu	(Nebraska)
archie.mcgill.ca	(Canada—first Archie site)
archie.funet.fi	(Finland)
archie.au	(Australia)
archie.doc.ic.ac.uk	(Great Britain)

Log in to an Archie site by typing "archie" and after a greeting you will see an "archie> " prompt. Enter Help as a command to receive instructions on using the "prog" command to search as well as Archie's other commands. Another feature of Archie is the Whatis database, which gives names and synopses of over 3500 public domain programs on the Internet.

Another program of interest is Gopher, whose first server is available at the University of Minnesota by Telnet (VT100 emulation) and by special MS-DOS, Windows 3.1 and Macintosh client programs. This Gopher and others offer databases and news groups, with University of Minnesota resources and computer-related information and electronic books and directories of some Internet resources special to this mother Gopher server at Minnesota. Gopher can be reached at consultant.micro.umn.edu. Log in from Telnet as "gopher." If you are coming in via an A-NET connection from an IBM host, log in as "a-net." The VT100 emulation is not very good on this server when compared to the software for MS-DOS and Macintosh which is distributed by boombox. micro.umn.edu. Over a thousand Gopher servers are now operating on the Internet. Gopher clients are available for Windows 3.1 from NOTIS, Inc. (WinGopher) and as shareware from several popular FTP sites (HGOPHER v.2.4, BCGopher).

VERONICA (Very Easy Rodent Oriented Net-wide Index to Computerized Archives) servers index the contents of Gopher servers. They usually limit the maximum number of items retrieved to 200 and are accessible through various Gopher servers. Sometimes the menu choice is "Search Gopherspace" instead of actually using the VERONICA name. Another index server is provided by WAIS (Wide Area Information Service). It searches collections of data, i.e., databases, on the Internet. Someone has to create an index for the server to use in a search. It uses a relevance score to order its search results and is not a Boolean system. To directly use WAIS, you can use a Telnet client to log into think.com or nnsc.nst.net. At the login, type "wais" to run a character-oriented interface. There are several client programs also available from popular FTP sites. Some Gopher servers provide WAIS search connections or implement WAIS-type indexing on their Gopher server content.

The World Wide Web (WWW) is a hypertext-based knowledge system with linking capabilities to other systems and resources similar to Gopher. The Hypertext pages are created with Hypertext Markup Language (HTML), and Internet resources are tied through Uniform Resource Locator (URL) addresses. WWW was developed at CERN in Geneva, Switzerland. NCSA has developed MOSAIC as a Windows-based client for WWW access. Another promising WWW client for Windows is Cello, developed at the Cornell University Legal Research Institute.

III. LOCAL AREA NETWORKS (LANs)

Local area networks create a building or floor-level network connecting personal computers or workstations to shared resources provided by computers acting as servers. Also, for smaller LANs peer-to-peer networks can be set up to provide printer and program sharing. Windows for WorkGroups, Novell Lite and LANtastic are the most popular of these. These dedicated servers on a server-based network, such as Novell 3.12, can be file servers supporting multiuser applications, special work group software or communications servers acting as gateways to remote host computers or other networks. They can also provide sharing of high quality or specialized print or other output devices and storage media such as CD-ROM or WORM units. Electronic mail systems are another obvious benefit from LANs. Multiple LANs can be interconnected for institution-wide networks that might span a metropolitan area or reach across a country or even the world. The metropolitan area network (MAN) and wide area network (WAN) build on the local area network concept, i.e., to enable data transmission between computer users and their computing resources for rapid communication and computer-based solutions to applications that could not be approached without these facilities.

A. Major LAN Architectures

Basic LAN technologies were actually conceived in the early 1960's when the earliest networks were built. These included IBM's building of American Airlines' SABRE airline reservation network, connecting 60,000 video terminals all over the United States to six large-scale computers in 1964. However, the first real computer network was the SAGE (Semi-Automatic Ground Environment) system for the U.S. Department of Defense. It was designed in the early 1950's at the Lincoln Laboratories of the Massachusetts Institute of Technology. By 1974, Xerox Corporation's Palo Alto Research Laboratories (PARC) developed the Ethernet local area network protocol. It was a refinement of a protocol invented earlier by N. M Abramson. (1)

Ethernet is the most widely implemented LAN, with its original specification based on a coaxial cable transmission medium. Currently, it can also be implemented using a thin coaxial-type cable called ThinNet or unshielded type 5 twisted-pair wire under the 10Base-T specification. Today, Ethernet handles 10-Mbps transmission rates on conventional LAN media. Implemented on fiber optic cable in backbone configurations, it can support 100-Mbps transmission rates. This is the 10Base-F protocol, which is composed of 10Base-FP, for passive fiber, and which uses an optical splitter at the hub, and 10Base-FB, which defines Ethernet as a fiber backbone network. These are being proposed as revised chapters of IEEE 802.3, which is the Ethernet protocol standard.

AT&T developed STARLAN as a LAN that can be implemented with either coaxial or twisted-pair cable. Its 1-Mbps transmission rate makes it a relatively slow LAN but one with excellent reliability. Datapoint Corp. developed ARCnet in the mid-1970's on coaxial cable media. It is the easiest to install and the least expensive to implement. It has a limit of 75 users per network and a 2.5-Mbps transmission rate. It is very reliable and is appropriate for smaller workgroup architecture. Its major drawback is its limited connectivity with bridges or gateways that are available with Ethernet or Token Ring architectures.

The last major LAN architecture is Token Ring, originally developed by IBM and now available from many other suppliers such as Proteon. It has been implemented in two variations: the original 4-Mbps and the newer 16-Mbps transmission rate. The 16-Mbps Token Ring uses IBM's premises wiring system or special type 1 shielded twisted-pair cable, while the lower speed version can be implemented on type 3 unshielded twisted-pair cable. Many Token Ring adapter cards for 16-bit bus systems are available as a 4/16 arrangement, permitting the card to be used with either speed network. Token Ring is moderately difficult to install, works best with the IBM premises wiring system and is the highest cost LAN to install. These combination 4-MB and 16-MB Token Ring cards are much more expensive than 10Base-T cards.

Today, the most popular physical LAN strategies are Ethernet in ThinNet and 10Base-T versions and 4-Mbps Token Ring from IBM or competing vendors. There also are some special-purpose LANs that use wireless technology and some nonserver peer-to-peer–type networks, such as LANtastic, which allow resources on one LAN-attached computer to be shared by other LAN-attached computers. Photonic's PhotoLink is an example of an interesting wireless LAN that uses an infrared light beam to transmit and receive signals using a line-of-sight technique for the infra-red light beam units. Microsoft's Windows for Workgroups v.3.11 is rapidly gaining market share in the peer-to-peer market.

MANs and WANs have ben made possible by the development of fiber optic cable technology used in fiber-distributed data interchange (FDDI) backbone networks. In these situations, different protocols may be supported such as Digital Equipment Corp. DECnet, which is based on Ethernet; OSI; TCP/IP; or Novell's IPX to link LANs into MANs and WANs. Value-added networks, such as GTE Telenet, Tymnet or Uninet in the United States and Datapac in Canada, also provide connections for WAN traffic. The development by AT&T of T1 service, which is a 1.544-Mbps telephone line equal to 24 leased lines with redundancy, and its even faster T3 line transmission have made it is possible to handle relatively high speed computer-to-computer traffic. Another advancement, which was conceived some time ago, is the Integrated Services Digital Network (ISDN) which is designed to provide telephone, data, and video signals for service providers to offer video, security, database or videotext services to an organization. ISDN is now finally taking off in the marketplace after a very slow start.

The International Standards Organization (ISO) pioneered the Open Systems Interconnection (OSI) Reference Model, which is a description of a layered communication protocol for computer-to-computer networking. Libraries embraced this reference model very early, as the Library of Congress Linked Systems Project was implemented as closely to the reference model as the then-current hardware and software technologies and products would permit. Some deviation was necessary as some definitions had not yet been developed or accepted as standards, nor were commercial programs available for implementation at each of the layers. Figure 1 shows the OSI Reference Model schematic. With the experiences of other network architectures and with lessons learned from actual implementation of the OSI Reference Model, there will be revisions to incorporate more emphasis on internetworking, as has happened with the Department of Defense network model. An excellent collection of articles on the OSI situation is in *Library Hi-Tech* 8(4): (1990).

Layer 1 is the physical interconnection level. It is implemented in the RS-232C physical serial device interface standard. Layer 2, Data Link, is specified in the Institute of Electrical and Electronics Engineers (IEEE) Standard 802 series. The ISO, under its 802 group, has accepted these IEEE standards. The IEEE LAN Standards Committee 802 has approached this layer by defining logical link and medium access control, with work still being done on layer 3. ISO 802.3 defines Carrier Sense Multiple Access/Carrier Detect network protocol, which is Ethernet's scheme to prevent contention on the network. ISO

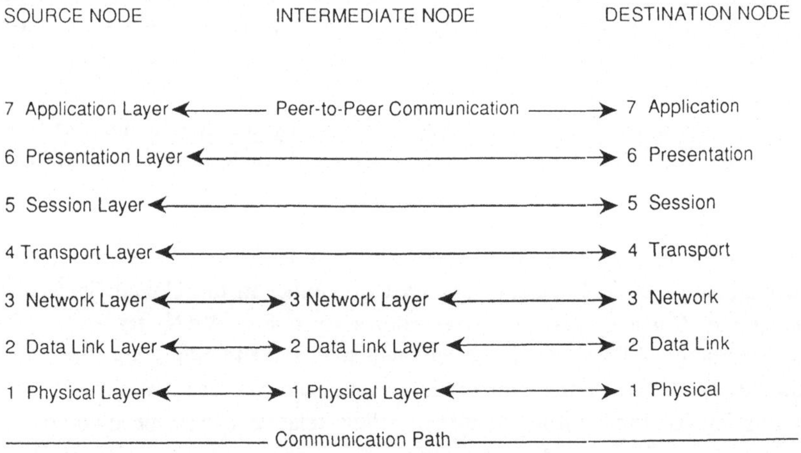

Figure 1 OSI Reference Model.

802.4 and 802.5, respectively, define Token Bus and Token Ring techniques, the latter used in IBM's Token Ring network.

The Internet Protocol (IP) is an implementation of layer 3 of the OSI Reference Model while the Transmission Control Protocol (TCP) is an implementation of layer 4. These protocols were created by Ungermann-Bass, Inc., and were put into widespread usage with the implementation of the Sun workstation, which used UNIX as its operating system. TCP/IP was implemented in UNIX to provide networking support. Currently, the Simple Mail Transfer Protocol (SMTP) handles layers 5 to 7 for Internet messaging. Telnet and FTP also handle layers 5 to 7. It will be quite a while before the full OSI protocol suite will replace TCP/IP on the Internet; however, current network directions indicate that eventually some modified OSI layered architecture will form the basis of many computer-to-computer networks and also be supported along with Novell's IPX and IBM's Netbios on LANs. As Digital Equipment Corp. and IBM move to develop OSI Reference Model-compliant products within their DECnet and System Net-work Architecture offerings respectively, these products will also change for the better.

There are two specialized networks that have been devised. The first is the Manufacturing Automation Protocol (MAP), developed by General Motors Corp. It uses the IEEE 802.4 Token Bus standard for its lower layers and the OSI Reference Model for its upper layers. It is designed for process control and factory floor automation. The second is Technical and Office Product System (TOPS), developed by Boeing Computer Services. It uses either IEEE 802.3 or 802.5 at its lower layers and the OSI Reference Model in the upper layers. Figure 2 shows a broad comparison among the layers of the most prevalent networking architectures currently implemented.

Advanced Peer-to-Peer Communications is IBM's term for its Logical Unit (LU) 6.2 service. LU 6.2 provides basic internetworking services where applications communicate as equal partners, sharing management responsibilities. Any LU 6.2–based application can initiate a session with another LU 6.2 remote partner. These partners negotiate the roles that each will assume. Low-entry networking allows this without mediation by the mainframe computer, although on older hierarchical SNA network sites, the mainframe must still mediate LU 6.2 sessions. The IBM Document Interchange Architecture and System Network Architecture Distribution Services (SNADS) are examples of LU 6.2 applications. They closely match the CCITT X.400 Message Header Support standard. It is this latter standard, along with CCITT X.500–Directory Recommendations, that enables interlinking of computers and electronic mail into a worldwide system, independent of specific computer manufacturers' hardware.

<table>
<tr><th>Layer</th><th>OSI/ISDN</th><th colspan="2">DOD</th><th>DECNET</th><th>SNA</th><th>IEE802</th><th>NETWORK DEVICES</th></tr>
<tr><td rowspan="2">7</td><td rowspan="2">Application</td><td colspan="2" rowspan="4">Process/
Applications</td><td rowspan="2">User</td><td>User</td><td rowspan="2">User
Application</td><td rowspan="5">Gateway (4-7)</td></tr>
<tr><td>Transaction
Services</td></tr>
<tr><td>6</td><td>Presentation</td><td>Network
Applications</td><td>Presentation
Services</td><td rowspan="3">Largely undefined
selected OSI
protocols used in
MAP and TOP</td></tr>
<tr><td>5</td><td>Session</td><td>Session
Control</td><td>Data Flow
Control</td></tr>
<tr><td>4</td><td>Transport</td><td colspan="2">Host-to-Host</td><td>End
Communications</td><td>Transmission
Control</td></tr>
<tr><td>3</td><td>Network</td><td colspan="2">Internet</td><td>Routing</td><td>Path Control</td><td>Logical Link Control</td><td>Router (3)</td></tr>
<tr><td>2</td><td>Data Link</td><td>Network
Access</td><td>CSNP
CSNP</td><td>Data Link</td><td>Data Link</td><td>Medium Access
Control</td><td>Bridge (2)</td></tr>
<tr><td>1</td><td>Physical</td><td colspan="2">Physical</td><td>Physical</td><td>Physical
Control</td><td>Physical</td><td>Repeater (1)</td></tr>
</table>

Figure 2 Comparison of network architecture layers with the OSI Reference Model.

B. Data Networking: Routing, Bridging and Future Network Directions

Today's large LANs often are an interconnection of different vendors' hardware and software, since networks grow over time, usually from a series of LANs designed to serve workgroup solutions. For example, a library may have installed a series of LANs to solve current problems. These might be for printer sharing, access to CD-ROM or access to an integrated online library system. When the number of networks is relatively small, interconnection is relatively easy and it costs about the same to connect each additional network. Figure 3 shows a graph of the relationship of network size, complexity and cost to internetwork. In this figure, when the network can no longer be supported at a reasonable cost, the complexity barrier is reached. Beyond that point, the network would be severely constrained and unable to grow or even continue responding to users' or libraries' needs.

For these connections of disparate LANs, there are two technologies—bridging and routing—that can provide a solution based on accepted standards. Since traffic bottlenecks at the point of LAN connections are often a problem, proper utilization of these technologies can assure satisfactory performance.

A bridge is a device that connects separate networks into a single logical network. A router connects separate networks into an internetwork in which each network retains its logical identity as a separate network segment. In terms of the OSI Reference Model, a bridge operates at the data link layer 2, while a router operates at the network layer 3. If extended network length is needed in a building, it is possible to incorporate devices called "repeaters" between LAN segments. These repeaters operate at the physical layer 1 of the OSI Reference Model. Repeaters merely regenerate signals to accommodate extended wire lengths. A gateway device is essentially a protocol converter and can operate at any layer of the OSI Reference Model.

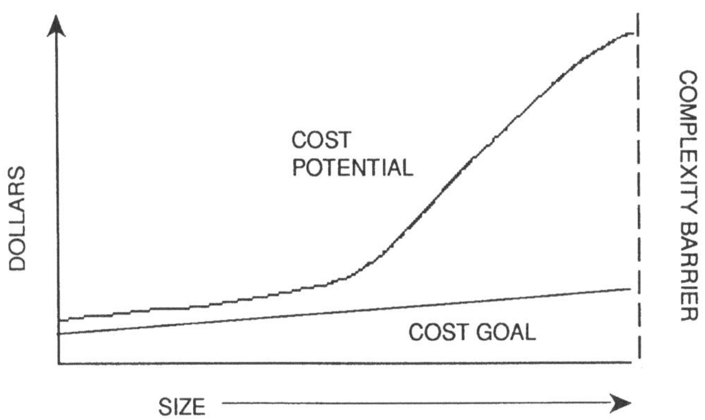

Figure 3 Support costs for internetworking as a function of network size.

Bridges work with device addresses and use these to determine what to do with data packets. Since information about paths or routes through the network is encoded in network addresses and these are accessible only to devices operating at the network layer, the bridge is a relatively simple device and therefore its cost can be kept low. Since routers operate at the network layer and know the network in both network address and path terms, they also "know" which path is the shortest or other details affecting choice of path. Because of this, routing software is more complex than that of bridges, while the actual hardware device itself may be the same. Today, the LAN suppliers build in the functionality through the software, creating more flexibility for network designers. The OSI Reference Model and the TCP/IP protocol are both vendor-independent standards for fully interoperable internetworking.

The products available in the interconnection market break down into local- and wide-area products. Devices meant for local use permit connection to local media and network backbones. These may be coaxial, twisted-pair or fiber-optic media. Local-area devices can connect dissimilar media of two networks. Wide-area devices are equipped with two or more long-distance communications ports and at least one local port. These long-distance connections typically are leased point-to-point lines with speeds of 19.2-kbps to 2.048-Mbps capacities.

How basically does a bridge work? It uses source and destination addresses to create a database. These devices "learn" on the basis of source addresses and they "forward" on the basis of the destination address. They also perform a "filtering function" if the destination address is on the same network segment as the source, the bridge automatically discards it. This prevents unnecessary traffic congestion on the bridge since only packets destined for the addresses on the other network segments pass over the bridge. If a destination address is not in the database, the bridge forwards the packet in a "flooding" process, sending it to all network segments connected to its ports except the port where the source address is assigned. Once the packet is received by the correct destination, this information is then added to the database.

Current router products are capable of handling multiple protocols through appropriate software. Protocols that do not contain a network layer, such as Digital Equipment Corp. Local Area Transport terminal connection protocol, IBM's LU 6.2 and IBM's Netbios, are not able to be handled by a router. These can be passed only by a bridge or passed through another network to a network destination address capable of handling that protocol. The router database contains a "routing table" with the actual path to be used. Although some devices in environments requiring absolute security are handled by the network administrator through routing tables built into a static routing setup, the more common method is a "dynamic routing," where the router itself broadcasts information when it detects network changes.

Obviously, in designing a network there are advantages and disadvantages to both bridging and routing. These are shown in Table 1.

Table 1 Advantages and Disadvantages to Bridging and Routing

	Advantages	Disadvantages
Bridging	Simple to install and configure Transparent to users Easily modified and reconfigured Networks connectable using different protocols without added software Computers can be added without configuring new newtork addresses Relatively low cost for high performance	Unable to take simultaneous advantage redundant paths in a network by load splitting Can slow down network from flooding when an unknown address packet is sent out Cannot prevent a "broadcast storm" when certain broadcast protocols cause packets to be flooded to every port No real support for fault isolation or other distributed management, especially problematical in large bridged networks Can prevent use of certain applications over the network if these need to use unique names on a network-wide basis, since two copies of an application running under the same name could malfunction and affect the whole network
Routing	More flexible than bridges and can differentiate paths by numerous factors such as cost, line speed, line delay and length No "broadcast storms," as incidents in one subnet do not affect other subnets Support for any topology as well as easier accommodation of extensive network growth and complexity Can load-split over redundant network data paths to make best use of available signal bandwidth	More difficult to set up and configure Movement of individual workstations more difficult as a new address must be assigned Configuration laborious and time consuming for static routing protocols Some low-level protocols cannot be routed

Presently, institutions usually construct a fiber-optic FDDI type backbone having 100–200 Mbps bandwidth. This FDDI can be installed as a growth vehicle on the same fiber used in an Ethernet/802 fiber-optic backbone LAN. Certainly, the future in data networking is to increase the bandwidth to accommodate heavier traffic. This implies an eventual extension of FDDI to the desktop in one scenario and might result in new LAN architectures that will extend the ISDN concept. 100-Mbps LANs will be needed to operate multimedia LAN applications involving sound and graphics.

IV. STANDARDIZATION EFFORTS AFFECTING LIBRARY INFORMATION TECHNOLOGIES

Automated library systems benefit from more standardization, both in data processing as well as applications. With standardization, it is practical for system developers to produce products with more acceptance and broader appeal. For the library, it also means that investments in information technology will use common and accepted parameters. This will ensure a wider choice of systems products for the future, with more preservation of hardware and software dollars already invested. For example, standards such as ISO 2709, which provides a magnetic tape record layout standard for data interchange, forms the basis for placing USMARC records onto magnetic tape, while USMARC defines the data element and logical layout of the actual bibliographic data. In a far-reaching way, other standards adopted by the National Institute of Standards and Technology (NIST) or Federal Information Processing Standards (FIPS) and those of other bodies, such as the IEEE, affect library information technologies. Now, let us examine the major player in developing American National Standards affecting library and information retrieval applications.

A. National Information Standards Organization (NISO)

NISO develops standards that, when adopted, become American National Standards (ANS). Its predecessor organization was known as the American National Standards Institute Subcommittee Z39 (ANSI Z39). Thus NISO's adopted standards carry the identification number Z39.xx, with the xx denoting the specific standard number. As of January, 1994, there were 29 active and adopted standards in force. Some current standards are in the process of revision, since every five years standards must be examined for possible revision and revoked or reaffirmed if not to be revised. Three new draft standards were being balloted.

Z39 standards have increasingly addressed issues that have been brought out by the use of computer and communication systems. Early standards were directed at items such as Z39.4–Basic Criteria for Indexes or Z39.5–Abbreviations of Titles of Publications. New standards are exemplified by Z39.58–Common Command Language, Z39.67–Computer Software Description.

Several standards currently having a wide impact deserve specific mention here as they will affect current and future library systems. The first of these is

Z39.50–Information Retrieval Application Service Definition and Protocol: Specification for Open Systems Interconnection. This is actively being implemented by major bibliographic utilities and system developers. The sixth meeting of the Z39.50 Implementor's Group at OCLC on September 8–10, 1991 saw over 25 organizations attending. They have developed a list of proposed enhancements for the next version of this standard, i.e., version 3. Version 2 has been adopted and version 3 is a work in progress. ISO's Technical Committee 46 also began working on its version 3 of their corollary standard. Z39.50 is the application layer protocol by which two computers can communicate. It offers the promise of designing intelligent front-end programs that will help and mediate access by users. Implementation of Z39.50 may be done using TCP for the immediate future since TCP is widespread, whereas full OSI support is commercially lacking. As of December 6, 1991 there were three interoperating Z39.50 implementations in test operation. These are Pennsylvania State University (PSU) on a VAX 9000 under VMS, University of California, Division of Library Automation (UCDLA) on an IBM 3090 under MVS/ESA and the University of California, Berkeley (UCB), on a DEC system 5810 under Ultrix v.4.2. In each case of interoperation an Init and Search cycle was completed and MARC records were returned. PSU was a server to UCDLA and UCB clients in one series. UCDAL was a server to UCB as a client and UCB was a server to a DLA client. Given the nature of this work, one thing can be assured. That is that later versions of this standard will be functionally improved since this sort of protocol technique requires staged development based on some experience. In 1994, all the major library automation system vendors are working on Z39.50 compliant clients and many also on servers. Several vendors have released commercial production versions of their products.

Also of considerable importance is Z39.58–Common Command Language. For library users and librarians, given the wide interconnection of library systems now possible, it would be nice if one set of commands could be learned and become the common basis for searching these disparate systems. Given the eventual trend toward graphical user interfaces (GUIs) as exemplified in current microcomputer software and workstation user interface shells under UNIX, it is only a matter of time that host-based library systems will also incorporate such GUI facilities, most likely adopting one of the UNIX GUIs such as X-Windows or MOTIF. When that occurs there will need to be some GUI standard, but most importantly, there will need to be a translation from the GUI to a common command language set if systems are to become more hardware and platform independent. Therefore, Z39.58 becomes an important cornerstone to the eventual emergence of future standards covering GUI approaches. This will assure the widest interoperability and interconnectivity on the application level for all bibliographic systems.

Z39.2 defined a format for bibliographic information interchange. However, another important thrust is being made through ANSI X12 organization electronic data interchange (EDI) work. The Data Interchange Standards Association, Inc., is the major group responsible for X12 EDI standards development, and the Book Industry Systems Advisory Committee and the Serials Industry Systems Advisory Committee are actively working with publishers, agents and library system developers to develop EDI between libraries and their material suppliers. Orders, claims, quotes and other financial and status data are all amenable to being facilitated by EDI application.

Standards development is a consensus process within the various standardization bodies. For example, anyone can propose a standard for NISO consideration. NISO's Standards Development Committee and Board of Directors examine proposals for new standards. If the review is favorable, which takes three to six months, the proposal is sent out to NISO's membership representatives for vote as a new work item. Then, it takes another three months for balloting, and if the proposal passes, NISO's Executive Director appoints a committee chair and together they recruit the committee members. That usually takes six to nine months more. Thus it is normal to see the initial standards development process for a new standard to take from 20 to 36 months, at which time a draft standard enters a three-month comment round to NISO member organizations or anyone else wishing to comment. Comments necessitate revision, which usually takes a further 12 to 18 months, with balloting on the resulting draft another three months. If the standard passes, the resolution phase begins. In this phase any "Yes, with comment" votes and any "No" votes (with their stated basis) are examined and resolved. This typically takes about six months. Once NISO has consensus, it passes the standard to ANSI for review, publication, publicity and implementation as an ANSI Z39 standard. This usually takes another nine months to complete. Thus, it typically takes 5 to 8 years to produce a standard from its original concept to final adoption. Then, every five years, the standard must be reviewed for possible revisions and reaffirmation or revised and reballoted. NISO had 57 voting members as of January 1, 1994.

B. International Standards Organization: Technical Committee 46—Information and Documentation

NISO is the U.S. Technical Advisory Group (TAG) on the work of ISO TC/46 and casts the U.S. vote on these ISO standards. There are ISO standards that are implemented in their U.S. form via Z39 standards. Subcommittee SC4 deals with computer applications within information and documentation. There are nine other TC/46 subcommittees and some of these are Common Command

Language, Transliteration, Data Sets (EDI/X12) and Electronic Publishing. There is active participation by NISO in these developments.

C. Other Efforts

The ANSI X.3 committee handles various telecommunications standards. With the increase in internetworking of systems, this work is integral to systems we envision in this decade. An exciting new development is the formation of the Coalition for Networked Information and its Architectures and Standards Working Group, which is working on standards for referencing networked information objects. A number of ad hoc solutions to identifying and referencing these resources have been developed, but these present major barriers to assuring full future interoperability. The Coalition's intention is to submit this work to the Internet Engineering Task Force as a draft RFC and also to NISO for adoption as an ANSI Z39 standard.

The Museum Computer Network has its Computer Interchange of Museum Information Committee (CIMI) developing protocols for exchange of museum information. This protocol would carry a variety of data types such as text, binary, image and graphic. It would support real-time, interactive and batch modes of operation as various applications might require. This group can be contacted by writing or calling:

John Perkins, CIMI Project Manager
5659 Market Street
Halifax, NS B3K 2J1 Canada
Telephone (902) 454-4077
Internet: perkins@dcd1jh.das.net

In a similar vein, the Art Information Task Force is researching the development of a framework of information categories for describing art objects. A data dictionary of art-specific data elements is under development. This task force is jointly sponsored by the Getty Art History Information Program and the College Art Association, with National Endowment for the Humanities support.

V. CONCLUSION

The enactment of the High Speed Computing Act and $3 billion of government-funded research into high-speed computing, including a 1-gigabyte bandwidth national backbone network to be undertaken on the NSFnet in the Internet, will result in the further evolution of the Internet. It may also happen that today's TCP/IP dominated internetworking will be replaced by OSI-based systems. However, for that to happen, it will be necessary for OSI to be modified to be more compliant toward this internetworking. Meanwhile, the major growth in LANs will continue, since individual productivity issues and workgroup computing solutions depend on reliable LAN technologies. These must grow or shrink to meet institution demands. Token Ring and Ethernet strategies for LANs will continue to divide the market, with Ethernet ruling the backbone network because of its inevitable implementation as a fiber optic media standard. LANs using Token Ring may slowly garner a greater share of the LAN market, in situations where IBM host computing solutions are the norm. However, expect Ethernet to dominate in institutions with non-IBM mainframes server-based LANs and peer-to-peer networks. NISO and ISO TC 46 will continue to dominate library and information field standardization efforts. However, other organizations such as the Coalition for Networked Information will evolve to play increasingly important roles in standards development, acceptance and implementation.

REFERENCE

1. Abramson, N. M. The ALOHA System, Another Alternative for Computer Communications. In: *AFIPS Conference Proceedings. 1970 Fall Joint Computer Conference 37*: 281-285 (1970).

5

EVALUATION, PROCUREMENT AND OTHER FACTORS AFFECTING THE SHAPING OF YOUR LIBRARY SYSTEM

Life was simple before World War II. After that we had systems.
— Rear Admiral Grace Murray Hopper
in a speech at The Ohio State
University, February 5, 1987

The most damaging phrase in the language is "We've always done it this way!"
—Rear Admiral Grace Murray Hopper
in an interview in *Information Week*, March 9, 1987, p. 52

I. INTRODUCTION

This chapter will discuss some procurement and evaluation factors together with marketplace directions which will undoubtedly influence the future of library systems. A library's procurement decisions are based on an evaluation of a number of vendor-dependent factors but also on some institution-dependent ones, so I want to explore these latter as well. Such an exploration should assist individual readers in assessing their own situations, whether they are adopting the perspective of librarians, systems specialists or line management.

It seems that there is always a case of "fud" (fear, uncertainty and doubt) over much of this, particularly over the more technical things such as the shape of the network, the computing platform, operating systems and standards of one sort or another. Therefore, I will discuss trends or currents to help assist individuals sort out the best selection for the near and longer term future. Since today's software investments will be for the longer term than those made several decades ago, overall system architecture may now play a stronger role in such selection. This is due to the higher cost of software and the much greater functionality of each software release to meet more application demands.

All of us should view computer-assisted processes as an extension of our effectiveness as professionals. It may be necessary to view a functional requirement that is present in a system as beneficial, even if the vendor's implementation of it does not appear well executed or if reaping the most benefit from the function requires us to change our way of doing something. To make a function work well, further modifications to our procedures may even be necessary. This sort of field experience can provide system vendors with valuable feedback for future improvements. Finally, viewing the direction of library automation systems on a broad scale, in the wider context of both your institution's information systems directions and of the library and information science profession as a whole, can make some specific procurement decisions easier than if you were to view prospective systems merely on the microcosmic level of library operational or service needs.

For libraries just getting involved with their first system procurement, the learning curve will be quite different than that of a library that has previously installed one or more systems. It is one thing to begin from scratch on every level, while it is quite another to make a conversion from one automated system to another developer's product, particularly when subsystems or applications are involved. Some factors will differ in their magnitude and complexity with the size of the collection, staff, service locations and such. Practicing "old fashioned common sense" and what other libraries might have done in the same situation can be helpful. However, your situation, while appearing identical, may not be purely so. In that case, you cannot merely duplicate the actions of another library to arrive at a best solution for your particular circumstance.

On a final prefatory note, remember that the most successful libraries, as far as implementing information technology, have both management and staff committed to the effort. A committed management and staff that can use interactive systems to bring about great improvements in library service can do much to engender commitment in the library's clientele and parent institution. I have even seen great commitment on the part of the staff overcome somewhat inept and ineffectual management of the effort, through the staff's taking the initiative to organize its own training or determine other critical factors. Unfortunately, in the highly line structured world of libraries, not always are all the levels of management able to be effective to the desired degree. So, ride with the bumps and preserve your individual commitment, despite the postures of others, and may you eventually succeed.

II. INSTITUTIONAL CONSTRAINTS

One may think that the usual institutional constraint on a library considering a new system is fiscal. However, this constraint, while certainly a factor, particularly in a tightening economy, is usually not the major one. It is true that a library must sell its need to employ computer technology or other related information technologies. Once a library has demonstrated the effectiveness of using new technologies and the institution has given its support, then other constraints will become apparent. The selling of a library auto-mation program has to take into consideration an institution's attitudes and policies, competitive situation, fiscal health, and key personalities—and these key players' hot buttons. An institution's chief information officer (whether or not with that title), together with the institution's operating units that provide central or networked computer support, are key players to bring into support of your library's program. Often priority is given to supporting and servicing a library system in a service center. One of the major constraints that usually develops after some funds have been approved for the library stems from computing directions set for your whole institution, including whether your institution has specific proprietary systems, has adopted an "open system" commitment for new systems, recognizes strengths of the service centers versus library strengths, and has broad system access views. Also, differences between the historical computing background of the institution and the library can provide other constraints. Finally, another possible constraint is the institution's views of interconnectivity and wide-area communications. This involves views of both internal and external access to information systems.

A. Management Information Systems and Computing Directions

Organizations have varied dependencies on computer and information technologies. Enterprise computing in industry, academe and government is now being influenced by the following trends:

A tightened economy, forcing more competitive strategies to increase effectiveness and efficiency of human labor

A longer term investment in software solutions, with the expectation of upgrades, changes and evolution of the software to meet new business needs

A downsizing of computing hardware, with an increase in computing power using distributed computing techniques

An emphasis on UNIX as a common denominator to increase system interconnectivity, employ fifth-generation development tools, increase software life and portability through hardware platform changes

A dependence on client/server application architecture using present and future workstation power, with role negotiation between workstation and its application server module counterpart
An increase in need for "user friendliness" to minimize user training and support, usually through a common graphical user interface (GUI) such as Microsoft Windows, Macintosh, OS/2 Presentation Manager or one of the UNIX GUIs, e.g., Motif
A LAN-based strategy for workstation, server, and host computer connectivity
A multimedia influence through advanced graphics and sound-chip technology.

Since the members within an organization differ in their responsiveness to implementing new, competitive strategies, it is critical to find out who your key employees are, where they stand in the organization, and what is needed to convince them of the soundness of your program. It is critical to develop an approach that will begin to build the library as one of the key information technology players and users for increased organizational effectiveness and competitiveness.

In large institutions information technology strategies may be either centrally or divisionally developed. Sometimes a combination of centrally planned and managed resources is coupled with divisionally organized and managed resources. Sometimes these strategies are deployed depending on the current fads in organizational structure, while in other situations a more reasoned approach is taken. Some institutions believe in employing only proven technologies, while others are willing to be more experimental and even go into some "bleeding edge" or high-risk systems where, if successful, a major competitive edge will be gained. Determining your strategy in planning your library system, taking into account these factors, will help sell your choice of technologies. Meshing the library's planning into the overall technology strategies of the organization may appear to be a difficult task, but it is a realistic approach that can pay big dividends in gaining organizational support. Let us examine these directions and how a library might capitalize on them in its planning.

1. Open Systems Versus Proprietary Platforms

Traditionally, organizations have based their information systems mainly on the computers and associated equipment and operating software supplied by one or possibly several computer manufacturers. In other words, a proprietary operating system such as IBM's MVS, Digital Equipment's VMS or Hewlett-Packard's MPE with the matching hardware formed these computing platforms. In early 1992, close to 90% of the computing systems installed worldwide were on such platforms. However, 12% of today's systems, which is an increase of 50% over the prior five-year period, are UNIX operating system based.

```
Source Node                  Intermediate Node          Destination Node
7 Application Layer <-- Peer-to-Peer Communication --> 7 Application
6 Presentation Layer <-------------------------------> 6 Presentation
5 Session Layer  <-----------------------------------> 5 Session
4 Transport Layer <----------------------------------> 4 Transport
3 Network Layer  <-------> Network Layer  <----------> 3 Network
2 Data Link Layer <------> Data Link Layer  <--------> 2 Data Link
1 Physical Layer  <------> Physical Layer  <---------> 1 Physical
```

Figure 1 OSI Reference Model showing the communication path.

Although the use of proprietary systems will continue into the foreseeable future, it is now far easier for application software developers to create new applications capable of running under several different operating systems. Therefore, new systems that will run on a version of UNIX and employ certain standards common across platforms in what has come to be called the Open Systems Interconnection (OSI) Reference Model approach will become increasingly prevalent. See Figure 1 for a schema of the layers in this model.

Currently, computer-assisted software engineering (CASE) tools on UNIX-based platforms, such as Sun's SPARC system, together with numerous cross-compilers to prepare target code for different proprietary platforms, make this possible. Similarly, writing to a common user interface standard—such as X-Windows in the UNIX world, MS-DOS-based Microsofts Windows or OS/2 Presentation Manager in the Intel microprocessor world—allows a program to be executed on all systems able to run that operating system. Products such as the DesQview-X from Quarterdeck Software allow a user with a non-UNIX system, i.e., an MS-DOS system, to run an X-Window-compliant program on a non-UNIX platform. Similar X-Window clients are available for Windows 3.1. This allows LAN workstations to have application program interface connectivity to UNIX-based applications along with applications that traditionally run under Novell IPX or Netbios environments.

The major host computer manufacturers, while still fighting to maintain markets in their proprietary operating systems, are also adding UNIX-based, open system-compliant products that will allow interconnectivity and preservation of their existing products in a more open system compliant total system architecture. Support for the TCP/IP protocol is an example of this. An increase in intersystem connectivity products assures that users of such popular systems as Digital's VAX series will have the ability to access applications on traditional IBM mainframes running VM or MVS. Key to this is appropriate terminal emulation for IBM 3270 family devices on the VAX and conversely proper Digital Equipment VT-100 family emulation within the IBM product line. All of the major computer equipment manufacturers—among them, IBM, Digital Equipment, Hewlett-Packard, AT&T, Tandem, Sequent, MIPS, Encore and Ultimate—have such interconnective products that claim some ISO OSI Reference Model compliance.

Although the shift to UNIX presently appears somewhat slow, it has been accelerating over the past half decade and will continue to pick up speed as new systems and new applications are developed. Application developers realize that users want to preserve more value in their software in the future. This gradual shift means that inevitably, as present computer lines begin to exhaust their expandability—such as is now the case with DEC's VAX line—some new systems must be designed and manufactured. These new systems need to be brought to delivery stage rather quickly. The widespread adoption of UNIX for supercomputer distributed operating systems has not taken place because UNIX is the best overall operating system but rather because of its incorporation of these good interconnectivity features.

Although there are still several major flavors of UNIX, there is increasing agreement on many features, such as the Berkeley extensions which are now incorporated in most UNIX operating systems. Since UNIX is well developed and supported, with relatively easy portability to a new processor family due to the concentration of processor-specific code in its kernel, its attraction for hardware developers is great. For example, NeXT computers could not have been developed as quickly or with such excellent interconnectivity and such a creative GUI had NeXT not adopted Carnegie Mellon University's MACH re-write of the original UNIX system. NeXT continues to use MACH in its NeXTStep system on the Intel 80xxx platform.

Another attraction of UNIX is its ability to run programs developed in any language; thus, the popular conception that programs must be written in the C language is not true. It is true that various C compilers are a popular development tool under UNIX, but many other languages such as Fortran and Pascal are also used. Recompilation of such programs from other platforms is possible, at least in part depending on the standards used in writing the program, its modularity and its user interface design. Certainly, modular programming techniques and now object-oriented programming using Object C and C++ languages will enhance a developer's ease in creation of multiple platform program versions. Thus, good software engineering practices by developers, adoption of standards and open systems adherence around new hardware platforms will go far in preserving a user's investment in application software.

The trend is toward increasingly OSI Reference Model-compliant systems, with bridges among commonly encountered proprietary operating system platforms. For example, there is no single system that offers a truly portable platform other than the PICK operating system, which can run on some 200 hosts. With PICK able to run as a guest under UNIX on many hardware configurations, the strengths in intersystem connectivity together with excellent database and application development environments are brought to the library's bibliographic applications for such systems. In this situation, both the PICK application and UNIX applications can coexist, running simultaneously in a multiuser, multitasking and multiprogramming mode.

Even Novell, Inc., has announced that it intends to support its IPX protocol on UNIX, incorporate TCP/IP support and generally bring its Advanced Netware LAN operating system into being the major LAN operating system under UNIX, MS-DOS and OS/2. This will not mean that proprietary operating systems will totally disappear; however, they will need to assume some different characteristics, particularly as more and more applications are designed around client/server architecture. By the year 2000, host computers will largely be background processors for large database access services, acting as servers for such networks, while the desktop client system assumes the major application processor role. In this role the workstation will manage all data entry, query formulation, error checking, user interface support, control of interprocess communications and provision of user tutorial and assistance functions. Library systems will take a leading role in this migration, with the most successful vendors demonstrating mature applications using workstation-based architectures compliant with current standards in the areas of open systems and library or bibliographic data. ISO and ANSI are actively developing added standards to facilitate this. These efforts are leading endeavors when compared with other potential industry areas for standards such as banking or retail.

It is critical that the library determine where its institution is heading with respect to its proprietary platforms and its directions in the UNIX/Open System area. If this direction is not advancing as expected, a library should try to see if it might provide the impetus for developing a more forward-looking posture, since library systems are dependent on intersystem connectivity if maximum benefit is to accrue to the institution. For example, suppose that an institution is currently dedicated to either an IBM VM/MVS platform or a Digital Equipment Corp. VAX/VMS platform. Given this constraint, it might seem more difficult or impossible for a library to consider any system not able to run on these platforms. However, this might be a perfect opportunity to effect change. If the library application assessment shows that another vendor's system written for UNIX or that could run as a guest operating system under UNIX would be the preferred system, this would be a good opportunity to prove the benefits of introducing an open system strategy. The library's system is an ideal candidate for such a test and evaluation since the application demands are a combination of complex query processing and real-time demands with connectivity to other applications such as accounting, electronic mail, human resource systems and other internal or external information databases used in research, marketing or product development. Thus, a pilot project using the library's needs for computing support is not only an excellent technical test but should be of manageable magnitude in perhaps all but the very largest libraries.

The operating costs of UNIX-based systems now operating on current generation systems such as those using the MIPS processors are considerably lower than IBM or DEC systems. Thus, convincing a cost-conscious management to undertake a UNIX-based pilot project, which would still offer excellent intersystem connectivity to present applications on the IBM or DEC systems, can be substantiated economically. If a pilot system is installed, it can prove to be the foundation for other new systems or revisions to present systems on the traditional proprietary environment. This would mean a more responsive and less costly information systems program institutionally for the longer term. With proper positioning of the library in the organizational infrastructure, this sort of thing can be—and has been—achieved. Certainly, each case will be different, but some commonalities can provide clues to your organization's real directions. These are:

Administrative history of computing
Staff morale in the MIS department
Reporting line for the chief information officer
Growth and dependence of computing
Necessity for competitive advantage

Your success in sorting out your institution's posture relative to computer and communications technologies and the library's or information center's strategy to mesh its technology implementation will enable you to develop and sell your plan.

2. Service Center Strengths Versus Library Strengths

Service centers provide computing services through central systems, development and maintenance of host software, and a variety of training, network and microcomputer support. Service center strength usually lies in the technical aspects of data processing and information technology. However, library strengths usually lie in the organization and retrieval of information as well as in numerous procedural factors on the application level which software must handle appropriately.

The complexity of present library systems and their interrelationship with other systems in the organization have resulted in a trend in many larger academic and private organizations whereby libraries use their data processing service centers as facilities contractors, particularly when their applications are resident on mainframe or superminicomputer hosts. In this arrangement, the hardware and central site software support is provided for a fee. There also may be a help desk and other user support provided for problem resolution. Where the organization has a systemwide backbone network, this also is maintained by the service center. However, where a library uses a LAN-based library system, it may be more desirable and responsive to have the library do its own network support involving its own servers and workstation portion up to that backbone connection.

In large systems where central computer facilities exist, a division of system responsibilities is one solution to explore. The computer center can provide direct hardware and operating system support with its specialists and facilities, while the library can concern itself with working with the vendor on the application installation itself in concert with a computer center programmer/analyst. The library can also handle its conversion, upgrade scheduling, train staff and do further system planning. However, if a library system has a low support priority in such a center, this will present considerable problems as the library will experience difficulties in installing new versions or modules for its system.

There are relatively few libraries that have on their own staff a well-rounded complement of data-processing professionals who can manage and operate a large computing system and network. Those organizations such as the University of California, with its systemwide MELVYL on-line catalog, are fortunate because they can direct themselves at specialized application areas and yet interact with other institutional computer service centers to codevelop interconnective aspects of systems and do pilot projects of major benefit to the library agenda that still fit into the institution's picture, without having to balance priorities of many differing user departments for personnel resources. They can also develop much greater application expertise regarding the library's systems needs. Such a situation is, in my view, the ideal for many large organizations, particularly those in academic settings. However, given the situations that presently exist in most large institutions, the library staff that can manage and operate a large computing system and network will probably remain an ideal that has little real hope of being widely achieved.

The coming of LAN-based systems may sidestep this situation since the equipment involved does not need special raised-floor, liquid-cooled computer rooms. Local LAN management can be done by staff trained in that function. Having all of the functions associated with the library's system serviced and controlled by the library's management can provide a more responsive and effective information system since the staff's priorities are not diluted by the need to respond to other departments' emergencies and applications deemed to be of higher priority.

By contracting with a parent organization's data processing unit, a library can hope to place its system in a more professional technical management facility. The library helps fund that unit's technical staff and facilities, instead of hiring its own library staff or building its own computer facility. This can be an attractive tradeoff, given that the library has firmly established its priority as relatively high. However, if the library system is considered low priority, then this arrangement will not be a very good one. Sometimes, despite a high priority, this sort of "outsourcing" can be less than ideal if the service center staff is not well managed and inexperienced. Thus, none of these approaches can be universally applied to every library. It is necessary for each library to determine what approach will be in its best interest—economically, politically and operationally.

While library strengths lie in knowing the application area and the needs and expectations of library users, their weak point in many cases is at the technological level. Thus, the management information systems organization in the institution is viewed as the source of such planning expertise and the library manager often is unable to interact at that level either when it comes to technological aspects or the institution's overall business aspects. For this reason, in almost every case, library managers and staff are well advised to gain expertise in information technology and in their organization's overall business needs and forecasts for using information technologies.

If the library finds that its institution's data processing department is relatively weak, with low status and low staff morale, the library could be in a stronger position to assume a leadership role in information technology, assuming that the library manager or key staff are able to demonstrate that they are skilled in this area. Gaining an understanding of the overall organization's need for information technologies and discussing this with key executives could open such a channel.

When assessing a service center's strengths in more detail, there are usually five areas to examine. The first is computer operations, where all daily computing jobs and their support is accomplished. Backups, tape mounts, central printing and job control are the more mundane aspects of operations, while the resolution of sticky system performance problems, system tuning for optimal interactive performance, physical storage organization and other more complex matters provide critical need for system programming specialists. The second area, systems programmers, follows from the above. They are the specialists who provide the necessary support to operations and to application programming through maintenance of the operating system, teleprocessing monitor, compilers and other critical tools used to fine-tune a system and assure its reliable operation. The third area is application programming, where both custom systems and commercially licensed packages are maintained and new systems not obtainable commercially are developed.

Custom applications might be developed by a specific group within applications programming, with or without outside contractor assistance. With flexibility in today's software controlled via parameter tables, an important function of the applications programmer is to work with these tables. The fourth area is networking and communications, which would include assistance with application installation on servers, routing within the network, central address management on the enterprise-wide network and maintenance of all LAN wiring. Finally, user support and training in use of enterprise systems is another to investigate. Although other functions may be incorporated into service centers, these are the key bread-and-butter obligations that need to be carried out satisfactorily. Also, probably within the systems organization will be some sort of microcomputer support either through the user support area, as a separate group, or attached to the group responsible for LANs and communications. However, such microcomputer support units are usually small and spread quite thin in assisting users, setting up new systems or handling malfunctioning equipment problems. For that reason, prudent libraries will plan to develop as much in-house microcomputer and LAN expertise as possible so that first line support will be prompt and oriented to the library's specific needs. These centers can then be relied upon for more serious problem resolution as a backup to the library's staff capabilities.

Lining up your institution's and library's strengths and weaknesses together with your own library's information technology directions will lead to a plan for information technology that meshes these strengths and hopefully works around the weaker areas by letting the library assume some leadership where voids may exist. Knowing what sorts of buttons to push and sound bites to use, together with appropriate presentation or proposal skills, can help put your action plan into operation. Although some excellent advice can be gained through various management texts, librarians need to develop their own repertoire of techniques to plan and implement systems in their own organization. This is an area where sometimes an independent consultant can help to depoliticize plans and proposals, give them technical credibility and relate them into the enterprise-wide scheme of priorities.

3. Access Issues

Since the earliest of times, access to library collections has been an issue with which librarians and curators have dealt. Prior to the twentieth century, and still later in some countries, access to books was a privilege of the nobility, rich merchant class or clergy. Today, librarians consider wide access necessary a factor in our culture as is our public educational system. Five hundred years ago it was sufficient to record a book by its author's name and possibly some sort of accession number and then place this information in an accessions book. Librarians and curators of the time were intimately familiar with their stock and users could approach these repositories only through this intermediary. While using the skills of curators is still key to truly effective utilization of scholarly collections, with the size and proliferation of scholarly work, it would be impossible for these intermediaries to provide quality service without more comprehensive and detailed indexing tools.

Presently, there is no less need for librarians' ability to facilitate access to collections. In fact, with society's increasing demand for remote access to services, i.e. electronic communications-based remote delivery, libraries have no choice but to use whatever technologies will enable delivery of their services without the user having to physically come to the library building. Location of materials and their availability is the first step in facilitating ease of use. Moreover, even though library user demand is increasing, the funding for libraries has not kept pace to increase staff or add new branch locations. Consequently, libraries are also faced with the dilemma of shrinking resources, yet expanding demand. Proper employment of information technology will ease this situation so that the library services by telephone, fax, and computer access can extend service to those users who prefer to use these access modes. In many private sector libraries, while staff resources have been curtailed, substitution of these electronic information approaches has been supported through increased equipment and telecommunications funding. However, this has not happened to the same degree in public sector libraries.

Users of all types of libraries are increasingly expecting to be able to secure document delivery independent of the document's location. The demand for these custom services is costly and library users who can pay for them directly are in the "information rich" sector. Corporate information centers, information brokers and those with sponsored research grants in academe are in this sector. Libraries and information centers can pass their costs on to these users such as has been the case with photocopy. Some organizations are recognizing that there should be an organization-wide funding of these document delivery services, at least for book materials, while article retrieval should continue to exact photocopying charges. The researcher's effectiveness is the tradeoff for such central support. But, what of that sector we may call the "information poor"? These are the myriad citizens who must use public libraries, who do not have access to computers and fax and who may have special access needs because of their location, age, physical health, employment or other circumstances.

The tradition of the Carnegie Free Library, where local taxes support community library services, is being severely taxed today. Where basic library services meant access to books, magazines and newspapers at the turn of the century, now basic access must extend to many new formats for published work and new access tools, many of which are useable or available only in either some computer-assisted form on a local workstation, or provided on some remotely accessible information provider's system. Where does a library draw the line in determining just what services are "free versus fee"? Our intention is not to answer this here but merely to point out that good interlibrary lending, facilitated through resource sharing agreements and library consortia, is essential for improving remote access to items and is now considered to be a basic cornerstone to library services. Therefore, no library can continue to operate without investing in computer-based and communications-oriented services and products. Remote access to the library's union catalog is one of the major selling points to increase library usage. Only through such demonstration of increased usage does the library have hope of proving its increasing effectiveness and worthiness to get its fair share of the institution's fiscal pie.

Currently, some individuals can be characterized as "information poor" not because they lack the money to pay for customized information services, but rather because they lack the education necessary to access computer-assisted forms of information—that is, via a personal computer, modem and software—to allow them to dial into their local library or other free or fee-based services. For example, many university and college computer centers will allow non-students in their communities to open up electronic mail or accounts limited to using Internet access facilities for a very low annual charge, i.e., under $100. With the proper education in basic personal computing and use of Telnet and FTP software, these users could have access to research library catalogs worldwide as well as software and other data repositories such as the Simtel mirror site archives. Public libraries and special libraries in the private sector are now rapidly increasing their access across the Internet. With further federal legislation, this network should grow into a state-of-the-art knowledge carrier which will become basic to ultimately providing information access to a large sector of the current "information poor" group. With information access techniques becoming established in grade school curricula, access to the "information superhighway" will ultimately be as ubiquitous as using the telephone—just taken for granted, no matter where one happens to be at the moment.

Perhaps the most interesting access development to library and other information collections is the emergence of citizen-governed and -operated public computing facilities. The National Public Telecomputing Network and its affiliates, such as the Heartland FreeNet, Cleveland FreeNet, Peoria FreeNet, and Tri-State Online (Cincinnati) FreeNet, offer as one of their services gateway access to both local library online catalogs and also some remote catalogs through Internet connections. These FreeNets have modest annual membership fees but these are not usually a requirement of gaining some level of access. Much as individuals who listen to a National Public Radio affiliate and really appreciate the educational radio service will feel a conscientious obligation to become a member at the appropriate rate, users will join their local FreeNet if the membership costs are kept low, i.e., $25-50 per year—roughly the same as public radio memberships. The FreeNets are supported by grants, donations and these modest user memberships. In return for membership, the member has voting privileges. Volunteers from many community sectors, together with cooperation from many community-based organizations, become the major information providers on the FreeNet. With terminals provided in many public locations such as libraries, shopping malls or supermarkets, the potential for the FreeNet in the United States is as great as the Minitel-based services have become in France. With the development of videotex services, such as U.S. West's Community Link, there could be an effective cooperative approach to information provision in a new public setting. That setting will ultimately be to the beginning of the 21st century what the concept of the Carnegie Free Library was to the beginning of the 20th century. We can all make this happen by actively supporting FreeNet development in our local communities.

If one really thinks for a moment, it is possible to see that no select group of library users should be left out of the loop of remote access. Even corporate special libraries, where many collections might contain proprietary or confidential material, should be able to offer remote access services to their employees, governed by a properly secured database and user account system on their computers. These employees should be able to order items from the library from their desks or travel location via their workstation or notebook computer. They should be able to use electronic mail, search corporate collections, and order items for delivery or purchase. Therefore, even in a small special library where an MS-DOS- or Macintosh-based library system might be employed, such a single-user-type system might initially suffice as a tool for the librarian to operate the library. But eventually the objective should be to have the library's database accessible via the corporate network, so that any employee can search and request materials remotely and use the electronic mail facilities of the network to request items or answer questions. This should be as important in a small—30-100 person—company as in a setting of several hundred to several thousand employees. This degree of access should be a goal for these systems in the near-term future.

Therefore, in considering access issues, it is clear that remote access is highly desirable for all online catalogs, independent of their size. It is also clear that it is also more critical to try to expand access to a clientele that is ever more comfortable with computer access via personal computers, having begun using such devices in their early school years. Remote access together with interconnectivity will continue to increase, with smaller libraries able to receive benefits now only enjoyed by the large research libraries with Internet connections. User education is also a key ingredient to diminishing numbers of users who now fall into the "information poor" sector.

4. *Historical Computing Background in the Institution*

Some organizations have strong traditions of highly centralized management and planning for information systems, while others have left to lower levels of management the task of dealing with information technology, such as at the division or plant level or collegiate level in a large university. Often, one encounters a centralized management and planning strategy, with subsidiary service centers providing actual end-user services. These usually include managing host computers, voice and data communications, and microcomputer/ workstation support. Now that more computing power is at the desktop than was available from the mainframes and minicomputers of the seventies and eighties, it is more critical than ever to develop institution-wide strategies to implementing enterprise-wide applications using the new tools. These new tools are open systems using standards for data and interprocess communications that will preserve software investment as newer more powerful hardware becomes available. Development tools, such as computer-aided software engineering, cross-compilers and workgroup software products such as Lotus NOTES, are typically found on these systems today. The use of a client/server architecture design in new applications is the targeted direction for virtually every commercial software developer. Applications on Sun Computers and other UNIX and Microsoft Windows systems already demonstrate this approach and its effectiveness in improving end-user computing satisfaction.

Although in 1992 some 88% of computing still employed proprietary operating systems platforms, there is a growing trend toward UNIX coupled with the concept of more open application system architectures that can be independent of hardware. While UNIX is not the ideal operating system, its architecture makes it possible for it to be ported to a new hardware environment more quickly than developing a new proprietary system possibly could. Also, the variances of UNIX are being brought under increasing control, so that there is an improved degree of compatibility among the various versions. However, it still is necessary to recompile applications under these variant UNIX versions.

A decade ago it was a relatively safe course for an information systems organization to choose a major vendor by examining where it wanted to spend its dollars, since prepackaged software was only just emerging as a constraint on of what computer environment would be necessary. Thus choosing one of the largest manufacturers such as IBM or Digital Equipment was relatively safe as some industry-specific software could be found on these platforms, while the rest, in any case, would require development or conversion from a previous system. Today, in typical enterprise computing, over 50% of the software currently running is commercially written. In some vertical markets this is even higher. Choosing a platform becomes increasingly important to preserve one's investment in software as the commercial developer is moving largely to UNIX for new applications or rewrites of older applications. This serves the developer, too, since now the developer gains a wider client base while being able to port the product to many different hardware platforms. This further increases the software's market potential. Also, downsizing of central computing, which increases reliance on networked computing solutions, is the current trend. Increasingly library turnkey systems vendors are also moving toward UNIX- and LAN-based systems solutions and away from single proprietary platforms requiring one vendor's equipment and operating system. The very large library system will be the last one to migrate away from proprietary operating systems as the development of systems like the NOTIS Horizon product is still in the early stages. This system is hosted on IBM RISC/6000 systems under AIX. Moreover, as these proprietary systems become POSIX compliant, these software investments can be preserved further.

Since end-user applications development in the commercial sector has not been a strong suit of the actual computer manufacturers, it is commercial developers or groups that have grown out of individual library institutions that are the key software providers to the library and information center today. Your institution may have adhered to developing its computer capability by using a single-vendor approach such as adoption of IBM's Systems Application Architecture. However, even IBM has increasingly seen that it cannot dominate the standards world and must support more open connections to its systems, such as introducing TCP/IP support in its products. The IBM user community had wanted this support for several years before IBM saw fit to respond here in the United States with these capabilities. Now, a strong commercial software development base exists, and newer organizations will adopt these fresh strategies to preserve their software investment and lower their hardware and operating costs. Older organizations will also be forced to do this also to preserve their competitiveness.

You will need to determine your enterprise-wide strategies for multi-vendor platform support and the move to open systems concepts, particularly as is meant by adopting UNIX and some of its family of computing standards. You need to find out if your information systems organization continually experiments and tests new computing products and is involved with new applications on UNIX-based systems. All of this information will stand you in good stead to justify your choice in a library system. You will weigh software functionality, user access, connectivity issues, longer term investment, vendor enhancement ease, vendor development progress and maximization of your software dollar and conversion investment. The factors described by the following statements can constrain your selection, and you need to develop ways to deal with them if they are present in your organization:

My organization only runs only IBM mainframes, so I must find software that runs on that platform.

My organization has no LANs and is not planning any, so I have to use either a single-user microcomputer or my organization's mainframe, neither of which is appropriate.

My organization uses only MS-DOS- (or Macintosh-) based microcomputers and specific LAN manager software, but my preferred solution is a UNIX-based, small multiuser system that can be run from a UNIX server with TCP/IP connectivity to other systems.

My organization uses only MS-DOS–based microcomputers, but my preferred library automation solution runs on a Macintosh and our LAN has no such provision.

The above situational list could be extended to encompass other, more constrained views that are often encountered by librarians from their information systems organizations. These constraints are somewhat artificially imposed constraints since there are technologies to deal with all of these situations. Yet, information systems managers believe that these constraints produce economic benefit and efficiency, without usually considering that employee effectiveness is the real issue that must be addressed. If effectiveness is enhanced, then the competitive posture of the organization is enhanced. Ultimately, this is what builds long-term productivity growth.

The marketplace alternatives for library automation range from microcomputers to mainframes, including employment of local area networks. All major functions in these systems, except generation of some printed products, are interactive and performed in either real time or simulated real time. Not only must the system be appropriate to the library's needs, but the functionality of software, its ease of use and operation, installation support and training, database conversion and continuing operating costs must be considered. Also, the vendor's record of enhancement, problem resolution, and announced future directions provide an indication of the vendor's long-term position in the market.

Since the needs of a library's system encompass many characteristics common to other business systems, a new library system provides an excellent chance for employing a workgroup solution approach that can be a model for other parts of the enterprise if none of the newer LAN- or UNIX-based solutions have been installed. The required external connectivity makes such a system an excellent candidate for connectivity prototyping, using UNIX and TCP/IP platforms with Internet connections. Since a library's function is supportive to a wide range of disciplined inquiry, private sector libraries have excellent justification for gaining access to the Internet and other external networked information services. Corporate librarians can explore these possibilities by joining their local UNIX users' group, making contacts with university and college computer organizations and exploring their local connection costs to their NSFnet participating state or regional network.

In conclusion, while the historical and present computing background will flavor the possibilities for library automation directions, the librarian must view these factors as enabling the library to make its best case for what it feels will be the best longer term solution. The better this approach can be tied to a prudent use of new-generation software and hardware that relates to the present organizational directions or seeks to remedy deficiencies in that direction, the more justifiable will be this plan. Certainly, I am not suggesting that organizational politics and the interests of key executives will not color the acceptance of the library's plan. But, such critical decisions as systems investments—in any organization that considers itself to be well managed and responsible to its stockholders or customers—need to be based on the concept that management wants to improve the effectiveness of its systems as a means to remaining viable as a business. Melding these considerations together with a knowledge of how to make the organization's political climate supportive of the library's plan are the ultimate goal that the librarian will have to achieve. In adopting technology, there are leaders and trend setters—the early adopters. Then there are the majority of libraries, which begin using the technology once the early adopters have reported positively to the profession. Finally there are some organizations that seem to lag quite far behind in their adoption of newer technologies. One must remember that if it were not for these early adopters, many of the advances we enjoy today would not have made it to commercial success. Your success will depend, too, on your ability to know when to be an early adopter and when to run with the pack. But in no case does one want to be in the third group, since this group will always experience more service difficulties than the first two.

5. Historical Computing Background in the Library

It has been estimated in the literature that some 8700 libraries have installed minicomputer based automated library systems in the United States. Estimates for microcomputer-based systems would probably add over 40,000 software packages. Worldwide, the figure is probably at least double that number. The library automation market is viewed by the industry as worldwide and increasingly multilingual. With over 14,000 libraries now having access to OCLC, it might be expected that in the United States there are hardly any libraries without at least one terminal or microcomputer. The fact remains that in the United States there are over 20,000 school libraries, over 4,000 college libraries and many thousands of public libraries. Therefore, the potential market for library systems in medium- and smaller-size libraries is really quite great, even if the very largest research libraries and consortia have been using automated systems for some years.

Only several hundred libraries were active in developing automated software applications in the 1960's when there was a surge of activity brought about through research grants and the increasingly widespread availability of punched-card equipment and the IBM 1401 stored-program computer. Ralph Parker, University Librarian at the University of Missouri, was believed to be the first librarian to employ punched-card technology in developing a circulation system in 1936. While a few pioneering librarians dabbled and experimented in the punched-card/paper tape medium of the day, the IBM 1401 in the 1960's, with its relatively common availability, made more serious systems possible. It took another decade before investors would believe that a market for automated library systems for operating libraries existed. With the advent of the early minicomputers, it became possible for the first time to commercially market systems to meet real library problems. The earliest group of librarians involved with library automation can look back on 25-30 years of experience, having gone through various generations and much standards development. Those whose background began with the early commercial systems will have some 20 years of experience, probably with two or three systems changes and as many different vendors. The next generation of librarians entered the field at the beginning of the early 1980's when there was some relative maturity of application development in more integrated and multifunctional systems, which were still largely minicomputer or mainframe based. The newest librarians have grown up with the microcomputer, local area networks and an even more mature local systems able to remotely access a number of services from other providers or on CD-ROM, or locally mounted as databases on the library's own system. Thus, a library staff's experiences will range from the early pioneer state to the very latest systems now being introduced.

The deeper one's background and experience with information technologies, the more understanding one can have of the positive and negative effects of coping with evolving systems and the changes that they necessitate. We must get used to the fact that planning, systems management, conversion problems and the like are going to be a continuing part of library activity. Thus we must try to be as effective at these as possible. Experience, both bad and good, can assist in providing some foundation for our systems efforts. However, this cannot substitute for building effective overall library management and staff involvement and commitment. All of the parties to the process must feel that they have a stake in the outcome if it is to be successful. Sometimes, there are impediments that must be overcome, and here is where experienced staff have the edge over less experienced individuals.

One of the most effective learning strategies in acquiring information technology is to put one's basic technological knowledge to use by actually implementing a project. Each new situation is then presented as a puzzle to be solved in the context of previous experience and knowledge. These solutions compound to form the spectrum of an individual's total experience and greater expertise, which adds value to the organization—but only if the organization properly utilizes this knowledge. Unfortunately, one of the most glaring failures in our libraries today is the inability of managers to effectively use the skills and experience of their employees. In installing an automated system, this problem comes to light more times than not.

The effective library manager able to successfully introduce a well thought out use of information systems technology will need to recognize the strengths as well as any weaknesses in her or his staff. The manager must take steps to remedy any shortcomings, especially poor morale or deficient knowledge. One effective way to do this is to arrange staff visits to nearby libraries where successful systems have been installed, particularly libraries using systems that are under consideration for one's own library. Another remedy is an investment in short courses on communications, local area networks, automated library systems, database services or other timely topics. It may be necessary to make an investment in staff time or appropriate to bring in outsiders to give seminars on site to the staff. The development of good diagnostic and troubleshooting skills can be fostered and will do much to assist in problem isolation and resolution once various equipment and software are installed.

The staff of smaller libraries might be more dependent on the parent organization's data processing support personnel, while in larger libraries the library's own personnel might be expected to take care of in-library systems such as LANs, workstations, and public-use microcomputers or terminals. Any workgroup using microcomputers should be able to accurately diagnose and install most add-on devices and manage its portion of a LAN, including the database server. Larger libraries need a staff complement whose special mission is to support the implementation and operation of information technologies. These first-line support groups depend on institutional level networking and computing groups for their backup and for more specialized situations. Even if organization service centers provide contract operation and support of a host-based automated system, it is still the library's responsibility to manage system upgrade priorities, additions of further software and databases, gateway access to other service providers, ongoing retrospective conversion and other decisions and planning for future systems. Thus, the library needs someone who can act as its own chief information officer, with some full- or part-time staff who can assist with these tasks.

It might be argued that under ideal conditions, the best strategy for a library would be merely to contract out for daily operational support for technology-based solutions, with the need for a only library manager to monitor and arrange for these contracted services. However, with that scenario, the library staff, who should be effective users and planners for information technologies, would never develop the necessary expertise nor real stakeholder positions in using the technology or having a voice in its future direction. A more effective and beneficial technology management strategy uses the capabilities within the library staff itself to the fullest, seeking out contractual arrangements only for those skills lacking in house.

For example, in a large library system, it may be determined that a facilities contract with the campus data center for actually operating the library's central site equipment might be the best solution, since the computer facility is present, the hardware may be already present or could be properly housed there, and the necessary operations and backup expertise are there. However, the library should assume full responsibility for setting priorities in operations, training its own staff to use the system, handing its conversion to the various subsystems and specific applications, and obtaining any needed in-library equipment. Depending on the size of the operation, it may be necessary for the library to set up one or more full-time positions responsible for working with their automated systems. It might be possible to float staff in and out of some specific assignments, such as training other staff when enhancements or a new version of the software are to be installed.

It would be easier if there were one prescribed way to manage information technologies in all libraries. However, that is not the case. I have seen situations where management of the automated systems effort was poorly structured, weak or ineffectual. Under those conditions, one would expect that a system implementation could not be successful. However, I have seen such situations nevertheless become highly successful because of strong staff commitment as stakeholders. The staff decided to do whatever it took to bring the system into operation as smoothly as possible despite management uncertainties and ineptitudes. In the process, the staff built a good base of experience. Conversely, I have seen how libraries with complete and talented systems staff in in-house information systems groups were not able to gain staff trust and confidence or build stakeholder commitment. This resulted in less effective implementation of the systems.

In my view, every library must have at least one individual who is committed to gaining and using information technology experiences—someone must shoulder the responsibility of chief information officer for the library. It might be the head of the library, another administrator, or a staff member whose position would be designed to include these responsibilities. This individual should be someone in whom staff and library management has confidence and she or he should be an integral part of the library's management group. An appropriate organizational framework must be provided for that individual and any support staff hired. This framework must permit effective communication for handling both present information technologies and for gaining approval for implementing new technologies and systems. Without such an institutional commitment to a library's future, it is difficult to assure a library's success at introducing, using and maintaining new technologies.

Let me present yet another example. Many libraries now employ numerous workstations for access to CD-ROM databases. Usually the library starts out with one or two individual microcomputers, each having a CD-ROM drive attached. Someone has to be responsible for installing each new version of the search software for each CD-ROM title received. And someone has to take responsibility for determining why something is not working, whom to call if a software or hardware problem cannot be corrected by routine troubleshooting, and the like. As the demand for CD-ROM services grows, the library turns to networking technology to increase the number of workstations per user and the ability for more than one user to access each CD-ROM title. This adds a further degree of complexity to the support needed. Even if the network is a relatively simple peer-to-peer type, with Lantastic as opposed to a server-based network using Novell's Advanced Netware, the need for knowledgeable support staff becomes even more critical as the complexity curve goes up. If the present staff finds it difficult enough to deal with several stand-alone CD-ROM stations, a more complex situation may bring total inability to cope if a problem develops and the necessary technical expertise is not present. If someone on staff can accept the responsibility of being trained to administer the LAN and can do an acceptable job, the move to that technology is more likely to work out well. If not—and if the necessary expertise cannot be brought in from the outside—then this sort of system will have considerable trouble with reliable operation and will more likely be deemed an ill-advised experiment.

To conclude, the track record of information technologies being evaluated should help a library determine just how rapidly and along what path to make its present and near-term commitments. To draw a parallel, even though a world-class athlete has the ultimate goal of winning a gold medal in the Olympics, there are many intermediate goals for the athlete to set and achieve leading up to that final goal. In setting high goals for your library's technology program, recognize that there are many intermediate and much less dramatic goals that need to be achieved first. The highest goal may be beyond achievement, but its mere presence presses one to strive for more and more success.

B. Interconnectivity and Wide-Area Communications

The library's catalog and other databases used for access to published or locally available information sources, together with many of the administrative functions performed by library systems, can no longer be viewed in isolation from other information systems in an organization. This means that interconnectivity to other systems and applications is rapidly becoming the norm instead of merely an advanced research curiosity. The interconnectivity and interchange of data may be purely local within the institution or may involve external connections to library suppliers, bibliographic utilities, consortia systems, and private database suppliers. They may even involve communications among libraries in a metropolitan, statewide or regional area. On whatever level—be it a private network, the Internet, or an X.25 packet-based network—support for such protocols as IEEE 802.3, the Ethernet LAN standard, and for TCP/IP are critical for achieving this physical interconnectivity. The NISO Z39.50 Common Command Language standard and its adoption by library software suppliers for their search engines has made possible a high degree of user effectiveness in accessing systems based on hardware and software other than that employed in one's own local library. Other NISO and ISO standards are defining various protocols for intersystem connectivity. Novell Netware's IPX protocol is the major LAN protocol in use today. Novell Netware using TCP/IP is a recently introduced product that should have appeal in the larger LAN if its bugs can be resolved satisfactorily.

1. Internal Institutional Access

In the mid-to-late 1980's, access to interactive library systems was provided mainly within the library or its own institution, sometimes with some dial-in off-site access allowed. Links from the library's automated system to institutional systems were somewhat primitive, if they existed at all. For example, a college's student enrollment database or its employee payroll database contain most of the requisite information for a college library's borrowers' file for circulation. Usually, the common practice would have been to extract the needed data periodically and then reload this data into the library system's borrowers' file as it had been defined. While such a practice certainly is still encountered, a better approach would be to have the library's system access institutional file only for those data elements not maintained in the library's own borrowers' file with its item links for each circulation transaction. A library system using a modern database management system (DBMS), particularly one supporting structured query language (SQL), could make this link to an SQL driven institutional database. The need for data duplication is reduced, while data currency is enhanced across all systems requiring access to the same data. Similar examples can be drawn from acquisitions, budgeting/ accounting and other functions.

The key to future viability of present library systems is how well their present subsystems are integrated, together with how far they have supported connectivity to other applications likely to be encountered in the library's parent organization.

Another side to internal access is that of the library user and library staff. Library users should be able to access their own library's databases and services via whatever terminal, microcomputer or workstation is installed at their office, laboratory, dormitory or home. Consequently, access via an organization's LAN or some dedicated computer access network, while now the norm, must also include a facility to dial into the system, since many users do work at home or use other computer systems where modem access is the best way to connect to a remote system. Therefore, when acquiring a microcomputer-based library system, one should verify that the system is upgradeable as to its license or version to support access on a LAN and dial-in access via an asynchronous LAN gateway, preferably for an appropriate number of simultaneous users. A LAN equipped with an asynchronous gateway allows users with accounts on the LAN to have dial-in access in addition to their on-site workstation. One should note that even a one-person library staff needs more than a single MS-DOS microcomputer, since the librarian may be doing a task on that system while a user in the library or a remote user wants to search the catalog. Therefore, a small LAN in this situation would also be in order or a UNIX-based multiuser system able to operate on a low-cost microcomputer such as an Intel 80486–based system. Unfortunately, the amount of library staff access, even in a small library, cannot be determined merely through a staff head count or formula for shared access.

For TCP/IP protocol systems, it may be preferable to provide institutional access to systems using an X.400 user account validation and the serial line interface protocol (SLIP), which emulates an Ethernet connection over a modem link. The same client software for use of various Internet resources can be operated from both Macintosh and MS-DOS/Windows systems. The Windows implementation requires running a Windows socket and Windows packet driver.

In libraries with a larger staff, while some access sharing of terminals or microcomputers may work out, the potential of microcomputers is maximized only when they are convenient, close at hand and equipped with software that provides the necessary tasks with some ease of use. That is the reason microcomputers are called personal computers. Users who use their microcomputers more frequently will become more proficient at using them as well, so it is in the interest of the library to make sure that all staff who need to use the automated library system have convenient access via an appropriate device in an appropriate work location.

While reference staff members may have access to their library system at public service areas, it is equally important that they have access at their office location since they will have to use electronic mail and will also need to search various databases in order to answer in-depth questions or telephone inquiries directed to them. If they are not initially provided with this access at their office desks it will not be long before they begin requesting such access, so it is best to figure on this in planning for the new system. In fact, the only reasonable way to begin staff access planning is first to assume that all library staff members need system access, at least for electronic mail, from their office and from any public service desk locations they routinely use. Then, by examining where and how specific staff will utilize automated systems facilities, one may be able to work out any acceptable sharing arrangements. Also, one can determine what sort of microcomputer or terminal and printer would be best for each location, depending on whether the individual working there is expected to perform other functions best done with microcomputer software typically used in business today or merely needs access to the functions supported on the host system.

Various authors have examined the question of how many library terminals are needed for patron access to a library's online catalog and other databases. Definitive catalog access studies at OCLC resulted in a number of published reports. While some formulas were applied, virtually all large library systems were initially installed with the number of terminals usually based on some count of the average and peak number of in-library catalog users. The libraries then discovered if there were sufficient terminals by watching how many people were waiting for a terminal or by receiving user requests for a terminal in a certain location, convenient to some stack area or collection shelving area. Some counts of users in the library can help determine a starting number of terminals. In my opinion, no library system should require users to wait for more than one user to finish a search in order for a terminal to become available. Unlike a supermarket, where optimal queuing is usually deemed to be not more than four customers waiting at any checkout station, a visit to the library may be a more optional one in many cases. For that reason, we should allow for less queuing in the case of catalog searches. Initial planning for the system should figure that within its initial year a complement of terminals will be added—possibly up to double the starting number.

While a formula can be applied to this aspect of library system planning, it may be just as productive and a lot less work in the end merely to examine usage patterns of your present microfilm or card catalog or automated system to determine a realistic minimum for your public usage workstations, with a possible doubling within a year. Certainly, if new branches or locations are in the planning stage these will also need to be included. For some libraries with remote access, it might be expected that most growth would come in that type of access and not necessarily within the library itself. I would expect this in the case of private special libraries serving a large and worldwide corporate clientele. Finally, it is best to view internal access rather broadly from both the staff and user perspectives. It is also desirable to gain an understanding of possible application level access links desirable for your library and organization, given its management information systems situation.

2. *External Institutional Access*

With the 1990's, there has been incredible growth in research library catalogs accessible via the Internet. Previously, there were widely accessed private network systems, such as the libraries of Bell Laboratories and IBM Corp. However, with increased need and interdependence on resource sharing among libraries, new avenues for determining locations and a specific item's availability are needed. Therefore, it is not unlikely that even relatively private libraries will need to permit some degree of external access to their non-proprietary or non-security classified collections. More and more organizations will be attempting to gain Internet access or provide some sort of gateway access via such subscription services as America Online, Compu-Serve or Community Link. It would be wise for librarians to examine the potential for being service providers via their library systems to such gateway services.

III. REQUEST FOR PROPOSAL

Readers may feel that this section should deal mainly with the creation and dissemination of the library system request for proposal (RFP). In my view, there are several good texts that quite nicely fill this order. (1,2,3) Also, the dangers or pitfalls to an RFP have been well stated by three noted library automation consultants. (4) They point out how wish-list specifications can be misleading as vendors do not gain a clear understanding of the mandatory features the library requires. One need not use only the RFP, as sometimes a request for information (RFI) or for quote (RFQ) is sufficient to select a system. These other requests stress the need to involve vendors early on, well before issuing any formal request.

The library also needs to see the perspective of the vendor in the process. While a vendor who wants to stay in business has to have as a goal the highest possible level of customer satisfaction, the vendor has only a limited amount of resources to allocate to gaining new customers and still support existing installed sites. Therefore, vendors will examine RFPs and will not respond to RFPs obviously based on a competing system, unduly complex or lengthy RFPs or ones that contain unreasonable performance requirements. If the vendor cannot meet the required features or if the RFP asks for hardware proposals and the vendor provides only software, the vendor is unlikely to respond.

Libraries that presently have automated systems have shared their procurement documents upon request with many sister libraries. Therefore, there are many procurement documents that can be obtained and judged on their respective merits for providing guidance in creating your own RFP, RFI or RFQ. For these reasons, I am not going to focus here on the details of every sort of procurement package. Rather, I want to offer some plain, easily understood advice that will allow you to develop your procurement package within your institutional setting using the above resources:

Consult your purchasing department for its requirements, which must be addressed in any procurement

Describe your library's service points, staff, operational volume, in-library and external access provisions, and holdings so as to provide some system sizing information

In plain language, explain just what operations in the library are to be automated, your source of cataloging records, your authority control situation and any other information about your present record base, machine readable or not

Give some indication of expected system growth in the coming 3–5-year period, such as items cataloged, circulated or ordered

Specify any standards that are mandatory for the vendor to incorporate such as the ANSI Z39 family or US MARC

Define any other services expected from the vendor beside the software and/or hardware, e.g., retrospective conversion, staff training, documentation, bar-coded labels, migration assistance from present system to the vendor's

Explain how the vendor should quote the system price, e.g., software, hardware or added services broken down into components

Provide a brief view of near and longer term system enhancements that your library might want to consider in its future planning, e.g., Internet connectivity, mounting external databases of several types and using electronic data interchange with library suppliers.

To this last point, vendors usually respond with lists of planned enhancements. You can readily see if any of your future views coincide with those on a vendor's list, as these lists are usually the product of input from their existing customer base or to meet some competing vendor's features.

A relatively short and concise procurement document sent to a selected group of likely vendors whose products have received preliminary examination in light of any institutional constraints will result in a well-handled procurement. Both the vendor and library will develop a better working relationship as a result. Investigation of such vendor qualifications as fiscal health, staff size, customer list, time in the market and record of customer service will sort out the viable companies, whether they are selling host-based or microcomputer-based products. The idea of a procurement is to acquire a suitable system that can be used over a relatively long term—at least five years—and during which you will be able to find a resolution to any problems that occur. Choosing a vendor carefully helps maximize the probability that the vendor will make enhancements that the library desires and that will go hand in hand with the vendor's desire to remain a market force in the future. After all, isn't that what selection of a library system is really all about?

IV. SYSTEM MARKETPLACE AND SYSTEM PLATFORMS

In recent years there have been dramatic changes in the system marketplace, with declining hardware costs improving the price/performance ratio every few months for microcomputers and every six months or so for larger systems.

Software costs have experienced inflation, but increased development efforts have resulted in greater software capability and complexity. Thus, the total system cost of hardware and software has remained somewhat stable for the last couple of years, while the dollar buys more powerful hardware. System platforms have moved from the traditional mainframe or superminicomputer to lower end minicomputers, workstations and personal computers, including LAN support for a number of packages. In other words, while several years ago a library would have been looking at a minimum of $100,000 for a minicomputer-based system, such a system might now involve a LAN license or single user license fee and whatever the microcomputer and peripheral equipment would cost, i.e., probably well under $10,000. One can easily have this much invested in a desktop publishing system if one configures a Macintosh Quadra, laser printer and Aldus Pagemaker. The following marketplace considerations will also assist your planning efforts.

A. Marketplace Directions—Open Systems

Although there is still a strong allegiance to computer systems using proprietary operating systems, e.g., IBM's MVS/XA or VM, DEC's VAX/VMS or Tandem Computer's Guardian, it is clear that the open system market is growing. Today, the term "open system" is coming to mean really a system using the UNIX operating system, although proprietary systems vendors like IBM are putting out products designed to make their proprietary operating systems more "open." An example of that is IBM's recently announced U.S. support for the TCP/IP protocols which it has supported in Europe for several years. In hardware, the trend is toward using reduced instruction set computing (RISC) hardware architectures. Currently, manufacturers of such hardware have chosen to implement UNIX, since this is relatively easier than designing a new proprietary operating system for the new hardware. Complex instruction set computing hardware is on the way out. DEC announced several years ago that it had topped out on its VAX series systems and was developing new systems as VAX replacements. I would bet that these new systems will use RISC on their new Alpha chip and provide some migration for software from the VAX/VMS over to the new system and that these new systems will be UNIX based. It should be noted that Alpha runs Windows NT from Microsoft, so that is another future library system platform. In another three years about 30% of the multiuser computer marketplace should be UNIX based. With the aging base of proprietary systems being replaced by new generation systems, probably only a few major vendors in the next decade will remain as suppliers of proprietary operating systems and the hardware needed to run those systems.

I believe that the move to open systems would be further accelerated if there were not some hindering factors still plaguing the UNIX marketplace.

First, U.S. and international standards bodies still need to refine system service definition standards. There is still divergence of opinion over this among key UNIX system suppliers. Second, while UNIX support remains the principal market requirement for the label "open system," the near-term success of open systems is closely related to acceptance of UNIX workstations as substitutes for high-end personal computers. Thus, workstation manufacturers have been introducing low-end products with that magic $5000 price tag, instead of the typical five-figure amounts usually encountered. Their hope is that their lower priced products will compete with high-end personal computers based on the Intel 80486DX2/66 and the Pentium systems. Market fragmentation and disagreement over some needed standards are the current problems facing UNIX. The ultimate goal of open systems is the protection of software investment, since the software will be portable at the binary level once it is recompiled on the target system. With hardware improving at such a rate, we will see quite a large used RISC system market open up since typically these systems will be replaced by more powerful ones every 3-4 years instead of the 5-7 years now seen in host computing platforms. Despite these factors, DataPro Information Services Group has forecast a $56 billion UNIX market for 1995.

One other interesting factor will be the impact of the IEEE's standardization effort, called POSIX. Instead of merely providing some standards for UNIX, POSIX resulted in a whole new operating system specification. Some major vendors such as DEC, Unysis and Tandem have promised to support development of POSIX. Just when such a new "open system" would actually be available is anyone's guess. Meanwhile, even if POSIX systems are created in the next five years, I am willing to bet that the migration to this will be one of the matters addressed and it will be migration from UNIX to POSIX.

Meanwhile, software development is moving in two directions simultaneously. First, systems designed for single users under MS-DOS are now available in LAN versions. Second, systems designed for one proprietary operating system are being rewritten, if not redesigned, for UNIX-based platforms. For example, VTLS has released a version that will use the IBM RS/6000 RISC-based system, which runs IBM's version of UNIX, called AIX. Systems heretofore available only on rather large hardware platforms are now available on smaller, lower cost platforms. For example, NOTIS Systems' KeyNOTIS runs on the much less costly IBM 9370 series supermini versions of its larger mainframe systems.

NOTIS AIX-hosted Horizon appears to have sufficient robustness to capture existing NOTIS IBM MVS sites as its feature set is augmented to match the capabilities of the original NOTIS. Similarly, DEC vendors are likely to migrate to DEC's Alpha processor family, aided by some migration tools for VAX/VMS applications.

Workstation hardware is now moving toward real multimedia capabilities. IBM, Tandy and several other manufacturers have announced special multimedia models, and the newest Macintosh models have had some strong multimedia capabilities. Imagine how graphic renditions, accompanied by sound, could enhance our online catalog. See the actual title page of the work. Hear some bars of that music score or the overture from that opera recording. Liven up your archive's finding aids by using a Hypertext-based index, with samples of artifacts captured in full-motion video and appropriate accompanying sound commentary. All of the above are not a dream but are, in fact, being worked on by numerous researchers now.

Who are the major market leaders in open systems? Hewlett-Packard, with the acquisition of Apollo, became the largest UNIX workstation supplier. The HP-9000 600/700/800 series RISC-based systems include workstations, servers and multiuser hosts. Hewlett-Packard's major open system problem is that its HP-3000 series medium-scale systems run only their proprietary MPE operating system. Hewlett-Packard is unwilling to cast this proprietary installed base into the open systems pot at this point. Thus, it must support two major computer lines. HP's major competition is Sun Microsystems, which offers entry-level workstations at about 50% of the HP lowest priced system. Sun also has promoted migration of popular PC software to its system, such as dBase IV and WordPerfect. However, Sun workstations have not kept pace with their competitors' performance in the millions of instructions per second (MIPS) ratings of their systems.

Another serious UNIX player is NCR, acquired by AT&T in 1991. It has sold mainly to the VAR/OEM market a system available in several models, called the Tower. NCR has a new system, called the 3000 family, which will use Intel chips, run UNIX and include sizes from workstations to loosely coupled multiprocessor systems ranging up to 100,000 MIPS. Unisys is also a major open systems provider, but one that is troubled by also having to support two proprietary lines—the former Burroughs and Univac mainframes. However, it is also trying to gain some market share for its Intel chip-based U6000 models.

DEC has long offered its ULTRIX, a UNIX derivative operating system on its VAX series. However, it still must protect its VAX/VMS investment. While DEC has promised to support POSIX on a future version of VMS, with its aging VAX line topping out, it seems that its new RISC-based Alpha systems will be one successor to the VAX. Alpha, which runs ULTRIX and Windows NT, is a very powerful system. IBM, although it has developed its UNIX flavor, AIX, to run as a guest under its VM mainframe operating system and on its RS/6000 systems, is now positioning to be a serious open system player. With its highly successful mid-range AS/400 replacement for its System 34/36/38, IBM is not going to drain off any AS/400 opportunities, if it can be avoided, to the RS/6000. But will the future hold any further AS/400 power improvements? It may be time for AS/400 high-end system users to start looking at other alternatives. Low-end users still have some growth possible but should be aware that the AS/400, while an excellent system for its time, is rapidly aging. However, as Figure 2 shows, support costs for all of this internetworking among disparate systems increases with the age and complexity of the systems. Improved software products should ameliorate this cost somewhat as more such systems become operational.

With two major vendor camps having developed around UNIX—the Open Software Foundation and UNIX International now joined by the X/Open international consortium—there are several major flavors of UNIX emerging. Who can say which is better? Right now this is highly subjective so that the purchaser has to make up her or his own mind after seeing the product. While this has some negative effect on the market, the downsizing of data processing operations in many market sectors means that applications will be off-loaded increasingly from mainframes to some other systems—LANs or UNIX-based multiuser systems are both likely candidates. Increasingly, the choice for such downsizing is a migration to UNIX-based systems using a client/server-type architecture. Ongoing operating costs can be lowered quite dramatically for such systems, given that eventually there is no need to keep the mainframe or that the mainframe itself becomes less costly to acquire and operate.

Libraries have been leaders in adapting and developing open system interconnection application layer (layer 7) protocols. All of this points to a gradual shift from proprietary platforms for today's library systems to UNIX-based systems. Moreover, if and when POSIX becomes an actual supported operating system, it might be offered to run as a guest under another system such as UNIX, much as the rather marvelous PICK operating system does now, to give users of PICK-based library systems some of the best of both worlds. If the above does not take place, there will need to be some further migration

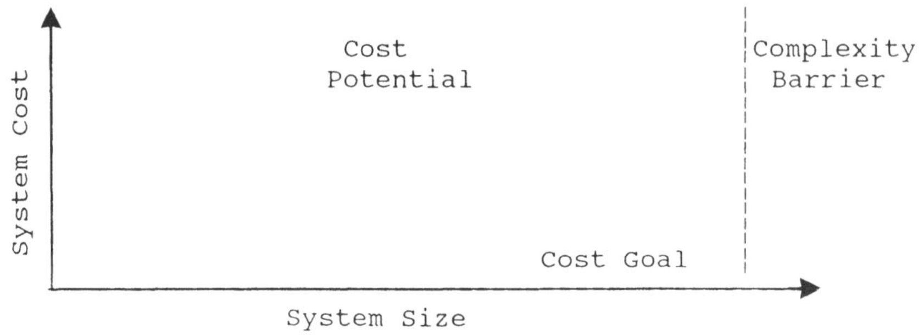

Figure 2 Support costs for internetworking.

paths laid out by all POSIX developers, but the path from a UNIX-based system may be the clearest through the underbrush. As competitive pressure develops further, one can expect to see that proprietary operating system mainframe- and minicomputer-class systems, as their lines age and top out, will be replaced by new RISC-based systems, most likely running UNIX, POSIX or Windows NT.

B. Marketplace Directions—Proprietary Platforms

From the above, I do not mean to sound a death knell for the major manufacturers' proprietary systems in the near term. However, for the longer term, i.e., 10 years and beyond, there is no doubt that the existing hardware lines running these proprietary systems will all reach the point of not being able to be further improved as to MIPS or other factors used to measure performance. There will still be some actual growth in this proprietary market in the coming several years, as the existing software base is still very strong for these systems. This is also true because user investment tends to concentrate on expansion of existing systems rather than on creating new ones. The minicomputer market will lose more ground as these vendors are having difficulty maintaining third-party software support and development of new software for this class of aging proprietary system. Proprietary vendors are embracing client/server architecture for their distributed systems in the hope of retaining their installed client base for a longer period. They are hopping on board the band wagon for POSIX compliance in the hope that this will also stem the tide of UNIX. I would not want to bet on that strategy as today's customers are knowledgeable and are going to do whatever they can to preserve their software investment. For example, some libraries obtained a library system on a proprietary platform but have negotiated for a low-cost upgrade to a UNIX-based product when that is ready from their vendor. Or they have chosen a vendor right now that has a UNIX-based system or one that can run under UNIX using another operating system as a guest.

IBM is the provider of the largest base of proprietary systems with its System/390 Enterprise System 9000 mainframe line and its AS/400 midrange systems. The AS/400 has much improved server capability, Ethernet and TCP/IP support. In an effort to get corporate UNIX workstation users to tie their LANs back through the IBM SNA network, IBM has announced the scheme of routing TCP/IP within the SNA network.

The number two player is Digital Equipment Corp. With its VAX architecture reaching its extensible end, it is planning a migration to its Alpha RISC-based processor family, with POSIX support under VMS. This, it believes, will attract UNIX software developers yet retain compatibility to the old VMS applications on the new computer line. These developments, together with the DECnet Phase IV product enhancements, have produced improved networking capabilities, and so DEC should present a serious entry into the open system market.

Hewlett-Packard's new MPX/E HP/3000 900 Series uses HP's Precision Architecture RISC technology as does its UNIX-based HP/9000/800. HP is also promising POSIX support under MPX/E and moving the HP/3000 series to client/server computing, and it is also selling Sequoia Systems fault-tolerant computers that use UNIX. UNISYS has finally consolidated its myriad host computer lines into the 2200, a Sperry-Univac architecture system descended from the Univac 1100 series and the Burroughs-designed A series. It is also supporting TCP/IP and moving to client/server support. Unysis continues to focus on online transaction processing and has a strong international market in these systems.

In 1990, NCR became the first major computer manufacturer to completely abandon proprietary operating systems in favor of UNIX. Its support by parent AT&T for the scalable architecture NCR 3000 could be a bellwether for the future of open systems. Second-tier vendors such as Tandem, Prime and Data General are all facing serious downsizing as their costs must be reduced in light of stagnant markets for their products. Tandem has a UNIX-based computer line of considerable power using the Silicon Graphics R4000 MIPS processor. This may be an eventual successor to its proprietary systems. None of these companies have an installed base large enough for sustenance without adopting open systems directions. Thus, the long-term viability of their proprietary products is uncertain at best. Although there has been some growth in fault-tolerant market systems, current conventional systems offer many features designed for increased reliability, resulting in improved uptime, so that for many applications, the added cost of a true fault-tolerant architecture system is not worth the added investment.

V. CONCLUSION

The application software capabilities and product enhancements that are available at the time of system installation—or that are highly likely to be in place soon thereafter—constitute the major system evaluation and selection criteria. Given a short list of several possible application systems, it is possible to further sort these out by examining their respective hardware platform options, their operating system requirements and the directions of their system developers toward open systems. Also, consideration needs to be given to other factors of conversion support, training, ongoing software support, record of past new version introductions and general fiscal health. Ease-of-use considerations may also be a factor of some importance, particularly to some customers. Remember that true elegance in computing is when a truly complex problem can be solved by reducing it to a simple and easily comprehended system.

We all know that some applications today support literally thousands of separate functional features. However, we also know from questioning users that the majority of them actually use and really need only some 20% of the functionality of any given program. This is why many users are well served by some simpler-to-use, basic functionality that is easily mastered and retained. Determining the 20% of the functional features that are used has taken many years of program evolution.

Setting realistic goals that are attainable in your selection of a system, biting off only what you can now afford but providing a good enhancement base for future years, will result in an easier systems transition. Your library staff and users will come out winners if due diligence, common sense and some wider perspectives are applied in your systems procurement effort.

REFERENCES

1. Boss, Richard W. The Procurement of Library Automated Systems. *Library Technology Reports 26*:629-749 (September/October 1990).
2. Boss, Richard W. *The Library Manager's Guide to Automation. 3rd ed.* Boston, MA: G.K. Hall, 1990.
3. Cortez, Edwin M. *Proposals and Contracts for Library Automation: Guidelines for Preparing RFP's.* Studio City, CA: Pacific Information; and Chicago: American Library Association, 1987.
4. Mathews, Joseph R., Stephen R. Salmon and Joan Fry Williams. The RFP—Request for Punishment or a Tool for Selecting an Automated Library System. *Library Hi-Tech 5*(1): 15-21 (Spring 1987).

6

OLD ESTABLISHMENT SILICON AND IRON
THE BIG CONCURRENT USER SYSTEMS

To err is human. but to really foul things up requires a computer.
— Philip Howard. *The Times*, February 25, 1987

I. INTRODUCTION

The systems covered in this chapter represent mainly long-term survivors in the library systems marketplace. These firms began generally during a time in which mainframes or minicomputers represented the only viable platforms for online, multiuser interactive systems. For the larger library and for the library dependent upon a shared host resource in its organizational setting, these systems represent solid, time-tested software for performing a set of integrated library operational functions using a central bibliographic database. As time has passed, so too has the era of platform-specific hardware and operating systems. Today's host computer platforms are 32-bit architecture. The old 16-bit systems, like the Digital Equipment Corp. PDP-11 series, are no longer on the market. Systems that once depended on mainframes now can run on smaller sized and lower cost midrange hardware, for example, KeyNOTIS on the IBM 9370 series as well as on the IBM 4300 and 3000 series hosts. These platforms contain advantages that may be significant for certain libraries. For example, very large databases still can be handled more easily in these storage environments than under a LAN such as Novell's Netware ™ or Banyan's Vines ™. Internet connections using TCP/IP (Transmission Control Protocol/Internet Protocol) are usually already in place in academic institutions, so the libraries can easily take advantage of these intersystems connections. Increasingly, more public libraries, public schools and corporations are establishing Internet access. Professional site management is in place in these facilities' computer organizations. These data-processing organizations are ready to contract with the library for computer time and application/operating environment support. System backup, including offsite storage, is available. This makes the library's investment well protected against normal malfunctions or system failures. With an increase in system interdependency and complexity, it becomes a necessity to have more expertise available than found in the normal turnkey operating environment in the library itself, with limited operations staff. The release of some client/server applications further enhances these mainframe or host applications, once dependent only on a standard character-based terminal emulation. The move to microcomputers on the desktop means that there is ample opportunity to use a desktop system in a more meaningful manner than merely as a terminal emulator. The user interface, in-context help and application logic can be handled at the workstation, with the host handling storage, indexing and data manipulation tasks.

Before moving to a discussion of these systems, it is appropriate to examine some system trends affecting all currently operating application systems, including library automation systems. It possible for any library today to realistically use some sort of automated library system software. This is true even in the one-person, small-school or special library for tasks heretofore possible only on the big silicon and iron systems.

II. SYSTEM TRENDS

There are six major trends that are affecting the system marketplace and software developments of both established and newer system vendors. The first trend is "rightsizing," which usually means the choosing of appropriately sized hardware and software platforms that are able to grow or shrink with organizational demands. The second is the mounting of external abstracting and indexing databases or other nonlibrary catalog databases—a virtual necessity for libraries—to provide broad access to these from their public user terminals and workstations. The third is the provision of Internet connections to other institutions' catalogs and information bases. The fourth is the move away from using CRT terminals and the move toward using microcomputers as intelligent workstations to enable a client/server design strategy for implementing the application. This maximizes resources at both ends of the system, permitting the host to do what it does best while the client workstation can power significant parts of the application without serious resource contention with the host. The fifth is the provision of system versions for more than a single operating system and/or hardware platform in order to reach a wider market and to provide more flexibility to prospective purchasers in arriving at a configuration able to be supported and grow in their organization. The sixth is the provision of system migration facilities and tools, since many libraries are procuring their second or even later system and are not remaining with their original system vendor. Moving bibliographic data is one problem, but moving many of the operational data records such as item, holdings, acquisition and circulation transaction data is quite another problem, which is compounded by whether migration tools are available or must be custom designed. Very soon most of the systems included in this chapter will have migrated to UNIX versions or will be replaced by newly designed UNIX-based systems using client/server architecture. However, it will be several years before these vendors' client libraries will have migrated to either their present vendor's UNIX successor or a competing system.

A. Rightsizing

The decade of the sixties brought initial experimental systems operated in batch mode and usually serving a single dedicated purpose such as circulation, acquisitions or some form of catalog or list production. Sequential files were used, and input was usually by punched card, although other mediums came to replace punched cards. Computers meant mainframes in those days. The seventies brought integration of multiple applications using a single bibliographic file using random access files. However, many of these early interactive systems did not dynamically update their files in real time. Instead, they used batch processing to perform this task. The computers of the seventies were usually still mainframes, although the seventies brought the emergence of the 16-bit-word-length minicomputer as a lower cost alternative. It was the early development of commercial systems using this platform that started the transformation of library automation into a vertical market of commercially developed solutions and away from locally developed systems, in all but a very few large libraries. By the 1980's the superminicomputer had emerged to provide a more cost effective platform for software previously mounted only on higher cost mainframe systems. As these systems became lower cost and increasingly powerful, equipped with larger mass storage systems, they provided a longer term growth path for the purchaser. The 1990's has brought a maturity of systems integration and features across platforms from microcomputer/LAN to mainframe, including emphasis on system interconnectivity through such standards as Z.39.50. (1)

The ability to provide a transparent gateway to other systems using the Internet and specific services such as CARL's Uncover periodicals database has brought a new expectation of the integrated library system. Currently, system functionality can be delivered to the user by software on a LAN as transparently as that delivered by a mainframe or superminicomputer.

Rightsizing usually means using some form of computing that includes lower cost hardware and software to deliver acceptable functionality comparable to that of the previous central computing hardware and software. It could mean operating several smaller mainframes or midrange systems in a network and splitting the load between them to reduce total cost and complexity of a single system. It could also mean, more typically, taking some mainframe applications and redesigning them so as to permit their operation in a LAN environment. Here, database and application servers substitute for the mainframe, and workstations perform some of the application tasks under a client/server approach. It could also mean using the mainframe as the server under a client/server application model. This often means moving to a popular RISC system using a UNIX version for that platform.

Using the client/server approach, one can have the workstation generate all the on-screen menus, help screens, graphics elements and reused data. The workstation can perform all error checking and correction of all or almost all data to be input, depending on the application. The workstation can alert the server when it has data to send or when it needs data from the server. All query formulation can be handled by the workstation and intermediate results passed from the server to the workstation for iterative reuse for further queries to refine the search. Thesauri can also be resident on the workstation, so that term checking does not have to be done at the server. Currently the practical limit for handling databases under Novell's Netware 3.12 is around 60–80 gigabytes per server, though Netware 4.0 will change this. This is one critical factor that will determine just how far into downsizing a given library system can go. Given 486DX2/66 or Pentium processors incorporated into desktop servers, it is safe to predict that the next two years will see the dynamic sorting and indexing of LAN databases of 40–50 gigabytes. Large industry LAN users are crying for such capabilities as this will make possible the rightsizing of systems having database sizes now typical of the 100 largest ARL type libraries or the 50 largest public libraries—typically 20–50 gigabytes. Using UNIX-based servers in a TCP/IP network does make it possible to handle these very large databases if the server is sufficiently powerful to handle the expected transaction load.

Computer industry experts are predicting that our desktop systems will have 250-MHz operating speeds by 1995, so one can expect multiprocessor servers for LANs to be as fast as today's current typical large mainframe. The real question will be whether the LAN operating systems producers, such as market leader Novell, can deliver the multiplatform support for Windows, MS-DOS, UNIX and Macintosh systems that will be needed if LANs are to completely replace typical host systems used today. The direction that suppliers of these old iron-based library systems must take is to reengineer their systems within the client/server model as more and more nonscientific computing applications will use the host for server-based functions for very large databases. Most large scientific computing has already departed for supercomputer systems, as these applications continually demand more memory resources and speed than even present supercomputers can deliver. This leaves small-scale scientific computing, classroom and business/industry administrative applications as the typical mix for present host computer installations. Even electronic mail today is performed largely by mail servers rather than by large host systems, particularly in the academic sector. These mail servers are usually UNIX based, such as Sun Microcomputers' SPARCservers or the Silicon Graphics Indigo series.

There is no question that smart administrators will have a desire to employ rightsized systems to save operating expenses and provide easier support and expansion. These systems' real power is in enabling an organization's staff to perform much more integrated business processes. However, to do this requires building a support organization that is close to the users, one that ideally is distributed within actual user departments and somewhat more loosely connected than the typical rigidly hierarchical data-processing service organization. In larger organizations this may be more difficult to achieve. The commitment to rightsizing requires considerable understanding of resource management, user support and communication infrastructures. It also requires that staff fully understand how rightsizing will affect their responsibilities, making them more empowered to directly affect a process outcome. Some administrators will find it simpler but not necessarily cheaper or more effective to maintain merely a support and operations contract with their central data-processing department, with a key staff member serving as the end-user facilitator between the central service and the library. However, more progressive organizations will see the need to build their own end-user support organizations as they bring more functionality to the desktop via a LAN or other rightsized systems approach. Central data-processing or information systems organizations tend to work best when end-user support, custom application design and LAN management are performed in a distributed mode.

B. External Databases

It is no longer sufficient to provide only an online catalog of the library's cataloged collections. Abstracting and indexing companies that provide CD-ROM and book format indexes are also licensing their products to individual libraries to install on the library's integrated library system computer, or on another system linked through a public menu choice. Networked CD-ROM databases accessible from public terminals, depending on licensing arrangements, are another increasingly necessary service. For cost/benefit reasons, the future appears very bright for CD-ROM publishers. Library system vendors are providing search software that permits these files to be searched on the system, with the citations held by the library to be linked into the catalog database to show local availability. Sometimes, the library will subscribe to databases hosted on other institutions' computers, such as the CARL Systems Uncover database. Then the library system's public menu can offer all of these databases to the library user.

Generalized loader programs are usually provided by system vendors to load these databases, but usually the loader program must be customized to the particular database. Both library system vendors and database vendors, such as BRS, are actively developing loader software for accessing third-party databases. Independent firms, such as Peter Ward and Associates, also offer this program assistance for specific products—in Ward's case, the NOTIS system.

Presently, these databases are mainly of the abstracting and indexing type. Or they offer limited text, such as Current Contents, or article delivery, such as that provided through CARL Systems Uncover. The future will bring an increase in full-text services and databases where the content involves multimedia data, including still and motion video, sound and animation. This will mean that system users will come to depend on networked workstations instead of merely host CRT terminal emulation since many of these capabilities will be the product of client software in a client/server design environment. Workstations are rapidly incorporating multimedia features such as sound, high resolution/high color graphics and full-motion video. This also means that as these large-scale systems evolve, they will increase their dependence on the microcomputer and LAN to drive these capabilities and decrease the amount of host involvement in the actual application logic processing. The host will move to a database server function, and more transparency to the user in the total system interface will occur.

It is becoming less and less important where an external database resides. Network provision for access, minimization of duplication, and more creative licensing will be driving forces to institutions as they grapple with issues of proving wider access to materials, while still being able to afford to improve user services through these developments. The question of providing a service such as OCLC's First Search versus the same abstracting and indexing coverage on CD-ROM becomes an issue of some importance from the viewpoint of cost, convenience, uniqueness of holdings information, updating frequency, and value-added enhancement. With present resource choices, the provision of more general interest databases through the library's integrated library system terminals and workstations is the direction most libraries will chart. More specialized databases of interest to smaller subsets of users will still be served mainly by LAN access to CD-ROM servers or in some cases stand-alone CD-ROM workstations in the library. Dependence on print abstracting and indexing formats will continue to decrease since searching the print form is so much more time consuming and difficult in most cases. At some future point, print forms of abstracting and indexing tools will be a rarity indeed!

For the near-term future, those libraries using host computer systems will still have storage advantages for mounting large databases in house but the direction that LANs are taking through increased support for UNIX servers to attach to a Novell network could vastly increase the present storage capabilities of current Novell users to permit the loading of many external databases to such LAN servers. Thus, eventually, users of microcomputer-based LAN version software could have virtually identical functionality in this area, plus the functionality of multimedia-based catalogs and collection materials.

C. Internet Connection

The Internet, as we know it today, grew out of ARPANET, the Advanced Research Projects Agency Network, established in 1969. By 1971, this network linked together numerous different vendor platforms located at the University of California—Santa Barbara, Stanford Research Institute, University of Utah, University of California—Los Angeles, System Development Corp. and Rand Corp. These West Coast systems were linked to the East Coast systems which included Case Institute (now Case Western Reserve University), Carnegie Mellon University, Massachusetts Institute of Technology's Lincoln Laboratories (M.I.T.—LL), Harvard University and Bolt, Beranek & Newman.

In October, 1983, ARPANET split into two networks. The first was the Defense Data Network (DDN), or Milnet. It had 160 nodes, with 24 nodes in Europe and 11 in the Pacific. The second was ARPANET, with 50 nodes in the United States and Europe. ARPANET was being phased out to be replaced by the new DARPA (Defense Advanced Research Projects Agency) INTERNET. Today, the DARPA INTERNET, now NSFnet, is commonly called the Internet. It is the world's largest network, connecting several thousand regional networks into a common worldwide network. The phenomenal growth in network technology, adoption of TCP/IP as the standard communications protocol on the Internet, improved high-speed data carrier links and recognition of the benefits of system interconnection have made this possible. The first true computer network was built by M.I.T.—Lincoln Laboratories for U.S. Air Defense. It was called SAGE (Semi-Automatic Ground Environment) and had 23 computer networks, each connecting 100 radar sites and ground-to-air data link sites to a duplexed computer system. As of January 1990, there were 2,218 networks connected to the Internet, according to the Defense Data Network's Network Information Center. Currently, the estimate is that the Internet is growing by 15% each month. In June 1990, DARPA finally shut down completely transparently to the network community users—in a switch to the present NSFnet of the National Science Foundation. NSFnet was originally founded in 1985 to connect supercomputer sites established under NSF grants.

Typical of the regional networks attached to the Internet is the Minnesota Regional Network (MRNet). It is an NSFnet affiliate that provides connections for the Minnesota Super Computer Center, the University of Minnesota campuses, the Minnesota State University system and many smaller traffic connection sites on a subscription basis. It also offers SLIP (Serial Line Interface Protocol) connections over 9600-baud modems on the low end and very high speed T1 or T3 leased-line connections for very large network users.

As previously mentioned, the Internet continues to operate using the TCP/IP originated by Ungermann-Bass, Inc., for early ARPANET implementation. Sun Microsystems brought TCP/IP into widespread commercial use by bundling this protocol's software into its UNIX operating system. Other UNIX system builders followed Sun's lead. Now TCP/IP support is a part of all UNIX family operating systems. Proprietary operating systems also began to offer TCP/IP software products, so that it became possible to connect different systems for both high-speed data/file transfer and for terminal emulation sessions using the Digital Equipment Corp. VT-100 series terminal emulation or, in the case of IBM mainframes, the IBM 3270 terminal. Today, it is possible to connect all currently marketed host computers to the Internet using commercially available software and the regional network affiliation in the particular geographic area.

Although much emphasis has been placed on the International Standards Organization Open System Interconnection (OSI) layered network Reference Model, it will be some years before such a scheme replaces the Internet's use of TCP/IP. The main weakness in the OSI Reference Model is its lack of internetworking emphasis, which necessitates using a separate layer for this function. No such layer is present in the OSI Reference Model (Figure 1). The simple mail transfer protocol (SMTP), file transfer protocol (FTP) and the Telnet terminal emulations for VT-100 and TN3270 operate in the equivalent of layers 5–7. TCP provides layer-4 transport services and IP provides layer-3 network services. In the case of both OSI and TCP/IP, physical link and data link services are provided by hardware components.

Various standards organizations are working on defining standards affecting networks and their interconnection. The IEEE and CCITT Study Group VII, responsible for the X Series standards, are two major players to watch. For example, many networks now implement CCITT X.500 Directory

OSI REFERENCE MODEL			INTERNET
Source Node	**Intermediate Node**	**Destination Node**	TCP/IP
7. Application layer ←	→	7. Application layer	SMTP
6. Presentation layer ←→	Peer-to-peer communication ←→	6. Presentation layer	FTP
5. Session layer ←	→	5. Session layer	Telnet
4. Transport layer ←	→	4. Transport layer	TCP
3. Network layer ←→	3. Network layer ←→	3. Network layer	IP
2. Data Link layer ←→	2. Data Link layer ←→	2. Data Link layer	Ethernet
1. Physical layer ←→	1. Physical layer ←→	1. Physical layer	Ethernet

Figure 1 Comparison of the OSI Reference Model and the Internet protocol.

Services, which allow a user to look up electronic mail addresses uniformly across a network. An excellent introduction to this work is provided by Uyless Black. (2) Similarly, John Davidson provides an excellent introductory treatment of TCP/IP. (3) Expect more progress on X.500 technology as AT&T, in February, 1993 entered into a cooperative agreement with NSF to provide directory and database services for the NSFnet. They will develop and maintain a directory of directories, which will serve as a pointer to numerous Internet resources. The Coalition for Networked Information also is working on similar aids to the location of Internet resources.

Many Internet guides and directories have been published. Some are electronically distributed through the Internet and discuss specific Internet resources. Clifford Lynch describes the library–Internet relationship in his 1989 article. (4) *Library Hi-Tech* devoted an issue to the OSI topic. (5) Ed Krol's work is a "must" read for those with Internet access. (6) For those interested in only a briefer treatment, Polly provides this in her article. (7) For librarians and others interested in searching library catalogs accessible over the Internet, the works by Barron (8) and St. George (9) are necessary guides. Of main interest to libraries are the worldwide access to other research library catalogs, numerous discussion groups such as the Bitnet Listservs or the Usenet News Groups, databank and switching systems implemented by Gopher server software and file repositories such as the Simtel20 mirror sites for shareware or public domain software for PCs and workstations. The above references will give a good overview of the major resources, but new resources are being added daily to the Internet, so one is advised to keep abreast of the latest periodical literature.

Also of great importance to libraries and the scholarly community in general is the electronic mail potential of the Internet. By the end of the decade, it will become necessary for virtually every sort of institution, company, agency or individual to be interconnected and able to send and receive messages within a global network. With postal rates continuing to increase faster than the rates for electronic communication, fax and electronic mail will be an increasingly popular form of transmission from sender to receiver for many kinds of documents. As message content moves beyond mere text or simple printed graphics, new possibilities in applications will open up to include true multimedia networked information.

Will it be necessary for every library to allow remote users to access their catalogs or other resources maintained through computer databases? In the public sector the answer is "yes." In the private sector, the answer is certainly "yes" for the primary clientele that the private library is serving and "maybe" for other libraries and users with networking and resource-sharing arrangements. Private libraries with unique resources that they are willing to share certainly will want to consider networked and remote dial-in access. With the improvements in user validation possible through global name server validation at the institution level, security and controlled access can be safely offered to a limited clientele in a public or private institutional setting. For example, in a public setting, certain databases obtained under commercial license can require that only those affiliated with the institution may use these databases. If each employee and student has an Internet address recorded in a user record that also uses password access control to the institution's systems, then either on-campus or remote dial-in access can be controlled. The user must have both the address and password merely to gain an access line into the institution's backbone network even before reaching any particular network host or server resource service.

The ability to provide transparent links to other computer systems from your local host's user menu includes hosts addressed through the Internet. This makes it possible to give library users easy access to a selection of most often desired external resources. The proposed National Research and Education Network (NREN), when it is funded, will provide even wider institutional connections, reaching down into the commercial sector, the K–12 public school community and local government agencies. The acceleration of the FreeNet community computing environments, which began with the Cleveland FreeNet and now have spread to some dozen U.S. and Canadian cities, will also open worldwide network access to anyone with access to a PC and modem.

On a related note, the library community has always been at the forefront of pushing the adoption of OSI Reference Model-based solutions. The National Information Standards Organization (NISO) affiliate of the American National Standards Institute (ANSI) has developed a number of standards relating to automated library systems. The Z39.50 standard provides the specification for an application layer protocol that permits one computer operating in a client mode to perform information retrieval queries with another computer operating in an information server mode. This means that a system user will be able to query another Z39.50-equipped system, through Z39.50-compliant facilities, using one's own system's command language or interface. The Z39.50 software and hardware will take care of translating queries into an intermediate form, which the server Z39.50 system will then translate to its own native query commands. Similarly, the response is translated by the server to the intermediate form and then sent to the client, where it is translated to that system's native query response form. While the Z39.50 protocol is quite general, its initial application has been to handle bibliographic database access. Specialized data such as digitized images may require extensions to the basic Z39.50 standard.

The Research Libraries Group (RLG/RLIN) system has announced its initial Z39.50 implementation, which would allow libraries using the NOTIS software to access RLIN using NOTIS query commands. NOTIS, Inc., has committed to this standard and its PACLINK and INFOBASE products are the first commercially available products in the library automation area to be released. OCLC is working on a server and client support for EPIC and its other systems. Data Research Associates also has announced its intention to build Z39.50 support into its automated library system to connect to Digital Equipment Corp.-based systems and to the University of California MELVYL system in a joint project with MELVYL. The MELVYL folks are also working with Pennsylvania State University to implement a MELVYL and LIAS implementation between the Division of Library Automation's IBM 3090 MELVYL system and the LIAS DEC VAX/9000 system. Carnegie Mellon University's Project Mercury electronic library project and the University of California—Berkeley are other institutions working on Z39.50 capabilities.

It is a virtual given that many libraries will make support and development of Z39.50-compliant products a part of their automated system specifications. This should spur all vendors to develop products using this standard, since federal government initiatives have shown that it is only a matter of time until greater connectivity becomes the norm.

D. Workstations and Client/Server Architecture

The earliest interactive automated library systems used character- and line-oriented printing terminal devices, much like electric typewriters. They advanced to using similarly featured cathode-ray tube (CRT) terminals and then to CRTs that featured full-screen operation, protected mode fields and fully addressable cursors in monochrome. Finally, color display capabilities came to be added, and since the beginning of the nineties, the transition to client/server application designs and graphical user interfaces essentially has spelled the end to the glass teletype terminal as a viable user interface product except for older character-based traditional host-implemented applications. But, at the point where such character-based applications are supplanted by newer architecture systems, the replacement of the CRT terminal by the personal computer and/or workstation will be complete. In a mere 20 years, the CRT terminal, a revolutionary human/system interactive device, has been nurtured through maturity and then rendered virtually obsolete.

While the advance from printer/glass teletype saw limited communication speed enhancements, it made possible new user interface designs such as "fill in the blanks" labeled fields, transmission of only changed fields back to the host, function keys to replace obtuse multiple keystroke combinations and selection from a menu of functions. Even though some host computer systems such as RLG/RLIN used host-downloaded microcode to drive their custom application terminals, these terminals could not be program loaded by a user, nor could they locally save information except possibly through printing it on an attached screen printer or through a host attached printer. Nor could such a device transmit machine-readable data to a host from local storage media such as personal computers use. By the mid-1980's asynchronous communications software for IBM PCs and Apple computers was in commonplace use to emulate host terminals. Today, there are over 100 asynchronous communications programs available for MS-DOS- and Windows-equipped systems. All other desktop systems have many possible choices of software for this purpose. Even host computers such as IBM mainframes and their midrange AS/400, which use proprietary terminal emulations controlled through remote or host attached controllers, have competing terminal emulation and file transfer programs available for a variety of hardware and workstation platforms under all of the popular operating systems and graphic environments.

Clearly, the personal computer in its MS-DOS and Microsoft Windows operating environment is the terminal device of choice for future systems. Some competition from IBM's OS/2 on Intel chip-based systems will occur. Higher end UNIX-based workstations will also take an increasing share of desktop real estate. Apple's Macintosh will continue to appeal to its traditional educational market and possibly make new inroads in the home market due to its recently introduced lower cost, PowerPC-based, competitively powered systems. With improving screen resolution and number of simultaneous colors able to be displayed, along with the GUI as the accepted user interface, today's 13" and 14" monitors will be replaced by 15" to 17" monitors for the typical desktop and 21" monitors for more specialized work. Given Novell's increased support for UNIX systems in a multiplatform Netware 4.0 LAN environment, the Intel 80486 series and the new Pentium microprocessor will continue to dominate the library desktop.

To realize the benefits of lower system operating costs, improved user/system interaction and overall resource utilization, more power must be apportioned to the client side of computing through software operating on the desktop system. Library automation vendors' present systems are largely conventional host-driven applications which are not client/server based. But for a few exceptions, such as found in the next chapter, client/server applications in library software really began in early 1993. However, the next few years will see this change rather dramatically as further vendor marketplace consolidations occur. Therefore, it is critical that libraries position themselves to take advantage of these developments by investing in sound desktop platforms and LAN technology when acquiring new equipment. The nineties will continue to be the decade of intersystem networking and the migration of today's traditional host-based, character-oriented applications to newer "right-sized" server platforms using LANs and workstations equipped with various client software. These systems will permit more gradual system upgrading and less disruptive hardware replacement to accommodate any changing characteristics in an institution's needs. Computing support will be redirected at improving network operations support and increasing more direct end-user assistance. Wise directional choices made today should be able to provide a good foundation for the coming decade of new system developments.

E. Multiplatform Systems

Users of computing technology are demanding versatility in the marketplace from their software vendors. It is no longer sufficient for a vendor to offer software or a turnkey library system based on a single computer model from one of the popular computer manufacturers. Even IBM, the manufacturer of NOTIS, a system directed at larger academic and public libraries and long an IBM mainframe product, has been moved to offer a turnkey system called KeyNOTIS, designed to run on the IBM 9370 series low- to medium-scale multiuser systems so as to appeal to a wider spectrum of libraries. Moreover, IBM has released Horizon, a UNIX-based, newly designed system to replace the mainframe version of its NOTIS automated library system. Horizon uses IBM's AIX version of UNIX on an IBM RS/6000 system, the latest models of which incorporate the PowerPC microprocessor.

Dynix, whose main integrated library system product was implemented under the PICK Operating System using PICK Basic compiler and database management facilities, produced the original transportable software. PICK has been implemented on over 100 different computers ranging from micro to mainframe. Now, with the ability to run native PICK applications under UNIX, the excellent communications and network support facilities of UNIX are complemented by the excellent data management and retrieval facilities of PICK.

Software developers are increasingly adopting tools and approaches that ease porting their systems to several popular platforms. A distinct trend is to offer at least one UNIX family version along with one or more proprietary operating system versions. Certainly, there are implications of more difficult customer support when a vendor offers multiplatform versions on several hardware platforms. However, the overall advantage is to provide users with a better choice of alternatives to fit their particular situation. Expect to see an increase in UNIX versions and in systems designed to operate on Novell Netware-based LANs. UNIX versions will be implemented on many different processors, ranging from such fault-tolerant systems as Stratus to lower cost servers such as Sun Microsystems. There will be an appropriately powerful UNIX version system at a realistic cost for virtually every library system to consider just as today there are appropriate systems on proprietary hardware and software platforms ranging from micro to LAN and multiuser host systems. Most importantly for the future will be the availability of the POSIX-specified applications interface so that software written to POSIX standard will be executable on any POSIX-compliant platform. The work of IEEE in developing a standard to make UNIX versions increasingly compatible has resulted in the specification for a whole new operating system that will assure software transportability across hardware platforms. Both UNIX and proprietary platform suppliers are incorporating the POSIX application program interface into their products. In some measure, POSIX compliance by the application quells the necessity to move to a UNIX platform, given that one can find and use an existing proprietary solution that works.

F. System Migration

Many libraries have changed library system vendors. Some have installed three or four different systems since the late 1960's. As library systems have become more multifunctional and integrated, some libraries have changed vendors to take advantage of these increasing capabilities. There are numerous reasons why a library would want to consider a new system vendor. From a group study, Lester Pourciau (10) reported on the ten most substantive factors in a group of libraries deciding to change vendors:

1. Unresolved system problems over an extended period
2. Unacceptably long system response times during peak usage
3. Obsolete hardware that cannot support current or projected system demands

4. Lack of confidence in the current vendor's future performance,
5. Abandonment of the system by the vendor
6. New emphasis on networking at the institutional level
7. Altered commitment by a parent institution to its library
8. Increasing sense by the library of the advanced age or dysfunctionality of its system in relation to its parent institution's system
9. Attractiveness of new products offered by other vendors
10. User complaints about system performance

System migrations have been more common among libraries that have had longer histories of using computer technology. These libraries purchased early vendor-supported systems that were mainframe or minicomputer based. Some of these libraries even earlier had used various systems developed in house, usually to perform one specific function such as circulation, creation of a catalog, acquisitions or various serials-processing tasks. Migrations are increasingly likely to occur in the future because some vendors are likely to go out of business or merge with other vendors. Also, some products are going to be dropped from support, and competing vendors will increasingly target one another's systems in their fight for domestic market share. Smart vendors are trying to increase their market share by expanding into foreign markets, offering lower cost systems to appeal to smaller libraries—which still represent a significantly untapped market—and competing for libraries with already established systems. To be successful in this last thrust, vendors need to provide considerable conversion assistance and conversion software products to the target library. Third-party vendors and consultants can be brought in for custom conversion programming, whereas the library automation vendor can concentrate on providing more generalized data conversion tools.

The move of vendors away from their own customized data management engines and to more widely used commercial database management systems operating on multiple hardware and operating system platforms will also make data migration to a new vendor's system easier. Despite these developments, libraries considering switching vendors will need to analyze very thoroughly how their present bibliographic and operating data will be mapped to any new system and whether the new vendor has tools practical enough to do a successful migration at an affordable cost. Moving to a new vendor is a serious undertaking, made more complex by these data migration problems now that systems are well integrated and multifunctional. Such a move is additionally complicated by further commitments to training staff in the new system. A full amortization of the investment in the previous system should be an added consideration to the substantive factors influencing a vendor change. Moreover, funds need to be allocated to both the new system procurement and the conversion from the previous system, and allocation may need to include provision for conversion of additional original non-machine readable data if the library is to take advantage of some new system features. Perhaps the new system can handle the college reserve book room. This will entail extra expense if items serviced by the previous circulation system now need to be bar coded. Also, these reserve items would not have linked item records, so they would need to be created in the new system. If the previous system used brief bibliographic records or did not include a full retrospective conversion of the library's holdings, then it might be necessary to do further retrospective conversion to take advantage of the new system's capabilities. Today, nothing short of full union catalog conversion should be an acceptable goal of any library. And, once that goal is reached, it will be necessary to look to retrospective conversion for material formats that were not originally treated in the library's main catalog, e.g., possibly archival materials, maps, government publications, vertical file materials, specifications, pictures, recorded media and music scores. Given the present capabilities of library systems, their extensive potential can be realized only if libraries make comprehensive use of them.

III. CONCURRENT MULTIUSER SYSTEMS

Concurrent multiuser systems range from microcomputer hosted to very large shared or dedicated mainframe computers. These systems permit many users to activate specific functions simultaneously. They also can provide—and most do—real-time file updating, with foreground and background processing for certain output generation. They can support large databases with numerous terminals according to the size of the system, its communications and memory features and its networking support. In this chapter I focus on the older, established systems, which use midrange to high-end conventional mainframes as hosts. Proprietary operating systems are the norm in this system category. These systems are installed frequently in large academic and public libraries, and for library consortia.

A. Proprietary Operating System Type

Operating systems in this category are products developed by their respective computer manufacturers to provide control and application services to a proprietary computer design. One notable proprietary operating system is IBM's MVS in its several versions for the IBM 43xx, 3xxx and ES/9000 series mainframes. Another well-accepted operating system is Digital Equipment Corp.'s VMS for its 32-bit VAX family computers that were the successors to the 16-bit PDP-11 series minicomputers. The VAX line ranges from desktop VAXstations to large multiprocessor superminicomputers that rival many IBM host systems for accommodation of processing load. Worldwide, VAX systems continue to be the second most popular multiuser operating environment. Hewlett-Packard continues to support its HP-3000 series systems using its proprietary MPX/E operating systems while offering its UNIX-based HP-9000 line. Tandem Computers' Guardian Operating System is the basis for these high-end, fault-tolerant and highly distributed architecture hosts. However, even Tandem is now offering a new UNIX system. All of Tandem's competitors, such as Stratus in the fault tolerant market, have adopted UNIX versions as their operating system, with differing flavors of add-on enhancements specific to their computer systems.

Since user investment in systems currently focuses on enhancement of existing systems, there will be some steady gradual growth continuing in the proprietary system market. Proprietary operating systems are also attempting to hold off competition from open systems by supporting client/server application designs, TCP/IP protocols, distributed application architectures, SQL-compliant databases, and the POSIX (Portable Operating System Interface) operating system interface standard. The POSIX work undertaken by IEEE focussed on UNIX directions but resulted in establishing a portable standard for operating systems of application interfaces that could be built as a complement to established operating systems and that could make UNIX versions more uniform. It is estimated that by 1995 the number of systems on which POSIX can be run will be nearly equal to the number of open systems running UNIX.

In a February 9, 1993 product announcement, IBM stated that its Enterprise Systems business is adding to the portfolio of S/390 applications by implementing industry standard interfaces such as the Open Software Foundation's Distributed Computing Environment (DCE) and the IEEE's POSIX. DCE will provide interoperability among multivendor platforms while POSIX will allow UNIX-based POSIX-compliant applications to run on the S/390 new microprocessor-based parallel computers, which are designed to work in concert with IBM ES/9000 general purpose host computers. IBM also announced MVS/ ESA OpenEdition Services for MVS/ESA SP 4.3 to support POSIX, which was released in March, 1994. Such advance announcements are designed to forestall customer base erosion and provide customers and developers with planning data, but they must be taken as only an approximation with regard to time frame. Most of the initial release dates are not met; further announcements are usually made as to a revised release date.

Consequently, the most important consideration for libraries is not necessarily the move to UNIX from a proprietary operating system, but rather the direction that these specific proprietary operating systems are taking with respect to POSIX and DCE as well as to other open system-compliant standards. A move to open systems insures that the hardware and software of varying manufacturers can successfully be interoperable in the same system.

1. IBM Host Family

The current IBM mainframe architecture family consists of systems from its Enterprise Systems business. These are ES/9370, ES/3090, ES/4381, and ES/9000 series systems. They run a variety of IBM operating systems and some models also run native PICK and UNIX. The ES/9370 series runs VM/SP, VSE/SP and IX/370. The ES/3090 runs MVS/SP, MVS/XA, ESA/370, VM/HPO, VM/XA and AIX/370. The ES/4381 series runs DOS/VSE, OS/VS1, MVS/SP, VM/SP, MVS/XA, VM/XA, VM/SP-HPO and AIX/370. The ES/9000 series runs MVS/ESA, VSE/ESA, VM/ESA and AIX/ESA.

Amdahl makes the 5990 and 5995 series systems, which run IBM's MVS/ESA, MVS/370, MVS/XA, VM/SP, VM/HPO and VM/XA in addition to UTS (UNIX System V). Similarly, Hitachi Data Systems EX series run MVS/370, MVS/XA, MVS/ESA, VM/SP, VM/XA, VM/HPO and VSE.

With this proliferation of operating systems, it is important to determine, in an existing shared facility, whether the application being considered will run in the existing setup or will need additions to the operating system. In a new dedicated system it is equally important to run the operating system version recommended by the application supplier, and if several are possible, the one that will have the best future facilities and support. This will ease operating system upgrading as new versions and add-ons are made available.

We note here that IBM has ceased to offer its DOBIS/LIBIS system. While a significant number of DOBIS sites existed abroad, there were only two North American sites. IBM has sold the system to ELiAS N.V. (60 Kopeldreef, B-3001 Leuven, Belgium; fax: 011-32-16-270319, tel: 001-32-16-270390). This company has formed a six-person team to develop the successor to DOBIS which will allow present DOBIS sites to compatibly move over to the new system. A model-driven entity relationship object-oriented development technique (MERODE) will be used to create this new system. I wish this group well as this software was neglected for a significant period of time by IBM, and many of the DOBIS sites really had few other alternatives to pursue.

a. NOTIS Systems, Inc.

In one way, NOTIS Systems, Inc.
  Is perfectly consistent;
To any change in this regard
  They're mightily resistant;

Each version of the LMS
  Displayed this awesome trait,
Which MDAS, GTO and Loaders
  Also demonstrate.

What trait is this, where NSI
  Can really not be beat?

From the very jaws of victory
They still can snatch defeat!

I like the tailored OPAC screens,
And LSYS makes me smile;
The fiscal close will make our books
Easy to reconcile;

Whoever thought of GTO
Was really on the ball;
And living without MDAS
Simply would not do at all.

But when you see the OPAC guides,
Or fight with GTO,
Or find out MDAS 1.1
Won't work with 5.0,

Or when you go to use some feature
You've relied upon,
And find only then and there
Your favorite feature's gone,

You've really got to wonder
How they came by such a knack,
Of matching each stride forward
With a dozen small steps back.

I wouldn't trade in 5.0
For version 4.6,
And many things they've bollixed up
Will get a ready fix;

They always try—I'll give them that,
But when all's said and done,
Don't even hope that things will change
With version 5.1!

— Alan Alexander-Manifold, Purdue University Libraries at the 1991 NOTIS User Group, as reported in a NOTIS-L listserv message dated October 10, 1991. (In NOTIS-L archives at NOTISARC@ASTERIX.LIB.PURDUE.EDU).

Manifold's poetry about the NOTIS Library Management System (LMS) is but one of the very pertinent observations about this system by the poet laureate of NOTIS users. LMS was originally developed at Northwestern University, which later spun off this activity into a separately incorporated company to continue its development, support and marketing beyond the Northwestern University Library. In 1991, this company was acquired by

Ameritech Information Systems, which also acquired Dynix. These acquisitions were undoubtedly spurred by system networking and information transfer considerations. As a telecommunications company, Ameritech stands in good position to profit from being a system supplier to one of the leading information transfer and networking market segments.

In 1990, NOTIS introduced its turnkey product, KeyNOTIS, which is based on the ES/9370 series IBM systems. NOTIS sells LMS as a software product and works with IBM jointly if a library needs to acquire appropriate hardware. NOTIS's market strength is primarily in the large academic research libraries and secondarily in the large public libraries. This is to be expected since in most of these settings there are parent organization IBM mainframes and data centers that can run the NOTIS software. LMS is an IBM CICS teleprocessing monitor application, and there are versions able to run under all IBM operating systems supporting CICS, i.e., the MVS family and VSE family on the smaller systems. NOTIS operates in two modes, a staff mode, which is command driven, and a public mode called, LUIS (Library User Interface System), which uses single-letter commands and guide/index screen item choices. The v.5.0 and 5.1 screens in the public catalog display labelled fields, replacing the previous version's card oriented screens.

LMS and KeyNOTIS feature acquisitions, fund accounting, public online catalog, cataloging, serials management, authority files, MARC record transfer via GTO (Generic Transfer and Overlay) and circulation for both regular loans and course reserve room short-term loan support. A system control file allows a customer to determine field labels for brief and long record displays. The new LSYS transaction allows menu-driven, in-library configuration of system parameters which formerly required a support programmer's services. LSYS controls all OPAC help screens, introductory, explanation and news screens, so the system's screens can be customized considerably. The new merged heading index for the OPAC provides "search under" and "search also under" references in OPAC index displays. "Search under" also handles search redirection to the preferred term. In addition, LSYS handles all NOTIS tables for security, circulation policy and calendars. The MARC Format for Holdings and Locations is fully implemented with v.5.0. Version 5.1 is now being installed by many NOTIS sites. The LMS is not a turnkey system and requires programmer support, including SAS programming if custom reports are desired.

Through its technical processing functions, LMS and KeyNOTIS use numerous action dates, which can be supplied as default values and operator overridden and changed to handle ordering, payment and receipt, claiming and other actions. The ACTINT field contains any four-digit number from 0001 to 9999, which is added to the date in the modification date field to determine a default action date. Catalogers can be supplied NOTIS MARC Tag Tables by running a batch processing job using the LB270 program. The system has full authority control, and large libraries like it for cataloging, as LC MARC resource files can be locally mounted and the records used to form the basis of the catalog record. Also, the GTO facility allows bibliographic record transfer from OCLC, RLG/RLIN and various CD-ROM-based products into the library's main database. Originally, transfer was implemented using a dedicated GTO PC gateway connected to OCLC or RLG/RLIN terminals. However, Vanderbilt University has implemented GTO from its Novell-based LAN which allows all of its stations to have simultaneous access to its NOTIS system and to OLC, and then to send records to OCLC. Its GTO scheme uses a Netware print queue in conjunction with a LANPress print server. The Netware login script contains a statement that redirects a nonexistent LPT3 device to the Netware print queue. The OCLC Passport software is then configured to use this LPT3 device to export records. Finally, this queue is serviced by the LANPress server, which is connected by serial cable to one of the ports on the HOSTESS multiport serial adapter in the GTO PC.

McGill University also has implemented its GTO in conjunction with its IBM terminal emulation gateway product, called NET3270, which is of interest to all potential NOTIS sites since it implements the full MARC character set. McGill's PCs run LaserQuest, a CD-ROM-based product on a network server and operate under Novell Netware. Again, Netware services are used to download LaserQuest records to the GTO PC and then sent up to the mainframe.

The MARC authority record format is used in the authority subsystem. Indexes to titles, main headings and added headings are generated online in real time. A merged heading index combines four staff views of the index (universal, authority, headings and music) with eleven search types (author, title, name, series, dictionary and six different subject searches). Merged heading index updating is dynamic. Keyword searching, formerly provided by a specially licensed version of BRS Search, is a batch update operation which needs to be run regularly to the keyword indexes available in public mode. These indexes are not searchable in staff mode.

LSER is the program that provides serials check-in and subscription support via acquisitions and claiming. Bindery preparation is not supported, so libraries need to develop their own approach for this. An example of such a bindery system is the University of Minnesota Libraries bindery support system, which was implemented in DataEase on a Novell Advanced Netware 3.11 LAN using Windows on the workstations and the Wall Data 3270 emulator for Windows, called Rumba. Bill Sozansky was the developer of this application at Minnesota. It has been extended to other University of Minnesota Libraries outside of the Wilson Library site via ipx protocol routing over 10Base-T Ethernet connections to the campus backbone. LSER provides workable support for serials, including defining captions used in holdings statements and six levels of enumeration to record a serial.

The circulation subsystem being rewritten for the next NOTIS release, v.5.2, provides the necessary features to support multibranch and varied, complex patron and material types. Support for the reserve book room will enable any academic library to gain some effective system support for that critical operation. The latest LMS version, v.5.1, supports location based catalogs, but it requires increased host resources to do this.

NOTIS has an optional front-end product, called Navigator, that provides single-level menu access to all NOTIS applications. One can set it up to allow multiple catalogs to be selected or multiple MDAS databases and non-NOTIS applications to be accessed. MDAS stands for Multiple Database Access System, which is the NOTIS-designed replacement for the previously licensed BRS Search to provide keyword and external database search engine support. One needs MDAS or the new NOTIS INFOBASE product to use Navigator. INFOBASE is NOTIS's first UNIX-based product to be released and is the first commercially available server to fully integrate the Z39.50 communications protocol. It operates on an IBM RS/6000 platform under AIX. INFOBASE allows patrons to use existing search commands and terminals for searching other databases and links searches to the library holdings in the main library bibliographic database. PACLink and PACSearch allow libraries to search remote online catalogs via the Internet. PACLink is a Z39.50 implementation as a client/server system. PACLoan allows patrons to electronically request interlibrary loans while searching remote catalogs, then define the method of delivery while online. Patrons are led through the necessary steps to search and make the loan request.

PROPAC, with a GUI version for Microsoft Windows and one for Apple Macintosh, is the client software to communicate with the Z39.50 products, such as INFOBASE, MDAS and eventually LMS. It was beta tested in March, 1993.

In 1990 NOTIS began an electronic data interchange (EDI) pilot project to send serial claims to Faxon. (11) The University of Minnesota Libraries became a beta site for this project. A working EDI system was brought up and continues to operate. An intermediate system, an IBM PC/AT is used to download claims from the NOTIS host. Then, this PC/AT runs the EDI software and calls Faxon's computer via modem to transfer the claims using Kermit file transfer to Faxon's VAX front-end computer. Only a minimally equipped MS-DOS personal computer is needed for this EDI function.

On the one hand, while NOTIS appears to be a rather traditional mainframe software supplier, it recognizes that users want to have a choice of platforms and increasingly are interested in implementing new systems on the client/server model. Its growth has been relatively steady, with over 225 sites now operating NOTIS systems. This vendor will be positioned well to continue to serve its large library customers while slowly improving its appeal to smaller academic and public library sites through further lessening the need for extensive programming and system level support for its software. NOTIS customers have their own support server, called NOTIServ, which has customer-written SAS programs and other useful items of which all NOTIS sites should be aware. Also a listserv, called NOTIS-L, is available to those with Bitnet/Internet access. It is filled with reports of glitches, problems, work-arounds, and questions and observations on diverse things users are encountering with this product's various releases. From early glimpses, NOTIS's new system, Horizon, appears to be a viable successor to mainframe NOTIS. Expect to see NOTIS continue to be a major player with increasing commitments to UNIX, client/server and networked applications.

b. Information Dimensions, Inc. Information Dimensions, formerly a division of Battelle Memorial Institute, is now a subsidiary of OCLC, Inc. Its product BASIS, a search-and-retrieval engine that has operated on several platforms, forms the core of its BASIS PLUS system targeted at organizations needing full text database support. This product operates on IBM mainframes, Digital Equipment Corp. VAX series and many UNIX-based computers. It was the only system of its type to also operate on Control Data Cyber mainframes under the proprietary NOS and NOS/VE operating systems. Using BASIS, Information Dimensions developed its TECHLib Plus integrated library system for the special library or corporate-wide network of information centers. Versions for IBM mainframes, VAX and UNIX provide multiuser capabilities over the full span of integrated technical processing, searching and outputs typically associated with an integrated library system.

The current version supports dynamic index and record updating. Searches can be performed on author, title, subject, keyword, call number, abstract, comments and table of contents. Soundex code searching is also a feature to assist in retrieval when exact spellings are not known. While the system's record structure itself is not MARC, any MARC record may be loaded and its content preserved. A MARC Management Module provides these loader services and can also produce MARC record output for record transfer to other systems. Serials check-in supports claiming and nicely customizable journal routing but does not support bindery preparation. The Acquisitions Module supports both electronic and hardcopy orders, invoices and payments. The Thesaurus Module can automatically switch a search term to a preferred, broader or narrower term and switch abbreviations or synonyms. Searches can be across all library locations and all material types or limited to specific locations and material types. Searches have three parts: field name, operator and search value. Field names include AUTH, all author fields; AU, author; TITLES, all title fields; TI, Title; SU, Subject; CA, Call number; KN, Key number; CO, Corporate author; CT, Catalog number; PHWORD, Phrase word. Operators are = (equal), ^= (not equal), INC (includes), > (is greater than),

< (is less than). The * (asterisk) and ? (question mark) are multiple and single wildcards that can be used at the beginning, middle or end of a search term. Online catalog searches use a labelled screen with fill-in-the-blanks data entry. Multiple entries on this screen are automatically ANDed together. A keyword search is equivalent to a Boolean OR search of author, title and subject fields. Full-set manipulation commands are provided to combine, review, discard, or choose items from a set and show summary or full records for selected items.

TechLib Plus is a well-designed and mature system to consider for the special library that needs wide system access throughout its organization. On IBM and compatible mainframes, it will run under VM/CMS, MVS/TSO and AIX operating systems. VAXes that run either VMS or Ultrix can run this software in its appropriate version. In addition, Hewlett-Packard HP-9000 systems under HP-UX, Sun Computers SPARC, Control Data Workstations (Silicon Graphics) and IBM RS/6000 series are all UNIX systems that now have TechLib Plus versions. Since these systems have penetrated many corporate settings, the special library should examine this solution in addition to examining LAN or PC-based solutions. Users with big-system interconnectivity needs will be better served by one of these implementations than the typical MS-DOS or Novell LAN-based solutions.

2. IBM AS/400 Minicomputer Family

IBM AS/400 systems range from very small systems, under $15,000 cpu, to dual processor, midrange systems with a system unit price of around $1,000,000. This range can support from several to 2000 workstations, depending upon the application. OS/400 is the proprietary operating system used across all AS/400 systems. These use an IBM 5250 terminal emulation which is similar in features to the IBM mainframe 3270 concept. The AS/400 systems are very user oriented, with excellent server capabilities, Ethernet support and TCP/IP implementation. They are widely installed in education, retailing, and service industries. As a successor to IBM's System 34, 36 and 38 machines, the AS/400 systems are equipped for versatile communications and for implementing easily supported turnkey applications. In February, 1993 IBM announced improved new models with 60% more capacity to replace existing AS/400 models. IBM also announced much larger models that are equals in throughput to most of the IBM 4381 series models. This should extend the useful life of AS/400 systems.

a. NSC, Inc. This small company offers its AARCS (Automated Record Control System), which includes A/V booking, cataloging, circulation, community information and referral, online catalog, serials management, acquisitions and system administration modules. The system supports bar code printing of CODABAR, 2 of 5 Interleave, CODE 39, CODE 128 and UPCA labels. MARC authority and cataloging are quite nicely implemented. A microcomputer circulation system for backup or remote book mobile operation is offered. The online catalog is fully authority controlled with "See" and "See Also" references. There are interfaces to most popular MARC record vendors' products. Fund accounting is fully integrated. Serials management includes check-in, claiming and routing but not bindery preparation. NSC licenses this software under various arrangements such as object-executable code only or both source and object code. Currently there are 21 customers, mainly public and special libraries. Screens have function key labels at the bottom, are character based and are nicely organized in a consistent manner. A new online catalog module is under development as is continued enhancement of the serials and acquisitions modules and expansion of the use of windowing capabilities. This is a well-designed system which could be used in small to relatively large settings as the range of AS/400 systems can support quite large databases and numerous simultaneous users. This system has good potential for its customer base to grow, given that the company can continue to offer its present customers enhancements and develop new software versions to take advantage of newer user interface techniques.

b. CMDS (Computer Management and Development Services). This vendor supplies a library automation system that is part of a larger system for smaller college and university or school district administration. It is called Teams2000, uses the Teammate relational database and is AS/400 based. Over 250 customers use this school administrative software. The whole system comprises admissions, financial aid, registration, advising/degree audit, general ledger, accounts receivable, accounts payable, purchasing, payroll, fixed assets, development/alumni and ED+ (which tracks diagnostic tests, creates individualized educational plans and learning outcomes). The other module is the Teams2000 Library system, which can operate outside of the larger system or as a part of it.

This system features an online public access catalog, which is menu driven, with fast path searches on author, title and subject by entering the first few characters in the string. One can page-forward and -backward through author, title and subject indexes from any point. Keyword searching using wildcards is provided. Search results can be printed into a bibliography or reading list. Cataloging in the system accepts OCLC and Bibliofile records, with interfaces to import other vendor records under development. Full MARC records and character set are supported. No special hardware beyond the AS/400 terminal is needed to enter diacriticals and special characters. Circulation and its printed outputs can be tailored to each library's needs. Bar code or keyboard entry of transaction data may be performed. The system produces a number of standard reports on circulation and catalog activity. The Teammate dbms (database management system) report writer facility can be used to generate custom reports. An acquisitions system works in concert with the

Teams2000 purchasing module. Using the BTLink software from Baker & Taylor, the bibliographic records can be loaded. There are no modules supporting serials or interlibrary lending, although the circulation system can be used to record charges to other institutions or libraries.

This system has a good start with its basic modules but could be enhanced considerably by further subsystem additions, which I am sure will come in the future. For educational enterprises looking to an enterprise business system, the Teams2000 system deserves serious evaluation. CMDS is an IBM Business Partner and Authorized Application Specialist firm.

c. Gateway Software Corporation. This company is relatively new, having been incorporated in 1989. It specializes in developing software for school districts, where often library system software is a subsystem of a larger school district's administrative system. This company would be a competitor to CMDS, above. Gateway's system is a well-designed IBM SAA (system application architecture) compliant menu and function key-driven system. It has excellent links and integration between its functions so that most actions can be invoked through a single key press. For example, in circulation, pressing the F6 function key will bring up any overdues that a current patron may have and pressing F9 will bring up the details of any fees due the library. Book discharging is very fast as a screen full of bar codes can be scanned and then sent to the system.

The online catalog can display its searches in either a card format layout or a labelled screen display. Librarians, but not patrons, have the ability to view a full MARC record display. Pressing F23 generates a program interrupt screen saying "Do not turn this workstation off. To do so could result in serious data damage." The program allows a temporary disabling of a workstation from the system and its reactivation by staff with a valid user identification and password. In cataloging and bibiographic maintenance, a full-screen editor is provided. Searches can be restricted to a specific library, group of libraries or all libraries. Subject heading lists and other searchable field lists can be scrolled and browsed in a window and selected as search values. Help is truly context sensitive and appears in a window with merely a function key press. For experienced users, the menus can be bypassed and a fast path command mode used. Title, author, subject, keyword, call number and Boolean searching are provided.

The circulation module can charge out equipment or other inventory items as well as conventional book and journal materials. Any bar code label not exceeding 24 characters can be accommodated but CODE 39 and CODABAR are the favored customer choices. The interlibrary loan module links to the circulation module to make interlibrary materials sharing easy and accurate. Acquisitions supports all ordering, tracking, claiming and fund accounting functions. There are numerous statistical reports included, but the customer can separately acquire IBM's Query software to create its own customized reports. This is the same approach that big-system supplier NOTIS uses where the SAS software is used to create batch query programs to extract and print various customized reports. SAS acts as the NOTIS Report Generator.

A separate Textbook Management System can be installed that will control textbook issuance to students and warehousing for a whole school district or specific schools. Student transfers and withdrawals and collection of any fees for lost or overdue items are smoothly implemented. Another separate module is Media Management/Booking, which schedules, tracks and inventories all types of media items. The system is fully integrated with the library management system's online catalog. Vehicles, conference rooms, training aids, delivery routes, loading lists and delivery instructions can also be handled by this system.

Gateway has twenty installations including one system with 25,000 students, 30 schools and 400,000 bibliographic records. An appropriately configured AS/400 with this software probably could handle the needs of all but a handful of the very largest of the school districts in the United States. This company has produced a well-thought-out system, one that it will be able to enhance and support into the future. I would expect them to grow in number of sites and become an even bigger player in the school market. However, the company below also will be a formidable school district competitor.

d. National Computer Systems, Inc. (NCS). The Education Systems Division (ESD) of National Computer Systems, Inc. (NCS) provides the Library Management System (LMS) as a module to its CIMS III Comprehensive Information Management for Schools software for school district administration. This system is very easy for children to use. System security is quite flexible and able to be controlled to the individual staff members' level for system functional access. Command-level security allows such a setup as each user must be authorized for each command allowed. It is not necessary to install the CIMS III software in order to use the LMS, but CIMS Student Management System student records can be used to create the LMS Patron records.

ESD's parent company, located in Eden Prairie, Minnesota, serves education, business and financial markets with optical mark reading, imaging scanners and forms for human resources administration, health care, sales administration and psychological assessment. It also licenses an asset management package for trust departments of financial institutions. In education, it is the leading supplier of forms-based data entry systems and test score capturing. Eighty-five percent of the nation's 1000 largest school districts use NCS test scanning systems. The Catalog Card Co. is another NCS division that provides retrospective conversion services for its library system and others.

LMS can be set up to provide user-defined media types, reading levels, categories limit descriptions, publisher usage, patron types and circulation rules.

Multiple or single libraries can be defined and added to the system at any time with no change in the software license fee. Both MARC and MicroLIF data can be imported into the system. A personal computer temporarily logged off the AS/400 can perform MicroLIF record conversion. The system can handle up to 40 media types, 60 reading levels, 40 categories of media genre and 10 alternate author types with a 9,999,999-item limit. Unlimited holdings and subjects can be accommodated. The subject authority file provides full cross-referencing using "See" and "See Also" in the public catalog. All records and indexes are dynamically updated in real time, including circulation status in the online catalog.

The system performs cataloging, circulation and online catalog functions. Inventory control via portable scanners is another feature, and the system can be interfaced to the CIMS III student database. It uses the IBM Query software as a report generator to provide customized reports from the system in addition to the many predefined reports. The cataloging module uses labelled display fields instead of MARC tags. Screens are uncluttered and quite consistent in data placement. System documentation is supplied on magnetic tape and may be printed by the customer on any printer attached to the AS/400 configuration. Each menu and command is explained in detail. Although the user manuals could include some additional data entry examples, they are excellent in their organization and coverage. At present the system I examined does not provide for any acquisitions or serials management functions. I do not know if these will be added in a later release, but prospective clients might wish to inquire about planned enhancements and any other features they desire but do not find in the product upon examination. Release 5.0 represents a well-designed and -integrated suite of functions for those modules presently included. K–12 school districts certainly should compare this system to the competing Gateway product, which, while from a newer and smaller company, does offer more modules to its system. It should be interesting to see if Gateway, CMDS and NCS can successfully tap K–12 school libraries with continually improving products. Prospective customers should examine these systems for their present features and expected future capabilities before deciding among them.

3. Unisys, Inc., PALS

PALS (Project for Automated Library System) was and is continuing in development at Mankato State University as the Minnesota State University automated library system. It had been marketed and supported also by Unisys, Inc., on whose Unisys 1100 and 2200 series mainframes it runs. It runs under the OS/1100 operating system which grew out of the former Sperry Univac rather than the Burroughs line of computers after Burroughs gobbled up Sperry Univac and formed the new company Unisys, Inc. Unisys has transferred PALS development and marketing to Dynix, Inc., an Ameritech company.

PALS has been known for its excellent software that has great ease of use coupled with considerable functional power. While PALS uses Unisys UTS terminal emulation, VT-100 terminal emulation has been added to the PALS workstation software so that a full range of internetworked systems can be accessed from a PALS system. Of appeal mostly to very large library systems or consortia, PALS has the drawback that it does not run on the most popular proprietary operating system and computer hardware. However, the Unisys hardware and operating system is one with a notable history of providing high-volume transaction processing support in demanding critical applications such as airline reservations and medicine. Therefore, despite the fact that there just are not the numbers of Unisys computers installed in academic and governmental settings that there are from IBM or DEC, this system remains attractive for consortia and large libraries.

PALS provides MASTERLINK, which allows a PALS workstation's client software to be updated directly on each library's system personal computer. Systems librarians at each site then need to transfer this software to their system's individual workstations.

The Minnesota system installation mentioned above and commonly referred to as MSUS/PALS has an online catalog of 3.4 million records, representing 50 Minnesota libraries, excluding the University of Minnesota which has almost 5 million bibliographic records in its NOTIS-based system, called LUMINA. MSUS/PALS, like LUMINA, is accessible via the Internet. The future of MSUS/PALS future is now being examined by a committee as the chief of the development of PALS, Dale Carrison, retired in early 1994.

PALS is a distributed system that uses a workstation program to provide considerable module functionality on Intel 80386 (or above) microcomputers running MS-DOS. PALS was a leader in providing functionality that made use of the microcomputer as more than just a terminal emulator in its first circulation system releases. The system consists of five subsystems: online public access catalog, cataloging, circulation, acquisitions, and serials control. PALS is programmed in COBOL and source code is provided under license. PALS is designed to be customer installable under the Unisys COMUS facility. The OPAC implements Boolean searching and use of search sets as well as the traditional author, title, subject, call number and term searching. Other fields of the MARC record can be indexed according to the customer's wishes when the system is set up. Users learn to search the catalog quite easily with this system. Help in context is immediately available. The circulation system is fully integrated with the online catalog and uses mnemonic commands. Transactions can be entered via bar code scanner or keyboard. PALS provides a PC-based backup circulation capability, whereas such a capability is not provided by NOTIS, one of PALS major competitors. Circulation also supports reserve room and course/instructor access to users.

The acquisitions subsystem is a fully functioning in-process system and can accept transfer of spreadsheet budget data into its fund accounting. The serials module handles all subscriptions of any type, including receiving, claiming, binding and holdings control. Issue arrival predictions are flexible and use a well-thought-out technique. An electronic interface to EBSCO has been recently announced and released. Most PALS libraries add records by processing an OCLC MARC tape, but PALS workstation software also provides a full-screen MARC editor to create and modify bibliographic records. PALS also supports third-party reference databases from Wilson and UMI using the same searching capabilities of the online catalog. The MARC editor can also be used to create special databases such as community information and referral. An interlibrary loan module was recently implemented, and it is fully integrated with the online catalog and the circulation system. Records are downloaded to a workstation from PALS to create interlibrary loan forms, and then the transaction is recorded in the circulation module if it is a loan to or a borrow from another institution for a PALS patron. One PALS system can include up to 36 separate libraries and can be accessed by a thousand or more users simultaneously depending upon the configuration and the network arrangements. PALS workstation software also supports the ALA MARC character set. A newly implemented authority control module provides full cross-referencing support. It also masks blind headings so no searches result from these. The authority file can be batch loaded and then also maintained with the MARC editor. The MARC editor runs on the PALS workstation, an Intel 80386SX (or above) under MS-DOS.

PALS public stations can be virtually any ANSI standard terminal or any personal computer. All modules used by staff support an MS-DOS–based personal computer as the access device. The computer needs to be at least an Intel 80286, but the MARC editor requires at least an Intel 80386SX system.

There is a Statistical Writer program that can produce off-line customized reports from up to 10 years of archived annual data from the system. Documentation is well organized and goes into excellent detail on defining the PALS profile definition and other aspects of setting up and using the system. Many worksheets are supplied as part of this documentation.

The current capabilities and its ease of use, coupled with significant power, make it an excellent contender, if not the winner, for top design honors among mainframe-class automated library systems. The foresightedness in recognizing the utility of the personal computer and the practice of continuing to build solutions that take advantage of developments in hardware on the desktop are to be commended. PALS will be in a strong position to provide future client/server architecture software using the OS/1100 operating system. Whether it will move in the direction of other vendors to offer a UNIX platform is not known. However, Unisys does remarket UNIX systems manufactured by another company as part of its product line. Also, it has been confirmed that the Minnesota State University system is looking at UNIX alternatives to its present Unisys proprietary systems. Therefore, it is likely that at some point PALS will move to UNIX. And, with Dynix supplying its systems to run under UniVerse, which runs PICK-implemented systems under UNIX, it certainly would be possible to begin a port of this system to UNIX, since COBOL can be recompiled under UNIX.

4. Digital Equipment Corp. VAX/VMS Family

The VAX family system range includes MicroVAX systems, VAXstations, VAXservers and large single and multiple processor VAX 9000 systems. These systems also can run Digital's UNIX implementation, called Ultrix. In this section I will discuss proprietary VMS systems but will also note if any other versions are available. VAX systems represent the second most popular host hardware platform in the United States.

a. Data Research Associates, Inc. (DRA). DRA was founded in 1975 and has provided hardware and software-turnkey and software-only systems using Digital Equipment computers. Over 800 libraries worldwide access DRA systems. These libraries range in size from 20,000 to 1.4 million titles and also represent a wide range in their respective number of patrons. This vendor is known for standards adherence and proselytizing to others about the virtues of library automation standards. While DRA was originally strong in public libraries with its flagship Cleveland Public Library customer, it now also has a considerable presence in academic and some special libraries. DRA is currently supporting and developing software in compliance with 17 library automation standards. It has opened offices in Australia and Singapore to tap the international market in the Pacific Basin. It also provides DRANET, its own private network to interlink its systems for messaging and access to its central computer, which has the MARC database loaded and accessible to customer libraries for cataloging purposes.

The DRA library system features acquisitions, online catalog, serials, cataloging, circulation, reserve room circulation and course reserve support, thesaurus, interlibrary loan, CD-ROM interfaces and MARC record interface. The system supports Boolean searches, the full MARC record, global changes and dynamic updating for all online activities. Batch record loads are updated during the batch processing run. DRA also sells a special system for libraries for the blind and physically handicapped which currently is the mainstay of the regional libraries established with federal government support to serve these users. Separately offered additional modules to the DRA library system are offered for media booking, union list of serials and newspaper indexing.

Variant module mixes are used when configuring the system for academic, public and special libraries to provide some distinct features for these types of libraries. Library networks and consortia are well supported through distributed databases, which allow each library to maintain its own parameters and system identity. DRA has considerable expertise in converting libraries from other systems to its own system. Networked cataloging access to its central MARC database and record transfer and overlay to the local database are provided.

DRA is working on a Z39.50 link connection with the University of California's MELVYL online catalog system. This was in test at this writing but not yet available to customers. It also has a workstation product under development using the IBM RS/6000 and Sun SPARC systems, and work is progressing on a DEC Windows desktop user interface and CJK (Chinese, Japanese and Korean) language support. DRA has announced commitment to support the Z39.63 Inter-Library loan standard. Electronic ordering is also an active project, with Brodart, Blackwell-North America, EBSCO, Faxon and several other vendors' systems involved. Its system supports the ALA MARC character set through DEC VT420 terminal emulation.

Here is a financially viable, growing company with 90 employees, with big plans to expand its market internationally as well as in the United States. To achieve this, the company is courting smaller library sites and pursuing software-only sales. Given that this system is flexible enough to accommodate the needs of a large public library as exemplified in its Cleveland Public Library site and yet also meet the needs of a large corporate library network at 3M Company, DRA's powerful system can be generalized or tailorable. With its push to use library standards and to aggressively pursue new market segments while providing sound support and enhancements to its existing customers, DRA should be a strongly positioned contender to continue as one of the market leaders in number of installations. In fact, DRA has almost the same number of systems installed in academic libraries as NOTIS, albeit mainly in somewhat smaller colleges and universities. With its VAX platform, DRA systems should be able to serve virtually any library, without regard to number of patrons or size of bibliographic database.

b. Centel Federal Services Corp. An integrated library system for the special library is offered by Centel. It is called DATALIB and has been installed in numerous federal government sites and private corporate libraries and information centers. The system is available as a VAX/VMS system, although a version is also offered for Data General minicomputers, which run the proprietary AOS/VS operating system. Originally, this system was developed on the Data General hardware. It is also available in a version to run under UNIX System V. Quite a diverse hardware spectrum, from small to large systems, can be supplied.

The system includes modules for acquisitions, online catalog, cataloging, circulation, serials and a thesaurus, and there is a MARC record interface. It is sold as a base system consisting of the online catalog and retrieval functions. Libraries can add the above modules as extra cost options. Acquisitions includes fund accounting and all the modules are well integrated. The online catalog features a graphical user interface, called PatronSEARCH, which is very much like Microsoft Windows on an MS-DOS personal computer. Mouse support, hot key commands, and point-and-shoot Boolean operators support sophisticated searching, including proximity searches. The serials module also supports bindery preparation.

Kunkel et al. give an excellent overview of this system in their article in *Library Hi-Tech*. (12) This is a system that special libraries should consider if they are searching for a solution that uses one of the system platforms for which this software is available. This is a mature system that has gone through numerous revisions and releases and has shown continued improvement.

c. Data Trek, Inc. While Data Trek has released a new Professional Series system for the MS-DOS and LAN environment using the C programming language and VBASE, its original system, called the Manager Series, includes a version for the VMS operating system. Manager Series is also offered on MS-DOS, Novell and Apple Macintosh. School and special libraries are the main purchasers of this system. Its VAX product offers circulation, online catalog, acquisitions, serials control and a MARC cataloging interface. It is the Manager Series micro-based product running under VMS on a VAX. See Chapter 8 for a more detailed view of the Manager Series product.

d. Dynix, Inc. Marquis, offered by Dynix, Inc., is the Dynix client/server architecture system for the VAX under VMS operating system, which was introduced in 1990. This system is available in versions that operate under UNIX versions on IBM RS/6000, Hewlett-Packard HP-9000, Sun and others. It can also be installed on a server under Novell Advanced Netware as a client/server application, with client software for both Intel 80386 (and above) workstations and Apple Macintosh computers. On Intel chip systems the client runs either OS/2 or MS-DOS and Microsoft Windows 3.1. The system is programmed in the C and Modula 2 languages.

Acquisitions, online catalog, serials management, cataloging and circulation are the Marquis modules known to be available at this writing. The system is a transportable client/server application using a GUI. It could be an indicator of the user interfaces that will undoubtedly be implemented in the near term by other competing vendors as the desktop moves ever more quickly to being dominated by the GUI instead of the DOS prompt. This is a system to watch as it is further developed. It will also be interesting to watch the sales performance of this product since it will test just how much real acceptance there is to actual deliverable client/server applications. Dynix offers other systems (described below) that are probably much better known due to their relatively large installed base.

Dynix Scholar is an Intel 80xxx-based microcomputer version of the original Dynix system; it is marketed mainly to school libraries. The original Dynix Automated Library System is a PICK implementation for a variety of platforms running PICK or UNIX with PICK, such as UniVerse. This is a very user oriented system, which library patrons really enjoy using. It features acquisitions, cataloging, circulation, reserve book room, backup/bookmobile, journal citation, serials control, PAC Plus, information and referral/community resources and media scheduling modules which, when run in concert with each other, are fully integrated. Libraries can license only the modules that they need for their particular system. Each Dynix system comes with the Recall Report Generator, which allows libraries to derive all sorts of custom reports from their system in addition to the many standard reports provided. Recall uses English-like statements as its query language. Dynix provides workshops for its customers on using this facility. Each of these modules has a standard set of reports, and using the Stat Manager menu, it is possible to define various statistical reports and instruct how the system will maintain patron and collection statistics. These modules are menu driven and the screens are very clear and consistent in data placement and logical use of the screen area.

The acquisitions module handles electronic order placement using the BISAC (Book Industry Advisory Committee) format. Interfaces for this are currently available for Baker & Taylor, Blackwell North America, B. H. Blackwell, Yankee Book Peddler, Ingram, Book House, Brodart, Franklin Book Midwest, and Professional Media Corp. The fund accounting system and other features of this module are all neatly executed to provide both smaller and very large libraries the features needed to handle any purchasing volume or complexity of accounts. During receiving of items, there is automatic routing, including rush and priority items.

The cataloging module provides a reliable and easy-to-use MARC record maintenance structure for catalogers. Automatic authority verification is performed online and records can be full-MARC, quasi-MARC or even non-MARC, which means that one can handle vertical file items, paperbacks and other furtive material not justifying the expense of full-MARC cataloging. Access points to the union catalog database are defined by the library. Search strategies are keyword, exact entry, root words and truncation. Boolean AND, OR and NOT are implemented. Searches may be limited also by search qualifiers such as date, language or material type. Tape loading of existing databases can be done to mount a MARC source file, for example. Optional direct interfaces to OCLC, RLIN, WLN, LSSI, Lasercat, Bibliofile, Autographics and others are available.

The Circulation module is designed for high-volume transaction processing and will support multiple-branch or consortium tracking of patrons. Bar code or OCR scanners are supported for transaction recording as is manual keying of the transaction. Up to six operator security levels plus dedicated terminals means that front desk terminals in public areas are secured even if staff have to temporarily move away from the desk area. Both small and large numbers of public service staff can be handled through this arrangement for maximum safety. Since only schools having reserve book rooms would need this module, Dynix has made it a separate, yet integrated facility in its system. Like the circulation module, it links to the online catalog, called PAC Plus, showing item status. Course/instructor support is a key part to this module and is well designed. Either general circulation terminals or specific reserve room only terminals can be used to perform these transactions. Depending on the security arrangements, other Dynix system modules can be accessed through a menu. The backup/bookmobile module uses a hand-held pocket calculator–size device to record transactions for check-out, check-in, logging of exceptions, patron blocks as it has a loadable patron block file. This device is the TELXON PTC-701 or 710, a 19-ounce pocket computer with a built-in bar code reader. Up to 6 hours of use on each of two supplied battery packs means that the bookmobile can recharge the sets when returning to the library at day's end.

The PAC Plus online catalog is a much enhanced version of the online catalog, maintaining and improving ease of use, power searching and many additional databases to the union catalog. The module includes Dial PAC, the American Heritage Dictionary, Best Seller/Reading Lists, Bulletin Board, patron information options and bibliography preparation with ProCite®. This module has as its companion the optional modules Journal Citation, Information and Referral/Community Resources, Citation Center, Gateways and Imaging. Library-modifiable, context-sensitive help is only a keystroke away at any time. Patrons can place their own holds on items. The Bulletin Board can contain site or systemwide bulletins and announcements. Searching can be by command mode for the experienced or by a window-prompted mode for new users. Each location can define how search results will be displayed. Summary screens, full bibliographic displays and column/field labels are all definable by the library. Fields to be used for limiting searches can be selected. A library modifiable synonym list, full authority control, full Boolean searching, unlimited indexing, cross-index searching, and automated tracings to related works are all features. Search tracking reports help a library evaluate PAC Plus use. The Best Seller/ Reading Lists can link to the online catalog and show status and allow holds. The Bibliography Manager supports multiple formats and allows saved lists to be named and retrieved, with options to save to disk in MARC or ProCite® formats. This module has many other slick options, making it a natural for student and faculty use in a research setting. Catalog records can be displayed in

MARC format or in labeled, formatted form. The Journal Citation module loads citations and abstracts from various vendors, links these to library holdings and full-text articles and provides searching identical to the online catalog. Vendors include ABI/Inform, EBSCO, H. W. Wilson, and Information Access Company. The Gateway module provides a modem or network access connection to remote computer systems selected through a directory of remote systems. The Linked Image databases provide for scanned images to be linked to bibliographic entries, displayed for preview in a postage stamp size on access workstations and in full image as desired. A Z39.50 Search and Retrieval engine provides a client program in both a graphical user interface and a character-based one. The server software supports TCP/IP protocols. The Citation Center offers Dynix citation databases via the Internet, with full-text article links for a monthly fixed access charge.

The Information and Referral/Community Resources module is another impressive facility to inform library users about clubs and organizations, events, fugitive facts, questions and answers since it has files set up for these purposes. The question-and-answer setup allows library patrons to ask any question of the library and receive a response in their patron personal record or to be viewed on the online catalog terminals. There is even a filter word list to screen out offensive language and counts of how many times a question is accessed by patrons. The electronic mail feature refers unanswered questions to other staff members. This module also provides newspaper indexing so all sorts of local indexing projects may be supported and accessed from any public terminal.

The Serials Control module really handles the job, including full bindery support. It fully links in with the online catalog, fund accounting, vendor file and full subscription management. Routing is flexible and able to serve virtually any imaginable organizational situation. This module will also produce brief and full serials catalogs which can be viewed online, printed or produced on microfiche. Dynix provides a publication pattern exchange based on other clients, so libraries can import accurate publication patterns to generate more reliable predicted arrivals for their check-in work based on other clients. This should save a lot of time in setting up serials records on the system.

The Media Scheduling module completes the currently offered modules. It provides scheduling, circulation and media catalog maintenance with the same excellent and flexible searching and reporting of the other Dynix modules. The Dynix system provides modules of depth and power that will be excellent functional models for transporting to Dynix's Marquis and Scholar products. Dynix systems serve over 1600 libraries of all types worldwide. This system can be implemented in any library or information center, handling both light and heavy duty transaction loads on its wide range of hardware platforms. Dynix customer libraries receive very sound technical product support in a timely fashion. Ameritech Information Systems, the parent of both Dynix and NOTIS Systems,

Inc., has two formidable players in the library market, each with sizeable, yet different segments of the market.

e. Gaylord Information Systems. Gaylord has offered various software to the library market for over a decade. As the largest supplier to libraries of supplies and equipment, Gaylord offers its customers a large and established company working on their behalf. Gaylord was founded in 1896. Its venerable Gaylord Model C charging machine, introduced in 1934, is still in use in some 6000 libraries worldwide. It began offering computer-based systems in 1974. The Galaxy System can be obtained as a software-only or complete turnkey system on an appropriate VAX computer system. The system has been popular with small- to medium-size public and college libraries. At this time nine school districts have installed this system.

Acquisitions, online catalog, cataloging, CD-ROM interface, serials management, interlibrary loan, circulation and reserve room modules are available. A report generator, Datatrieve, is used to produce customized reports. The catalog is fully authority controlled. The CD-ROM interface is LC's CD-MARC for cataloging records import into the system. SuperLINK is a new online communication facility between Galaxy and other systems via an OSI, NISO Z39.50 and X.400 compliant module to transfer electronic mail and queries. SuperSEARCH extends a Galaxy database by accessing Wilsondisc and Infotrac CD-ROM databases. SuperSHARE allows Galaxy to share its files with other academic, corporate or local computer files such as student/faculty college and university administrative systems to provide Galaxy with its patron file for circulation. SuperCAT cataloging uses the above LC MARC database, including an optional foreign language title disk. Galaxy also supports importation of OCLC Prism bibliographic and authority records.

There is a portable Galaxy for bookmobiles and circulation backup that uses an MS-DOS laptop computer. The online catalog is Z39.58 Common Command Language compliant, just like several of the library systems in use by very large libraries. A map of the library showing collection locations can be displayed on patron stations. This is a fully functional, well-integrated system that shows its developers do know libraries and library operations. Screens are nicely laid out and easy to scan quickly. Menu choices also are easy to understand. In the circulation system, a useful public or school library feature is the linking together of patrons, so a family's children can be linked to one or both parents, and the parents similarly linked. There is even an Easy Access System (EASE) for the visually impaired that uses a braille screen printer, screen magnification on demand and a synthetic speech/voice synthesizer.

Make no mistake; even though this system has been initially targeted for installations of 30–60 terminals, this system has large-system features and robustness. On an appropriate VAX configuration even the databases of the largest ARL libraries can be operated. A modest VAXserver 4000 system can handle up to 12 GB of disk storage. Gaylord should be a powerful competitor in the market in any targeted direction it tries to take this system. Its 215-terminal installation in New York State has been quite successful.

f. Comstow Information Services

Comstow has offered its Bibliotech software to the special library since 1980, with some 50 libraries continuing to operate it and receive high levels of satisfaction. Its clientele are all long-term customers, which attests to Comstow's excellent support and provision of enhancements desired by its customers. (The two customers that have left Comstow did so not because of dissatisfaction with the product. Rather, one company closed its library because of a merger and the other was required to use a microcomputer instead of the company's VAX.) I know of no other vendor with such a loyal and satisfied customer group. Users report that their Hotline Customer support is top notch as are their annual user group meetings. This is nothing short of remarkable performance.

While Bibliotech is a VAX/VMS product, Comstow has recently begun offering a UNIX version called Bibliotix, which runs on Sun Computers SPARC systems and Hewlett-Packard Apollo workstations. Basic Bibliotech includes catalog maintenance, authority control and an online catalog with a 4GL (Fourth Generation) command language and report writer. There are numerous batch data conversion programs for Dialog, OCLC, LC, MARCive and Bibliofile records. Provisional entries can be made in the authority file. Terms automatically transfer from authority to the catalog record when cataloging on the system. The optional thesaurus module adds hierarchical cross-references. Searching is menu driven, with the Thesaurus used to pluck terms for the search. A browse mode covers 14 different indexes and permits right-hand truncation. Boolean searches using AND, OR and NOT can be limited by other qualifiers such as date and type of material. The report writer comes with 18 predefined formats, including claims, orders, spine labels, overdue notices, route slips and even catalog cards. Periodicals Control and Circulation modules are integrated so as to provide seamless circulation of individual periodical issues.

Lynda W. Moulton, President of Comstow, is the author of a text on designing databases for special libraries which should be a must read for all librarians contemplating system implementation. (13) User documentation is very well organized and clearly written, and the system can be smoothly adapted for the corporate library within a shared VAX as it has excellent resource utilization. A CD-ROM access module allows VAX network-connected workstations to access CD-ROMs on a Virtual MicroSystem V server with a Meridian CD-ROM jukebox under Novell Advanced Netware 3.11. An article in the electronic journal Automatome, published by the American Association of Law Libraries, Automation and Scientific Development SIS, describes one law library's experiences with Bibliotech in a most positive way. (14) The firm is Pillsbury, Madison and Sutro in San Francisco, with four branch offices and 621 attorneys.

5. Hewlett-Packard HP-3000 Family

HP-3000 series systems are based on proprietary RISC architecture processors and range from small microcomputers to large systems with over 30 MIPS speed and with support for up to 85 GB of hard disk. These systems run versions of the proprietary MPE operating system.

a. Inlex, Inc. This company recently acquired the MS-DOS- and LAN-based program called The Assistant, formerly offered by Library Automation Products, Inc., which should appeal to smaller libraries and special libraries. Inlex in turn was acquired by Data Research Associates in late 1993. Inlex's main product is the Inlex/3000 library system based on Hewlett-Packard mid-range systems. Customers are mainly public and college libraries, with over 100 systems installed. Counter to the general trend of system suppliers, Inlex has developed its own terminal called the Inlex 200 series to support the ALA MARC character set and provide other features. Inlex/3000 offers acquisitions, online catalog, cataloging, circulation and interlibrary loan. Additional modules consist of inventory control, community information and referral, external computer gateway, portable circulation, report generator, authority control and smart bar code processing. The acquisitions module supports electronic ordering from Ingram and Blackwell North America. In 1992, periodical databases from IAC and Wilson were added. Serials and media booking are currently in development but a release date is not known. Circulation can be complemented by a reserve book room module for academic settings. Inlex is also working on integrating a CD-ROM jukebox system interface. The Inlex/3000 catalog has been described by Howard Pringle (15), and Waller and Pearce have discussed Inlex system enhancements in *Library Hi-Tech News*. (16) Users interested in this Hewlett-Packard platform will need to compare this system to the VTLS system discussed below. Inlex sales have been mainly in the United States, whereas VTLS has enjoyed increasing popularity abroad.

b. VTLS, Inc. The original Virginia Tech Library System (VTLS) operated on Hewlett-Packard HP-3000 systems under MPE. This version continues to be a mainstay product of this company, which Virginia Tech formed to continue development, support and commercial marketing of VTLS. One-half of current VTLS sites are installed in foreign countries, mainly Europe. VTLS has also developed an IBM mainframe version operating under VM/SP, VM/IS, VM/XA, and VM/ESA using SQL/DS. A UNIX version is available. Its other product is MicroVTLS, which is a compiled dBase III Plus implementation designed to run on a Novell LAN with MS-DOS 386 or 486 systems as server and workstations. VTLS has also have developed InfoStation, a multi-media workstation based on the NeXT workstation and this product links to the VTLS online catalog. (17) Now that NeXT has ceased hardware production and offers its NeXTStep software on Intel and other microprocessors, VTLS InfoStation uses NeXTStep on the Intel 80486 system.

VTLS is an established and mature system possessing good integration. It uses standard DBMS products in each of its versions. Acquisitions, online catalog, cataloging, CD-ROM interface, interlibrary loan, serials, circulation, reserve book room and a thesaurus are major modules offered. The system supports full-text searching using Boolean operators. Some users have complained over the quality and features in the online catalog's user front end, which runs on MS-DOS computers, so that one could expect VTLS to make improvements in this area or possibly face one of its user sites to create a better front end. Public, school, university and special libraries are present customers of this system as are some consortia or multiple library cooperatives. Of interest to prospective system customers will be the Proceedings of the First Annual VTLS Library Directors' Conference. (18) For Internet connected users, there is a listserv called VTLSLIST@VTVM1.BITNET. A good basic descrip-tion of the system was provided by McGrath and Lee in 1989, but since then, there have been considerable enhancements and new products. (19) VTLS has been a leader in pushing multimedia-enhanced systems, and it has been a leader in providing multiple platform products to appeal to a broad spectrum of dif-ferent types and sizes of libraries. VTLS is likely to increase its strength, particularly in the foreign market.

6. Tandem Computers: CARL Systems, Inc.

OCLC's systems are based on Tandem fault-tolerant computers as is the UTLAS network in Canada. Presently, only the CARL (Colorado Alliance of Research Libraries) system appears to be available on this platform. CARL has assumed support of all UTLAS T/50 series systems, which were the former DataPhase ALIS III systems. All but two of these have replaced their T/50 software with CARL software. CARL's goal is to convert all of these systems to the CARL software. A related development, the acquisition of marketing rights to the Tacoma Public Library's ALICE-B system by Ameritech could bring this system back to the market, but my inquiries to Ameritech produced no response as to the fate of ALICE-B. At the Tacoma Public Library ALICE-B uses a CD-ROM–based online catalog but performs technical processing and public service functions on a Tandem computer system. (20) Want to bet that Ameritech continues to remain silent on ALICE-B?

CARL is programmed in TAL, Tandem's proprietary language. It provides acquisitions, online catalog, CD-ROM interface, serials management, cataloging, circulation and reserve book room support. CARL's own system provides the Uncover article database on subscription via Internet and modem connections. Uncover2 document delivery is another fee-based service to libraries. CARL is designed to serve as a library consortia and multi-institutional system. CARL's 27 installed sites are all big systems with 4,976 total dedicated terminals and Internet connectivity. Another current goal is to develop a graphical user interface to its online catalog.

Clearly, large libraries will be interested in examining CARL as a competing system to NOTIS, DRA, PALS, DYNIX and VTLS as suppliers of very large networked library systems. Some six years ago, the Triangle Research Libraries Network (TRLN) developed an online catalog which was a module in its integrated bibliographic information system—a system that was never really completed. It was based on Tandem hardware, but because of the aging hardware base and need to significantly upgrade the hardware to run Tandem's current operating system version, the Triangle development ceased. TRLN has now chosen to install a DRA VAX-based system. TRLN had the old Tandem TXP processors. The Guardian Operating System version c30 was not to be supported past December 31, 1993 on these systems. While Tandem was at one time a much more popular host system for large libraries, this is not now the case. Lower cost and increased reliability of conventional systems have obviated the need for truly fault tolerant and fully redundant systems in all but a few settings. However, the architecture of Tandem systems, its leadership in distributed database development and rugged, high-performance software and hardware will appeal to very large sites.

While Tandem systems still represent the Rolls Royce in fault-tolerant architecture and online transaction processing, Tandem itself will be re-examining its directions. If it can adopt POSIX standards as a part of Guardian, it probably will continue to compete well in its relatively narrow market segment. Otherwise, it may suffer the same fate as some of the other mini/superminicomputer manufacturers, either going out of business or reshaping into a very different company with more standardized product lines. Somehow I find the marketplace realities sad, as I have always had a high regard for the capabilities of Tandem hardware and software.

IV. CONCLUSION

The largely proprietary operating system-based solutions presented here represent many years of continued development and refinement. They are workable, competitively priced solutions for libraries, with numerous current customer sites to which prospective clients can refer. As computing technology developments march on at an accelerating rate, expect to see changing roles for today's midrange and mainframe systems as they take on more server functions in a client/server implementation strategy, made inevitable by the desktop revolution. Rather than considering moves to UNIX and away from proprietary systems, libraries should instead be considering the directions library software developers and computer manufacturers take to implement POSIX-compliant applications and operating system application program interfaces. Also, customers should be concerned over maintainability and release of new product features by vendors in addition to current customer support proficiency. Finally, libraries that really want to be on the leading edge are going to have to be willing to help vendors as beta test sites and as continued devil's advocates for necessary enhancements together with insistence on standards adherence. Customers served by the vendors included in this chapter are the libraries most likely to play dynamic roles in improving access to information resources since these libraries are relatively large, serve considerable scholarly communities or populations and many have interconnections via the Internet.

APPENDIX: VENDOR CONTACTS

CARL Systems, Inc.
3801 E. Florida Avenue
Bldg. D. Suite 300
Denver, CO 80210
(303) 758-3030
(303) 758-0606 Fax

Centel Federal Services Corp.
11400 Commerce Park Drive
Reston, VA 22091
(800) 762-5632
(703) 758-7000
(703) 758-7380 Fax

CMDS—Computer Management & Development Services
1661 Virginia Avenue
P.O. Box 1184
Harrisonburg, VA 22801
(800) 999-2637
(703) 432-5275 Fax

Comstow Information Services
249 Ayer Road
P.O. Box 277
Harvard, MA 01451-0277
(508) 772-2001
(508) 772-9573 Fax

Data Research Associates, Inc.
1276 North Warson Road
P.O. Box 8495
St. Louis, MO 63132-1806
(800) 325-0888
(314) 432-1100
(314) 993-8927 Fax

Data Trek, Inc.
5838 Edison Place
Carlsbad, CA 92008
(800) 876-5484
(619) 431-8400
(619) 431-8448 Fax

Dynix, Inc.
151 E. 1700 South
Provo, UT 84606
(800) 288-8020
(801) 375-2770
(801) 373-1889 Fax

Gateway Software Corp.
10 S. Montana
P.O. Box 367
Fromberg, MT 59029
(800) 735-3637
(406) 668-7661
(406) 668-7665 Fax

Gaylord Information Systems
Box 4901
Syracuse, NY 13221-4901
(800) 962-9580
(315) 457-5070
(315) 457-4760 Fax

Information Dimensions, Inc.
5080 Tuttle Crossing Boulevard
Dublin, OH 43017-3569
(800) DATA-MGT
(614) 761-7446
(614) 761-7290 Fax

Inlex, Inc.
One Lower Ragsdale Drive
Building #1, Suite 200
P.O. Box 1349
Monterey, CA 93940
(800) 553-1202
(408) 646-8600
(408) 646-0651 Fax

National Computer Systems, Inc.
Educational Systems Division
1201 S. Alma School Road
Suite 9500
Mesa, AZ 85210-2013
(800) 736-4357
(602) 464-0023

NOTIS Systems, Inc.
1007 Church Street, 2nd floor
Evanston, IL 60201-3622
(708) 866-0150
(708) 866-0178 Fax

NSC, Inc.
428 W. Ryan Street
Brillion, WI 54110
(800) 624-5720
(414) 756-5305
(414) 756-2359 Fax

Unisys, Inc.
P.O. Box 500 MS B140
Blue Bell, PA 19424-0001
(215) 986-6423
(215) 986-6583 Fax

VTLS, Inc.
1800 Kraft Drive
Blacksburg, VA 24060
(800) HOT-VTLS
(703) 231-3605
(703) 231-3648 Fax

REFERENCES

1. *Information Retrieval Service Definition and Protocol Specifications for Library Applications. American National Standards Z39.50-1988. National Information Standards Organization. Approved Jan. 15, 1988.* New Brunswick, NJ: Transaction Publishers, 1989.
2. Black, Uylesses. *The X Series Recommendations: Protocols for Data Communications Networks.* New York: McGraw-Hill, 1991.
3. Davidson, John. *An Introduction to TCP/IP.* New York: Springer-Verlag, 1988.
4. Lynch, Clifford. Linking Library Systems to the Internet. *Library Hi-Tech 7*(4): 7-18 (1989).
5. *Library Hi-Tech 8*(4) (1990). Special issue on Open Systems Interconnection.
6. Krol, Ed. *The Whole Internet User's Guide & Catalog.* Sebastopol, CA: O'Reilly, 1992.
7. Polly, Jean A. Surfing the Internet: An Introduction. *Wilson Library Bulletin 66*(10): 38-42, 155 (June 1992).
8. Barron, Billy. Accessing On-line Bibliographic Databases. Available via anonymous FTP to unt.edu in directory LIBRARY/Libraries.TXT.
9. St. George, Art. Internet Accessible Library Catalogs and Databases. Available via anonymous FTP to ariel.unm,edu in directory /Library Internet.Library.
10. Pourciau, Lester J. Automated Library System Migration in the United States. *The Electronic Library 10*(2): 103-108 (April 1992).
11. Schwartz, F. E. The EDI Horizon: Implementing an ANSI X12 Pilot Project at the Faxon Company. *Serials Librarian 19*(3-4): 39-57 (1991).
12. Kunkel, Barbara K., Lerinda L. Frost, M. J. Stivers et al. DATALIB: Information Resource Management System. *Library Hi-Tech 8*(3): 61-69 (1990).
13. Moulton, Lynda W. *Databases for Special Libraries: A Strategic Guide to Information Management.* New York: Greenwood Press, 1991.
14. Howell, Betty. Bibliotech Software. *Automatome 10*(3/4): 6-7 (Summer/Fall 1991). Also, Howell, Betty. Choosing an Integrated Library System—The Pillsbury Experience. *San Francisco Bay Region Chapter of Special Libraries Association Bulletin* (November/December 1991) pp. 5, 11, 16.
15. Pringle, Howard. Inlex Online Catalog. In: *The Online Public Catalog*, edited by Walt Crawford. G. K. Hall, 1992.
16. Waller, Earl and Melvin Pearce. Performance Issues of Automated Library Systems: Enhancing Inlex—A Case Study. *Library Hi-Tech News* (May 1988).
17. Lee, N. S. InfoStation: A Multimedia Access System for Library Automation. *Electronic Library 8*: 415-421 (December 1990).
18. Boucher, Rick and Frank R. Bridge et al., eds. Proceedings of the 1st Annual VTLS Library Directors' Conference—Linking Multimedia Digital Libraries: Where We Are, Where We're Going. Blacksburg, VA. *Information Technology and Libraries 11*(1): 40-61 (March 1992).
19. McGrath, Deborah H. and Carl R. Lee. The Virginia Tech Library System (VTLS). *Library Hi-Tech 25*: 17-28 (1989).
20. Mischo, Lare. The Alice-B Information Retrieval (IR) System: A Locally Developed Library System at Tacoma Public Library. *Library Hi-Tech 8*(1): 7-20 (1990).

7

THE NEWER BREED OF CONCURRENT MULTIUSER SYSTEMS

We are in an engineering age, an electrical age, with its physical, commercial, industrial and social changes, with its new conditions, new opportunities and new responsibilities.

—Charles F. Scott, 1903 AIEE President's Address,
June 29, 1903. [*AIEE Trans.* *22*: 3-15 (1903).
AIEE and IRE were forerunners of the IEEE.]

I. INTRODUCTION

While many of the companies featured in this chapter have been in the library system market for some years, their product lines have received substantial revision in many cases. Their previous systems were usually based on some proprietary operating system and sometimes used highly customized hardware in their turnkey systems. Many of these vendors have adopted the open system path by moving their products over to UNIX-based systems. There is no doubt that as UNIX further coalesces into fewer variants and also adopts POSIX application interface standards that these systems will be strongly positioned to compete against systems based on major proprietary operating systems. However, proprietary operating systems are also becoming POSIX compliant. I have included information on three European systems as they are in wide use abroad. In the case of Information Management and Engineering, this system is actively marketed in the United States. Databasix is marketed in Europe. BookShelF, from Specialist Computer Systems and Software, Ltd., is marketed in Great Britain. However, with the market for software becoming global, this could change at any time.

Unfortunately, there is no single correct path for all institutions to follow in their desire to have more open architecture systems with increased levels of software portability and maintainability. If this were the case, there would not be the diversity of opinion among system vendors and librarians as to how to reach this elusive nirvana state.

All that can be said for certain is that systems of the future must increase their maintainability, their robustness when dealing with ever larger and more numerous complex records, and their flexibility to accommodate new record structures to handle digitized materials—scanned images of text, graphics, and recorded sound. Future systems will employ new development tools to improve these characteristics. This will make it easier for vendors to build their new releases for existing platforms and for new hardware as these systems replace older hardware. With newer computers based increasingly on RISC architecture microprocessors, such as DEC's Alpha chip, there will be further accelerations in the UNIX market since it is most likely that vendors planning to use these chips will have new UNIX ports made instead of developing a whole new operating system. Similarly, POSIX will develop on these new systems because of its portable design. The cost of RISC chips has continued to decrease. Today, a porting house can deliver a UNIX port for a new microprocessor normally in under six months, since it is only the UNIX kernel that must receive the rewrite. Contrast that to a totally new operating system development that would take 2–3 years and much expense. Market economics make it clear that many new multiuser hardware platforms will support a UNIX, a UNIX with POSIX features or a full POSIX operating system if there are perceived deficiencies in the UNIX product when compared with what might be created from ground zero.

Libraries should follow their parent institution's data and information processing developments very closely. Since mixed-vendor installations are becoming more the norm today, libraries are going to be faced with a wider array of realistic choices that will be consistent with the systems directions being taken at their parent institution's highest level. In some institutions, e.g., large colleges and universities, it is possible for the library's systems needs to be a driving force behind the institution's systems planning. In these settings every campus network connection must be capable of accessing the library's online catalog, a database that usually represents one of the larger, if not the largest, mass storage repositories among campus administrative and research computing. In institutions where the library is a much smaller collection and where there is more flexibility as to remote access options for the library's clientele, such as in the corporate sector, there are much wider options to consider. While examining these directions, bear in mind that the inexpensive hardware as exemplified by today's desktop PCs of under $2000 and the low current licensing fees for LAN-based products are only part of the cost of acquiring, installing and becoming operational on an automated system. Data conversion, staff training and maintaining/upgrading software are other aspects. Another key aspect to consider is your library's and your institution's ability to provide system support. The emphasis in the nineties is on wider inter-networked user access to complementary data resources. There is also acceleration in implementing applications using scanned image data and multimedia features. These significant factors, together with database size and transaction load, will influence whether a library chooses a host-based system or a PC/LAN-based solution.

II. NONPROPRIETARY OPERATING SYSTEMS

Nonproprietary operating systems are those based on one of the UNIX operating system versions: AT&T's UNIX System V from UNIX System Laboratories, University of California—Berkeley's UNIX or another version from a commercial firm. Another category of nonproprietary operating systems includes those systems that are implemented using the PICK operating system. PICK is proprietary to PICK Systems, which has created versions of its truly portable system for over 100 computer models worldwide. Moreover, there have been ports where PICK is able to run as a guest or on top of UNIX, thereby making it possible for applications coded in the PICK BASIC language to operate under a UNIX system and use the TCP/IP networking features of UNIX while preserving the data manipulation and searching strengths inherent in systems implemented using PICK BASIC and the built-in DBMS features of the PICK operating system. Another approach is the separation of these DBMS functions, which makes it possible to use PICK BASIC for the application language while using a SQL-compliant DBMS under the UNIX operating system. UniVerse is an example of an operating system where PICK-based systems can run, along with UNIX applications and TCP/IP networking.

Most expansion of the open systems market is occurring through the increased sales of workstations such as Sun Microsystems, Hewlett-Packard Apollo, Silicon Graphics and DEC's VAXstations, all of which use UNIX. The question for the future is whether these workstations will supplant an MS-DOS/Windows or possibly an OS/2-equipped personal computer on the desktop. To the marketplace, open systems have come to mean UNIX-based systems, with software portability considerations the main force driving users away from proprietary platforms. With proprietary platforms there is still fear that hardware will be dropped and application migration made much more complex or totally impractical. Witness in history the demise of DEC's PDP-11 series systems, which ran RSTS and RSX operating systems. RSTS systems with applications implemented in BASIC PLUS could migrate more easily to DEC's new VAX series. However, depending on the language used, RSX systems posed numerous additional hurdles when trying to rewrite for the VAX. At the time of the VAX introduction, this was still the normative state of computing, as new architecture hardware designs made earlier systems obsolete.

Normal daily business situations tend to reenforce expansion and enhancement of current systems, rather than the adoption of radical changes of direction that are represented by moving from a proprietary system to the UNIX world. While UNIX applications are widely portable in source code form, vendors cannot protect their software rights with source distribution. Therefore, commercially supported systems must be delivered in binary form. This means that library system vendors need to do the port to a variant UNIX platform. UNIX providers, such as Santa Cruz Operations, have espoused a binary compatibility among Intel 80386 (and above) implementations. Binary compatibility allows "shrink-wrapped" software distribution in the UNIX world, something that could increase the sales of UNIX applications.

With the IEEE POSIX work resulting in an operating system specification completely independent of UNIX rather than fulfilling its original intention of resolving the major variant differences within UNIX family systems, what has occurred is that both UNIX and proprietary vendors are moving to implement POSIX standards in their respective products. This means that the eventual goal will likely be a convergence toward POSIX. This future universal multiuser platform will preserve software investments better as hardware continues to improve at an accelerated rate compared with software.

Today, there are two trade consortiums that have split the UNIX market into two major portions. The Open Software Foundation (OSF) includes market leaders Hewlett-Packard, Digital Equipment Corp., and IBM. The UNIX International group includes UNIX System Laboratories (AT&T) and Sun Computers. On the international level the X/Open consortium is increasingly influencing the directions taken by both OSF and UNIX International. OSF is pushing adoption of its Architecture Neutral Distribution Format (ANDF) as the way to develop the retail market for open systems. Perhaps the key to determining future directions will rest with the cost of microprocessors. If new RISC-based microprocessors such as DEC's ALPHA are comparable to Intel's new Pentium—as both have come onto the market at relatively the same time—there could be even hotter competition between UNIX-based platforms and Novell Advanced Netware or Windows NT promised features. One thing that makes UNIX systems of increasing interest to libraries is that there have been substantive transaction processing enhancements which make UNIX a desirable, high-performance system for libraries having large numbers of online, real-time transactions such as circulation and inventory.

Current UNIX workstations can deliver 100-MIP-class performance. This is over twice the performance of typical late 1980's mainframe systems. Expect similar power from Motorola/IBM/Apple's PowerPC at very competitive prices. The future is still somewhat clouded as to whether automated library systems will be better off under UNIX or a proprietary system. Systems yet to be delivered might be a future route for some vendors. The move to client/server applications under UNIX or to client/server applications under current LAN systems such as Novell or systems such as Microsoft's Windows NT is influencing future choices, too. Microsoft is saying they will port NT to numerous microprocessor platforms, so it is ready to take on the UNIX open system head to head. Since Windows NT supports TCP/IP and the new Unicode, 16-bit character set, the foreign language support makes it attractive for systems marketed worldwide. Digital Equipment Corp.'s Alpha-equipped systems now run Windows NT. The future marketplace will ultimately be decided as customers vote with their software and hardware dollars.

III. CONCURRENT MULTIUSER SYSTEMS

I present here some popular systems that have been traditionally based on mid-range minicomputer class hardware, using mainly UNIX or PICK as their software platform. I am including several proprietary systems that are newer, as is the case with Grom-Hayes, or are more specialized to the media center, as is the case of Dymaxion.

A. UNIX and PICK Systems

With software outside of that provided by PICK systems generally not portable, vendors have adopted one or more of the following approaches to designing for platforms of the future. One group believes UNIX to be the future wave and that only through this path will truly open systems become reality. Another group believes that, given the variants within UNIX, it really cannot be considered one operating system platform so that movement of this software is no easier than movement of software among proprietary systems. A third group maintains that while maintaining one's original, mainly proprietary platform versions, one can rewrite or through some technique port one's existing systems to UNIX and/or develop new systems using UNIX while adding these functions to one's original systems. For the purchaser, the more important consideration may be POSIX developments on that platform and POSIX compliance in the library application. Also, library products developed using the Z39.50 standard have become a competitive requirement. Just as there is an operating system battle for the desktop between IBM's OS/2 and Microsoft's MS-DOS/ Windows and Windows NT systems, there is a similar struggle taking place between proprietary and nonproprietary operating systems in the multiuser, midrange to high-end systems. UNIX is gaining ground in this struggle but slowly.

1. BRS Software Products

BRS/SEARCH in both its C version and mainframe version is a full-text searching engine which allows a multiplicity of applications to be supported such as bibliographic database search and retrieval, litigation support, campus information systems, product support manuals and documentation. Toolkits for developers to integrate BRS/SEARCH into relational DBMS, imaging or other software can be licensed. The C version is available on MS-DOS personal computers and can be run on the Intel microprocessor under Xenix, Digital Equipment VAX under both VMS and Ultrix, NCR Tower UNIX systems, Pyramid, Sperry, Cray supercomputers, Unisys, Data General, Pyramid, Sun Computers and other UNIX systems. The C version will also operate on a Novell LAN. The mainframe version is an IBM MVS/ CICS or VM/CMS product. This search engine is essentially the product to which one compares all other competing text search-and-retrieval engines.

This product is very powerful. Because of its relatively costly license fees, potential users need to have substantial applications requiring this level of search sophistication. Large research libraries and special libraries are the potential customers for this mainframe or VAX/VMS software. The C version is more affordable, with license fees starting around $2,500 and rising according to the size of computer and specific target system.

2. Carlyle Systems, Inc.

Carlyle was founded in 1981 and initially offered a library automation system using a distributed architecture hosted on Intel microprocessors. In January, 1990 Carlyle was strategically redirected into a mainstream UNIX platform systems house. Its Voyager series was introduced in January, 1992. Carlyle is a privately held company owned by several venture capital partnerships of Technology Funding, Inc., and Carlyle employees. It has 39 employees, 18 of them in software engineering. The Voyager series is directed toward academic and public libraries. It uses the OPEN LOOK graphical user interface and supports X terminals and ASCII terminals using Sun Microsystems, Inc., and servers and workstations under SunOS, which is the Sun version of UNIX. Since both Intel 80xxx series and Motorola microprocessor-based systems can be configured to emulate an X terminal with emulation software, both MS-DOS and Macintosh family systems can be clients in a Voyager configuration. As an example, one can connect an MS-DOS, Microsoft Windows–equipped micro-computer to a TCP/IP Ethernet network using the NetManage TCP/IP for Windows product, called Chameleon v.3.1, for basic Telnet vt-100 emulation. For full X-terminal support under Windows, one could run an X-Windows product such as PC

Xview by Network Computing Devices of Mountainview, CA, or HCL-eXceed by Hummingbird Communications, Ltd., of Markham, Ontario, Canada.

The modules that constitute this integrated system are image/OPAC, cataloging, circulation, online public access catalog, acquisitions, CD-ROM gateway, serials control, interlibrary loan and authority control. This system uses a full MARC database driven by the Ingres™ Intelligent Database. Ingres™ is a high-performance relational database management system which uses standard SQL (structured query language) for querying and updating the database. Carlyle uses a client/server architecture to implement this system, programming it in the C language. It uses multiple processors in the network to distribute processing so as to maximize performance. Voyager uses the most advanced distributed processing and system integration technology presently available to developers. This system is architecturally very advanced when compared with many of its competitors.

Image/OPAC is a state-of-the-art linked database of scanned digital images that can be associated with bibliographic records. These images can be true color. A database editor is used to create new records and edit existing ones. The records can describe an image or be a bibliographic record linked to an image. This module sets Voyager apart from most other integrated library systems, although this capability is under development by other system developers. The cataloging module services the bibliographic, authority and holdings data with a full-screen MARC editor. It also has flexible facilities for importing, exporting, and managing MARC records. Incoming MARC records from tape, disk, communications links or Ethernet can be saved to a work file where they may be reviewed for local authority and data validation in the cataloging process. These records also can be directly imported into the online catalog. Pop-up scrolling windows for data field selections are used throughout. A scrolling list of special characters and diacritical marks makes it easy to enter foreign text. The circulation module is fully featured for regular public service points and has a reserve book room feature for course reserves by instructor and course. Reports and notices are generated by the Ingres™ SQL query facility. The OPAC online public access catalog reflects all changes in status as all updates are real time. Full search, browse and display facilities are provided. Libraries can control the fields to be indexed. Here is where pop-up windows and pull-down menus really make this an easy-to-use system. Short, normal, long and MARC displays can be selected with a mouse click.

Acquisitions allows downloading of electronic data from vendors to allow bibliographers to select from title lists and catalogs. Purchase orders can be created by selecting titles and creating line items in one easy step. Any order complexity can be handled. Fund management supports multilevel transactions within and across separate fiscal years with automatic tracking. Voyager maintains funds through journaling and permits general ledger review of all fund and budget totals. Again, the SQL query facility is used for both standard and customized reports. The CD-ROM gateway provides access for an unlimited number of users to an unlimited number of CD-ROM products on the same terminals used for OPAC and other Voyager access. LC CDMARC names and subjects and any other CD-ROM product can be searched. Both ISO 9660 and High Sierra CD-ROM file structures are supported. Voyager also supports Ethernet CD-ROM server configurations. A CD-ROM server is required for this module. The serials control module provides full bindery preparation support. Issues can be routed and claimed, and issue arrival is predicted through the use of flexible check-in templates. The serials module is really powerful and relatively easy to setup. The interlibrary loan (ILL) module is an addition to the circulation module. It manages the borrowing and lending of items between libraries and between consortium or network members. Voyager includes accounting for the ILL module by using the acquisitions module's accounting facility. Borrowing requests are checked against the union catalog. Patron files of the borrowing library are checked to see if a patron is blocked. Voyager prints ILL request forms, bills, invoices, purchase alerts and other products. The authority control module integrates with the cataloging and online catalog modules to perform the essential functions related to maintaining a fully authority-controlled database. Drag-and-drop mouse support allows an authority record to be loaded into the full-screen editor using the mouse with a simple point, click, drag and release motion.

This system should be able to accommodate virtually any size individual library or group of libraries due to its full use of the Sun architecture and SunOS networking facilities. These use Ethernet and TCP/IP protocol connections both to Voyager servers and to the external Internet. The Sun Microsystems hardware handles very large database sizes and relatively large transaction processing loads. Potentially, here is a system that could replace most mainframe automated library systems, given that an appropriate number of Sun computers were used in the network. Voyager should serve large academic, public and special libraries very well, particularly as the profession moves toward more and more serious interest in linking images with our text-based records. I like what I see in the product direction not because of UNIX, but because of the distributed architecture approach. This will make overall system operation and maintenance for both large and smaller systems much easier. Voyager has the ease of use features desired and maintains the ability to handle complex transactional situations.

3. CLSI, Inc. (now GEAC, Inc.)

CLSI was one of the earliest turnkey system vendors to libraries having been founded in 1971. It was acquired by GEAC in 1993, which continues to sell CLSI's system in addition to its other product lines. CLSI systems have undergone vast transformations from several hardware and proprietary operating system platforms using considerable custom hardware to highly standardized UNIX systems using the Informix relational DBMS product. CLSI has sold its systems mainly to public libraries. While this company has suffered some customer erosion to other systems, it appears that many of its over 300 customers have ordered and installed various system upgrades. With CLSI's LIBS 100 PLUS system under UNIX able to operate on IBM RS/6000, Sequent and Altos models, there should be wider appeal across all sizes of public libraries for this system. CLSI's competitors—among them, Dynix, NOTIS, IME and Sirsi—also offer RS/6000 implementations, and so it will be interesting to see if CLSI can widen its installations beyond its public library base into academic settings. CLSI is ready to supply software-only solutions where existing UNIX hardware is in place. This is a departure from its previous turnkey hardware/software system approach.

CLSI has had some notable achievements as the first established turnkey library system vendor. It offered the first online catalog commercially available and the first system capable of supporting multiple distinct libraries while preserving their individual parameters. In 1985, it offered the first local system capable of processing Chinese, Japanese and Korean bibliographic records.

LIBS 100 PLUS is a menu- and command-driven system. A menu bar is always available at the top of the screen. Message windows pop up when needed. Help is context sensitive. It supports the full ALA MARC character set on ASCII terminals. In cataloging, text labels and MARC tags are both used to insure that each field is properly recognized. Novice catalogers need not remember every MARC numeric tag. Pull-down menus give good ease of use to the user interface. Entering fixed field codes is easy since the system uses a pop-up window to show each field label and value. Circulation supports loans from 1 hour to days, weeks and months. Use of Informix, which is an SQL- compliant DBMS, means that queries can be made for custom reports in standard SQL. Earlier, CLSI had benchmarked several relational DBMS products and chosen Ingres (1) but later it migrated to Informix. This shows that this vendor is doing its utmost to assure that it can enhance and upgrade its systems using as much standardized software as possible. If an embedded proprietary DBMS had been used, such a change would have entailed rewriting the whole application. LIBS 100 PLUS screens are clear and highly user attractive. The online catalog adheres to the Common Command Language Z39.58 standard. The journal citation module currently allows databases from Information Access Co., H. W. Wilson, UMI/Data Courier, EBSCO and several other suppliers to be indexed and searched using the same commands as in the online catalog. All MARC fields can be indexed. The catalog is authority driven, so "See" and "See Also" references are present. Keyword browsing, right-hand and embedded truncation are search features.

Boolean operators AND, OR, NOT, <, >, and = are used in Boolean searches.

The Sequent computers used by CLSI feature 2–30 tightly coupled Intel 80486 microprocessors that share common memory and run Dynix/ptk, which is a POSIX-compliant UNIX for Sequent Symmetry computers. This system supports the AT&T System V interface and other open system interfaces including POSIX 1003.1, FIPS Pub. 151-1, and X/Open XPG. Programming languages supported are C, C++, COBOL, FORTRAN and Pascal. When parallel processing just began commercially, CLSI demonstrated its growth potential. (2) The Symmetry computer's VME bus interface links to an Ethernet LAN and to synchronous and asynchronous terminal line controllers with Network File System and TCP/IP support. Other communications protocols and standards are also supported for excellent internetworking of a Symmetry system with other established platforms within an enterprise.

CLSI has its DataLink, Z39.50-compliant database access product in late development with a GUI interface. Since LIBS 100 PLUS is a UNIX-based system, UNIX mail underlies its own LIBS 100 PLUS mail front end. CLSI is working on other system enhancements and has steadily released LIBS 100 PLUS new features in subsequent releases.

The question of LIBS100 is whether this system will be able to expand its main market beyond the public library setting. The ease-of-use features and hardware platform choices are sound in light of present capabilities and price/performance considerations. The IBM RS/6000 should broaden sales into educational and commercial settings, where these systems have immense popularity. CLSI has good customer support and a history of being willing to make considerable changes in its systems to meet current and future market directions. Under GEAC, it is expected that this good customer support will continue. The real question for the future will be whether GEAC, with its Advance and its older GLS product, will continue to develop both Advance and LIBS100.

4. *Cuadra Associates, Inc.*

Cuadra has offered the STAR system for over a decade to libraries, museums, government agencies, law firms, record centers, marketing departments and other organizations that need a powerful multiuser database management and information retrieval program. When STAR was first conceived, it was offered as an Alpha Micro supermicrocomputer application under its proprietary AMOS operating system. Then, as the hardware platforms evolved, so too has STAR evolved to take advantage of the best available suite of hardware and modern operating systems, with its migration to UNIX.

This system combines the best features of menu- and command-driven approaches. Virtually any type of text and image files can be set up as a database. It is designed to be managed by end users, with good tools for assigning passwords, performing backups, monitoring job status on the system and checking disk space. In-context help is only a keystroke away at any moment. Data entry is facilitated by a powerful yet easy-to-use text editor, instantaneous addition of repeating fields, automatic translation of input codes to fully spelled-out values, automatic checking of input against user-defined authority files and user-specified help messages for each field. Searching is fully Boolean with word adjacency and word proximity operators. There is explicit nesting of previous searches and explicit parentheses to force expression evaluation order. All fields can be searched by ranges and by truncation. Records with no data in a field can be found by "null" searching. There is a flexible report generator, and in STAR databases it is easy to define as how one wants to enter information and search it, have standard reports available, and create security levels for each database and field within a database. There are global operations that make loading external data, maintaining data and changing data quick and easy.

Libraries and information centers can use STAR to manage traditional collections and more specialized collections such as patents, specifications, laboratory notebooks, company reports, central correspondence, and nonprint materials. The library can have a conventional online catalog for some materials and special database designs for other materials. Starter kits with prototype databases and documentation and conversion programs to load machine-readable sources such as MARC records are available. The MARCplus input screen and displays/reports are an example of one of these prototypes that can be put to work as is or altered to meet the users needs. This data can then be laid out to be displayed in a MARC-tagged format and a traditional card format. Subject- and author-sorted reports are also shown. One can construct a labelled display for the online catalog or printed output as well. The LIBCAT Multi-format Bibliographic Catalog provides a non-MARC bibliographic catalog design, several standard reports and model authority file design. There is another database for circulation with a borrower database design that comes in the MARCplus or LIBCAT versions. There are acquisitions and serials definitions also. These provide workable full-function capabilities as delivered but can be tailored by the customer to fit any special needs. For libraries, a lot of time can be saved by acquiring these predefined applications and working with them to make any needed changes.

If you have image data to use and maintain, STAR uses a personal computer–based image manipulation system as an add-on module. The STAR records in a database can be full ASCII text records. To get the images into the system requires a scanner and a personal computer to create a scanning workstation. The Kofax KF9250 High Performance Document Processor board in the personal computer supports the image-scanning process and compresses the scanned image before storing it as a binary file. A laser printer is used to print out image data. The stored image binary files can be on a hard disk attached to the UNIX computer that runs STAR, or they can be located on another computer acting as an "Image Server" on a LAN. On a LAN this "Image Server" can be a single high-capacity hard disk, a WORM drive, an optical disk or jukeboxes. The average document page requires about 50 kB of disk storage for each compressed image. A special image identifier field contains the link to the scanned image in the STAR database record. Monochrome images are currently supported, and this vendor is working on color image-scanning support. The image file format used is the Tagged Image File Format (TIFF). Novell Netware and Sun NFS (TCP/IP) networks are supported currently. Ethernet is presently supported, with support for Token Ring networks to follow.

The theoretical limit on number of records in a STAR database is 268 million but the actual limit will be determined by the respective computer and storage configuration to support acceptable performance. Records can be variable length, with each record having up to 32,000 lines of text (about 1.9 million characters). Each record can have up to 500 fields defined, and fields can occur multiple times. Multiple-occurrence fields are limited to 1000 characters per occurrence.

STAR runs on over 200 different hardware platforms including the IBM RISC/6000 under AIX, The Hewlett-Packard HP/9000 under HP-UX, SCO and AT&T System V UNIX on Intel 80386/486/Pentium, Sun Microsystems Sun-3 and SPARCstation computers under SunOS and SOLARIS, and Alpha Micro supermicros under UNIX or AMOS. Those interested in user ratings on this software will be pleased by the high marks given in *Computers in Libraries* in the review by Pamela Cibbarelli. (3)

5. Databasix Information Systems, B.V. (DIS)

Adlib Information Systems, Ltd., was the original developer of the ADLIB system, which operates on Prime Series 50 minicomputers using Prime Information, the implementation of PICK on Prime computers. ADLIB LITE is a personal computer–based version of the ADLIB Library and Collection Management System.

ADLIB is an integrated library system with multilingual features. It can be set up to accommodate many different languages. It features an online catalog, cataloging, acquisitions, circulation and serials management. It has data import features that permit virtually any MARC format record to be used for its database. There is a thesaurus which controls indexing vocabulary and cross-referencing. A complete statistics module generates a good repertoire of standard management reports. In addition, system facilities under Prime Information allow for custom report generation. This system has variable-length fields and records, repeating fields, and B+ tree indexing, and it is composed of the following system building components that allow the library the freedom to tailor the system:

ADAPL	BASIC-like programming language
ADLIBUT	Data dictionary definition
ADIN	Screen management
ADOWT	Report generator
ADTERM	Free text
MENUS	Menu database

The system is menu driven. Boolean searching is implemented using AND, OR and NOT Boolean operators. This is a well-laid-out and organized system with appeal to special libraries and colleges particularly. There are many installations in Europe.

The ADLIB LITE system is a Novell LAN-based version of the minicomputer version with database compatibility and the nice look and feel of its bigger brother. It can run as a PICK implementation on an Intel 80386/486 platform. Like its sibling, it can handle ISDB and normal labelled printed outputs. Also, all of its screens and associated language dialog are held in parameter files. This makes it possible to translate the system into any language interface that can be displayed on a microcomputer. English, French and Dutch translations have been done, with additional languages being translated at other client sites. Like its parent, the help screens are user modifiable. Pull-down menus and pop-up windows provide a nice appealing interface. For software protection, licensed users are issued a "dongle," which is installed on the parallel port of their server or host system.

Both of these system versions are mature, full-function products that as to functionality and tailorability can compete with similar systems developed in the United States in their intended college and special library markets. To my knowledge, this system has not been marketed in North America, but it would not be surprising to find its market expanded in the future.

6. Dynix, Inc.

This company has accelerated its efforts to gain smaller library clients to expand its market. In 1991 it sold over 90 systems that had one to four terminals, with 61% of the sales having eight or fewer terminals. Like NOTIS Systems, Inc., Dynix was acquired by Ameritech. This should complement NOTIS, since Dynix's installed base is strong in public libraries, though it does have over 150 of its more than 950 installations in academic libraries. Dynix is trying to expand in the public school market with its Dynix Scholar system using UNIX and PICK on Intel 80486 personal computers. Dynix has at least 15 sites that are quite large, with over 200 terminals. Dynix has signed an agreement to take over the marketing and support of the Unisys PALS software described in

Chapter 6. No other details of this are known at this writing, but readers are urged to watch the library trade press for further developments with vendors or to contact these vendors.

The original Dynix system supports acquisitions, cataloging, online catalog, serials control, circulation with a reserve book room capability, media scheduling, journal citation files, information and referral database and a report generator. There are interfaces to OCLC, RLIN, Bibliofile, Baker & Taylor and other MARC record suppliers. Also, there is connectivity to Novell-based networks. Versions operate under either the PICK operating system or under a version of UNIX that supports PICK such as UniVerse. Quite a few hardware platforms are in use and currently supported. Among them IBM RS/6000 and System 9370, Sequent, Sequoia, Prime, MIPS, DEC's VAX and Ultimate. The system is being marketed abroad in Asia, Australia, New Zealand, France, Germany, Ireland, Netherlands Antilles, Tahiti, Great Britain and Iceland. System migrations from other vendors systems include CLSI, CTI (no longer in business), DataPhase (no longer in business), Data Research Associates, Gaylord, GEAC, OCLC LS/2000 (no longer supported), PALS, Sydney, ULISYS, UTLAS and others. There are users groups in the United States, Australia, New Zealand, Canada, Great Britain and Ireland.

The journal citation module currently supports loading external databases from ABI/Inform, EBSCO, H.W. Wilson and Information Access. Commands are the same as for the online catalog, and these files are physically separate but linked to the online catalog for holdings information. Each system module can produce standardized reports, and these can be controlled by how data is categorized using the STATMANAGER facility. Also, the RECALL Report Generator, which uses English-like statements, can be used to produce customized additional reports. The library can specify which fields will be indexed in the online catalog. They can customize instructional and display screens. Multiple library installations can optionally display holdings for all locations or just selected locations. Displays are clear, use labelled fields and are very quickly read by the searcher. Optional touchscreen terminal devices are available which may be appropriate for some clientele. System security is flexible and dependable. The serials module works in concert with the acquisitions module to provide check-in, claiming, copy distribution and bindery preparation support, while the acquisitions module handles subscription support. Routing slips, accounting information, brief and full serials catalogs can be viewed on screen as well as printed out. Serials catalogs can be output to tape for microfiche production. The acquisitions module supports electronic ordering using the BISAC format with numerous popular vendors such as Blackwell, Yankee Book Peddler, Ingram, and Brodart. A backup and bookmobile circulation capability is provided by Telxon PTC-701 or 710 calculator-size computers having a built in bar code reader. The Telxon comes with two battery sets that each operate for 6 hours and recharge in 8–10 hours. Those users wishing to read more detailed descriptions of Dynix should consult the book by Jacqueline Gilmartin. (4)

On the larger end, two Dynix installations are the Ramsey County Library in Roseville, Minnesota and the Fort Worth, Texas Public Library. Ramsey County has seven branches, 294 terminals, 596,000+ volumes and a circulation of 2.2 million per year. Its system is a Hewlett Packard 9000 model 870s/100. It is positioned for excellent growth in both database size and number of simultaneous users, since this computer can handle more than double the terminal load and up to 85 GB of mass storage. The Fort Worth system uses a MIPS 6280 to support 195 terminals and a 4.2 million circulation of 1.8 million copies and 475,000 titles.

Dynix is a mature, robust and very user oriented system supporting full MARC records. It is widely installed in virtually every type of library and offers quite a variety of flexible hardware choices in its turnkey form. Over 90% of Dynix sales involve both hardware and software for a turnkey system. However, I would expect that more software-only sales will occur as institution-level UNIX platforms emerge. Dynix should continue as a strong vendor to virtually all library segments, particularly the smaller to midrange organizations but also to large enterprises, as exemplified in the above-mentioned systems.

7. GEAC Computers, Inc.

GEAC is a Canadian company that manufactured its own proprietary hardware, the GEAC 6000, 8000 and 9000 series. It was also a software company with focus on financial systems and library systems. The GEAC 6000 and 8000 were hosts for GEAC's first automated library system called GLIS. Its current system is ADVANCE, a product it acquired by purchasing a company that had spent numerous years developing a PICK-based integrated library system. ADVANCE is available to run under PICK and to run under UNIX on Data General, IBM RS/6000, DEC, Motorola, Pyramid, C. Itoh, Fujitsu, Ultimate, Bull and ICON systems. This is a broad spectrum of possibilities from small to very large multiuser installations. GEAC system installations appear to be rather evenly divided between public and academic libraries, with some consortia and special libraries represented in its foreign installations. Those users interested in detailed experiences with GEAC library systems should consult the book by Westlake and Clarke. (5) Of further note is GEAC's acquisition of CLSI and its LIBS100 system in 1993.

ADVANCE has foreign language user interfaces for Dutch, Italian, French, German, Russian and Croatian—in addition to English. The system supports all MARC formats, including foreign and Unimarc. It will import and export to these formats and is fully real time in updating files and indexes. ADVANCE will support single libraries or multiple institutions. The database can be a shared union catalog or individual private files. Standard ASCII terminals are supported as are microcomputers in an Ethernet LAN. TCP/IP network support is used. The modules supported by ADVANCE include acquisitions, cataloging, online catalog, CD-ROM interface, interlibrary loan, media booking, circulation and reserve room circulation, serials management, thesaurus, authority file, and journal citation. The serials module does not support bindery preparation but handles serial arrival prediction and enumeration and date chronology very nicely. It also generates routing slips. The system has over 200 standard reports and outputs defined. It runs under the UniVerse operating system and uses a generalized report writer to produce custom reports. The acquisitions module supports BISAC ordering and receiving with Baker & Taylor. There are interfaces for online record transfer from OCLC, UTLAS, WLN, MicroEnhancer and Bibliofile. In cataloging using MARC screens, one can display instructions for every valid MARC tag, subfield and indicator upon demand or during the session until logged off. There is a microcomputer-based circulation backup system and a hand-held bar code unit with software to permit physical inventory in the stacks. The online catalog gateway permits access via TCP/IP connections to remote systems catalogs, i.e., Internet connections. It also supports modem connections using dial access or leased asynchronous line communications.

A new product is IMAGEPower, a personal computer image scanner that captures and catalogs photographs, negatives, slides, tables of content, or diagrams and links these to a corresponding bibliographic record by adding a unique image number in a specially defined record field tag. It can be used with both the older GLIS and the current ADVANCE systems.

The online catalog supports keyword searching on title, author, subject and/or series words in both separate indexes and in combinations. Boolean AND, OR, NOT, and exclusive OR with left-to-right evaluation are provided. Labelled brief and full displays may be chosen by the user. A vocabulary-controlled hypertext feature can extend a search to other works by the author, other titles in the series and/or other records with the same subject heading or to browse the shelves by call number. Optionally, online catalog users can view a full MARC tagged record. ADVANCE supports screen image printing and directing print to system or local side printers. Bibliographies are in brief format, formal bibliographic citation (Chicago Manual of Style based) and full bibliographic and holdings format. This last includes all tracings and cross-references. The system can be set up to allow patrons to view their own circulation record and place holds on items.

GEAC has teamed with SynreVoice Technologies, Inc., as codevelopers of a voice processing system to interface with both ADVANCE and GEAC's earlier GLIS system. The GEAC Library Voice Information System (LVIS) allows libraries to automate the traditionally labor-intensive tasks of mailing various notices such as recalls, overdues and bills for lost materials. Instead this module delivers them by telephone. It also allows patrons to perform telephone renewals online. It includes an audiotext system that can provide callers with a 24-hour information service. Early 1993 saw the introduction of affordable voice-incorporated applications to run mail order businesses, shop by phone and numerous other applications. I predict that this capability will become very popular with larger libraries having sizeable circulations.

ADVANCE is a smoothly integrated, many featured and powerful system. Its hardware platform base is sufficiently broad to accommodate virtually any transaction load or database size. It does not have the hardware and software limitations and lack of smooth integration that were problems of the previous GLIS system based on the GEAC proprietary hardware and operating system. With this system, GEAC could recapture some of its lost market, appeal to a wider range of customers and continue its foreign market penetration.

8. Highland Library Systems, Inc.

Highland Wings originally was a system that operated under the native PICK operating system. It was directed at smaller libraries using Intel 80386/80486 processors. However, its new system runs under DR/DOS multiuser, which is a product of Digital Research. It also sells DR/DOS in its single-user form as a compatible replacement for MS-DOS. Digital Research was a recent acquisition of Novell, Inc. Using a multiport DigiBoard serial interface, very economical small multiuser systems with two to six stations can be configured. The stations can be CRTs or can be low-cost microcomputers, even Intel 8088 or 80286 systems. Community colleges, public libraries, law libraries and others form the current 24-library customer base.

This system is multiuser. Yet, it does not require either a LAN or a more complex operating environment such as the original PICK or PICK under UNIX. There is much to attract small- to medium-size libraries to this system, since system support has been made as simple as possible. Wings will run in a LAN configuration for larger installations or those that already have a LAN in place. With Pentium processor–equipped systems, it should be possible to run a setup of a couple dozen stations with mass storage of around 4–6 GB on a stand-alone Pentium running DR/DOS multiuser. With an estimated 150-MB storage needed for a 50,000-title database, including all sorts of indexes and records of other modules, a relatively small processor platform is capable of supporting somewhat more stations than most would think possible without a server-type LAN. Highland sells a complete turnkey configuration of software and hardware or software alone. Wings can be leased via Consolidated Financial Resources, Inc. It should be possible for virtually any smaller library to afford a solution such as this. On a LAN configuration, there could be as many stations supported as are allowed under the LAN operating system being used, for example, 256 stations under Novell Advanced Netware 3.12 on a single server.

At the time Wings was originally conceived in 1985, PICK offered unlimited growth, true multiuser operation, good response time and reasonable price. With the improved performance of microcomputers, Highland has now recast this system to not only preserve the above benefits but also to take advantage of memory-mapped monitors to display its pop-up window-designed screens. Remote branches can be connected to a multiuser DR/DOS system via dedicated phone line or with a lower cost option by using dial-up lines to transmit updates to the central system. These remote locations use Highland's branch software and bookmobile software as add-on modules. This is a very user friendly, yet fully MARC-based online catalog and circulation system. It uses labeled catalog displays, invokes a browse feature at the press of the PF5 function key and has help just a PF1 key press away. The online catalog asks users to enter their search word(s). It then displays selection lists to further narrow the search. It drops the last character of a word and re-searches until either hits are found or two characters remain and no hits are found. Users need not be concerned with author, title, subject, Boolean operators or other complexities. While this type of searching will work nicely in smaller catalogs, it presents problems in large union catalogs where there might be thousands of entries under such terms as "Shakespeare" or "Bible." MARC records can be imported from diskette. One could use a product like Bibliofile to capture MARC records and then import them into this system. Bar code labels and readers can be used in the circulation module, or this transaction data entered on keyboard.

Libraries needing the two basic modules of online catalog and circulation and that are looking for a highly cost effective and user friendly system with as minimal a support requirement as possible should examine the Highland Wings system.

9. Information Management and Engineering (IME)

The Information Navigator integrated library system has been installed in over 1800 sites worldwide, in 22 languages in 35 countries. Academic, public and special libraries have found this system able to meet their needs. This system has the TinMan database software at its heart. When it was first released in 1984, it was called TinLib. It features hypertext-like navigation searching using query by form and query by example. The database is an object-oriented entity-relational database. Its records are variable length as are its fields. The system has modules for online catalog, cataloging, circulation, serials management, acquisitions, record import and export, communications and a report generator—all elegantly integrated. The serials management module includes all functions for purchasing, receiving, claiming, routing and accounting for serial holdings and subscriptions except for bindery preparation.

The elegant feature integration makes using this system a distinct pleasure. This is a well-designed, highly maintainable program code system with considerable tailoring possible by the individual library. Where multilingual needs are important, Information Navigator has the facilities to support such access and handle a database of foreign materials. The only limiting factor on this system is the amount of hard disk storage provided on a server. However, that limit is more than sufficient to meet the needs of even the larger of the ARL libraries. TCP/IP networks can be designed to support thousands of users. This system, like the Carlyle system, makes use of the latest in program development concepts, is a client/server, and is "rightsized" for a wide range of libraries interested in having either a Novell LAN or TCP/IP and UNIX type solution.

The Information Navigator is supported in its UNIX form on Sun Microsystems servers and workstations and Hewlett-Packard HP 9000 RISC-based systems. It is also available as an MS-DOS single user system or on a LAN license for Novell Advanced Netware. IME markets this system through 30 distributors located in various countries worldwide. Within this market there are 18 user groups that meet twice annually. In 1991, IME sold 26 systems in the United States and 164 systems in Europe. It should be noted that the U.S. Library of Congress is using seven UNIX systems equipped with the Information Navigator for running its overseas field offices in Cairo, Jakarta, Karachi, Nairobi, New Delhi, Rio de Janeiro, and Washington, D.C. A book jobber/distributor module will be added to the existing system to perform these support functions. These systems will support multiple foreign languages and character sets, including Arabic. The Canadian distributor for IME is Crozier Information Resources Consulting, Ltd., Edmonton, Alberta, Canada.

10. Innovative Interfaces, Inc.

This company was formed in 1978. It provided the first data transfer interfaces between systems such as the CLSI LIBS-100 and OCLC. In 1982, Innovative started to offer a system called INNOVACQ for acquisitions and one called INNOPAC for an online catalog. Now, its integrated system is called INNOPAC, with release 8 of the software delivered in January 1993. Modules include acquisitions, circulation, online catalog, serials control, materials booking and reference databases. Interfaces to import MARC records from virtually all suppliers exist. This company has a history of positive growth and profitability with considerable investments in product improvements through the years.

INNOPAC is popular in smaller to upper middle sized libraries, with its largest installation having over 200 terminals and a 1.5-million title database. Recent growth in installations has been through the sale of systems to smaller libraries although a few 100-terminal sized systems were newly installed in 1992. INNOPAC is distinguished by excellent integration, ease of use, and flexibility in establishing parameters. It maintains excellent response time, reliability and provides comprehensive management information. Support for customers is rated quite well by INNOPAC users. The INN-touch newsletter to clients is quite informative and well written. Customers are mainly academic and public libraries but include some special libraries. Tri-College Consortium (Bryn Mawr, Haverford and Swarthmore Colleges) is an example of a consortium user. Over 300 libraries in five countries are users of this system.

Berkeley (California) Public Library has used its INNOPAC to bring up the Berkeley Information Network community information and referral service. This busy service records over 3000 searches per month. The University of Maine has put the Maine Union List of Serials up on its INNOPAC. This database has 20,000 titles and 45,000 holdings statements for 80 academic, public and special libraries in Maine. This union list is also linked to Information Access Corp.'s Expanded Academic Index database to show holdings for articles indexed in that product.

Release 8 of INNOPAC has several advanced features. Support for scanned images to be linked to the bibliographic database permits libraries to scan archival materials, photographs and other documents and include these in their databases, displaying their content on any terminal using X-Window software under UNIX. This release also includes Z39.50 client software which has been tested with the following systems: OCLC, RLIN, MELVYL, LIAS, AT&T and NOTIS. This option is part of the Electronic Gateways feature. INNOPAC libraries that acquire this feature are able to allow their patrons to search systems using the same INNOPAC user interface that have Z39.50 server software/hardware in place. The University of Arizona is the first library to install this option in its system, called SABIO.

Innovative's system also provides an electronic mail application that is based on UNIX mail. Through its gateway feature, it can connect to the Internet and Bitnet or to other networks supporting TCP/IP, DECnet, and Ethernet. The DARPA Simple Mail Transfer Protocol (SMTP) is supported. Portable bar code scanners are supported for inventory management. This module produces both summary and detailed reports. Currently, reference databases from H. W. Wilson, Information Access Corp., UMI and EBSCO can be loaded, and others will soon be supported. Acquisitions supports electronic ordering. INNOPAC serials control also includes bindery preparation support, including production of pull slips to retrieve unbound issues from the shelf. All of the system outputs can be tailored by the library to its specific needs. This serials module is one of the slickest features to this system from a technical processing view. Circulation includes extensive support for the reserve book room. It also generates numerous management reports, including tabular and graphed formats. The online catalog supports CJK and the full ALA MARC character set. In late 1992, Innovative started offering an enhanced terminal for use with its system to display the full ALA MARC character set. This is a modified Wyse T160, which has been renamed the INNOPAC T160E. It emulates a DEC VT-100 terminal.

Innovative software operates under UNIX on a variety of computers, including models from Digital Equipment, Convergent, MIPS, Hewlett-Packard, Sun and IBM. All updates are real time. INNOPAC features are excellent for research libraries and also public libraries where wide intersystem connectivity is desirable. With its excellent repertoire of features, this system has positioned itself to be a leading contender for the research library market and already has quite a few top university clients. Innovative is making good progress on bringing substantive new major versions to its clients. The company is financially strong and should be able to attract the attention of large libraries that want to move away from proprietary-based systems to a UNIX platform.

11. Keystone Systems, Inc.

The Keystone Library Automation System (KLAS) performs holdings management, cataloging, online public access, acquisitions, circulation, serials, branch/bookmobile support and equipment service, and materials booking/audiovisual support. This system is created using PROGRESS, a fourth-generation relational dbms for UNIX. It can be implemented on IBM RS/6000 UNIX computers, other UNIX, AIX and Xenix computers with the latest release of PROGRESS dbms software. This system began in 1983, when Keystone responded to a request for bid for a turnkey computer system for the North Carolina Regional Library for the Blind and Physically Handicapped, in Raleigh, North Carolina. For this reason, KLAS features extensive reader-related features in addition to the standard circulation control and cataloging functions. Originally, this system was implemented using the Unify relational dbms on Xenix, and now it is a PROGRESS application. KLAS is designed for medium to large library collections.

KLAS features pop-up screens, and users browse and pick from the items on the screens. Moving between modules is only a couple of keystrokes. There are 15 user-defined fields, 3 text fields, 3 numeric fields, 3 date fields, 3 logical (yes or no) fields and 3 report fields for use in flagging fields for custom reports. There are extensive predefined reports, but since a Report Writer is part of PROGRESS, any client library can use a facility designed for non-programmers to access all fields in the system and create custom reports. There are many levels of security so that the system administrator can limit staff access to the specific module, functions or data needed to perform that task. Each user has a menu that controls which functions are available to them. Online help is only a key press away, with the F2 key providing in-context help at any point. There are extended free-form note-taking fields to put in important data on patrons or holdings. The author and date of the note are maintained for each note entered. Extensive statistics are tracked on period-to-date, year-to-date and lifetime basis.

The holdings management module is the base-required module for the system. It contains all the basic required functions for a library to maintain holdings and provide simple check-in and check-out functions. An infinite number of loan periods can be defined, with a table of loan codes to allow for different loan periods for different items. The "Find" function locates items based on an ID number assigned to that item. Holdings can be searched by ID number, title, author or subject code. The user can select the number of items one wishes to find.

The catalog management module has full USMARC record capability, with the MARC record base online on CD-ROM. Items can be cataloged under multiple authorities, e.g., LC and a local catalog authority. Catalog searching is by author, title, keyword and text string. The circulation control module features individual, minibatch and batch modes. Batch mode allows a large number of items to be entered into the system and then processed later. Minibatch mode allows the user to perform either check-in or check-out for a number of items, and any messages regarding these items are displayed and dealt with at that time. Individual mode allows the user to process items in real time, item by item. Mailing labels and cards can be printed to use in mailing items to library patrons. The on-line public access module has a menu-assisted search capability for patrons which uses indexed fields such as title, author or subject to query the full MARC records. The branch library/bookmobile management module provides inventory and circulation management to a unit when interactive access to the KLAS system is not possible. The transactions are later uploaded to the KLAS host. The patron services module allows the library to maintain its patron data, which also includes patron reading preferences and other specialized information that goes beyond the normal borrower file usually found for circulation. Nightly, the KLAS computer can service library users in need of materials by running their patron profile against the library's database and selecting items that the patron has not yet read. The serial control module stores data on individual serial titles and issues for subscription maintenance, renewal, and issue holdings and, in addition to the pre-defined for these purposes, features 15 user-defined fields. The Acquisitions module handles all purchasing and fund accounting. It can provide a gateway to serials control for subscription and binding, circulation for fees and fines, and equipment service for repair costs.

The equipment service module keeps track of any machines or items that are library property. Even a repair history is part of this system. A bar code circulation label can be used on each piece of equipment just as for books. Equipment can be checked out and in just like books. Extensive notes can be attached to each item record. The materials booking/audio-visual module schedules use of any holding that a library wants to preschedule. It can produce an offline printed catalog of holdings and it has interlibrary loan functions. Communications services is a gateway for KLAS to connect to other systems via TCP/IP or Internet using custom programming to create the needed interface.

This system will be attractive to libraries for the blind, physically handicapped or other special or public libraries with needs for the extensive patron-tracking features. Software pricing is by module and by number of concurrent users, with prices for 1–2, 3–8, 9–16 and 17–32 users. An all-module license does not receive any discount price, so there does not appear to be any advantage for a library to license all modules at once. Without such a discount, it is more advantageous for the library to license each module as the library becomes ready to implement it on its system. In my opinion, vendors should be using pricing techniques that encourage licensing of multiple or full modules in a system by offering some discount on the total license price. This is justifiable since it simplifies customer support and training once the initial installation is up and running.

12. Multicore Library Services (MultiLIS)

MultiLIS is a product of the Sobeco Group, Inc., of Montreal, Canada. It grew out of the University of Quebec integrated library system to which Sobeco had acquired the rights. In the United States the distributor is Multicore Library Services. Although there is a version of this system for Digital Equipment VAX processors under VMS, this product is originally UNIX based under UNIX System V on NCR, Bull and MIPS hardware. It has also migrated its software to Intel 80386 and 80486 microcomputers. Although software-only packages have been sold, most systems are turnkey and are sold as hardware with software. The State University of New York (SUNY) has chosen this vendor to supply its 42 campuses with systems during the next three years.

Academic and public libraries as well as some special libraries and school systems have installed this system. Half of the MultiLIS customer base is in Europe, with the remaining systems mainly in Canada, although sales in the United States are growing. Work is proceeding on Minitel and Videotex interfaces, mainly for European customers. One distinguishing feature of MultiLIS as it is installed in Canada is its collection exchange module that permits block relocation loans from a central site. This should appeal to public and school libraries and serve to set this product off from many of its competitors since it is available now in the U.S. English language system version.

The system supports acquisitions, cataloging, online catalog, CD-ROM interface, serials management, circulation, reserve book room, MARC record interface, and a thesaurus. It has a PC-based remote circulation workstation for bookmobile or branch use. MultiLIS also publishes a quarterly newsletter

(ISSN 1188-3839). There is a Bitnet discussion group listserv for MultiLIS for those with Bitnet/Internet access. To subscribe send an e-mail message to listserv@albanyvm1.bitnet and place the following in the message body: SUBSCRIBE MULTILIS FIRST NAME LAST NAME.

Documentation for this system is in ring binders. It appears to be produced with very readable and professional desktop publishing layouts matching the good technical writing. This system can be set up to work bilingually in French and English or just one language. All versions of this system use the same file and index structures so that a library can easily move from the VMS version to the UNIX version or vice versa. Two-level indexes are used which make it possible to manage up to 4 million records with a maximum of two disk accesses per record. Keeping disk accesses to a minimum in automated library systems produces much faster transaction processing and much less wasted machine resource which can be allocated to the application instead of to the overhead of system resource management.

Modules have linked, prompted help always available for each input field. When cataloging on the work form displayed on the screen, one can have the system display selection screens from the authority file and tag lists that can be chosen for use in building that record. On terminals connected to the system, if one hits function key F17 and a letter in edit mode, a menu of diacriticals will be shown. The online catalog displays diacriticals but ignores them in building its search indexes. Bibliographic records retrieved in catalog searches can be displayed either in card format or in labelled screen format. Search is by author, title and subject. Additional searching can be collective author, uniform title, keyword, person as subject, call number, series, publisher, document type, record number, item bar code number, ISBN, ISSN or LCCN. Boolean searching is supported using AND, OR and NOT with truncation. Searches can be saved in sets and these sets later combined to use in further searches. A report module allows creation of reports from a command file containing a series of instructions similar to a source program in a higher level language. End users can choose from pre-prepared command files and supply parameters when the system requests them. Programmers have full access to all fields and all files of a MultiLIS database. Custom command files can be prepared. These appear rather like a Pascal language program. In the documentation I reviewed, these commands were in French. For example our English "writeln" would be written "ecrireln." I had no problem deciphering this, and probably with a bit of work I could have written a command file using this report generator language. Although now somewhat dated, Kelly has provided a description of MultiLIS in an issue of *Library Hi-Tech*. (6)

This system should compete well internationally because of its multilingual features. The hardware platforms are sound and offer quite a range. Smaller libraries as well as larger or multiple library systems can install this product and have good network connectivity and functionality across the basic modules, which are nicely integrated.

13. Ringgold Management Systems, Inc.

Ringgold has offered its NONESUCH system to libraries using a range of micro- and minicomputers. For Intel 80xxx platforms, this system has versions for MS/PC-DOS, UNIX and Xenix. It will also run under UNIX or on a LAN for larger systems. Currently, NONESUCH Acquisitions and NONESUCH Circulation are the two modules available. An online catalog module is in beta test but has not been released at this writing. The acquisitions system has an interface to load MARC records from OCLC's Prism system, WLN's system or from a CD-ROM-based MARC file. Up to 200,000 orders can be kept online with full-fund accounting and electronic ordering. This latter function supports BISAC variable and fixed formats, Baker & Taylor, Brodart and others. The NONESUCH Acquisitions system has been used by Ringgold customers since 1986. It has matured into a full-function system with excellent reporting and is suitable for all types of academic, public and special libraries. Basic2 has been used to write this software. Ringgold licenses it separately from hardware but also provides turnkey hardware/software solutions. Software licenses include both binary executable code and source code. Although a library probably will never need to use the source code, having the source and a compiler for it makes the system lower risk for the library. Only a few other commercial systems such as NOTIS supply both source code and object code under their user licenses. Twenty-five college, university, public and special libraries are using NONESUCH Acquisitions.

The NONESUCH Circulation system is designed to handle up to a million titles, copies and patrons. It fills reserves on a specified copy or first available copy basis. The system can also accept batch input from a back-up system or remote system such as on a bookmobile. Loan periods for any item can be varied even when the item is checked out to a user. This system is highly functional, yet very easy to use, and supports bar code input. Eight college and public libraries are current users of this system. COBOL has been used to write this software.

The new online catalog module will provide key word access to all MARC records and will use Windows and color VGA. When used with the other modules above, the program will be integrated to show item status in the online catalog. Judging from the reliability and well-tested nature of the acquisitions and circulation programs, I would bet that when the online catalog is released, it will be a high-quality product for the largely microcomputer-based market to which it is directed.

Ringgold has served libraries for over a decade in numerous consulting capacities. Its systems are designed to meet the needs for advanced support in the functional area covered, at an affordable cost and with good tailoring features for the individual library.

14. Sirsi, Inc.

Sirsi has been providing its Unicorn integrated system to libraries for over a decade. Like other systems on the market that have undergone numerous releases, this product is a mature, full-function system. Its current enhancements focus on external database searching and addition of electronic ordering capabilities to acquisitions. A new online catalog module is also being developed. Unicorn operates under virtually any version of UNIX on platforms ranging from Intel 80486 to large mainframes running a UNIX version operating system. Popular platforms for Unicorn have been systems from Unisys, DEC, NCR, IBM, Arete, Sun Microsystems, Inc., and others. Over 175 sites have been installed in college, university, public and special libraries.

The system is now in version 6.0. Unicorn comprises the following twelve modules. The core module is bibliographic and inventory control, to which any or all of nine others may be added. These others are enhanced public access, retrieval interface manager, circulation, academic reserves, acquisitions, serials control, authority control, electronic mail, and materials booking. The core module offers a full-text database able to store MARC, non-MARC and full-document text. A document management system is a part of this core module. Enhanced public access is provided through the BRS/Search engine for full-text, Boolean searching. Retrieval interface manager allows searching of up to four local or remote databases simultaneously with unlimited availability beyond the four simultaneously searched databases. Retrieved information can be downloaded into the local Unicorn databases. The remote databases currently offered are BRS, Dialog, DROLS TR, DROLS WU, NASA RECON, and 14 others. The serials control module uses SISAC (Serials Industry Systems Advisory Committee) numbers as a means of title identification. Bindery support is part of this module. There is a bibliographic record loader which also features a CD-ROM interface. OCLC records can be imported as can Bibliofile records from the Bibliofile CD-ROM.

Modules are quite flexible and can be set up to handle virtually any library's needs. Unicorn distributes some of its functions to software on the personal computer workstations. The system does not use menus or hot keys by a user to convey user desires. For example, to place an item online, the phrase CREATE ITEM can be issued by pressing function keys for each term. The system uses combinations of nouns and verbs meaningful to a library user. Screens can be tailored to the particular user function. For a description of the Unicorn Collection Management system, consult the article by Young. (7) Later developments to this system are reported in another article. (8)

For version 6.0, two new software modules have been introduced. The first is STILAS STINFO (Scientific and Technical Information) tracking and accountability. The STILAS STINFO tracking module is a complete projects management system that tracks the stages associated with a contract. Key dates and deadlines and six stages of project are featured. This software can be interfaced to the DTIC (Defense Technical Information Center) WUIS/TEAMS database. An operator can search links to the STINFO records in the catalog, save the retrieved set and translate it into the DROLS WU format used for uploading to the DTIC WUIS/TEAMS system. Many years ago, I got my start in the library world in a defense contracting firm's special library, before the computer was seriously considered for most record-keeping tasks. I would have gone to the ends of the earth for the capabilities in this module as I now reflect on the manual record keeping I did for the numerous contracts I handled. The second new module is the inventory of accountable material, which allows authorized operators to create reports of accountable materials by location. Location might be an individual, a storage container, a classified material vault, etc. Transmittal forms are required for sending classified material out of a facility and this module will produce these. This application also supports destruction control, including numbered certificates of destruction on demand. Again, harking back to my special library days, having this module would have been a dream come true!

Unicorn is a system with wide appeal and with distinctive features for special, academic and public libraries that really sets this pioneer UNIX system apart from the pack. With its wide platform choice, virtually any size library can be accommodated at a reasonable cost. Software is licensed by the size of the library collection. Sirsi, Inc., has been a pioneer in numerous areas of library system development, having been the first UNIX-based product in the market. The commitment really shows in version 6.0!

15. Specialist Computer Systems and Software, Ltd.

BookshelF is an integrated library system marketed in Great Britain by Specialist Computer Systems and Software, Ltd. It originated out of a British Library research project that investigated the requirements of small- to medium-size libraries. Cataloging, acquisitions, circulation and serials are implemented. The cataloging module uses a thesaurus module to control subject terms and cross-references. This system is implemented under the PICK operating system and will run on any of the over 100 computers able to run PICK. One of the more popular systems in Britain is the Prime minicomputer family running Prime Information. It will also run on PICK under UNIX systems such as UniVerse and UNIDATA.

Peter Leggate and Hilary Dyer were the principals in the original system specification effort. This work was funded by the British Library under a research and development grant. Logical Choice was the original development firm. A single-user version implemented in Revelation on MS-DOS systems is now offered. This version, called Heritage, will also operate on a Novell LAN system. It uses a CD-ROM–based catalog. It also has a Windows interface.

The BookshelF system can be accessed by MS-DOS personal computers running Windows. A public library user system called BookshelF PLUS was released in MARCh 1992. It includes an online catalog on CD-ROM, a mobile BookshelF on a laptop/notebook computer with graphical output of management reports.

Any MARC format can be accommodated via defined tables and MARC record conversion programs. Each module includes a menu option "Reference Data," which allows library-defined parameters for that module. An area code definition allows multisite libraries to limit reservations to its own site, a group of sites or all sites. Separate order streams for acquisitions can be defined if ordering is decentralized. There are 26 general media description (GMD) codes implemented in the online catalog. The status information displayed includes: available, binding, hold, labelling/in process, on loan, on order, reserved, and in transit. The online catalog can be command driven or use two different menu-driven formats. The first of these provides fewer options for field specific searches, while the second of these provides the thesaurus. A community information menu can list town history, places to visit, library news, cinemas, museums, and other cultural or civic events. Journal articles can be entered and indexed via a journal article screen. The serials module provides for all serials management tasks except for bindery preparation. For college library use, it should be mentioned that BookshelF will support reserve reading room short-term loans and access by course and instructor.

This system has had a long and careful design and development history with proven installations in public and college libraries in England. Those interested in details of BookshelF should read the volume by Fisher and Rowley. (9)

16. TKM Software, Ltd.

This Canadian firm has purchased the rights to distribute the University of Brandon's BuCAT software, which is a VAX/VMS integrated library system. Presently, it is an online catalog and circulation system. Acquisitions, serials, interlibrary loan and media booking are under development. One can choose to display records in different formats. A library can specify which fields will be indexed. Boolean searching is supported, and with an add-on, full-text searching program called EDICS, one can do these searches tied to either BuCAT or its microcomputer version described below. BuCAT will allow the mounting of external databases as a complement to the online catalog. Some 15 customers, mainly Canadian community colleges, are now using this software.

If TKM can continue to make enhancements and get this product fully equipped with the modules under development, BuCAT could be a competitive VAX platform system outside of its present Canadian customer base. TKM's other products include a microcomputer-based online catalog called MicroCAT, distributed in the United States by The Highsmith Company, Inc. Highsmith has been a long-time supplier to the library market. MicroCAT is available to run under Xenix on an Intel 80386 or 486 system as a multiuser product, as a single user MS-DOS product and as a Novell LAN multiuser system. MicroCAT is a microcomputer version of BuCAT designed for the school library market, with sufficient flexibility to be used for basic online catalog and circulation in any school or smaller public library setting.

I was able to examine and run a new product for the Canadian Library interlibrary loan department for processing both loan requests from other libraries and requests to be sent to the National Library of Canada and other libraries for borrowing. This program, called Interlend, conforms to ISO 10161-1991, which is the international standard for interlibrary loan messaging. It generates Envoy electronic mail messages. This software runs on any MS-DOS system with at least 3.6 MB of hard disk space for the program. Although developed for the Canadian market, this program could be parameterized with U.S. library data, such as National Union Catalog symbols, instead of National Library of Canada symbols. It is programmed in Lattice C with FairCom Corp.'s C-Tree file handler. There are even compiled phone-dialing scripts written in a C-like language for Easylink, Envoy, Agrinet, Inet and Hayes modems. The only problem I had in running Interlend on my Everex 486/25 system was a QEMM memory manager exception error, which I resolved through a re-optimization of the system. However, when I tried to run the package on a Zeos 386SX notebook computer, with 593 kB free RAM, the ill.exe program froze the system, and much as I tried to resolve this, I never did get the Interlend program to run on this system. This is one mighty slick inter-library loan program despite this mysterious glitch on the Zeos. However, I must admit that this particular Zeos has also failed to run some popular shareware distributed software. Thus, I suspect that the bug lies not in the Interlend software but rather somewhere in the Zeos motherboard!

B. Proprietary Operating Systems

These systems are based on Digital Equipment Corp. VAX systems under VMS, but in the case of Inforonics a UNIX version also is available. These systems were not covered in Chapter 6 because they are either a relatively different product, such as what Dymaxion produces for media resources center operation, or they are new products to the commercial market.

1. Grom-Hayes Library Automation System

This system was developed by Dr. Larry W. Yother, who was Librarian of Hartford State Technical College. This college was incorporated into the Connecticut Community College system and is no longer in operation. Yother has an agreement with the State of Connecticut that enabled several other libraries to install this software at no charge. Now, he is trying to establish some arrangement that would permit this software to be sold as a commercial system. However, object code is available at this writing that would allow a library to try this software on its Digital Equipment VAX system using the VMS operating system. The system derives its name from the first librarian of Hartford Technical College.

Grom-Hayes is programmed in VMS Basic and is an easy-to-use, menu-driven system with an online catalog incorporating cross-references, circulation, acquisitions, periodical control, community information, and inventory control. Dialing into the system at an installed site hosted on a micro VAX produced lively response doing author, title, subject, or author, and title searches. Other searches such as call number and accession number are also offered. This system should meet the needs of college and public libraries and should be relatively easy to install and bring up. It has the advantage of being developed by a librarian who is an expert programmer to boot! The question is whether this system can be offered commercially and thus establish a firm customer base which in turn will allow it to continue to evolve along with competing systems.

The February, 1987 issue of *The Electronic Library* tells the story of the development of this system. (10) If the State of Connecticut can help establish this system with a firmer footing, many libraries would find it could meet their needs. Meanwhile, several other sites have been using this system for a number of years and are quite satisfied with its functional evolution, performance and low operational costs.

2. Dymaxion Research, Ltd.

This firm offers its media center management software, called MEDIANET, having developed its earliest form of the system in 1975. This system was first used at the National Film Board of Canada (NFB), which then designed its own system. That system ran between 1980 and 1988, when Dymaxion was contracted to develop a new system. Now, the NFB system operates on Digital Equipment MicroVAX nodes in Edmonton, Ottawa and Montreal. MEDIANET has been enhanced through customer suggestions. This is the media center system against which all automated library systems having media center modules should be evaluated. The current version is 6.1, with v.6.2 in beta testing.

This bilingual system has an accounting system, booking calendar and on-line catalog. There are over 50 installed sites, including the University of Minnesota where the film collection is not administered from the university library but is a part of another collegial unit. The basic system books films, handles shipping and receiving, and generates all the necessary reports and notices. The online catalog is an added module as are staff summary statistical displays, booking by remote clients, evaluations and acquisitions, relend and interlibrary communications. Further modules are also available that will generate a phototypeset catalog, handle duplication, and arrange booking by time of day. A campus services capability enables closet or building inventories, special delivery/pickup/return reports, optional receipts, work orders, room facilities and other details to allow media management in remote buildings and specific rooms.

My online demonstration with Dymaxion's Peter Mason was great. This system is replete with neat features that enable both small and very large media centers to have a system concentrating on their needs. The system imports and exports MARC records, enabling such data to be included in an online union catalog. The user interface really does an excellent job of minimizing keystrokes for the experienced user and yet allows the beginning user to use the menus and online context-sensitive help at any time. Depending on the function, the system anticipates the operator's next action, making this system very powerful, flexible and able to meet high-volume media transaction processing. The system is programmed in VMS BASIC and operates under VMS on any Digital Equipment VAX system. Dymaxion is also investigating a port to UNIX if it can find a suitable quality VAX BASIC-to-C translator. Currently, Dymaxion feels that VMS and its BASIC work very well and Digital's new Alpha microprocessor chip will provide a new family of systems from Digital with improved price and performance across a range of system sizes. These systems currently can support very small multiuser needs and grow to around a thousand simultaneous users.

Dymaxion is primarily a Digital computer and microcomputer vendor but derives around 20% of its business from software, with the bulk of that revenue generated by MEDIANET.

3. *Inforonics, Inc.*

This is a privately held company established by Laurence Buckland in 1965. It has provided computer composition and database processing for publishers, special libraries, professional associations and other clients since that time. Its text-processing service (TPS) is a total service from source data to typeset publication from an online reusable database. The Blue Sky database forms the heart of this service. It uses "heuristic keys" which may not actually exist in the data or complex program-generated text, e.g., Henry the Eight, Henry VIII or Henry 8th. Blue Sky can be licensed to a customer site or run in a time-sharing mode on Inforonics' own system. It is written in the C language using Modified B-Tree indexing. Versions are available to run under Digital's VMS operating system on the VAX processors and under UNIX on a variety of systems. This dbms is the basis of the INPAC and INFOCAT software products.

INPAC (Inforonics Public Access Catalog) is a product directed at special libraries. Many special libraries have been customers of Inforonics for MARC-based catalog products and other database services that use software running at Inforonics, accessed via remote terminal or microcomputer by customers. INPAC can take MARC records from an in-house source, bibliographic utility or commercial cataloging source, with new titles added through batch input from disk, magnetic tape or telecommunications. OCLC, CD-ROM or RLIN are all supported. The system offers a choice of three user interfaces. Menus are used for novice searchers. Commands are used for frequent users. An intermediate form is an advanced menu with storage and combining of search sets. Records can be displayed in labeled, catalog card, short-MARC and full-MARC forms. Searches are by keyword in the entire record as well as by the conventional author, title and subject. When searching for a title, author or subject, all keywords are also searched in the field. The publication date, range of dates and record type can be used to further qualify searches. All the knowledge numbers in a MARC record are also searchable. Print files can be exported for printed output, typesetting or desktop publishing input for very polished printed products.

INFOCAT is a MARC II cataloging and searching system. It provides the source records for the INPAC module above as well as two other products. One of these is BIBCOMP, bibliographic compilation. The other is MARCSOURCE, centralized cataloging. Both single and multiple libraries can be users of a system. All MARC formats are supported and field and subfield validation is a feature. A full-screen record editor is used for creating and changing records. The same user search interfaces are present as in INPAC, and record display choices are the same. Users can define non-MARC–record formats and create these records with INFOCAT, store them in the Blue Sky dbms and then search them using INPAC. Make no mistake; this is a slick and easy-to-use system. Some 50 libraries are using the INFOCAT and INPAC software. The American Antiquarian Book Society is one typical customer.

With the UNIX version of this software, it is possible to run this system on an Intel 80386 or 486 platform. Also, a version for a Novell Advanced Netware LAN can be licensed. This product, while nominally thought of as a DEC VAX/VMS product because of its origins and the long history of Inforonics' use of DEC computers, does present a choice of options to prospective users.

IV. CONCLUSION

As many libraries examine their positions with their present library automation vendor, they will examine other potential systems suppliers. The move to open systems, i.e., UNIX, seems to be a trend that software purchasers believe will preserve their software investment and facilitate internetworking of varying systems resources both within and outside their parent organization. However, one must bear in mind that both proprietary operating systems and these nonproprietary solutions are aimed at bringing POSIX compliance into their application repertoire. It is this factor, coupled with improved TCP/IP and Novell networking support, that will determine whether real client/server application designs can be installed and operated. When we look at current automated systems, we still see a large dependence on dumb terminals for system access. Today, a library patron workstation that will run Windows and access a network can be put together for around $1500 if one does not buy only a name brand, Intel-based system. A new CRT that emulates a VT-100 can be obtained for around $500. So, even though librarians recognize the value in moving to the personal computer as the patron and staff workstation, there is still a large dollar problem to be overcome to fund such an approach. However, our institutions will have to come to grips with this problem if any improvements in productivity and effectiveness are to come from adopting the latest generation technologies.

Librarians should not believe that moving from a proprietary operating system platform on a mainframe or superminicomputer to a nonproprietary platform composed of UNIX servers, a TCP/IP network or a Novell LAN solution will necessarily bring improvements. They should also bear in mind that UNIX still has distinct variations that impede real software transportability across popular UNIX hardware platforms. Any move would need to be accompanied by the necessary technical infrastructure in the library. And in many cases such support is now provided by a central computing facility that is not necessarily in a position to perform support for a distributed architecture system. UNIX systems, no matter how much they hide the underlying system from the user by a friendly shell program, always will need support gurus. Therefore, libraries considering client/server applications and "rightsizing" need to put in place their own on-site support and training infrastructrue. If they cannot do that, they will be better off staying with a central host-driven computing solution. UNIX or PICK under UNIX is not a panacea to solve systems problems. It can be a decided improvement if the library can provide the necessary infrastructure, is willing to assume responsibility for its own computing environment within the institutional context and work cooperatively with other centers of computing expertise in their organization. In other words, distributed systems are great, but only if one realizes the total implications of such an approach on the daily needs and operations of the library.

VI. APPENDIX: VENDOR CONTACTS

Adlib Information Systems, Ltd.
Marlborough Business Centre
Claverton House, Pelhams Court
London Road, Marlborough WILTS
SN8 2AB
England
(44) 672-515525
(44) 672-515828 Fax

Best Seller Library Management, Inc.
3300 Cote Vertu, Suite 303
Saint Laurent, Quebec, Canada
H4R 2B8
(514) 337-5007 ext. 290
(514) 337-7629 Fax

BRS Software Products
8000 Westpark Drive
McLean, VA 22102
(703) 442-3870
(703) 827-0686 Fax

Carlyle Systems, Inc.
2000 Alameda de las Pulgas
San Mateo, CA 94403
(415) 345-2500
(415) 654-0464 Fax

CLSI, Inc. See GEAC, Inc.

Cuadra Associates, Inc.
11835 West Olympic Blvd., Suite 855
Los Angeles, CA 90064
(800) 366-1390
(310) 478-0066
(310) 477-1078 Fax

Databasix Information System, B.V.
Rijnzathe 8, 3454 PV De Meern
Postbus 179, 3454 ZK De Meern
The Netherlands
(31) 3406-62455
(31) 3406-65033 Fax

Dymaxion Research, Ltd.
5515 Cogswell Street
Halifax, NS, Canada B3J 1R2
(902) 422-1973
(902) 421-1267 Fax

Dynix, Inc.
151 East 1700 South
Provo, UT 84606
(800) 288-8020
(801) 375-2770
(801) 373-1889 Fax

GEAC Computers, Inc.
14140 Midway Road, Suite 105
Dallas, TX 75244
(214) 490-3482
(214) 960-9728 Fax

GEAC, Inc. (formerly CLSI, Inc.)
320 Nevada Street
Newtonville, MA 02160
(800) 365-0085
(617) 965-6310
(617) 969-1928 Fax

Grom-Hayes Library Automation Systems
One Linden Court
Bloomfield, CT 06002-1788
(203) 243-1083 (home)
(203) 527-4111 (office)

Highland Library Systems, Inc.
1350 Heather Ridge Boulevard
Dunedin, FL 34698
(813) 734-7300
(813) 733-4791 Fax

IME Information Management and Engineering
990 Washington Street
Dedham, MA 02026-6790
(617) 320-0303
(617) 320-0793 Fax

Inforonics, Inc.
550 Newtown Road
P.O. Box 458
Littleton, MA 01460
(508) 486-8976

Innovative Interfaces, Inc.
2344 Sixth Street
Berkeley, CA 94710
(800) 878-6600
(510) 644-3600
(510) 644-3650 Fax

Keystone Systems, Inc.
P.O. Box 31066
4513 Creedmore Road, Suite 301
Raleigh, NC 27612
(800) 222-9711
(919) 782-1145

Logical Choice
3, Newtec Pl., 66-72 Magdalen Road
Oxford, OX4 1RE
England
0865-727946
0865-790853 Fax

Multicore Library Services
6631 Commerce Parkway
Dublin, OH 43017-3239
(800) 753-0053
(614) 792-5211 Fax
or U.S. Branch Office
3452 Losey Boulevard South
La Crosse, WI 54601
(800) 658-9453
(608) 787-8333 Fax

Ringgold Management Systems, Inc.
P.O. Box 368
Beaverton, OR 97075-0368
(503) 645-3502
(503) 690-6642 Fax

Sirsi, Inc.
689 Discovery Drive
Huntsville, AL 35806
(205) 922-9825
(205) 922-9818 Fax

Specialist Computer Centres, Ltd.
(Systems and Software, Ltd)
James Ho, Warwick Road
Birmingham, B11 2LE
England
(44) 21-766-7000
(44) 21-773-3986 Fax

TKM Software, Ltd.
P.O. Box 1525
839 18th Street
Brandon, Manitoba, Canada R7A 6N3
(800) 565-6272
(204) 727-3873
(204) 727-3338 Fax

Total Access, Inc.
3812 West 51st Street, Suite 105
Minneapolis, MN 55410
(612) 926-8914

REFERENCES

1. Shekhel, Alex and Mike O'Brien. Selecting a Relational Database Management System for Library Automation Systems. *Library Hi-Tech* 7(2): 17-20 (1989).
2. Shekhel, Alex and Eva Freeman. Parallel Processing Creates a Low Cost Growth Path. *Library Hi-Tech* 5(2): 19-25 (1987).
3. Cibbarelli, Pamela. Automation in Review: User Rating of STAR Software. *Computers in Libraries* 12(8): 1-4 (September 1992).
4. Gilmartin, Jacqueline. *Dynix: A Guide for Librarians and System Managers*. Brookfield, VT: Ashgate Publishing Co., 1992.
5. Westlake, Duncan and John Clarke. *GEAC: A Guide for Librarians and Systems Managers. 2nd ed.* Brookfield, VT: Ashgate Publishing Co., 1992.
6. Kelly, Glen J. MULTILIS: A Description of the System Design and Operational Features. *Library Hi-Tech* 6(3): 67-79 (1988).
7. Young, Jacky. The Unicorn Collection Management System: Its Structure and Features. *Library Hi-Tech* 6(1): 61-66, 86 (1988).
8. Companies in the News. *Wilson Library Bulletin* 66(10): 17 (June 1992).
9. Fisher, Shelagh and Jennifer Rowley. *BookshelF: A Guide for Librarians and System Managers*. Aldershot, England: Ashgate, 1992.
10. Yother, Larry W. Systems Development at the Grom Hayes Library. *The Electronic Library* 5(1): 34-42 (February 1987).

8

MICROCOMPUTER/LAN-BASED BIBLIOGRAPHIC SOFTWARE

Microsoft is doing what IBM did in the past. If you think the outside of the Temple is nice, wait 'til you see the inside. Once they get you inside, they lock the door and throw away the key.

— Bob Holmes quoted in *InfoWorld 15*(3): 3 (January 18, 1993)

I. INTRODUCTION

There are many integrated library systems and related programs available that work on current popular microcomputers. This chapter presents software that performs either those functions commonly part of larger multiuser integrated library systems or some specialized function often needed in a library. The programs in this chapter use mainly Intel 80xxx hardware that runs IBM's PC-DOS v.3.3 and above and/or Microsoft's MS-DOS v.3.3 and above, including the recently released v.6.2. IBM has released its own PC-DOS version 6.1, which incorporates some variant external command features from the MS-DOS version from Microsoft. Consequently, it may be desirable to check with the software vendors as to their compatibility with MS or PC-DOS version 6.x if you intend to run such a single-user or LAN workstation system. Many of these products also will operate on a LAN, usually a Netbios-compatible LAN such as Novell Advanced Netware 3.11 or 3.12. Some of the products in this chapter have Macintosh versions available but are thought of mainly as MS-DOS systems since they originated under that operating system.

Another operating system player that can be classed with the above is Concurrent DOS, a small multiuser and multitasking system that emulates MS-DOS. This system permits small multiuser systems to be implemented using a multiport serial interface card, such as the Digiboard in an Intel 80386/80486 microcomputer and either VT-100–type terminals or lower powered Intel 80286 or 80386SX systems to be used as terminals. A two- to four-user system can be configured with acceptable performance using this approach, with much lower maintenance and operating costs than installing a similar LAN-based system. The LAN-based system provides for growth and remote connectivity that the Concurrent DOS implementation would not. But if growth and connectivity are not needed, then this little-known system would be ideal. If you are interested in a system using Digital Research's Concurrent DOS, inquire about operating an MS-DOS–based system under this with the system's vendor. Even if not mentioned in configuration specifications, it should be possible for most MS-DOS software to run under Concurrent DOS since they are quite compatible. Digital Research also sells DR DOS which has just been released in version 7.0. It will run programs designed to run under MS-DOS, including Microsoft Windows.

A competitor to MS-DOS/Microsoft Windows combination of single-user, multitasking system is IBM's OS/2. This system will run MS-DOS programs in a compatible window as does Microsoft Windows. Currently it offers only Windows v.3.1–level compatibility for Windows-specific applications. However, with IBM no longer having access to Microsoft program code, OS/2's future Windows compatibility may be problematic. OS/2's main attraction is for those users who have OS/2-specific applications, can afford quite powerful Intel 80486 systems operating in a Token Ring–based LAN and are willing to equip these with at least 8 MB RAM—although 16 MB RAM systems are a more realistic minimum for running OS/2. OS/2, while it offers full 32-bit operation in its native application mode, will probably remain a niche player for those with IBM PS/2 microchannel architecture systems—which are themselves much less popular than IBM's own ISA bus Valuepoint and PS/1 clones. IBM is attempting to popularize OS/2 by pre-installing it on many IBM PS/2 microchannel–equipped models, but this does not guarantee that OS/2 will ever equal Microsoft's Windows and related products in number of installed systems.

Microsoft is also offering its Windows for Workgroups v.3.11 program that allows peer-to-peer networking, similar to the Artisoft LanTastic network. With the lower costs and rapidly increasing popularity of Ethernet in its twisted-pair form, called 10Base-T, this LAN topology and structure is growing at a much faster rate than IBM's Token Ring. LanTastic is a much more mature and stable product, enabling better and larger growth currently than Windows for Workgroups. However, this could change in the future depending on what Microsoft is able to do with this new product. Windows and Windows for Workgroups are still 16-bit-mode systems. To tap the full potential of the Intel 80386/80486 and its big brother the Pentium, will require a full 32-bit operating system. That system could be a 32-bit OS/2 from IBM as an out-growth of its alliance with Talagent and Apple. However, such a system might be UNIX based if NeXT, Inc., and Steve Jobs were successful in their May, 1993 introduction of their NeXTStep operating system on Intel and other chip systems. It should be noted that NeXT has stopped all hardware manufacture and sold its hardware manufacturing facility to Canon. Canon recently announced Intel 80486 systems specially optimized to run NeXTStep. Silicon Graphics has licensed NeXTStep's interface for incorporation into its MIPS-based systems. More likely will be the emergence of Microsoft's Windows NT (New Technology) as the dominant operating system for the Intel chip-based desktop/LAN. This is a full 32-bit-mode system and, like NeXTStep, is offered on Intel and Alpha processors, with other ports in the works.

Another factor complicating our knowledge of what will occur in the marketplace as to future microcomputer operating system directions and thus likely moves by application developers is the release of Novell's Advanced Netware v.4.0. Actually, it is UNIX based and incorporates support for mixed LANs where UNIX servers would coexist with traditional Novell Netware servers. Like Advanced Netware 3.12, it provides enhanced support for Apple Macintosh connectivity. Novell has bought UNIX Systems Laboratories, the company that AT&T spun off to develop, support and market UNIX System V. UNIXware is another related product that Novell has released. This product attempts to make UNIX a more attractive desktop system.

Some of the programs in this chapter are available for the Apple II family systems. There are other systems no longer considered competitive mainstream products. For example, I have not covered Apple II family software. The Apple Macintosh is a current mainstream system that keeps getting better all the time. Apple recently introduced quite powerful models incorporating the new PowerPC chip at very competitive prices. This makes them very attractive user-oriented systems. MAC System 7 is multitasking and also provides good support via the SuperDrive on current Macs for data transfer between Macs and MS-DOS–based systems. SuperDrive will write out an MS-DOS–formatted 3.5-inch, 1.44-MB floppy and also read it so that data can be imported between these platforms with increased ease even without the benefit of having a mixed-platform network and electronic transmission. Macs have built-in AppleTalk or Ethernet network connectivity. For heavier duty LANs it is more desirable to use these systems with a full 10-MB Ethernet LAN versus the 2-MB capacity of the AppleTalk scheme. I would expect that the niche users such as the education market, which has or had large Apple II investments, to stage their hardware replacements toward Macintosh systems and upgraded networks using Ethernet.

Prospective purchasers of microcomputer-based systems such as these represented here need to examine their current and future needs as carefully as those purchasers of larger and more expensive systems. Single-user MS-DOS systems cannot really provide adequate retrieval capability since even the smallest library needs to allow for simultaneous access by a librarian and a patron. Therefore, any library must consider that it will need a system able to be accessed by at least two users simultaneously if the system is to perform the most basic tasks associated with an online, integrated library system, e.g., access to an online public catalog and circulation control. That is why a Concurrent DOS or a LAN solution for these systems makes it possible for the smaller library to gain as much needed functionality as only larger systems used to provide, yet at an affordable cost.

II. PC/MS-DOS AND LAN FAMILY PRODUCTS

These systems form the mainstream of our desktop microcomputers used in business, education and government today. With competition providing a continual decrease in price relative to performance, the average desktop system today can be acquired for around $2500 or even less depending on the actual components specified. These systems can perform more interactive computing in integrated library systems than mainframe computers were able to do until the early 1980's. The ever-improving price/performance ratio, the continual rise in labor costs and the need to provide better access and retrieval to growing numbers of library users mean that no library today can remain totally noncomputerized. The market will see new companies introducing new software in an attempt to acquire some market share. The Appendix to this chapter includes several new companies that may lack a track record but have deliverable products.

1. APAK Systems, Ltd.: SEARCHME™

This Canadian company was established in 1979. SEARCHME™ is a registered trademark of the University of Guelph. The cataloging portion of this system was jointly developed at the university with APAK and provides client/server architecture systems to public and university/college libraries. London Ontario Public Libraries and the University of Guelph are two larger customer sites. The University of Guelph, replaced its GEAC GLS system, an 835,000-title database and 150-workstation system, with a SEARCHME CD-ROM catalog and integrated library system. Other sites use this product to back up their GEAC GLS systems. The INCOLSA library network in Indiana is a large U.S.

customer. This system can operate as a stand-alone MS-DOS product or as a UNIX-based system and within a TCP/IP network. The SEARCHME catalog can be a CD-ROM or hard disk-based system. It can be kept up to date via a supplementary file on hard disk when a CD-ROM catalog is used. Searching this medium is transparent to the user. The library can define many different system parameters, display screens, fields to be indexed, look and feel of the user interface and multilingual operation. With its network-linking capability, users can have access to multiple resources on an institution network from the microcomputer workstations in the library. The circulation subsystem can serve remote locations through this network. SEARCHME uses a UNIX file server. Searches of the online catalog can be saved to disk. The same record format can be modified prior to saving the search output for producing personal bibliographies. Records can be printed by sequence or individual record, limited by number. Print formats can be modified prior to printing.

The cataloging system can run stand-alone or networked via its client software. There is an online coding manual for MARC, context-sensitive help, interactive error checking during editing with a central database on any UNIX server to which the MS-DOS-based workstations are connected via TCP/IP protocol. Multiple library databases are supported, including loading of LC or National Library of Canada MARC tapes. This is the platform for producing a CD-ROM catalog or operating the online catalog from a central bibliographic database. The circulation system and other SEARCHME functions use a fourth-generation database management system. Fully customizable reports may be generated from this system. Similarly, the acquisitions subsystem is a client/server implementation or can be implemented on a single workstation if that is all that is needed.

The online catalog can optionally index by media or material type so that searches can be made by these criteria. Keyword access to the entire record and full-text indexing are also options. Field labels on display screens can be changed by the library. This system uses programmed function keys on the workstation keyboard to perform specific commands such as "Find by title" or "Display results." Two keystrokes and a user's search term retrieve most records. When using the PF key mode special keycaps provide labels on the keys. A library does not have to use this mode but can instead choose to use a menu-based interface where the user chooses items by cursor keys and the Enter key. The user search interface is provided in two forms: a novice mode—where author, title, subject and call number are used most commonly for known item searches—and an expert mode. This latter mode implements full Boolean searching either via PF key or menu. AND, OR, NOT, ET CETERA operators are used. The user creates the search one term at a time as index displays are retrieved to assist. These Boolean searches can be qualified by location, material type, and publication date if the imprint field has been indexed in the ALL Keyword Index.

An UNDO key permits removal of search conditions. The system uses implied truncation when typing a character string. The ETC (ET CETERA operator above) is a special SEARCHME feature to have the system automatically process a Boolean OR on successive terms in an index list. Once a record is retrieved, the user can browse the items surrounding that record. The system is excellent at handling compound personal names. For example, the name "De La Roche, Maria" can be located by any of the following, "Maria de", "La Roche, Maria De", "Roche, Maria De La", or "De La Roche, Maria." Diacritical marks are translated to the IBM character set on the workstations to display on screen.

If a CD-ROM catalog is used at individual workstations, these can have their hard disks updated with new additions either through loading from a floppy or a portable magnetic tape unit. Or, the system can operate from a central server. Bibliofile, various sources of MARC tapes and other MARC record sources can be integrated to provide local catalogers with MARC data records on which to base their work.

This integrated library system offers excellent functionality coupled with some cost-lowering options such as the CD-ROM catalog, designed to minimize the server storage needed. Very large databases can be accommodated either on the UNIX server or in a CD-ROM approach. An Ethernet TCP/IP LAN provides sufficient transaction capability to support relatively large circulation loads—certainly those found within academic libraries and even larger public libraries. This system represents a good growth capability for the smaller library also as they can start with a small CD-ROM based system. The fact that SEARCHME has been used to replace these larger and older GEAC GLS online catalog and/or circulation systems is a key indication that this system has the performance necessary for current and future institutional demands for interactive networked services.

2. *Auto-Graphics, Inc.: IMPACT, AGILE III and IMPACT/SLIMS™*

The IMPACT system is a CD-ROM catalog with a separate but integrated module for interlibrary loan. AGILE III is Auto-Graphics' host-based central online cataloging system and network in which shared file users can use all other shared files while private users are restricted to their own files. IMPACT/SLIMS is the Small Library Management System which incorporates an online catalog, cataloging, circulation, reporting and system administration. It can link to the IMPACT CD-ROM catalog or to other CD-ROM data.

Both IMPACT systems can be customized to the library's data needs, descriptions and search provisions, record downloading and screen time out. Databases have complete union list-of-serials capabilities and can be for a single or multiple institution or location. OCLC, RLIN and other MARC record sources can be used. Auto-Graphics provides central cataloging database support for libraries under contracts via the AGILE III system. This includes database preparation, CD-ROM mastering, and authority control. Auto-Graphics also offers many other services such as smart bar code generation, conversions from one system to another competing system and special database cleanup to isolate records not meeting LC MARC standards. One customer of this IMPACT CD-ROM system is Arrowhead Cooperative Library System in Minnesota. The CD-ROM catalog uses the standard 10-function-key IBM PC keyboard, with brief and full record displays using labelled fields. The library can decide which fields will be shown to the library user. One can have selected stations switch between MARC record–type displays and full labelled displays by doing an ALT-M keystoke combination. The ALA MARC character set diacriticals display over or under letters as appropriate. Author, title, subject or a combination of the above feature browsing access. Browsing by Dewey or LC call number is optional. There is a separate keyword search of author, title and subject using an implied AND. All-word indexing searches keywords in all indexed fields, with AND implied. An all-word index is required to support the research-level software module. This expert level supports additional searching of standard control numbers, location-based searching, the use of OR and NOT operators plus other search qualifiers such as language, publication date and wildcard characters. This system is programmed in the C language and a variant known as Vitamin C.

The IMPACT interlibrary loan module produces printed forms or will forward electronic requests via a file server when installed in a LAN environment. Novell Netware LANs or LanTastic also can be used for the LAN. Any IBM-compatible personal computer with at least 1 MB RAM can be used with MS-DOS 3.3 or above on the individual PC. In the LAN interlibrary loan, the server can dial each branch's interlibrary loan station each evening and collect the outbound requests for next-day processing. The system assigns a serial number and acknowledges that the request is in process. Requests are forwarded through a referral list to each lender until the request is filled. The system automatically flags overdue items, time-expired requests, renewal requests, and any other request needing action. It also maintains statistics and generates a transaction log which can be printed. Auto-Graphics will sell hardware and software for this system or the software and CD-ROM for installation on the library's own hardware.

The IMPACT/SLIMS system is designed for libraries under 45,000 titles. Auto-Graphics will custom quote prices to create the database for this system. Bar code scanners can be used optionally for recording circulation transactions. This system is currently in version 3.0 and is appropriate for school, special, public and academic libraries. It can operate as a single-user, stand-alone MS-DOS system or in a LAN using LanTastic or Novell Netware 2.11 at minimum. It probably would work with Novell Lite, although I have not actually tested it in such a configuration. It is programmed in the C language and uses Btrieve for its indexing. One can operate IMPACT/SLIMS along with IMPACT, where the local library database is in the SLIMS system and the IMPACT CD-ROM system is a union database. This system can also be used to generate a hard-disk update to the CD-ROM, which can be installed on the hard disk on each workstation to keep the CD-ROM current between its remastering. The library can import MicroLIF records as supplied by various dealers. Although searches between IMPACT/SLIMS and IMPACT on CD-ROM are not transparent, it takes only a couple of keystrokes to toggle back and forth.

This is an attractive system for consortia or individual smaller libraries and can be operated quite economically according to the extent of the LAN used and the frequency of remastering the CD-ROM catalog. Since standard CD-ROM drives can be internally incorporated into the main chassis of the microcomputer, these stations can be attractively packaged but use relatively inexpensive hard disk-equipped Intel 80386SX systems.

Auto-Graphics' central system uses several host platforms to provide its various services. A Sperry 90/80 superminicomputer together with a Data General Aviion workstation having two 16-MB central processors operating at 20 MHz, two 1600/6250-bpi tape drives, two 2-GB cartridge tapes, one 150-MB cartridge tape and 16 GB of direct access storage devices and a printer provide these services. In addition a Meridian Data CD-ROM publisher is used to produce the CD-ROM catalogs. The Aviion is connected via Ethernet to a Xyvision XFPS 55–typesetting system with four Xyview workstations, a Linotronic L300 typesetter with 250 type faces, two Linotronic laser proofing devices and a Linotronic 202 typesetter. In addition there are microfilm processors to produce microfiche products.

Auto-Graphics has a good history of providing service to its library clients. It has provided the IMPACT computer systems since 1987. Morrow and Lee have written about this product in some detail. (1,2)

3. Balboa Software: Library Master

This product is a bibliographic and textual database manager. The current version is release 2.0 which has added over 100 new features to an already abundantly featured product at its introduction. This software is available either as an MS-DOS single-user license or as a LAN multiple-user license. Prices are very competitive with competing products such as Pro-Cite, BRS/Search, Inmagic and Zyindex. The network version will operate under Novell or any Netbios-compatible network. This software will run under MS-DOS v.2.0 and above and on systems with 512 kB RAM available after loading MS-DOS. For small databases, even a dual 720-kB floppy system could be used, but a hard disk is really necessary for serious, continued production use.

In the network version each user can save her or his own default settings. Public read-only databases can be put up, personal databases in private subdirectories and shared databases for workgroup projects are all supported. Multiple users on the LAN can search simultaneously in a database. Automatic record locking ensures data integrity as individuals update databases. One of the strengths of this product is its ability to produce bibliographies in many styles. Turabian 5th ed., Vancouver 4th ed., American Anthropologist, American Chemical Society, American Ethnographer, American Sociological Society, ANSI and the Biochemistry and Linguistic Societies of America have style sheets prepared. Bibliographies can be by subject, author, or even by authors, editors and translators. Authority lists of authors, subjects, journals or other fields can be printed. A catalog of books and an index to periodical literature cross-indexed by authors, subject and journals are other products from this system. Titles can be italicized or underlined. This program supports PostScript output and interfaces to WordPerfect v.5.1 or above in MS-DOS or Windows versions.

The custom report capabilities through enhanced style sheet features are very nice. One can treat names in many ways, such as converting first names to initials and multiple names beyond a set number to "et al." in the citation. Suffixes such as "Jr." or "III" also may be treated several ways. Letter case conversion to capitalize all words or just the beginning of the field or each word and an option to keep capitalization for foreign languages where capitalization rules differ, such as German or French, are another slick feature. The Format File options also allow centered lines, joined lines, records indexed and grouped under any field, special treatment of records with empty fields and special processing if a field is the same as or different from the previous record.

Records can be imported into a Library Master database from MELVYL, NOTIS, GEAC, University of Toronto Online Library Catalog, Chemical Abstracts STN, Compact Cambridge MEDLINE v.4, EPIC, RLIN short title catalog, ABI/INFORM, AGRICOLA, religious and Theological Abstracts CD-ROM. Notebook II and NB Citation data formats can also be handled. The optional, separately priced Data Magician program can import and export MARC records. After a search, records are displayed in a browse-mode, brief-view display presenting seven records at a time. The fields displayed can be chosen. A single record can be formatted and printed as well as a whole listing. One can edit a record without leaving browse or search modes. It is possible to search a subset retrieved by a prior search, and search strategies can be named and saved for reuse. One can spell out Boolean search operators AND, OR and NOT in the search. Record number and record type searching is supported. For color monitor or laptop gray-scale monitor use, the system has complete color customization. Dates can contain non-English month spellings. There is a utility to repair a damaged database and an option to retain original record numbers. A .PIF file is supplied for running Library Master in a DOS Window under Microsoft Windows v.3.1.

This is a very price competitive product for its features. It has an improved manual and a basic tutorial that will help the user get up to speed quickly. Balboa's upgrade prices are also reasonable and based on the version being upgraded. Library Master is well named. It is a competing product to Personal Bibliographic Software, Inc.'s ProCite, previewed later in this chapter.

4. Brodart Automation (a Division of Brodart Co.): LePac, Precision One, P1 Integrated System

LePac is a CD-ROM online catalog introduced in 1985. It also serves as the online catalog for the Precision One (P1) Integrated System. P1 is a retrospective conversion and cataloging system for school and public libraries that use a CD-ROM MARC database. The P1 Integrated System is implemented using the LanTastic LAN to provide circulation, public access to the LePac catalog, cataloging and database maintenance, interlibrary loan, local authority control, holdings maintenance, bibliographies and an interface to the Precision One MARC record database. Collection Development and Acquisitions support was under development at the time of my inquiry to Brodart, so prospective users of this system should be confident that this module will be released to round out this system's capabilities.

LePac can store up to one million titles on a single CD-ROM disk using a proprietary data compression scheme. The system has a nice browse feature done by scrolling alphabetic lists of authors, titles or subjects. An express access by typing in an author name, subject or title brings the user quite quickly to the desired records. A single library or a union catalog database can be constructed as a location field is provided. Searching uses the implied "AND" when multiple terms are entered. To implement the OR operator, one merely encloses terms in parentheses, while a tilde (~) before a term implements the operator NOT. Cross-references produce the actual bibliographic record when the enter key is pressed. The LePac CD-ROM can be supplemented without the expense of remastering the whole CD-ROM via either a supplemental CD-ROM disk or downloading current records to the workstation's hard disk. Using the P1 Integrated System, these supplements can be fully integrated.

An add-on to LePac is the QuILL interlibrary loan software. It will produce printed ILL forms, download records to disk and enable a centralized processing center to form an ILL network using an MS-DOS microcomputer. Modem connections over telephone lines can be used to communicate with ILL software-equipped systems in the individual network libraries. This system can operate unattended, making its calls each evening on a predetermined schedule, then transferring requests and replies. It can make 20–40 calls per hour and store up to 30,000 ILL requests. The downloading to disk-type operation is used by systems that use an electronic bulletin board system for request and reply distribution.

Precision One features over 1.2 million MARC records on CD-ROM and has particularly high hit rates on audio/visual records. Libraries can subscribe to monthly current cataloging with LC MARC and audio/visual records created by Brodart. These are cumulative so only two disks are ever searched.

The P1 Integrated System complements the above systems to form a well-integrated application suite. Using this system to create local supplements to the LePac CD-ROM database allows a currency of records just as with a fully hard disk-stored database system. The P1 system will generate spine and pocket labels as well as shelf list cards or complete card sets. Records with added holdings or other modifications are stored on the system's hard disk and replace the CD-ROM record in a catalog search.

The Collection Development and Acquisition module under development will be a separately priced subsystem with a database built on Brodart's Books' file of titles in print. It will supply MARC record, title information, in-print status, age level and review source. Then, in the acquisition phase, a new program called PC Rose Plus from Brodart's Books is going to be integrated. A BISAC format disk will be used to transfer electronic orders to Brodart or other vendors. An interface to the circulation system will support bar code label production and building item records.

In addition to these systems, Brodart provides vendor conversion services using its over 12 million cataloging record database, mainly for school and public library customers. For this service and as a separate service to libraries it also uses its central Interactive Access System to store each customer's database at a fixed monthly cost. This system features full-screen editing with author and title searching for the cataloger. The personal computer interface software can download records to the workstation, where the record is processed with considerable flexibility. Brodart has a long record of service to libraries and certainly has systems installed in sufficient numbers to prove its worth in the marketplace.

5. Cactus Software, Inc.: MINARET—Collection Management Software

This system is designed to provide museum collections with support for bibliographic and artifact databases. It is equally at home in an archive and manuscript setting, slide collection, art works collection, or photography library. It uses a MARC II record structure and locally defined fields to extend MARC to cover these specialized materials. The user can specify which fields will be indexed for faster retrieval. It supports all seven MARC formats, including the Authority Format and the new Integrated Format. Record transport features allow the conversion of non-MARC databases to MARC and the MARC database to other, non-MARC formats. These are dBase .dbf format, R:Base, SQL and word-processing formats. Records may be up to 65,000 bytes each in this system. The system will print inventory reports, collection guides, catalog cards, and folder and slide labels. Searchers use browsable indexes, wildcards and keyword searches in any field. Browsable indexes in pop-up windows make the user interface appealing and easy to use. The accessioning support is quite full, printing deed-of-gift forms and other outputs customary to museum and archive collection administration. The authority system is fully invoked to provide search terms and record-building terms to the cataloger. Various receipt and record transfer forms can be generated. The accessions screen actually incorporates the cataloging information on further record pages which can be built later in brief or full form. The system can also mimic RLIN or OCLC record displays for users already familiar with these.

The National Archives of the Episcopal Church is one of some 200 clients using this software. Donald Firsching has written of his experiences with Minaret. (3) The other package that implements the Archives and Manuscripts Control (AMC) MARC format is the MicroMARC:amc system developed by Michigan State University, which is presented later in this chapter. Firsching is particularly impressed with the authority file features of Minaret, the addition of keyboard macro capabilities and the use of record layouts that can be copied, then modified to generate new MARC formats not supplied with the system. For example, he created an OCLC books format by modifying the AMC format copy. The system is conceived around the use of a construct known as an "environment," which brings together groups of records with the forms they will use. The records in a particular group will be of the same structure, i.e., with the same database field definitions or layout. Some 30 forms are already defined in the system as provided. The F9 key activates a menu bar at the top of the screen, but this bar is not of the pull-down type, so multiple menus must be paged through when performing some tasks. He also described Minaret's searching power as "somewhat primitive" compared with a standard database management system. Queries can be entered in three ways. The first is "EZ," which uses any blank fill-in-the field screen template. The second is Boolean, which offers operators that work only within fields. The third is "free form," which uses a Query language. The searching in this system, while adequate, probably could be improved through some user interface and index-building changes.

This system is available as a single-user MS-DOS system, as a Netbios-compatible LAN version and as a UNIX System V, release 3 program. Thus multiple-user systems of some considerable size can be implemented or very small systems supported with the same functionality in the software. Minaret is an interesting system, with a specialized market niche for museum and archive organizations. It is priced competitively, has excellent growth potential, and a good design foundation, and should continue to receive enhancements to keep it competitive in its specialized market.

6. CTB Macmillan/McGraw-Hill: Columbia Library System

The Columbia Library System is a product whose main market is in schools, with only 20% of its sales going to other types of libraries. These others are mainly public and college libraries. This system can handle up to 300,000 catalog records either as an MS-DOS-based single-user system or as a multiuser system running under a Novell LAN. Each of the modules is separately price but fully integrated. Cataloging and online catalog, circulation, MARC record interface, acquisitions and serials constitute the currently offered modules. The LAN version is in use by 67% of customers. The average collection size for these customers is 14,000 titles, although the largest site has close to 200,000 titles.

Columbia uses pull-down menus and is a system that will appeal to most users. Columbia originated in Regina, Saskatchewan, Canada and was originally developed by ABALL Software, which licensed it under the name Ocelot Library System. In Australia it is still licensed under the Ocelot name. Dr. Alan Ball was its principal designer. Further development of the software had been underwritten by the Canadian network UTLAS. In 1986 ABALL sold it to Columbia Computing. In 1989 this system was completely rewritten. It should be noted that a form of this earlier software is still supported by UTLAS and is called the M/Series 10 product, but it has only online catalog and circulation modules.

This system offers some menu customization to integrate MARC record source products such as Bibliofile or Mitinet/MARC. One can provide a gateway to a LAN electronic mail facility, a neighboring library's online catalog or a union catalog via an asynchronous modem-type connection. With an Internet gateway connection, a shared CD-ROM resource on the network can be accessed from the library's workstations. The system's browse and Boolean searching are very flexible and easy to learn. Pressing the F1 function key on the PC keyboard brings up context-sensitive help. The system uses its menu colors on a colored screen very pleasingly. The main menu offers the following choices: catalog, circulation, MARC, acquisitions, serials, utilities, files/DOS and quit. Catalog searches are displayed in a card format. For libraries that still use cards, the system will print card sets or shelf list cards and spine/pocket labels. The circulation system has some features that will appeal to schools. For example, one can generate lists of overdues by homeroom instead of merely generating individual student overdue notices. The sample reports from the system are nicely laid out, clear and can be generated on differing frequencies. The system exports its records in MicroLIF and a similar format called NearLIF. Records can be imported into this system from LaserQuest, OCLC, UTLAS, WLN, MARCive, Bibliofile, and different book vendors. The serial check-in uses a familiar metaphor—the Kardex—as its interface. It can predict expected issues using a start date coupled with the MARC standard frequencies from daily to triennial to establish its prediction calendar. The system maintains bindery information and issues bindery alert lists, but I did not see any indication of it printing bindery instruction tickets.

Columbia customers are sent Libra News, a newsletter covering Columbia news. They also have an 800 number for support if they have purchased an annual support agreement which costs roughly 10% of the original license fee for each module. There is also an electronic bulletin board. This system is competitive in its features with other MS-DOS–based products and in some cases really offers special features that will appeal to the school market. But other types of libraries within its database size range are advised to examine this system before jumping to the conclusion that it is only for school libraries. Columbia has been reviewed by William Saffady. (4)

7. Computer Assisted Library Information Co., Inc. (CALICO): LION

CALICO has provided library automation software to small libraries, mainly schools, since 1981. In the spring of 1993 the Macintosh version of LION was introduced. CALICO did not have a demonstration system to send me but invited me to come to St. Louis, Missouri to see the system in action in Principia Upper School where LION has been in use for six years. LION is an online catalog and circulation system designed for school libraries. It has had well-satisfied customers since its introduction in 1985.

8. Data Trek, Inc.: MANAGER Series, ULS Professional Series and GoPAC

Data Trek was founded in 1981, making it one of the pioneer companies to produce microcomputer software for the library market. Its original product, the MANAGER Series, is a MARC-compatible, menu-driven system. The new ULS Professional Series is a fully integrated MARC-standard product for libraries requiring full-MARC compliance. GoPAC is a Microsoft Windows–based online-catalog-search front end for all Data Trek software. Both MANAGER and ULS Professional run on MS-DOS–based computers as single-user systems or on Novell LANs for multiple-user versions. The MANAGER is also available on the Apple Macintosh and as a minicomputer product as mentioned in Chapter 6. MANAGER is functionally equivalent across its three platforms.

The MANAGER Series, implemented in dBase III and C language, is composed of separate but integrated modules: cataloging, online catalog, circulation, serials, acquisitions, DataBridge, report generator, audio/visual handler, and corporate documents. Hard disk storage estimates for this system are 2 MB per thousand titles, with hard disk capacity as the only limit in either single user or LAN versions. A full-screen editor is used for creating and changing records. The cataloging module will print catalog card sets or can be used in conjunction with the online catalog. It will generate new acquisitions lists. Spine and pocket labels are also a feature. The online catalog features both browsing and a power search facility that uses Boolean operators plus right- and left-hand truncation. Search results can be sent to the screen, the printer or to a disk file. A Hypersearch is possible through highlighting a word on a search result screen and then retrieving all other items containing that highlighted word. The circulation module also supports loans by the minute for college reserve book room use. Bar code labels and wand readers or scanners can be used or transactions keyed in for low-volume situations. The serials module features single-keystroke check-in, issue routing, and table of contents routing slip generation. It prompts the operator when items are ready for binding and predicts next expected issue. There are optional online vendor interfaces and claiming. A full subscription history is maintained and there is support for bindery preparation, including printing binding tickets and packing slips. The acquisitions module also has optional online vendor interfaces. Fund accounting, invoice tracking/processing, order file maintenance and order creation are all nicely implemented. Boolean searches on the order file can be sorted by up to three keys. The system generates order letters, claims and cancellations for all ordering situations. The DataBridge subsystem performs MARC import for LC MARC, OCLC, MARCive, NLM, WLN, MicroLIF and quite a few other MARC sources. There is a CD-ROM and an online interface. Transferrable local MARC tags can be specified. Field selection is user defined. The report generator has over 150 user-customizable reports. It features full editing, repositioning and elimination of fields, margin controls, page length and compressed print controls. Reports can be sent to any printer or to an ASCII text file for later printing or transfer to a word processor. The audio/visual handler supports media collections, while the corporate documents module provides special record definitions and features for these collections to be integrated into an automated system. The MANAGER Series uses a non-tagged-form record into which MARC data is loaded. It is complete enough for most libraries to use for their operational and public service needs. Multiple fixed-length standard fields are used in MANAGER Series modules. MANAGER Series also uses multiple dBase-compatible bibliographic record files for its respective modules.

The ULS (Ultimate Library System) Professional Series uses a full-MARC record for storage, downloading, editing and output. It is programmed in the C language. The EasyMARC feature lets a user edit MARC data without being intimate with each MARC record tag, subfield or indicator. The system then creates a correctly tagged MARC record. In the displays a user can switch between a MARC format and an attractively labelled display with no data loss. It has true variable length and repeating fields, with variable length records. Zoomable fields, pull-down browse lists and pick lists make this an attractive system from the user's view. This product uses a single integrated bibliographic database, with all modules accessed from a single menu. The Power Search capability is integral to the system, and there is an optional add-on called USM. The ULS product has more features than its older sibling and so may be a bit more complex to learn expertly. ULS modules for cataloging, online catalog, circulation, DataBridge and serials were available at the time I examined this product. An acquisitions module was under development and appeared that it might be released soon.

The GoPAC graphical user interface for the online catalog for either of the above systems is really well designed. It, too, is a C language implementation. The point-and-click searching makes catalog searching easy and invites one not to rush through an interaction with the system as it really appears fun! An EasySearch browse by author, title or subject will probably locate most known item-type searches. An Expert search using Boolean operators is easy to do. A user can send comments to the librarian or library staff. The output from searches can be in ascending or descending order by publication date or in alphabetic order by title. One can turn on and off automatic truncation. GoPAC is an excellent example of a Windows implementation of an online catalog user interface. Libraries using this system should plan to implement GoPAC on their public workstations as a minimum and preferably on all workstations within the LAN where the online catalog can be searched.

There are some 2000 customer libraries around the world that use these products, with some modules available in French, Spanish and Italian. Data Trek has distributors in New York, Ohio, Canada, France, England, Spain, Australia, Poland and Turkey. Special libraries are the main customer, but other types of libraries are represented in the customer base as well. If you are considering an MS-DOS-based system or one that you will run on a Novell LAN, then you will need to examine this product very seriously and make comparisons with its competitors' systems. Data Trek has had the longest history of continuously enhancing its MANAGER Series, and with the introduction of the ULS product in 1989 and the GoPAC in 1992, it is continuing the production of very competitive, feature-laden systems using the latest in software technology and current platforms.

9. Dawson UK, Ltd.: OASIS

Open Access Strategic Information System (OASIS) consists of interlibrary loan (AIM), serials management system (SMS), acquisitions, circulation and online catalog designed to operate on Intel microprocessor systems in a Novell network. The AIM module was jointly developed with Leicester Polytechnic and it provides electronic access to the British Library Document Supply Centre or to any other lending source. Another nice feature of this system is the file reformatter and automatic text editor, also jointly developed. It will handle diverse database downloaded records, extracting records from full-text retrievals. The serials module provides check-in, routing of issues with reader ranking and integration with the acquisitions module for subscription and payment details. Acquisitions handles the full spectrum of possible order types and information needed for accounting, invoice payment and claiming. The online catalog provides the expected author, title, subject and Boolean access. The system supports the main European languages. The catalog is authority based and provides cross-referencing and global control through its authority system. This is a user-friendly system with pop-up windows, fill-in-the-blanks forms, and scrolling windows to pick choices to fill in fields.

The integrated workstation (IWS) used in this system is an IBM or clone computer with client software for access, manipulation and formatting output from this system. Special libraries, public libraries and college libraries are the major users. A relatively small server with a 200-MB hard disk will handle a 40,000–60,000 record database. Dawson encourages schools and colleges as customers by offering this software at a discount. The system is available in separate yet integrated modules for either single-user MS-DOS operation or on a network license, priced depending on the number of PCs in the network. The prices quoted in pounds sterling do not include Britain's 17.5% value-added tax.

This system is competitive in its features and design to similar U.S.-developed software but does not appear to be marketed outside Europe.

10. Educational Solutions, Inc.: SURPASS/2

This system has gone through several major revisions. It was formerly called MELVIL. It is a MARC record-based inventory, circulation and online catalog/cataloging system designed for the school library market. Some 80% of SURPASS/2 customers are schools. This system is very easy to use, so easy that young children can be taught to look for topics and items in the online catalog quite quickly. There are eight security levels built in which should be sufficient to provide protected access to its staff- and patron-oriented functions on a LAN. Given a school-implemented Novell LAN, access to this online catalog can be brought from the media center to each classroom. The system will import both full-MARC and MicroLIF records from any known CD-ROM or commercial service source. The circulation system can be set up with parameters controlled by grade level as well as patron type. Defining your MARC database uses a scrolling MARC tag list and windows with the subfields shown where you fill in the subfield name or label as it will appear on your OPAC and data entry screens. Even support for nonfiling indicator values is provided. The user can control alert tones from workstations for caution or warning messages on overdues or fines. If the library still wishes to provide a card catalog, it can generate card sets and book label sets from this system. At year's end it is very easy to purge graduating students and to advance students to their next grade level. The system comes with some utilities such as printer. exe, which one uses to define the printer(s) available to the system. An editor called smenu.exe and a menu maker called menu.exe are two others provided.

The use of color, pull-down menus, flexible system setup, allowance for full or abbreviated amounts of bibliographic data in the records, scrolling windows and comfortable and familiar catalog card image that OPAC displays make this a good system to install where students and staff have been long accustomed to a card catalog. The online catalog uses either scrolling windows for selecting search terms or a direct entry of author, title or subject. Searches can be saved for later reuse or printed out. Search results can be in MARC or MicroLIF format. The Boolean operators AND, OR and NOT are supported. Keyword searches are done by capitalizing the word instead of entering it in lower case. Another slick feature is that one can access from the catalog screen published reviews and bulletins authored by users, and users can choose to submit reviews for this published review collection. This file can also be complemented with tables-of-content of the collection for patron view.

The circulation system uses bar-coded labels and stores its item records as Tag 901 in the bibliographic record. It is flexible enough to handle any school circulation need. The report writer permits custom reports definition and is easy to use.

While some users have operated this system in a peer-to-peer-type LAN such as LanTastic, the less problematic way to provide multiple user access to this Clipper-programmed system is to use a server-type network with the preferred LAN software, Novell Advanced Netware v.3.12. The system can be packaged as a turnkey hardware and software solution or, if the customer already has the necessary equipment and Novell LAN in place, as software only. Adding workstations is quite economical, with inexpensive license fees. This system will have strong appeal to school students, make teaching library skills to young students a pleasure and yet be a good price/performance value to the school system. System support for those customers purchasing it is provided through a toll-free telephone number.

11. Eloquent Systems, Inc.: Eloquent Librarian

This company's original product was GENCAT, an online catalog and cataloging system programmed in Revelation, which was introduced in 1986. A separate system for media center management, called The Eloquent Media Manager, is a sister system to the integrated online library system, called The Eloquent Librarian. This latter system is discussed here. The Eloquent Librarian is programmed in Revelation. The license fee is based on the number of titles in the catalog. The base system provides cataloging and online catalog, spine and pocket labels or printed catalogs. A research-only system can be licensed to provide search-only capabilities on a workstation. There are further modules for circulation, media management, acquisitions, serials, MARC import and MARC export. All of the above systems run on stand-alone MS-DOS PC/AT class systems or Novell LANs.

The Eloquent Librarian's base module can come as a predefined configuration for school library, media resource center or special library. The developer recommends working with a small test database if one decides to customize these setups as once the database is built, it is more difficult to make field changes to it. One can add or delete fields, change field names, add user codes and modify code names. After a database is built, one can still add fields, but not delete certain fields if these are titles in the database, nor can one select a new standard configuration. The system uses operator levels of trainee, search, research, data entry, all and system to control security. There is a French language module for libraries requiring French and English. The basic config-uration has the first comment field used for storing the edition, place, publisher, physical description and general note. To differentiate these data elements, a two-character code is used.

For those used to MARC-tagged work forms, setting up this system may appear a bit cryptic since the workforms do not contain any MARC tagging labels, indicators or subfield designations. A nice feature of this system is its global synonym authority file capability. British and American spelling forms such as "Centre" and "Center" can be indexed under a common form, yet still be located if the nonpreferred form is entered. Global stopwords have been defined, but these can be changed from their "the," "an," and "a" form. There is a spelling assist feature that can be turned on or off. Both MARC and MicroLIF formats can be imported or exported from this system. Each title record is limited to 64,000 characters but can contain repeating and variable-length fields. If one needs to print catalog card sets and book label sets, this module will produce these to the quality of the printer used.

Searching in this system is flexible and powerful. There are four different search screens used, three of which are basic templates, with the fourth providing expert search. Keyword searching looks for words in the title, variant title, summary, all authorities and comment fields that have been chosen for indexing. The second search screen permits basic author, title and subject searching, while the third provides multiple keyword, title and subject combinations. The expert search screen provides one or multiple access points with Boolean logic operators, including nested bracketed, parentheses or braces evaluation notation. The AND, OR and NOT operators can be written also as symbol codes and both right and left truncation are features. A search can also have a "must contain" value by enclosing the value in brackets like this: [steam]. Search results can be saved as lists and also the search strategy saved for later reuse.

I had no problem installing this system on an Everex Step 386/20. The circulation and MARC import modules were then installed from within The

Eloquent Librarian without any problem. The in-context help screens work very nicely and printing to the HP Laserjet through the supplied printer driver was faultless. This system was a pleasure to use and should have wide user appeal. Given that these systems use the very flexible GENCAT system basic modules at their heart, it is possible to set up this system to meet many variant conditions likely to be encountered across the present customer base of school and special libraries. As an example of this flexibility, the University of the West Indies selected the GENCAT software to support its institutional archives and records management as this product came the closest to fully supporting the emerging international descriptive standards for archival materials. Eloquent Systems will be implementing the highly regarded "Rules for Archival Description (RAD)" developed in Canada. The Eloquent Librarian has been reviewed in the literature by William Saffady. (5)

12. Feld Technologies: DATARoute

Through the years there have been quite a few microcomputer programs written to provide periodical issue routing labels, but DATARoute appears to me to be the best of this genre. It can run on a hard disk or floppy-only system. It is an MS-DOS program with dBase III file structures. The three files it creates are READERS.DBF, PUBS.DBF and LIST.DBF. Each reader has a three-character code—usually the reader's initials. Each serial title/copy has a five-character code. The reader record also includes a department (4-character abbreviation), telephone number (7 characters), location (4 characters) and status (4 characters). This last field shows the reader's status or seniority within the pecking order of routing. Routing slip assignment can use this seniority code to determine what readers will be on which routing slips for a particular copy of a publication and their order on the slip.

Operation of this system is quite smooth. If you press PF3 in the Change Readers menu Edit function, a menu of reader names pops up and you can select a reader. Soundex codes are also used to index readers so "sounds like" searches can be performed where the inexact spelling of names will still produce valid hits. For browsing through a list, the Zoom feature displays the first entry that matches a string in an exact-match mode search. The manual accompanying this program is quite complete except for no mention of the exact size of label stock needed for the regular or oversized label option printing. The samples appear to use half of an 8½" by 11" sheet for oversized and 2" by 5" for regular. The form length can be set for 1.5" with one-eighth inch line spacing and 3" for oversized with that same spacing. This program allows you to choose its menu colors to suit you and your monitor's preferences. Regular sized labels will hold up to 12 names and the oversized up to 32 for routing. Data entry is rapid, operation is bullet-proof and reliable for both novice and experienced computer users. If all you need is routing slip production because your present automated system does not adequately provide it or you have a manual serials operation, this routing program will be an invaluable work saver.

13. Follett Software Company: Circulation Plus et al.

Follett Corporation is composed of six companies serving the education market through wholesaling textbooks, operating college bookstores, and providing software to elementary and secondary schools and public libraries. Over 20,000 customers use this software. Follett's approach to automating these libraries is the "crawl, then walk, then run" technique in which small steps are taken before large and complex multifunctional solutions are approached.

Therefore, the products range from single-function programs such as the CardMasterPlus to the Circulation Plus and Catalog Plus systems. CardMaster Plus is a MARC-based database for producing catalog cards and label sets. It can interface to Mitinet/MARC for current cataloging source data. The Union CD Plus is a CD-ROM union catalog. MAC Search Plus station is an add-on to the Circulation/Catalog Plus products which uses an Apple Macintosh as a user station on a Novell LAN. For libraries still equipped only with an Apple II, there is Circulation Plus, which allows bar code–reading devices to be used, just as with systems based on more powerful computers. For retrospective conversion, Follett has Alliance Plus, a CD-ROM file of MARC recon records. Follet also offers retrospective conversion services to libraries. The Circulation Plus and Catalog Plus have features comparable to minicomputer- and mainframe-hosted systems with these functions but operate in a Novell LAN or as single-user MS-DOS programs. They also feature a hand-held scanning device called PHD+ to perform inventory control in the stacks and then transfer this data to the Circulation Plus system. There is no comparable inventory software or scanner provided with the NOTIS mainframe-based system which is directed at large libraries. Could it be that large libraries are thought not to need such a feature or that they can just develop this capability themselves with a bit of Turbo Pascal and any commercially available portable scanning device?

The Follett software is competitively priced, particularly its LAN versions of Catalog Plus and Circulation Plus, which most client libraries operate as an integrated pair. Follett's systems can be a solution for a single school or a school district, given the LAN configuration, use of asynchronous gateways and the Union CD Plus catalog. Customers have a firm with a long history of financial stability, bringing products to the education market and providing good support service. This product is reviewed by Saffady. (6)

14. GMUtant Software: BIBL

If you want to experience a real gem in software distributed as shareware, you need to get BIBL, the creation of Clyde W. Grotophorst. This program licenses for $39 for a single user, and its LAN version, called BIBL/NET, licenses for a mere $150 per server no matter how many simultaneous users access the server. BIBL is a full-featured catalog program for an individual's personal library or for a corporate or project library. It features multiple databases, full-text retrieval, mouse support, Boolean searching, keyword validation and over 13 reports. One can import ASCII files and with the numerous utility programs that GMUtant has, it is possible to import records from CD-ROM sources, ERIC, PsychInfo, Medline, ABI/Inform, AGRICOLA and others. BIBL gets regular updates and has been distributed from Grotophorst's bulletin boards (BBs) at George Mason University Library, through shareware distributors such as Public Brand Software and various other BBs such as the University of Minnesota Libraries BBs. I would seriously advise those looking for a program to manage their personal references for their publication and research projects to give BIBL a try since it is such a super software value. Moreover, it is easy to learn, the documentation is in the archive file distribution and there should be little need to have much help in using this software. The beauty of shareware is that you get to try it before licensing it so you need not have a problem with returning and getting a refund if the program does not fit your needs as you would with regular commercially distributed programs. FidoNet-connected BBs should also be able to get copies of this program and its ever-increasing number of utility programs via a File Request to the George Mason University Library BBs.

15. GRC General Research Corp.: LaserQuest and LaserGuide

GRC's LaserQuest is a competitor to Bibliofile and other retrospective MARC record sources on CD-ROM. LaserQuest CDROM cataloging workstations serve libraries for current and retrospective cataloging. Its database comprises over 7 million MARC records. Access is via LC card no. and title. Once a search produces a record, the record can be modified and saved to diskette. Records can be uploaded to an online system via modem, used to produce catalog cards, sent to GRC for creation and maintenance of the library's database or uploaded to GRC's sister product, an online CD-ROM–based catalog called LaserGuide. LaserQuest will operate on an MS-DOS system having at least 512 kB addressable memory available or it can work in a Novell LAN, with multiple workstations sharing the CD-ROM database in a tower CD-ROM server. One to six CD-ROM drives can be used in a stand-alone workstation or the Pioneer 6 disk changer used to hold the six disks constituting the database.

The LaserGuide online catalog uses the MS-DOS CD-ROM extensions. Its LaserMerge facility allows updated records stored on the workstion's hard disk to update the CD-ROM transparently between re-mastering of the CD-ROM. Staff can display records in a MARC-tagged display and can modify the local screen colors. Searching is through keyword in author, title and subject indexes. Bibliographies can be printed from selected records. A library map feature can show a flashing arrow for book location. By placing hyphens to connect words or quote marks around words, one can perform a phrase search. An asterisk (*) is used for a truncation character in these searches. Boolean AND, OR and NOT are implemented through a "fill in the appropriate area" on a search screen. There is a shelf list browse available, too. This system has easy-to-understand screens, is simple for the library user to learn and will perform the standard kinds of searches expected of an online catalog. This online catalog can be operated on stand-alone workstations or on a Novell LAN. LaserGuide was one of the early CD-ROM catalogs. Both LaserGuide and LaserQuest have been marketed since 1987, so they have proven themselves in the field. They are suitable for any type of library.

16. Information Transform, Inc.: MITINET/marc

Information Transform was founded by Hank Espstein. Some years previously, he was the Director of the Ballots Project at Stanford University. Ballots later became the software on which the RLG/RLIN network offered its members interactive mainframe cataloging, acquisitions and other services. It is evident that not only excellent programming but a thorough knowledge of MARC and cataloging standards form the underpinning to MITINET/marc. While its initial customer base was mainly school libraries, it is now used by hundreds of libraries of all types. It can be the MARC record source for over 60 different commercially available library automation systems.

This cataloging system is available on Apple II, Macintosh and MS-DOS microcomputers. It is programmed in the C language. It was originally developed in 1986 by Information Transform and the Wisconsin Department of Public Instruction as a joint undertaking. The beauty of this system is that it conforms to the AACR2 and ISBD rules, implementing 118 punctuation rules to make cataloging much easier for the novice. One can use this in conjunction with a MARC source such as Bibliofile or another CD-ROM MARC database to catalog all non-MARC record match titles. All MARC formats are supported, and the General Materials Designation (GMD) is assigned automatically after all cataloging data is entered. The operator can have screens prompted in plain English, in a terse form or in MARC-tagged form. The nonfiling indicator is set correctly for the English "a," "an," "and," "the" and 96 other foreign language leading articles.

There are versions set up to feed records to specific systems. For example, the MS-DOS versions include Follett, MOLLI, Dynix, Bibliofile, and Winnebago in addition to the regular version. Be sure to check with this company on your specific automated library system as additional versions have been issued and will undoubtedly continue to be produced. New versions of this software have been regularly released, and it is now in its third major release. These variant versions implement different local holdings field tags depending on the system. For example, the regular version uses the MARC tag 852 for local holdings, while the Dynix version uses MARC tag 949 and a different subfielding. The manual is very well organized, clearly written and replete with numerous cataloging examples.

Using this system makes cataloging a pleasure for both novice and experienced librarians as well as permitting easy training of nonprofessionals to do cataloging work. If one were to award marks as for an Olympic gymnastic performance, this product would score a perfect 10 for every routine—and it even keeps getting better with each new software release. The Macintosh version is Mac all the way and yet implements the same capabilities as in the MS-DOS version. The MS-DOS version is programmed in C language, while the Mac version is done in object-oriented C. The latest in programming techniques and a superb understanding of a very complex operation make these implementations rock-solid performers. Certainly, no software is a substitute for the professional expertise of the cataloger as to choice of entry, proper classification, descriptive treatment and subject analysis, but a tool such as MITINET/marc surely makes a cataloger's work so much easier and leaves the cataloger more time to be concerned with professional content instead of with learning lots of the arcane punctuation and form that is a part of both AACR2 and ISBD. Information Transform's service and support are also excellent.

17. International Library Systems Corp. (ILS): SYDNEY PLUS

This system has matured over a decade of versions and migration from its original Datapoint minicomputer implementation. It is oriented toward special libraries and operates as a Novell Advanced Netware LAN product. It is MS-DOS-based in its single-user version. A Digital Equipment VAX version is also available. The VAX version implements media booking, interlibrary loan and reserve book room modules, which are not a part of the microcomputer version—at least at the time I was able to examine this product. Special libraries, schools and colleges are the major customers of these versions.

The SYDNEY PLUS system starts with a base module which provides cataloging, queries, thesaurus and system management. There is an unlimited number of copy records, and the system has excellent cross-referencing support via its thesaurus. Any bar code reader and label code standard can be used for circulation. The MARC record interface supports Bibliofile, DOBIS, MARCive, OCLC, RLIN and UTLAS. Records can be exported in MARC using the output format generator program and export conversion program. The acquisitions module has full fund accounting and also permits billing user departments for materials and services. One can prepare online abstracts of items and incorporate these in the online catalog. There is an imaging module that supports optical scanning of documents, viewing and cataloging them, and incorporating image data in the online searchable database. The circulation system is flexible enough to handle many special and academic settings. The serials module allows operators to easily modify expected issue arrivals and perform the complex operations associated with maintaining large serial collections. There is a remote public access catalog module also. This is a nicely color implemented, menu-driven system with considerable customization features. Security is handled by module and by function, with 99 levels possible. The online catalog has a public check-out capability so that routine self-charging can be done by users.

The report generator produces customized reports and the syntax of commands is much like Inmagic or DataEase. A SYDNEY PLUS database uses approximately 4 MB for each thousand catalog records. The programs comprising all the modules require about 22 MB of hard disk space. So a relatively modest 340 MB hard disk system could easily service a 50,000-item collection. Of course, if the imaging module were to be used, disk requirements would go up considerably. However, one can obtain SCSI-2 hard disks that have 2.1 GB capacity for around $2100. Therefore, a very large database system could be implemented, particularly within a LAN environment.

SYDNEY PLUS is one of those products that has proven itself in the long-term market, and it just keeps getting better. Special libraries acquiring automation software should consider this product—in either the MS-DOS/Novell version or the DEC VAX version. New competitive capabilities are being added by ILS, and system prices are competitive.

18. Inlex, Inc.: The Assistant

This system is installed mainly in special libraries. It was formerly a product of Library Automation Technologies, Inc., which was acquired by Inlex. This is a polished, menu-driven system with acquisitions, cataloging, online catalog, circulation and serials modules. It is MARC based, and the online catalog is able to display MARC-tagged records and catalog card format in addition to its regular labelled catalog display. Pull-down menus and selection lists make this system a pleasure to use. Unlimited notes can be added to records. The authority file provides cross-references and powerful global change facilities. All file maintenance operations are easy to understand and to perform in this system. Security is quite flexible and can be tailored to the particular staff member's needs. Key entry and bar-coded labels scanned for circulation transaction entry are both permitted. Circulation has good calendar control and features to handle any loan periods and as many patron and material types as needed in any library situation. Library users can inquire of their own record of books checked out, overdue items and fine amounts. MARC records can be imported from many external sources such as OCLC or Bibliofile. The serials module is particularly strong as would be expected for a special library-oriented system. The issue routing has good flexibility and uses the patron record as does circulation. One can position a user on a routing slip in any order for a given copy of a journal. A patron can be added to multiple title routing slips in one operation through a selection of the titles in a scrolling window. This system is competitively priced to encourage LAN licensing.

Inlex has been acquired by Data Research Associates and operates as a subsidiary, with continuing support and development of the Inlex product line. There is a published review of this software. (7)

19. Inmagic, Inc.: INMAGIC Plus

This software has been used by numerous special and academic libraries as well as nonlibrary clients for over a decade. The original INMAGIC was implemented on Digital Equipment minicomputers. When MS-DOS systems became the desktop standard, INMAGIC became available for them and for LAN installation. There is a version for Digital Equipment VAX series computers, and INMAGIC for MS-DOS systems will also run on a Macintosh using DOS emulation software. The beauty of INMAGIC is its completely variable length fields and records, its repeating fields at a keystroke and its indexing options. There is no maximum record size and any record can have up to 75 defined fields and up to 100 indexes. The number of INMAGIC databases that can be set up is limited only by hard disk storage capacity on one's system or LAN server. Geared to handling text, this software is popular for customization not only for library operations and bibliographic search support but also for such applications as litigation support, documentation tracking, personnel/human resource systems and numerous other applications that can take advantage of its variable fielding and indexing strengths.

A nice feature of this software is its relative independence from the hardware on which it runs. For example, except for the text editor which was intimate with the IBM system architecture in versions prior to this completely new release of INMAGIC Plus v.1.0, release 1.0, I could run this software on a non–IBM compatible system such as the Victor 9000 under its customized MS-DOS. These files were then completely transportable over to the later MS/PC-DOS versions running on conventional IBM and clone computers. Traditional relational and flat file database software is oriented toward fixed length data and manipulation of numeric data. Text retrieval systems, on the other hand, are set up to treat text as a single large field or a group of related paragraphs. INMAGIC is engineered to handle both text and numeric data. Any field in any record can be any length. Any field can be indexed or globally changed. Unlimited repeating fields can be added any time during record editing without rebuilding the database. Searching can be by word, word stem, phrase or proximity to another term. Ranges of data values and Boolean operators are part of the search provisions. Performance of this software is superb. Even very complex searches on very large databases can be executed in a few seconds. The search screens are fill-in-the-blanks with clear, unbroken labels. Each of these screens can contain up to 10 prompts and each prompt can search up to 20 fields at once. One can browse through a field and paste a term of choice into a prompt. Validation look-up tables, format criteria and range values are techniques used to maintain data accuracy and consistency. The Report Writer can produce products ranging from labels to full-blown reports with added custom text, columns, page numbers, headings and arithmetic operations on rows and columns.

INMAGIC Plus has added menus and pop-up windows to the traditional command line interface which is maintained as an optional interface. Phrase and proximity searching and the prompted search mode are further enhancements. These give power and improve ease of use for both novice and expert user. Another strong plus of INMAGIC is its very well done system documentation, with a booklet covering its installation and another covering upgrading from an earlier version of INMAGIC. The installation guide covers both a stand-alone MS-DOS system and installation on a Novell LAN. A command reference, user's manual and the library guide are the other portions of the documentation. A companion product called SearchMAGIC is a search-only run-time engine for INMAGIC databases. Using a SearchMAGIC license at lower cost and packaging any INMAGIC created database could enable distribution of the database as a self-contained application to remote sites not equipped with LAN access. A small library could put up a user searching station on a separate computer at lower cost than a LAN and run the full INMAGIC Plus on the librarian's microcomputer and distribute database copies to remote users periodically.

The numeric date fields and the @DATE command are controlled by the country statement in the CONFIG.SYS file. One must have 500 kB of DOS-addressable RAM to install this software for full operation. INMAGIC will take about 1.2 MB of hard disk space for its program files. With 485 kB, one can run INMAGIC but not run its utilities from within the program or shell out to MS-DOS. Below that RAM, the program may not function or load. With MS-DOS 5.x or 6.x memory management or use of a memory manager such as QuarterDeck's QEMM to load high drivers, files, buffers and DOS itself, one should easily be able to get 500 kB from any 386/486 class system that is equipped with at least 2 MB RAM. Even on 286 systems equipped with QRAM from QuarterDeck and with at least 1 MB RAM, some loading high drivers will produce at least 500 kB. As an example, my 386/20, with 8 MB RAM and QEMM running MS-DOS 5.0, has been optimized to produce 623 kB of addressable RAM.

The Library Guide features database structures and report formats on diskette with an extensive manual covering the setting up of INMAGIC systems for library automation operations. It is quite easy once one has learned the

Report Writer and system to customize these to any individual situation, but many users may not even need to do such customizations. The previous versions of INMAGIC had a companion called the Biblio Guide that is now replaced by this Library Guide. Print formats are provided for both laser and dot matrix printers. European language support is via the extended ASCII characters entered by holding down the ALT key and typing the ASCII value from a table provided on the numeric keypad. With an MS-DOS version price of $1250, this is a solid value, and INMAGIC has always provided reasonable prices for its major version upgrades. Various dealers also sell and support this software as well as provide customer training and consulting. If you want excellent flexibility and fast search performance and have needs that may even stretch beyond the traditional online catalog and processing support, then this software will definitely show a strong capability to fully meet your present and future needs.

20. LEX Systems, Inc.: LEXIFILE

This system is a database management system geared toward special, school, church and small public libraries where several systems on a small LAN are all that is needed. The current software (v.4.01) does not presently provide a full-blown online catalog but does allow string searching, which should be ample for smaller collections. It also prints out catalog card sets. The software is implemented in Borland's C++ and uses function keys to do basic commands. The system uses a dBase file format and dot commands like dBase. One can save records in ASCII, USMARC and MicroLIF. One can also save file records in list, card, bibliography, display and labelled formats. LEXIFILE supports circulation of items via the .CIRC command. The program has a nice customization for printer, help messages, programmable keys, use of password security, and colors. The online manual is well done. The card printing and label printing is worked out quite well in this software for those needing these features. This program has a sound design and numerous installations, mainly in Canada although it has been marketed in the United States.

My expectation is that subsequent versions of this software will provide improvements and further functional support beyond the database and circulation subsystems. One of the strong points of this software is its pricing, which is done on the size of the database for single-user systems, with a LAN license adding only 30% to the cost. Add another 50% for the circulation program. This pricing definitely encourages LAN installation. The search and circulation programs are separately priced modules. An example of such pricing is to imagine a library wishing catalog support and circulation for its 10,000-title library collection. The search program would license at $695 ($995 for an unlimited size database). The circulation program would license at 50% the cost of the search program, i.e., $347.50 and a network license would be 30% of the search program, or $199.50. This totals to $1242 for the software.

21. The Library Corporation (TLC): Bibliofile and Total Library Computer System

The Library Corporation was founded in 1975 and was the first library-oriented company to use CD-ROM data storage technology in its Bibliofile product, a database of USMARC cataloging records and a cataloging system. TLC is also among the top 100 PC-based network integrators in North America according to *LAN Magazine*'s LAN 100. Over 4,000 libraries operating 10,000 stand-alone and networked PCs use TLC products. Through the years TLC has had an excellent record of customer service and support together with good product evolution.

The Total Library Computer System revolves around modules that are implemented on a Novell Lite or Novell Advanced Netware LAN, depending on the size of the installation. The online catalog is CD-ROM based and can be accompanied by circulation, acquisitions, the Bibliofile cataloging system, and MARC record import/export. TLC also has developed PACLink, a means for linking a Bibliofile online catalog to an existing circulation system. The first of these installations is at Queens Borough Public Library (New York) where the Bibliofile online catalog is linked to the Data Research Associates (DRA) minicomputer-based circulation system. TLC is working on other PACLink systems and is trying to enlist support from a number of library system vendors. The Bibliofile database and cataloging system does have direct online interfaces to both NOTIS and CLSI systems and bridging software for Dynix, DRA, GEAC and Innovative Interfaces.

Operating the Total Library Computer System on a LAN is improved through the use of Server Down circulation software which allows any work-station on the LAN to continue to spool circulation transactions until the server is restored and then to update the server. The circulation system is a robust, large-system-featured application. There is a Mark Reshelving Carts function that can help stack staff presort checked-in items by a shelf destination and a reshelving cart number. The cart numbers are set up in the system setup. One can also define a lag period to cover the number of days after check-in for an item to get back on the shelves. If the circulation system is accompanied by the Intelligent Catalog, the item will not display as available until after the lag period is up. A reshelving message is the status shown on the online catalog when this lag period is in effect. This system is function key driven and is firmly integrated with the Intelligent Catalog.

The public access catalogs for this system are ColorCat, AutoCat, Generic Catalog, BibCat and the Intelligent Catalog. These products use a different user interface. The Intelligent Catalog and Generic Catalog offer additional advisory features to suggest recommended fiction and incorporates dictionary or Boolean searching, KWIC and divided catalog searches. Type a single letter to begin a search and the right side of the screen fills with a word list that narrows as each added letter is typed. Then select words from that list to incorporate into the search. The labelled display asks "What would you like to find in the catalog?" The Generic Catalog offers the same capability as the Intelligent Catalog except that it does not use the special custom keyboard of the Intelligent Catalog. ColorCat is a color screen version of the Generic Catalog. There is a remote DialCat facility that can be licensed for a LAN system to allow remote users to search the catalog on a modem connection. The Intelligent Catalog also simulates artificial intelligence features with its AI expert system, hypertext, syntax analysis and thesaurus substitution techniques to prevent search failures. These catalogs provide a choice of card image, fully labelled or MARC record displays. The LAN server stores updates to the CD-ROM catalog to provide real-time currency between CD-ROM remastering completely transparently to the user.

The acquisitions system can import items into its consideration file from the Bibliofile cataloging CD-ROM databases. There is a publisher database of over 20,000 publishers on CD-ROM that can be used with this module. The system supports printing on any Epson-compatible printer. Further enhancements to the circulation and catalog are anticipated since this writing. Also upgrades to multibranch systems features and a release of serials control, interlibrary loan and media booking modules will soon flesh out this already strong, well-integrated and cost-effective system.

When using the Bibliofile cataloging system, I noted that the system expected to find MS-DOS 3.30, so I had to use the SETVER.EXE facility within MS-DOS 5.0 on a test system. When I did this and set Files=100, I had no problem installing and running this software. Those interested in some further information on Bibliofile products should consult the review by William Saffady. (8)

22. Library Technologies, Inc.: BIB-BASE

Besides offering this MS-DOS- and LAN-based integrated library system called BIB-BASE, Library Technologies, Inc., has offered retrospective conversion services to libraries for a decade and has prepared databases for most commerically available automated library systems from OCLC tapes and its own USMARC source records. Library Technologies, Inc., is a privately held company and has a number of service distributors in the multitype library network area such as Bibliographical Center for Research (BCR), SOLINET, NELINET, PALINET and WILS.

There are over 350 U.S. and Canadian libraries that have installed modules of this system. In the network version of this system Novell, PC Network and

LanTastic are all supported, so one can select depending on the size and physical layer network desired. The system starts with the Core module comprising a text editor, search-and-retrieval and the database management system required for all other modules. The Cat module provides catalog card and book label printing. The Public module provides patron search by author, title, subject, series, call number, ISSN, ISBN, OCLC/RLIN control number and a library-defined field. The Acq module is a full acquisitions, fund accounting, order tracking and purchase order production system. The Multiuser module adds LAN support for serving multiple simultaneous users, while the MARC module enables loading OCLC MARC records into BIB-BASE and exporting MARC records to other systems. There is a BISAC module that supports electronic ordering in the BISAC format and licenses for $395. Libraries have 180 days of free customer support and then can subscribe to annual support for 10% of the purchase price of the BIB-BASE modules they are using. At the time of my examination, the Core and Public modules were priced at $795, Multiuser was $995, and Acq, Cat and MARC were each $595. These are reasonable and competitive prices for the functionality of this product.

The performance of this system is excellent and its ease-of-use features are very well conceived. It uses clear menu-driven screens. Its MARC display is easy to work if one has some familiarity with MARC tags. While the online catalog uses simple searching, without Boolean operators, if more than one record is retrieved, a brief list is presented for browsing and selection of the specific entry. The record displays are clearly labelled. The system can store a full or partial MARC record. The system's major lack is the omission of keyword indexes so the search must be entered in the exact word order. If a search fails to produce any hits, a rather arcane message to the effect that "Search Request is not in the ________ Index" is displayed. Just a simple misspelling or typing could produce such a result. It would be better if the system put the user in the proximity of the search in the index entries. Documentation for the system is well organized but does not have a glossary or any section tabs separating the numerous chapters. This system focusses on creating and maintaining quality bibliographic records. It is suitable for academic, public and special libraries, particularly those able to implement this on a LAN since the real utility of any of these microcomputer-based systems is their ability to be simultaneously accessed by both library staff and library users.

23. Media Flex, Inc.: MANDARIN

This system was introduced in 1987 and was one of the early MS-DOS-based integrated library systems. The current version is v.2.52. MANDARIN has a full MARC database at its heart. It is programmed in the C language to assure accommodation of the field structures suitable to MARC record processing and good portability to future operating system and hardware platforms.

The user may define up to 100 different databases. Libraries decide what fields to index or map to related fields for simultaneous searching. Parallel fields permit creation of synonym fields which can be mapped to the subject index for cross-reference support. All records are stored as MARC records and can be exported in USMARC to another system. One can mix MARC records such as USMARC, OCLC, UTLAS, UKMARC, MicroLIF or CD-MARC. This system on a LAN can coexist with a MARC or other CD-ROM database on a CD-ROM server. Apple Macintosh users can access a MANDARIN database from Mac Attach interface software released in October, 1992. All commands and menus can be displayed in up to 10 languages, with English and French currently available. This system serves multicultural needs well and stores diacritics, correctly displaying them on the PC screen.

The online catalog opens with a bulletin board where library announcements can be placed and changed at will. Searching uses Boolean operators AND, OR, NOT, XOR, < , and >. For simple searching, a screen with lines for entering author, title or subject is presented, and the above operators can be typed in on this screen to invoke the Boolean features in a search. A function key press brings up an Advanced Search screen that looks quite like one from Dialog. It allows saving search sets and searching any indexed field, including the Boolean operators between and within fields. There are summary and expanded display formats that can be defined by the library. Patrons can print out selected search results up to a maximum number determined by the library. When the circulation system is in operation, the item status is shown for each cataloged item.

The circulation system allows library definition of fields in the borrower database and 20 different borrower categories, each having its own set of privileges. Self-service check-out can be set up when the system operates on a LAN. An inventory module allows the use of a hand-held bar code reader to perform data collection in the stacks. Code 39 is the preferred bar code scheme but the module will also accommodate CODABAR codes. Items found missing can be marked in the online catalog. Eradication of missing items can be done via a global delete after a period of time. The Data Spindler data transfer utility will permit loading of records from OCLC, UTLAS, USMARC, MicroLIF, OCLC Screen Save, dBase, ASCII, GEAC, DOBIS, EBSCO, Bibliofile, LaserQuest and many others. Records can be manually entered and edited in any MANDARIN database. The system also features a diagnostic and repair utility to handle corrupted indexes and databases. The report generator has many standard reports and outputs specified, even catalog cards and book/spine labels. There is a toll-free customer support line for U.S. and Canadian customers. MANDARIN is also implementing other external databases such as the SELECT Annual Database, which cites curriculum-related material in print and other formats favorably reviewed in *Booklist*, *School Library Journal* and other school material review sources. The newest feature is an interlibrary loan subsystem with a graphical user interface, implemented in the C++ language. If your system is on a LAN, you can receive direct dial-in customer service to your system via modem connection if your server has an asynchronous gateway.

For full-MARC record storage estimates, it is recommended that you multiply the number of titles in the library by 3000 characters for each record and its index overhead. The pricing for this system is competitive and encourages LAN implementation among its predominantly school and public library customer base. There is a price discount on license fees for schools. Even some college libraries, such as St. Lawrence College in Ontario, Canada, use this system. This college has 3000–4000 full-time students, 8000 part-time students and a 60,000-item library collection.

Melchior Management Systems, Inc., of Montreal, Canada is the developer of MANDARIN, and Media Flex is its U.S. Distributor. In Canada, Bibliofiche of Montreal and United Library services in Calgary handle customer licensing and support. This system has considerable power and features but occasionally appears somewhat cryptic to the user, such as in its short mnemonics for some of its function keys. Despite that, the system is relatively easy to learn, and once learned, it should not present any major problem.

24. Michigan State University, University Archives, Historical Collections: MicroMARC:amc

This system was developed at the University Archives of Michigan State University and is backed up by a solid understanding of the MARC archives and manuscripts record and the other MARC record formats. It is composed of an editor module to create and modify records, and a search module to search the first word or all words in a string when searching names, corporations or subjects. Accompanying these base capabilities are modules for MARC record input and output that create a standard MARC:amc–formatted file that can be transmitted to systems such as OCLC or RLIN. A report module allows access to any field in the database and generation of custom reports. There are predefined reports for accessions, processing status, future action, index terms and several other miscellaneous reports. The AUXINDX module allows the archivist to define any leader or fixed- or variable-length field as an index to search.

This system was the first to implement the MARC amc record in a microcomputer system. The work was funded in part by a grant from the National Historical Publications and Records Commission. Licensing of this system supports its current enhancement and support. Version 2.0 was released in early summer of 1988. In 1989 there were some 60 users of this software. The system does not yet use color displays. A greater drawback is that the single-user MS-DOS program apparently has no LAN capability or license provision to enable multiple simultaneous users. Otherwise the system is well documented and has positive views from its users. Landis (9) and Honhart (10) each give a good view of their experiences using this software. There is a user support group within the Society of American Archivists. MicroMARC:amc remains a very good program for providing a basic level of collection access support to an archive. I would hope that sufficient resources are generated through its licenses to continue enhancement and particularly to enhance the software for LAN installation and color screens.

25. Midwest Library Services: MATSS

This is an excellent MS-DOS or Novell LAN-based acquisitions system with a menu-driven interface. Specific functions can be password protected. Ordering, fund accounting, claims, cancellations and standing orders are all handled effectively. Bibliographic records can be selected from bibliographic utilities or from CD-ROM cataloging sources such as Bibliofile. Book orders can be printed either in 3" by 5" or 8.5" by 11" formats. The BISAC fixed-length format is supported for electronic ordering. The screens are uncluttered and quite consistent in overall appearance and position of fields. There are few noticeable delays in moving between functions and in the menu and data entry screens. In-context help screens really do make this system relatively easy to learn. The very large manual in 8.5" by 11" format is quite complete but does lack troubleshooting and tutorial sections. While this software licenses at a rather premium price, it is a premium product that also effectively utilizes color screen capabilities of current microcomputers. Security is quite good, with three levels of users: master supervisor, supervisor and user. Each user has the menu items specified to which he/she may have access. Users can also be set up for inquiry only.

When this system is installed on a LAN, the PCAnywhere program and a modem are used to provide support. The online help files contain over 35,000 words of documentation. Midwest Library Service provides invoices on diskette. Baker & Taylor, Blackwell NA, Academic Book Center, Ambassador Books, Yankee Book Peddler and Coutts Library Service are examples of dealers accepting MATSS electronic orders using the BISAC format.

If you are doing an order for a title with multiple ISBNs, a window displays each ISBN and its binding and price. Paperback and price fields then will reflect the chosen ISBN. This system was obviously designed by people who know the book-ordering business. If you order the low-cost demonstration disk, its cost will be applied to the system license if you decide to license this product.

26. Nichols Advanced Technologies, Inc.: MOLLI

This system is designed for the school library but does have about 10% of its customer base with public libraries. MOLLI appears to be the easiest library system I have seen. It handles full-MARC records and does keyword searching. The system is modular, with circulation, searching (OPAC), cataloging, inventory and reporting. Separate acquisitions, serials, borrower conversion and custom label printing programs are also available. Help is always a keystroke away with an F1 key press. The consistent menus and good use of color screens are another bonus. For a stand-alone configuration, an Itel 80386SX is required at minimum. Circulation supports bar code readers of either light pen or laser scanner type. For multiple users either a Novell- or LanTastic-based LAN using either Ethernet or Token Ring physical hardware can be used. A 486 server with 386DX or 386SX workstations with at least 2 MB RAM is needed. A 70,000-item collection would require a 210-MB hard disk on the server at minimum. This is a pretty good disk utilization for MOLLI records, the LAN software and the MOLLI application programs. MOLLI requires at least 515 kB addressable RAM in your computer under MS-DOS.

MOLLI has a demo/tutorial disk available with an accompanying booklet that is a marvel of clarity in showing this system's catalog searching and circulation functions. This system uses passwords to protect system functions. The master password allows the system administrator or librarian access to all MOLLI functions. Menu passwords allow control of who sees which menus and their commands. The circulation password allows eligible personnel to perform circulation functions. The current release of MOLLI (v.5.0) allows backup and restore functions to be carried out from within the program. The restore function is password protected to assure that only trained staff perform this critical operation and ensure that files are not overwritten with old backup data. Even the printer usage can be restricted by requiring a printer password. In the event that the master password is somehow forgotten, there is a utility provided through a password recovery program. Workstations can be made "search only" or "quick search only" and separate collections can have separate passwords.

The quick search is used for searching on simple single keyword. For example one could type "science fiction" and see a list of the search results in a short, long or MARC format screen. On the short display up to seven items are presented with title, author and call number. Pressing the number on the short display of the item will bring up the long display, which shows the circulation status in addition to full descriptive and tracing information. Commands such as Next, Previous, Left, Right, Display, Holdings, Print and Exit appear at screen bottom. The Left and Right commands show the item that should be on the shelf to the left or right of the selected item. The Display command allows the choice of a different display format, including the MARC display. The full search allows up to three search terms to be combined using AND, OR and NOT Boolean operators. On full search there is a bibliography menu to permit printing the search results as a bibliography, changing its sort order, limiting a search by material format and adding a search to an existing bibliography. Bibliographies can be printed in short, long or MARC format. Call number and accession number searches are supported also.

The beauty of this system is that it provides the necessary functionality to the school library, having incorporated customer suggestions in subsequent revisions, while maintaining an ease of searching that enables users of all ages and reading levels to perform searches and interpret results on the screens. A newsletter offers helpful hints on using MOLLI, typical problems that users have encountered and their solutions, and various technical tips and news of staff and product development at Nichols Advanced Technologies, Inc. This is a competitively priced system with over a thousand installed sites. William Saffady has reviewed this software. (11)

27. Novara Software: BIBLIOTRAC

Novara's system is an integrated library system that gives the appearance of a Microsoft Windows graphical user interface even though it is an MS-DOS- or LAN-based program. One can choose the language of the prompts and screens to be English, French or Spanish. The catalog is authority based to provide cross-referencing. Searching uses a fill-in-the-forms–type screen, and if the search does not produce a result, the system will perform a soundex code–type search and try to produce a result that way. Boolean searches are supported using the AND, OR, NOT operators. Various listings can be produced from the "Files" command on the main menu screen. These include bibliographies and card/label sets. The catalog display uses a card format analog, which can depict a multiple display of results as a row of file cards. Hitting Enter blows up a catalog card in the foreground. The next version of this software will support full-MARC records, but the current version allows import of MARC records into the BIBLIOTRAC data format. The circulation system provides the features expected in a product aimed at the school library market.

This system's customer base has been mainly Canadian school libraries, but the system is now being actively marketed in the United States. BIBLIOTRAC was originally developed for the Inverness County District School Board in Nova Scotia. It shows excellent ease-of-use features, and the next version will be able to compete better with those MS-DOS and LAN systems that are able to support full MARC. The system is programmed in ZIM from Zanthe Information, Inc., to achieve its good graphical user interface. This system can also operate under the QNX multiple-terminal operating system from Quantum Software for a small multiple-terminal installation which probably can be put together more cheaply than a LAN. Saffady has reviewed this software in *Library Computer Systems and Equipment Review*. (12)

28. Personal Bibliographic Software, Inc.: Pro-Cite 2.1 et al.

Around eight years ago, Victor Rosenberg, founder of Personal Bibliographic Software, Inc., envisioned software able to produce quality bibliographies according to the prevailing standard styles and adapt to any new bibliography citation standards that might emerge. From a modest beginning using the UCSD-P native Pascal operating environment, this software has evolved as MS-DOS and then Apple Macintosh versions. Formerly this program was called the Professional Bibliographic System; several years ago it was renamed Pro-Cite 2.0. Pro-Cite has become a market leader in software for managing references and producing bibliographies in numerous styles. In my work with this program on pre–MS-DOS and later MS-DOS systems, I have been impressed with its flexibility, accuracy of production of each bibliographic style and ease of use. Although I have seen the Macintosh version demonstrated, I did not use that version for this preview. At the time of my examination, the current MS-DOS version was 2.02, while the Macintosh version was 2.0.

This software uses a workform approach to data entry. It includes 22 fully developed workforms representing 22 different material types that might conceivably be included in a bibliography. The program is nicely customizable to recognize default directories, database settings of various sorts, quick search fields, authority lists, punctuation files, stop lists and foreign language character sets. You can design your own customized workforms in addition to those supplied. In fact, you can tailor this program to produce just what you want as to the format of any bibliography so that if you write papers for many different journals that each use different styles, you can select the appropriate citations from the database and produce them in the style you need. You can determine the record number interval to be used and determine the first record number to be assigned to a citation. This permits an alphabetic order accessed via the record number.

This system has authority lists for art and chemistry journals, author names, composers, drama and film journals, MLA journals, *Index Medicus* journals, general journals, music journals and playwrights. The user can easily establish new authorities, and existing authorities can be modified by adding, changing and deleting entries. These authorities are stored in .LST files in either their own subdirectory or in the Pro-Cite subdirectory. A clever feature of the authority file is the alternative text feature. With this, one could use a very shorthand journal abbreviation to have the authority list supply the correct fully descriptive title. Punctuation files control the bibliography format and 29 of these have been predefined. You can define other custom punctuation files to produce totally customized bibliographies to meet a new, previously undefined style.

The utilities menu selection allows copying selected records and workforms or workforms only. Here you also can perform import and export of records and repair a corrupted Pro-Cite database. This repair creates a new uncorrupted database under a new name.

The program comes with printer drivers for Epson-compatible printers and for Hewlett-Packard LaserJet or compatible laser printers, but if you have your printer manual with its printer codes, you can define your own custom printer driver. If you routinely create bibliographies that you would like to make available to others on a LAN or their own workstation there is a Pro-Cite read-only program for both platforms to allow distribution of Pro-Cite databases in a public access setting.

Pro-Cite for MS-DOS requires at minimum a 640-kB RAM, Intel 8088 or above microcomputer with MS-DOS v.3 or above, hard disk and printer for output. The software in this version ships on either a single 3.5-inch double-density (720-kB) or two 5.25-inch 360-kB disks. After its installation from its compressed state, it requires 1.7 MB of hard disk space for the basic program and its small sample database. A read.me file on the distribution disk updates the excellent manual with any last-minute changes or pertinent installation information.

Pro-Cite is a comprehensive and flexible bibliography generator. It is relatively easy to learn to use the program from the well-organized and -presented manual as you proceed on your first bibliographic project. Each aspect of the program is thoroughly covered in the manual. For example, Chapter 11, "Creating Character Sets," discusses how Pro-Cite sorts records by its default character set and that any character not included in this default set is ignored. So a custom character set can be selected that includes those characters not in the default. The chapter walks the user through altering these characters in their sort order and defining a new character set. There is no limit to any Pro-Cite database except your physical hard disk space. Each record can have up to 32,000 characters of information. In short, Pro-Cite is truly a classic piece of software for its intended purpose that only keeps getting better with age! This program runs well in a DOS window under Microsoft Windows. Perhaps the future might bring a Windows-compliant version of this program. Pro-Cite retails at $395 for the full program and $195 for the read-only version. A demonstration disk is $75 and the price of these latter two products can be applied to licensing the full program, so you cannot go wrong by getting the demonstration disk.

This company also has a suite of accompanying programs to Pro-Cite that are called Biblio-Links. These are programs that allow the import of records from numerous other online services into a Pro-Cite database. There is a Biblio-Links Library Package that covers DOBIS, DROLS, MUMS, NOTIS, OCLC, SCORPIO and USMARC for $295. The IBM Biblio-Links packages are $195 each and in addition to the above databases offer DIALOG, MEDLARS, SilverPlatter, STN and DGIS. There is an online Biblio-Links package for the IBM system that allows user access to BRS, DIALOG, MEDLARS, SilverPlatter and STN. The Macintosh Biblio-Links package will import records from BRS, DIALOG and MEDLARS into the Macintosh Pro-Cite version. It is priced at $295. On April 19, 1993 Biblio-Link II for the Macintosh was released for a license fee of $195. This is a single program that can transfer downloaded files from DIALOG, MEDLARS and SilverPlatter databases. It needs no customizing to read any of these files. Users can change the settings in Biblio-Link II to place information into different Pro-Cite workforms and fields. System administrators can create custom configuration files that will permit the transfer of downloaded information from any other database or local in-house system.

Personal Bibliographic Software also has a product called Pro-Search, which is a specialized front-end program that will simplify the DIALOG databases search sessions. This program uses a menu interface and puts Dialog's blue sheet data on disk. One can construct and store search strategies offline to reduce online connect time and charges. There is a built-in accounting feature to track online charges. An optional quarterly subscription service includes free program upgrades and keeps the bluesheet disk up-to-date. The MS-DOS version is $495 and the optional subscription service is $150. The Macintosh version is $295. Customers are supported well by this company and their software upgrade prices are quite reasonable. Personal Bibliographic Software is known worldwide for its reliability and flexibility, and the good ease of use of its programs.

29. Rachel's: RCCP, RLibrary/Cards

Lest I forget that there are some libraries that are not yet ready or cannot yet afford to install an online integrated library system, I want to include Rachel's software since programs from this company have been available for almost a decade. The first of these programs is Rachel's Catalog Card Printer (RCCP), which is available for Apple II series systems, MS-DOS systems and Macintosh systems at $27, $32 and $44 respectively. This program allows the librarian to perform level 1 cataloging with four subjects and two other added entries and use up to a three-line call number. This program prints catalog cards on standard stock pin-feed catalog card forms available from several popular library suppliers. If your library needs only to print catalog card sets to these specifications, then this low-cost program is just the right answer. Over 1000 school libraries have purchased RCCP since its introduction in 1984. Demonstration disks for this program are $2, $3 and $5, respectively, for the above versions.

RLibrary/Cards is a Macintosh program licensing at $144, which does level 2 cataloging, including GMD, edition, details, series, ISBN, ISSN and LCCN. Ten subjects or added entries can be assigned and five lines used for call numbers. Again, the catalog cards printed by this program on an Apple printer are high quality. It also prints book spine and pocket labels. The RLibrary/Cards II program is a $274 Macintosh program with Apple Laser printer support and network compatibility for libraries whose Macintosh is connected to a network or that have a laser printer. This program also prints book spine and pocket labels or spine labels by themselves, and it offers a choice of fonts and point sizes. The Apple Library User's Group Newsletter of January, 1990 includes an article discussing the problems of printing catalog cards, the Rachel's program for the Macintosh and how most of these problems are addressed by the Rachel's programs. (13) These are basic programs and are a great value for the library needing to find a good, low-cost way to print catalog cards and label sets.

30. Research Information Systems, Inc.: Reference Manager and Reference Update

Reference Manager is a database program for managing citations to materials of many different formats. It has an optional slide manager to enable a separate 35-mm slide database to provide lecture support. The program comes in both MS-DOS (version 5) and Macintosh (version 2) forms. It uses compatible database formats for complete record exchange compatibility. It is available in a special version for NEC 9801 microcomputers which are Japan's leading desktop system. Another optional program is the Splicer TSR that allows the full retrieval power of Reference Manager from within your word processor and the ability to paste a retrieved reference identification number in a manuscript within delimiters for later bibliography generation.

Reference Manager uses a lookup menu to show lists of names. One can mark words in titles to use as keywords with @ and connect multiple words in phrases with an underscore. Text formatting supports underline, bold and italicized fonts. Search and retrieval uses Boolean AND, OR, NOT and also browsable windows in each parameter type or field, or keyword search. If you have any of the following word processors you can load Reference Manager citations into these manuscripts: MASS-11; Multimate; WordPerfect 4.2, 5.0 and 5.1; Visiword; Volkswriter; Microsoft Word v.4.0 and 5.0; WordStar v.6.0; WordStar 2000; and XyWrite. You can also load into an ASCII text file written with a text editor. There is an optional capture module for importing records from more than 50 different databases—some online, some CD-ROM. The user can edit records during the import to add keywords. There is a duplicate record check made at the time of loading. This program will appeal to those who publish numerous scholarly papers. There is a special student edition of this program available for $79 that makes it attractive to the college student. Depending on the options above, Reference Manager licenses from $299 to $499. This program also is a potential competitor with Pro-Cite and Balboa's Library Master, and one is advised to compare all three.

Reference Update is available for the same computer platforms as Reference Manager. It is a microcomputer-based current awareness service that provides a weekly diskette containing table-of-contents information for over 1200 scientific journals in biology and medicine. The search software comes with the initial subscription, and searches can be saved for later reuse with each subsequent weekly disk. The user may print lists of references or request cards and export selected references to Reference Manager or download them to another disk file. Optionally in this subscription one can have article abstracts on disk, by modem or fax, or use the Abstract Express Unlimited service to download abstracts from this company's central system for a fixed annual fee. The central service bills per downloaded abstract and either the customer calls a toll-free number and pays connect charges or a toll number and does not pay connect charges. Abstract Express will also generate reprint requests to authors, allow use of document delivery services for the article from the Information Store, Inc., in San Francisco or print a generic document order form for use with another document delivery service.

If you work in the biological and health sciences these Reference Update disks can be an invaluable way to maintain current awareness.

31. Right On Programs: Super Circulation Control et al.

This company is the largest producer of micro-based software for libraries plus some hospital, medical, law and veterinary support programs. Some of its over 35 programs have LAN versions for MS-DOS–type LANs. These are Super Circulation Control, Circulation Control, Online Catalog Plus, Online Catalog Enlarged, Periodical Manager, Subscription Manager, Magazine Article Filer, Acquisitions Manager and Complete Inventory Control. Over 18,000 libraries worldwide have ordered programs from this company. Prices for these programs range from $479 for Super Circulation Control to $129 for Magazine Article Filer. Right On Programs sells bar code readers to use with its system to complete your circulation system needs.

Super Circulation Control combines Circulation Control and Online Catalog and is an easy-to-learn program as are the others offered in the catalog. These programs are available in MS-DOS and Apple II versions in their standalone forms. Right On Programs offers a step up to the next level of automation for the smaller library and the school library from single function programs that print catalog cards or perform some other similar task. Its programs make automating routine library housekeeping and patron services easy and quite affordable when one considers the amount of staff time saved and improved service resulting from their use.

32. Scarecrow Press: Librarian's Helper, Librarian's Helper Online

Librarian's Helper is a product that has been on the market since 1985. It prints catalog cards and book spine and pocket labels. It will handle any material types but does not store the material type in its record. There is even a more basic version of this program that does not offer any data storage feature. The program prints cards to AACR2 standards. It is menu driven but does not have a full screen editor, only a line editor. The enhanced version allows data storage and reprinting of cards and labels from the saved datasets. The enhanced version permits data transfer to other programs but the data is not saved or output to a MARC format. In the basic version, 32 fields can be entered, with up to 10 subjects and 10 added entries. Call numbers can be up to five lines on cards and labels, with a sixth line on the label for volume number. For multiple volume works, multiple label sets are generated. The enhanced version will allow up to 78 fields, with a total record size of 3000 characters. The enhanced version for MS-DOS systems is licensed at $250 and the CP/M version to run on an Apple II equipped with a CP/M card is $350. The basic version is $175 for either MS-DOS or Apple CP/M version. This product could be improved by a full-screen editor and the use of the PC keyboard's arrow keys and insert/delete keys. Otherwise, for the library merely needing basic card printing and label preparation this is still an excellent program in its output, albeit somewhat dated by its user interface and lack of MARC record format for data storage.

Librarian's Helper Online (LH Online) is an online catalog and cataloging system that is designed for the small library or for a special collection within a larger library. It displays its records in a card catalog format. Users can produce reports sorted by author, title, publisher or call number. Also, author and title authority reports can be produced. It can run as a stand-alone MS-DOS program licensed at $600 or on a Novell or LAN BIOS–compatible LAN. For a $900 license a LAN version with up to five users can be purchased. For a $1200 license a LAN with 6 or more users can access this program. Upgrading the single-user license to a LAN license is $300 for the up to five user system. To run this product you need Intel 80286 or above computers. The record storage is a variable-length record instead of the fixed-length record used in the above Librarian's Helper Enhanced program. Simple and complex searches using Boolean operators are featured of author, title, subject, publisher or keyword. Records can be entered from the keyboard, from Librarian's Helper Enhanced and MicroLIF format. Although this program is relatively easy to use and does permit a satisfactory amount of cataloging information to be stored, it does not appear to store MARC records nor export or import full MARC. The librarian works from a special expanded version of the program which includes all patron features plus maintenance and administrative functions. If you need a simple online catalog for a small collection and do not need to transport full MARC records into the catalog, then this program may do the job for you.

33. Western Library Network (WLN)

The Western Library Network (formerly the Washington Library Network) serves over 750 subscribing libraries for cataloging and acquisitions support in Washington, Oregon, Idaho, Montana, Alaska, California, Arizona, British Columbia, and other states and Canadian provinces. It originally operated as a division of the Washington State Library, but in 1988, WLN was established as a private not-for-profit corporation. There are two categories of member libraries: those that add records to the database and those that do not. Contributing online members use microcomputers to contribute original cataloging and holdings information while contributing offline members send their records in magnetic tape or other batch methods. Many of these libraries use WLN's LaserCat, CD-ROM catalog. The offline libraries do not have online access to the WLN database. Union list members add original cataloging and serials holdings for the purpose of participation in a union list. Search-only members can access the WLN database for reference, bibliographic verification, interlibrary loan or other purposes but are not obligated to contribute. Some 8 million catalog records, 8.2 million authority records and 17.4 million holdings statements were reflected in the WLN database at the end of 1992. The central system offers members an acquisitions system and interlibrary loan system in addition to the union catalog and cataloging system. The LC Name and Subject Authority files and the WLN Authority file are searchable as are the bibliographic and holdings data.

The WLN LaserCat system was introduced in 1987. It currently provides some 4 million records and associated indexes in 4 CD-ROM disks and several years of current MARC records to use in cataloging. GPO, CATLINE and NLC records not held by WLN members are also included. Searching is very flexible as exact match, browse and keyword searching on multiple access points is provided. LaserCat subscribers also get the Ultracard/MARC program from Small Library Computing. This program permits MARC record creation, editing, catalog card printing and spine/pocket labels. In 1988, WLN introduced LaserBridge. This program converts downloaded Lasercat records into comma-delimited ASCII text that can be imported by dBase II or III, Lotus 1-2-3, PC-File III and many other microcomputer software packages. LaserCat subscribers receive quarterly updates. LaserCat requires an MS-DOS 3.1 version on a computer with at least 640 kB RAM, two disk drives or one floppy and one hard disk. Either color or monochrome monitors are supported. The MS-DOS CD-ROM extensions must be loaded and at least two CD-ROM drives need to be attached to a single interface card. As of December, 1992, 540 libraries subscribed to LaserCat. A new graphical user interface for LaserCat was released in December, 1993, and both MS-DOS/Windows and Macintosh versions of LaserCat have been developed. Libraries or groups of libraries can procure their own records on a CD-ROM basis in a product called LaserPac.

It uses the same search software and interface. LaserPac can be updated on a frequency selected by the library, with additions being entered on a hard disk to supplement the LaserPac CD-ROM.

The CD-ROM LaserCat and LaserPac products have a very powerful search engine. Searches can be limited by particular file, library, date, type, language, government publication, juvenile work and large print classifications. Exact searches can be done on record identification number, LCCN, ISBN, ISSN, author, title, subject and all fields. Keyword performs searches on author, title, subject, contents and all of these fields. Browsing can be done in the author, title, subject or all of the above. In addition, other record identifiers such as GPO and CANMARC numbers can be searched. The index displays in-clude cross-references and codes to tell if the heading is authorized, authorized without any records, unauthorized or a children's heading. The brief record display screen lists up to four records resulting from a search. The title, author and publication information in the imprint fields is shown. The full display uses labelled fields, or the user can display a MARC format display. The holdings screen display is also nicely formatted for clarity. The MARC display labels each tagged field with a field name.

The WLN mainframe system's software has been licensed to numerous national libraries abroad. Biblio-Techniques, Inc., now no longer in business, based its BLIS system on the WLN host software, which uses ADABAS as its dbms. In 1986, when Biblio-Techniques ceased business, its five customer sites—Indiana University, Columbia University, Brown University, University of Cincinnati, and the Metropolitan Toronto Library—formed a consortium and became a WLN licensee. Also, the University of Missouri and the University of Illinois had used WLN software to create an online catalog.

WLN products are high quality and will meet continuing long-range needs of members as is witnessed by the growth of this network despite the dominance of OCLC among the bibliographic utilities generally and the popularity or RLG/RLIN in the research library community. WLN has grown from a small regional network to a major network spanning Western North America.

34. Winnebago Software Company: CIRC/CAT, UnionCAT and LAMP

Winnebago was founded in 1982 and has shipped thousands of programs to school libraries since that time. Public libraries also constitute a significant customer base for Winnebago software. Winnebago packages a thoroughly professional product. The documentation is in ring binders that are slip cased just like the older, expensive microcomputer programs that we grew used to such as Lotus and WordPerfect. In addition to the programs previewed here, Winnebago offers numerous other programs to perform specific library tasks.

CIRC/CAT is a circulation and online catalog that work together as an integrated public services system for the school library. Saffady has written a review of this program in *Library Computer Systems and Equipment Review*. (14) The MS-DOS versions of these programs—version 3.1 was the one I examined—are licensed for $1295, while a comparable Macintosh version is available for $1495. Separate LAN licenses are also available so that a school or school district LAN can operate this software for access at numerous locations. The circulation system handles up to 300,000 items and 100,000 patrons. There are 300 different material categories that can be assigned their distinct circulation set of circulation parameters. There are 99 different patron categories possible. One can attach up to five messages to any patron or material record. Bar code labels for both books and patrons can be printed on 3.5- or 2.5-inch label stock if one obtains the add-on bar code program. This program will print Code 39, Label Code 4 or Codabar on laser and Epson-compatible dot matrix printers. If one wants to maintain text book issuance and control, material types 200–300 are reserved for this purpose and do not display in the online catalog or circulation system. These also do not count on a patron's limit for number of materials checked out. The database is a MARC record and records can be exported in MARC or MicroLIF. This MARC import and export feature is provided by another add-on program called the MARC Compatibility Module. Import from CD-ROM cataloging sources such as Bibliofile or from diskette is supported through this module. Another optional capability is a CD-ROM interface so that a CD-ROM–based database can be used in conjunction with the online catalog. A shell out from the main menu and then a return to the catalog is how this is done. The online catalog uses a fill-in-the-blank or browsable window search. On a retrieved record, one sees the catalog card type display but pressing the M key will change the display to a MARC-tagged record display. The MARC-tagged display also has English labels on each tag for the beginning MARC user to understand easily.

The circulation system prints all the needed notices and reports to manage the collection and its usage. Over 30 reports can be generated by CIRC/CAT. One can assign bar code ranges to denote specific libraries in a multilibrary system such as a school district. The system will recognize materials belonging to another location on any library location for a systemwide circulation approach. There is a separate input module that lets one build patron and material data on floppies for loading into CIRC/CAT. In the online catalog, searches can be limited by reading level, interest level and material type. The library can choose the tags that will be used to provide keywords. One can browse through the list of keywords shown and activate or deactivate specific keywords. If one deactivates a keyword and later wants to reactivate it, there is a Keyword Rebuild feature that will rebuild its record pointers. The online catalog is searched via character string match or keyword. Search results can be sorted into a call number sequence. Keyword searching permits up to three words to be entered, linked by AND, OR and NOT Boolean operators. Adding, editing and deleting MARC records is provided with three screen formats: condensed, easy entry and full entry. The whole MARC record including leader and fixed fields can be edited.

This system uses its menus effectively. However, it is the use of the pop-up scrolling windows that makes this program a joy to use. But the circulation system, with its initial blank screen and "Ready" prompt, which is expecting either a patron bar code or patron name entry, could have been made a bit clearer and more friendly by an appropriate label or text box. This system should be a strong contender for school libraries, particularly those with LANs or district wide automation using a LAN. Customer support is free the first year and then is available for a competitive fixed charge each subsequent year.

As an example of how one high school has provided some wide access on its system, the Farmington, Missouri High School has linked its CIRC/CAT system to the local Farmington Public Library, using PC Anywhere. The high school students can access the public library's database by typing a command to call a predetermined phone number, entering a password and performing a search just as if they were at the public library. The public library patrons can do the same from their system to the school system. An area community college is also planning on using the Winnebago software and PC Anywhere to link into this arrangement as are some other schools in the area.

Winnebago's UNION CAT is a district-level online catalog for the MS-DOS operating system and provides all of the features of the CAT program above with provision to handle an unlimited number of locations and hundreds of thousands of bibliographic records in MARC format. The version current at the time of examination was v.3.0, which superseded version 2.62—which I have also examined. UNION CAT v.3.0 now includes the MARC Tag 852 for local holdings and the user-defined field is now tied to tag 961, subfield u. Several new reports have been added since the earlier version. In the card image display format the note field now displays up to 765 characters. The card image displays are in AACR2 format. One can choose whether to allow two or three keyword fields to be entered during keyword searching. There is a new keyword update utility that builds keywords for added records and it performed quite fast on our test 386 20-MHz microcomputer. CAT and UNION CAT would be strengthened if they were authority based as they do not provide cross-references.

LAMP, the Library Acquisitions and Management Program is a dBaseIII/Clipper application also using some Turbo Pascal and assembler routines. It has a consideration for purchase file, prepares purchase orders, maintains book fund accounting and performs invoice and account reconciliation. Old records can be archived to floppy according to rules the user sets up. It is possible to send orders to a vendor by modem. This is a simple system to learn and should fill the needs of most small libraries. It requires an MS-DOS system and if the modem transmission for orders is used with a book supplier, then an appropriate speed modem would be needed. An Epson-compatible or laser printer can be used to print the outputs from this system.

Winnebago users have both national and local/regional users' groups. A quarterly newsletter, which has excellent layout and is full of news, tips and such, is sent to licensed users of the software. This is a strong company with a good record of customer service and continuing evolution of its programs.

35. Zylab Div. of Information Dimensions, Inc.: Zyindex

Zyindex for MS-DOS systems has been an established text retrieval package for almost a decade. In June, 1992, the Microsoft Windows version of Zyindex became available. Both versions will also operate on Novell-, Banyan-, 3COM- and Netbios-compatible LANs when licensed for LAN use. *Infoworld* said, "Zyindex for Windows is easily the best program for general text retrieval in Windows." Version 5.0 added features to the current MS-DOS product. It builds indexes twice as fast, with a 30% overhead for its indexes. You can launch an application program from within Zyindex, with a quick return to Zyindex when finished with the other application. You can archive multiple versions of a file after a search and view any and all versions at will. Bookmarks can be inserted to mark your place to return at any time. Link points of interest in or between files and traverse the link at any time. Another neat feature is being able to add your own notes—which can be indexed and searched—and not compromise the original file integrity. Links and notes can be personal or public. If graphics are embedded in the file or linked, they can be displayed on the screen. TIFF, PCX, BMP and EPS graphics formats are displayed. If you have dBase format files, even with memo fields, these can be searched by Zyindex for Windows. Zyindex will search WordPerfect, WordPerfect for Windows, Microsoft Word, Microsoft Word for Windows, MS-Write, WordStar, AmiPro, Displaywrite, Xywrite, Multimate, Volkswriter, Total Word, ASCII, and ANSI file formats using the IBM PC character set. There is a runtime version of the search engine available for those who want to distribute a published text database application. Searches in Zyindex take from one to five seconds on an Intel 80386 at 33 MHz, while building indexes on such a machine takes an hour for 10–12 MB-sized files.

Zyindex searching is really sophisticated, with words, phrases, Boolean operators and wildcards all used. Unordered proximity searches are possible where word A is within *n* words of word B. Ordered proximity searches also are implemented where word A is up to *n* words before word B. Many other advanced search features to either narrow or widen a search among documents or defined fields are provided. This is a full indexing and retrieval package in a class with BRS Search on the search engine side but able to handle a variety of common text formats. The noise word or exclusion list can be modified as well as the default character set. The Windows version of Zyindex implements the Windows standard interface of dialog boxes, buttons and pull-down menus. For index building particularly, this program will perform much better with the faster microprocessor systems. The same is true for search speed, although typical searches are already sufficiently speedy to satisfy even the speed demon user. The conventional microcomputer software ring-bound documentation is well organized and clearly written. Zyindex for Windows licenses for $395 for a single-user and $995 for a three-user LAN license. If you have the MS-DOS version, you can update to the Windows version for $149.

There is a companion program called Zyimage, which is a complete electronic document filing system that unites Zyindex search and retrieval with scanned text documents produced by Calera's Wordscan OCR software. It preserves both text and image files of the document. This program is available in LAN license at $2459 for a five-user license, $3995 for a ten-user license and $5495 for a twenty-user license. A single-user license is $895.

This program is optimized to handle from 1 MB to 10 GB of text in a single index. The Zyindex Developer's Toolkit High Level Programming Interface (HAPI) provides direct program access to the index building and search engine to enable a developer's application to perform essential text retrieval functions. Create, add or remove documents in an index; search an index; obtain a list of retrieved files with number of hits and comments and text with hits from retrieved files. The HAPI add-on is $3995 and is available for MS-DOS, Windows and UNIX on 386/486 systems.

III. MACINTOSH SYSTEMS

There are quite a few specific library function programs that are available for the Macintosh. The previous section examined software that is thought of mainly as MS-DOS platform products but which some developers have also implemented on the Macintosh. I have not attempted to cover programs that perform a single task such as writing overdue notices, Hypercard-implemented applications such as bibliographic instruction or collection guides. I chose to separate these Macintosh systems because they are all integrated, online, multifunctional library management systems designed to compete with similar offerings on an MS-DOS or LAN platform in many cases. For the library or institution with Macintosh systems and Mac networking, these programs offer some competitive choices that should be examined before determining whether it would be advisable to move to an MS-DOS or other platform to implement online library computing support.

1. Caspr, Inc.: Library Works and Other Products

At the Caspr Library Center, Caspr, Inc, has computer labs, CD-ROM production, training facilities and a multimedia demonstration library to show its library automation products: Library Works™, Library Browser™, and LibraryDisc™.

Library Works™ is an online catalog, cataloging, acquisitions, serials and circulation system which is designed specifically for the Apple Macintosh family systems. MARC records can be imported and exported. AACR2 cards and label sets can be printed. The system provides Boolean searching and left and right truncation. With the Expand feature one can scroll through author, title, subject and keyword indexes. The serials module supports routing but does not provide any bindery preparation support. For a multiuser system one can use an Appleshare server, a Novell Advanced Netware server or a Digital Equipment VAX-server. This system handles up to a million records, with special versions available to handle even larger databases. School libraries are the main target for this system, although it has been installed in many other types of libraries.

Library Browser™ is the client software for public access to the above online catalog. It uses a card drawer metaphor in presenting search results on the Macinstosh. Records can be displayed in card, short, medium or long formats. There are client versions of this program for the Macintosh, MS-DOS/Windows systems and Apple IIe and IIgs systems. Any of these systems attached to a LAN running this software is able to perform searches. The search sets can be saved to disk or printed.

LibraryDisc™ uses the Library Browser™ interface to search CD-ROM databases. Currently these are the MARC School Edition™, which is produced by the Catalog Card Company with Dewey Classification and Sears subject headings; ERIC Journals™, which is the CIJE section of the ERIC database; Magazine Article Summaries™, which contains indexes and abstracts to magazine articles from EBSCO Publishing; and National Newspaper Abstracts from University Microfilms, Inc.

Caspr's products are well laid out and the documentation has a tutorial included. The Macintosh user interface is well implemented and therefore this software will be easy to use for users of all levels. Caspr also has a catalog card and label-printing program called MACCARDS for the Macintosh. If you are looking for a system that uses the Macintosh platform, this system should be included in your serious examination.

2. *Chancery Software, Ltd.: MacSchool Library and Advanced Booking*

These systems from Canada are a part of a series of software directed at school systems. The larger system is called the MacSchool System. Its other modules are Student Information System (SIS), District Student Management (DSM), Fund Accounting and CSL Precis. This last program is a simplified administration system for smaller schools with up to 750 students, with demographics, discipline, daily attendance, report cards and teacher gradebook. MacSchool

Library is the integrated library system module of this larger system. Advanced Booking is another module aimed at media center support.

MacSchool Library and its sister modules will run on a single Macintosh or on a LocalTalk™, PhoneNet®, or Ethernet network using MacTOPS™, Appleshare or Novell Advanced Netware. This library system supports cataloging, an online catalog and circulation using the typical Mac interface of pull-down and pop-up menus, dialog boxes, radio buttons, scrolling windows, and other familiar Mac interface features. Up to 65,000 bibliographic records and 5000 user records can be handled by this system. There is an optional MARC record import module that is separately licensed and can handle records from many different CD-ROM or book jobber sources. There is a report manager that provides for customized reports from this system. MacSchool Library has desktop publishing features to incorporate graphics and free-form text, allowing reports from this system to have quite a professional appearance. An unusual feature is that the online catalog displays bibliographic records in a spreadsheet-like tabular format for browsing. A vertical scrollbar is used as with many other Mac programs. Using this type of display eliminates the need for horizontal scrolling on the Mac screen. The user can double-click on a title for a full bibliographic display in a catalog card image format. When a question mark icon within a title column is clicked, an annotation will come up in a pop-up window. Searching can be based on any bibliographic field. Keyword searches can be on titles, subjects and annotations. Boolean AND, OR and NOT operators are supported. This system will also print catalog cards, individually or in sets, and spine and pocket labels. The separate advanced booking module, probably most useful for media and equipment items, permits advance reservations for specific items. It generates pick lists for reservation dates and will check out items on those lists, and it can print shipping labels to route materials to borrowers. The circulation portion of this system integrates with the MacSchool Student Information System, or borrower records can be key entered if that program is not being used.

This is a competitive product with good appeal for school district implementation as well as for an individual school. There are a variety of single and multiple licensing arrangements with prices competitive with other Mac software products. For a LAN installation the server should be at least a Mac IIci, IIvx or one of the Quadra models. Workstations should run system 7.0 and have 4 MB RAM or higher. A Mac SE/30 with at least 4 MB RAM is needed to run the single-user version of this software. MacSchool Library has been reviewed by William Saffady. (15)

3. COMPanion: Alexandria

This system was introduced in 1988 and has been released in three subsequent versions. This Macintosh integrated library system features cataloging, online catalog, circulation, acquisitions, serials and audio/visual equipment modules. There is a separate textbook module called the Textbook Librarian. This system is aimed at schools and school districts. It appears to have the largest installed base of the integrated library systems available for the Macintosh. It is available as a single-user system or as a LAN.

Hardware requirements for this system are a Mac running system 6.0.5 or above and equipped with floppy drive, at least a 40-MB hard disk and a monochrome or color monitor. A compatible printer is required for report production. For system 6.0.5 at least 1 MB RAM is needed, while system 7.0 will require 3 MB minimum. Servers and workstations in a LAN will need one MB additional memory. Alexandria can operate in AppleTalk or Ethernet LANs and a dedicated server is not required.

This system is built around a MARC format database. Bibliographic records can be key entered or imported from a variety of sources. Record displays can be either a labelled card type display or a MARC display shown in a scrolling window framed by a file tab card as for the card image display. When entering records an operator can use a labelled display that automatically converts its fields to MARC tags or directly type in the MARC tags, subfields and such. This allows a person that does not have MARC knowledge to perform data entry. Browse mode does a good job of emulating the browsing one does in the card catalog. For libraries that need to print catalog card sets, this software is capable of doing this. Alexandria searches for specific words or phrases in fields chosen by the user. Boolean AND, OR and NOT operators with up to five search specifications can be processed. Initial search results are presented in a brief display which can be expanded to a full-card or MARC-type display. The circulation system provides a good level of support for school libraries and those other libraries that do not have complex patron categories. Alexandria also integrates with Brodart's Precision One CD-ROM-based MARC record service. Version 3.0 provided acquisitions and serials capability but was not available when I examined v.2.02h. Finally, Alexandria is able to produce 84 different reports and send them to screen, printer or a file on disk. Self-mailing notices are used for notices sent to patrons. Backing all this up, COMPanion has 24-hour toll-free telephone support. Licensees receive free software upgrades for a year and there is a user group newsletter. To sum up, this program is intuitive, able to be used by library users of all ages and backgrounds, totally integrated and well designed to take advantage of all the strengths of the Macintosh platform. Certainly, the more powerful models of the Macintosh will run this software more quickly, but performance of this system is nevertheless very good owing to appropriate software design and implementation. Moreover, this system is very competitively priced. *Library Computer Systems and Equipment Review* carried a review of v.2.02. (16)

IV. CONCLUSION

Truly, there is a program out there that should satisfy most needs for an integrated multifunctional MARC-based library system from among those previewed here. System development is continuing to bring improved products to the marketplace. New products are also entering the market and competing with more established ones. Your software investment will be protected if your records can be exported in MARC or MicroLIF format to another microcomputer-based system. For the future, I expect that more of these products will move to client/server designs for their LAN implementations. I also expect to see moves to develop and release Microsoft Windows- or Windows NT-compliant programs soon. The graphical user interface and multitasking operation is now an accepted mode of computing on the desktop. If a library can afford to acquire a microcomputer, it should also be able to begin planning for an integrated system so that it can, at the very least, cease its reliance on printing catalog cards or circulating books manually. Service will improve as a result, with staff time able to be redirected to more meaningful tasks than the clerical work associated with many manual processes. Bear in mind that hardware is rapidly improving and costs are becoming lower to achieve the necessary computing platform. While software improvement is also continuing, albeit at a slower pace, your careful choice of software will assure your satisfaction level with the system over an extended period as you grow with your vendor through installation of new software releases and improvements.

V. APPENDIX: VENDOR CONTACTS

APAK Systems Ltd.
5405 Eglinton Avenue West, Suite 215
Etobicoke, Ontario, Canada M9C 5K6
(416) 620-5841
(416) 620-1819 Fax

Auto-Graphics, Inc.
3201 Temple Avenue
Pomona, CA 91768-3200
(800) 776-6939
(714) 595-7204
(714) 595-3506 Fax

Balboa Software
P.O. Box 3145, Station D
Willowdale, Ontario, Canada M2R 3G5
(416) 730-8980
(416) 730-9715 Fax
e-mail: hahne@epas.utoronto.ca

Brodart Automation, Div. of Brodart Co.
500 Arch Street
Williamsport, PA 17705
(800) 233-8467
(717) 326-2461
(717) 327-9237 Fax

Cactus Software, Inc.
15 Kary Way
Morristown, NJ 07960-5604
(201) 540-0980

Caspr, Inc.
635 Vaqueros Avenue
Sunnyvale, CA 94086
(800) 852-2777
(408) 522-9800
(408) 522-9806 Fax

Chancery Software, Ltd.
4170 Still Creek Drive, Suite 450
Burnaby, British Columbia, Canada V5C 6C6
(800) 999-9931
(604) 294-1233
(604) 294-2225 Fax

COMPanion
3755 Evelyn Drive
Salt Lake City, UT 84124-2305
(800) 347-6439
(801) 278-6439
(801) 278-7789 Fax

Computer Assisted Library
Information Co., Inc. (CALICO)
P.O. Box 6190
Chesterfield, MO 63017
(800) 367-0416
In St. Louis, MO: 863-8028

DataTrek, Inc.
5838 Edison Place
Carlsbad, CA 92008
(800) 876-5484
(619) 431-8400
(619) 431-8448 Fax

Dawson UK, Ltd. Technology Division
Cannon House, Park Farm Road
Folkestone, Kent CT19 5EE
England
0303-850537
0303-850440 Fax

Educational Solutions, Inc.
4863 American Road
Rockford, IL 61109
(800) 443-3229
(815) 227-0527
(815) 227-4035 Fax
(815) 227-4034 Modem

Eloquent Systems, Inc.
25-1501 Lonsdale Avenue
North Vancouver, British Columbia, Canada V7M 2J2
(800) 663-8172 U.S.A.
(604) 980-8358
(604) 980-9537 Fax
or P.O. Box 3379 Blaine, WA 98230

Follett Software Company
809 N. Front Street
McHenry, IL 60050-5589
(800) 323-3397
(815) 344-8700
(815) 344-8774 Fax

GMUtant Software
Route 1, Box 296
Hamilton, VA 22068
(703) 993-2219

Information Transform, Inc.
502 Leonard Street
Madison, WI 53711
(800) 824-6272
(608) 255-4800
(608) 255-2082 Fax

ILS International Library Systems Corp.
320-2600 Granville Street
Vancouver, British Columbia, Canada V6H 3V3
(604) 734-8882
(604) 734-8854 Fax

Inlex. Inc.
One Lower Ragsdale Drive, Bldg. #1, Suite 200
P.O. Box 1349
Monterey, CA 93942
(800) 553-1202 outside CA
(408) 646-8600 CA
(408) 646-0651 Fax

Inmagic, Inc.
2067 Massachusetts Avenue
Cambridge, MA 02140-1338
(800) 229-TEXT
(617) 661-8124
(617) 661-6901 Fax

LEX Systems, Inc.
Box 280
Lucky Lake, Saskatchewan, Canada S0L 1Z0
Sales and support:
Jim Bruce
10622 129th Street
Edmonton, Alberta, Canada T5N 1X3
(403) 455-7942
(403) 451-2754 Fax

The Library Corporation (TLC)
Research Park
Inwood, WV 25428-9733
(800) 326-7159
(404) 591-0089
(404) 591-0295 Fax

Library Technologies, Inc.
1142 E. Bradfield Road
Abington, PA 19001
(215) 576-6983
(215) 576-0137 Fax

Media Flex, Inc.
P.O. Box 1107
Champlain, NY 12919
(518) 298-2970

Michigan State University
University Archives—Historical Collections
EG-13 Library Building
East Lansing, MI 48824-1048
(517) 355-2330

Midwest Library Service
11443 St. Charles Rock Road
Bridgeton, MO 63044-2789
(800) 325-8833

Nichols Advanced Technologies, Inc.
In U.S.A.:
3452 Losey Boulevard South
La Crosse, WI 54601
(800) 658-9453
(608) 787-8333 Fax
In Canada:
1100, Royal LePage Building
10130 103rd Street
Edmonton, Alberta, Canada T5J 3N9
(800) 661-4109
(403) 424-0091
(403) 428-7644 Fax

Novara Software
95 College Street
Antigonish, Nova Scotia, Canada
B2G 1X6
(902) 863-3361
(902) 863-2580 Fax

On Point, Inc./TLC
Total Library Computerization
2606 36th Street N.W.
Washington, DC 20007-1419
(202) 338-8914
(202) 337-7107 Fax

P.S.S. TAPESTRY
265 Northgate Drive
Warrendale, PA 15086
(800) 835-7863
(412) 934-1660
(412) 934-1640 Fax

Personal Bibliographic Software, Inc.
P.O. Box 4250
Ann Arbor, MI 48106
(313) 996-1580
(313) 996-4672 Fax

Rachel's
111 Insbruck
Clayton, NC 27520
(800) 869-7390

Research Information Systems, Inc.
Camino Corporate Center
2355 Camino Vida Roble
Carlsbad, CA 92009
(619) 438-5526
(619) 438-5573 Fax

Right On Programs
755-A New York Avenue
Huntington, NY 11743
(516) 424-7777
(516) 424-7207 Fax

Scarecrow Press
52 Liberty Street
P.O. Box 4167
Metuchen, NJ 08840
(908) 548-8600
(609) 424-2595 Technical Support

Scribe Software, Inc.
(Media One for Windows K-12 Schools)
4435 N. Saddlebag Trail #1
Scottsdale, AZ 85251
(800) 443-7890
(602) 990-3384
(602) 990-3505 Fax

Winnebago Software Company
310 West Main Street
P.O. Box 430
Caledonia, MN 55921
(800) 533-5430
(507) 724-5698
(507) 724-2301 Fax

Zylab, Div. of Information Dimensions, Inc.
100 Lexington Drive
Buffalo Grove, IL 60089
(708) 459-8000
(708) 459-8054 Fax

REFERENCES

1. Morrow, Blaine. Optical Product Review: IMPACT Public Access Catalog. *CD-ROM Librarian 4*(1): 22-26 (January 1989).
2. Lee, Joel M. IMPACT. In: *The Online Catalog Book*. Edited by Walt Crawford. New York: G.K. Hall, 1992.
3. Firsching, Donald. Information Sharing Through Standardization: Minaret at the National Archives of the Episcopal Church. *The Southwestern Archivist 16*(3): 6-8, 32 (Fall 1992).
4. Saffady, William. The Columbia Library System. *Library Computer Systems and Equipment Review 14*(2): 27-31 (July-December 1992).
5. Saffady, William. The Eloquent Librarian. *Library Computer Systems and Equipment Review 14*(2): 32-36 (July-December 1992).
6. Saffady, William. Circulation/Catalog Plus. *Library Computer Systems and Equipment Review 14*(2): 23-26 (July-December 1992).
7. Saffady, William. The Assistant. *Library Computer Systems and Equipment Review 14*(2): 8-11 (July-December 1992).
8. Saffady, William. Bibliofile. *Library Computer Systems and Equipment Review 14*(2): 12-17 (July-December 1992).
9. Landis, Lawrence A. Cataloging Software and the University Archives: Micro-MARC:amc at Oregon State University. *The Southwestern Archivist 16*(3): 6-8, 32 (Fall 1992).
10. Honhart, Frederick L. MicroMARC:amc: A Case Study in the Development of an Automated System. *American Archivist 52*: 80-86 (Winter 1989).
11. Saffady, William. MOLLI. *Library Computer Systems and Equipment Review 14* (2): 56-59 (July-December 1992).
12. Saffady, William. Bibliotrac. *Library Computer Systems and Equipment Review 14* (2): 18-22 (July-December 1992).
13. Turitz, Mitch. RLibrary/Cards. *Apple Library User's Group Newsletter 8*(1): 77-80 (January 1990).
14. Saffady, William. Winnebago CIRC/CAT. *Library Computer Systems and Equipment Review 14*(2): 64-69 (July-December 1992).
15. Saffady, William. MacSchool Library. *Library Computer Systems and Equipment Review 14*(2): 42-46 (July-December 1992).
16. Saffady, William. Alexandria. *Library Computer Systems and Equipment Review 14*(2): 3-7 (July-December 1992).

9

INFORMATION TECHNOLOGY
THE TOOLS OF TOMORROW

> The flashiest graphics will never save a poor user interface. Sexy graphics are like lipstick on a bulldog. Lipstick may make the bulldog look better but you still don't want to kiss it.
>
> — Norm Cox, designer of the Xerox Star

I. INTRODUCTION

This last chapter examines information technology as one of the major tools of tomorrow to shape our society and our institutions—particularly our libraries as one of the most important influences in education, culture and society. Increasing societal and economic pressures are driving our continuing evolution. Competition in almost every significant activity or industry is global. For some years now, most economies have been in a global downturn, although 1994 has brought evidence of some economic turnaround. Insufficient education continues to contribute to unemployment, which fosters stress and tears at the societal fabric, undermining the quality of life for all. Our educational and cultural infrastructure must change to meet these challenges, addressing them through new and creative educational techniques. In a world that has become more visually oriented, our education and information infrastructure must develop techniques to incorporate these changes. Information technology, through the melding of computer technology with communications, digital imaging, and full-motion video and sound, can be a powerful ally to improving education and thus improving skills for gainful employment. But, in order to do this, libraries and librarians will have to change. Real-world problems can be approached on an educational level by developing an infrastructure of high-quality information technology. If the right changes are made by libraries of every persuasion, there should be a good future for automated library systems and related information technologies. These systems can and should become major information delivery systems to a wide variety of societal segments.

II. THE SURVIVAL GAME: BUILDING THE INFORMATION TECHNOLOGY INFRASTRUCTURE

In order for librarians and libraries to survive as a profession and as an institution, respectively, they will need to lead their institutions in building improved information technology–oriented infrastructures. The numerous evolving problems to be overcome will present further opportunities to foster improvements in information delivery, in a continuing, closed-loop feedback process.

A. Changing Libraries

It has been evident for over half a century that libraries can no longer comprehensively collect in a wide variety of subject areas. Thus, a long history of cooperative networking and interlibrary lending has been the mainstay of satisfying ever widening and interdisciplinary subject material demands of research, scholarly and student users. New publishing techniques such as CD-ROM, multimedia interactive computer works, machine-readable text files on the Internet, and collections of scanned materials stored in image and character formats are increasingly becoming key parts to library resources. These collections are accessed and controlled through specialized retrieval software and LANs with Internet connections. The new publishing formats and systems are pushing the envelope of the library community to supply and service clientele using these new mediums. The local area network, with its ability to provide wide CD-ROM access as well as institutional connectivity to both the library and to the Internet, is the underpinning communications system of today's forward-looking library. A host computer–based automated library system providing technical processing, online catalog and circulation support is not sufficient in itself to provide all the information technology resources needed for today's libraries. This is certainly true for academic and special libraries, and increasingly is becoming the case for public libraries. The library user has become more comfortable using microcomputers, electronic bulletin boards and online services such as the FreeNet-based systems, CompuServe or America

Online. Through school exposure to computers, greater numbers of children are introduced to information technology earlier in their school experience. Many more families are seeking to provide themselves further enriching experiences through purchasing CD-ROM and multimedia publications for use with their home computer system.

At some point in the not too distant future, cable television companies will undoubtedly begin offering carrier services to allow individual homes to connect to such networks as the Internet, with software and connections that are easier to use than today's modem communications. With present 14.4-Mbps modems priced below $150 and the next wave of modems to include voice mail capabilities with double that data transmission speed, more and more owners of personal computers are acquiring connectivity tools that allow them to access remote online resources. Today, even bulletin board system operators can subscribe at reasonable cost to a service called Planet Connect to bring file distribution networks, Usenet News Groups and FidoNet echo conferences to their systems and users. As the prices of these information technology products and services drop, a wider market is generated for them.

It is still true that there is a population segment that is disadvantaged economically and socially and is hampered from learning and using information technology-based educational or recreational resources. This situation needs to be addressed by the public library community in cooperation with local schools and FreeNet kinds of public computing efforts to assure universal access to electronic participation in educational, social, occupational or political affairs. Erosion of the family, confusion of the values of right and wrong and many other serious societal problems grow from poor economic opportunities, inadequate education and lack of motivation. The public library will need to be a key player, along with the school system, higher education and other community agencies in addressing these problems. Building imaginative information delivery systems is a key component to providing the necessary foundation.

Taxpayers are going to have to invest in building a progressive technology-based delivery system if our cities are to address the problems of unemployment, lack of employable skills and crime. The frightening irony of the increase in use of information technology-based delivery is that an increasingly large segment of our population will become "information poor" as the costs of access to services are borne more and more by the individual. In other words, the expectations of an equal level of "free" service across a library's clientele, so well exemplified by the expansion of the free public library through the Carnegie building program over 80 years ago, seems to apply less and less each year. Libraries have been forced to institute fees for service for many tasks that, prior to use of information technology, were free to all users. User searching of indexing and abstracting databases, which has replaced the laborious and lengthy comprehensive searching of book form indexes, is now only beginning again to be a basic free service as more libraries have created host-based search services to accompany their public online catalog or increased their use of CD-ROM media as the delivery format. Given operational costs, the likely scenario is for more growth in CD-ROM-based delivery rather than for more host computer-operated databases in local institutions or at database search service companies such as BRS or Dialog.

Libraries are going to have to develop ways to manage access to materials available in electronic format and to effectively share them much as they have shared print resources for over a century through interlibrary lending. Traditional hierarchical library organizations are going to have to adopt a more team-oriented work environment where a more varied task responsibility is shared by both library professionals and technicians. Specific mission-directed teams, which may change in composition as clientele needs change, will come into being. For example, in a university setting there might be library teams that concentrate on all aspects of service and support for specific subject areas. In turn, these teams would be assisted by other specialists in particular information technologies such as LAN, automated library system and imaging system support, end-user training in information resources, in-depth problem examination, and Internet resources. The traditional view of the library as a public services and technical services hierarchy overseen by an administrative services structure will disappear. This traditional organization has proven increasingly unable to deal with contemporary library service delivery, where extensive intercooperative relationships are needed, resources are scattered and staff need to have wider latitude and skills development.

Managerial overhead must be minimized as these resources are needed to reshape libraries through investment in electronic infrastructure and training. When staff can have responsibilities that range from determination of a client's needs to the fulfillment of that need, there will be a more responsive and satisfying working situation which will result in increased overall productivity. With staff able to perform tasks through such a continuum, it will be easier for the library to maintain operations when staff are on leave. Such a climate creates a win–win situation for the library user, who will no longer be forwarded around a large and specialized library system, but will be able to maintain contact with a given staff member until the information need is satisfied.

B. Changing the Information Profession

The nineties have been said to be the information age, and yet since the eighties, some famous schools of library science such as Columbia University's have ceased to operate. Still others such as the University of California at Los Angeles are facing reorganization and/or serious questioning of their appropriateness in the present and future scheme of graduate education. This has not happened as much to other programs such as schools of business or computer science. Is it that today's industry and education leaders expect some other profession to take over the organization of knowledge and its delivery? It seems that this may be the case, partly due to the perception that librarians lack the necessary information technology and business skills that are deemed critical to the success of organizations in an increasingly competitive climate. Schools of information science increasingly have moved in the direction of emphasizing skills involving information technology such as database design, online search strategy development, bibliometrics and various statistically based studies of information use and value. While these schools produce students better trained in information technology, they do not necessarily produce individuals better able to manage and provide the specialized skills needed in curatorial, archival and research library operation. Neither do they produce professionals having better organization of knowledge and reference service skills.

I believe that really what is needed to maintain and improve the viability of libraries as our knowledge centers is to meld some traditional organization of knowledge perspectives with practical business-oriented skills involving communications, strategic planning, budgeting and information technology. A combination of management information systems and information science and library curricula would provide a modern, professional basis for the 21st century library. One can see the difference in the success of various computer-assisted services between libraries that know how to manage and support these fundamental tools and those that do not. The library must have a staff that can understand the necessity of its involvement in the development, support and operation of in-library systems and how to manage evolving cooperative arrangements with data-processing and networking centers within their organizations. Librarians who believe that the library should merely budget funds to engage a unit outside the library to provide total system support will not even be equipped to determine if such an arrangement is providing the best service at the price being paid. Moreover, such central services usually cannot give immediate priority to each user's system problems. Only through an experienced and knowledgeable staff that is are willing to assume roles from intelligent consumers of information technology to on-site immediate trouble-shooting, user training and support will there be sufficient understanding to deal intelligently with managing and supporting library systems in a most cost-effective and service-responsive way. More than ever, this decade is one of distributed computing, involving development of customized information solutions using an accepted repertoire of commercially available software with content and data manipulation features that involve a form of programming. Examples include access to SQL-based data, using various SQL data extraction programs, using instructional course-building programs such as Asymetrix's ToolBook, or creating Ask blocks in a Gopher Plus server on the Internet.

Arrangements for managing and supporting information technology will take differing shapes depending on the size of the library, the size of its parent institution, the institution's existing computing and communications resources and the capabilities of the library's management and staff. At minimum, desktop user support should be provided initially within the medium to large library itself, with the goal that the majority of problems be resolved without the need for outside specialists. This means that someone on the staff should be able to troubleshoot basic malfunctioning software and hardware. If more extensive repair is required, this individual should make the necessary calls for such service or information. The same would be true for both stand-alone and small personal computer networks and for any in-library automated library systems that are operated outside of a central computer operations site. Institution-wide support for wide area network access and for systems operated out of central data processing centers as well as back-up advanced technical support for LAN problems or other in-library situations would be a part of this solution for typical institutions such as higher education, government or corporations.

In smaller institutional settings, where the libraries are very small, dependence on centrally provided or contractually provided services may be the only way to support information technologies. For this situation, the librarian will need to be quite savvy as to how to assure that a satisfactory arrangement is provided at a fair cost. Consultants, provided they are equipped with the needed technical knowledge, can be engaged to provide support services. The librarian who manages the library must provide the necessary leadership to set the direction for information technology evolution in the library and have the necessary judgment to channel consultants' work effectively.

C. Problems Facing Libraries Today

Having been in the library and computer field over 30 years, almost all of them spent specializing in applying computer and data processing technologies to improving library operations and services, I have formed some opinions of the problems facing our libraries and the staff who operate them.

Currently our societal values do not place a very high value on education and the accompanying and related organizations such as libraries. This is evidenced in the reward system and the relatively low salaries paid to teachers, college faculty and librarians. Professions such as engineering, accounting, human resources management and general management are paid higher average salaries throughout a career than are librarians. Chief librarians or directors of large academic libraries often are not paid as much as their peer management counterparts in other areas of their institutions. The library profession suffers from the image of still being a female-dominated field even though increasingly there are more males in the field. Traditionally, female-dominated fields that are infiltrated by increasing numbers of males at some point experience a relative increase in average salary. An example is nursing, where salaries have improved as more males have entered the field. This has not occurred to the same degree in librarianship. However, the graduates of information science programs are receiving higher starting salaries and larger raises as they move forward in their career development. This is because information science graduates are perceived as having more of the necessary skills for today's information technology-based knowledge resources.

The profession needs somehow to increase its perceived value in the educational area and in the critical area of providing key knowledge to institutions and organizations to enhance their overall productivity and responsiveness to changing societal and economic conditions. This may be difficult, but it is not impossible, as certain segments of the library and information field already have made gains in status. This is the case in some large private sector companies and in some governmental libraries. Until there is a higher perceived value granted by society to librarians it will be increasingly difficult for libraries to gain a fair share of their institution's budgeted resources.

The library profession must attract and retain individuals who can master increasingly complex information technology skills and operate in a professional business and managerial climate. Currently, techniques such as Total Quality Management have helped large organizations improve operations and be more responsive to their customer base. Such techniques when employed in the library have resulted in model service climates in their institutional settings. The 3M Company and Cargill, Inc., are two examples of private companies where significant improvements in information services have resulted through use of modern management techniques and the infusion of information technologies throughout their organizations coupled with individuals who have the necessary skills to operate in such a setting.

The above problems are exacerbated by the need to make more costly investments in information technology and in training library staff in its use while overall library operating budgets are shrinking as a percentage of their parent institution's total budget. What this means is that libraries may be forced to make hard choices between materials purchases for their collections and information technology investments. While some balance is needed as these choices loom, it is evident that the same collection expenditure strategies, centered on book and journal format resources, cannot continue into the foreseeable future. The move to networked CD-ROM format access is an example of employing an information technology that can be maintained and operated at lower cost than identical services provided through the more traditional mainframe computer operation and associated search software maintenance. However, without the prior investment in a good LAN strategy and connectivity throughout the library and institution, neither of the above approaches can be brought to the individual student's or researcher's bench.

The investments in information technology and the redeployment of a library's budgetary resources will determine just how successful that particular library will be in the coming years. Burgeoning electronic publishing and resources made available via digital imaging facilities are replacing direct hard copy print resources. If the right decisions are not made to invest in building the needed skills and technology infrastructure, some libraries will face even more serious problems in meeting their users' needs. Libraries in higher education and in specialized research facilities will be most seriously affected. Public libraries will be affected in their partnership ability with schools and social service agencies in addressing community educational and economic problems.

It will be only a matter of time until all libraries will be forced to use resources beyond the traditional printed book and journal. Society as a whole is becoming increasingly computer literate and more visually oriented. Some evidences of this are the increase in electronic bulletin boards (BBs) such as those represented in the FidoNet network, which connects some 100,000 systems, operated mainly avocationally by individual citizens rather than institutions. If one consults local city or county listings of the available BBs, it is probable that for every FidoNet-connected system there are some 20 other systems that operate independently or as part of another smaller BBs network. Since this BBs phenomenon is worldwide, wherever telephone connections exist, the current estimate of such systems is about 10 million. With an estimated 80 million personal computers being used worldwide, this phenomenon will continue to grow. The Internet also is growing worldwide at a fast pace. Some 20 million individual scholars, researchers and other computer users can access Internet resources such as Usenet News Groups, electronic mail, Listservs, Gopher and World-Wide Web (WWW) facilities through their university, governmental or commercial connections. Increasingly, the previously independent online subscription services such as CompuServe, America Online, Prodigy and Delphi are allowing their members some Internet connectivity. To illustrate the growth in these resources, during the period September to November, 1993, there was an increase of over 2000 new Usenet news groups available to Internet users. Some 7800 of these news groups existed at the end of 1993.

The above situation will accelerate the need for having the necessary information technology infrastructure. The mere survival of libraries as societal institutions will depend on how wisely today's library administrators make these budgetary redeployment choices. The key ingredient will be to improve the library's toolkit to build the needed self esteem and perceived worth of the library as compared with other organizations within an institution.

III. SURVIVING BY IMPROVING THE TOOLKIT

As I pointed out previously, our libraries must build their perceived value within the parent institution. This begins with libraries investing in staff training and continuing education, assuming full partnership responsibilities with computer-related departments of their institution and embarking on their own applied research projects to pilot and sell the beneficial aspects of full-scale information technology investments—all obvious ways to improve the skills toolkit of the library's staff.

In the sixties and seventies librarians dreamed of the increase in services they could provide if their union catalogs could be more widely accessed through online computer resources. To make this possible, libraries had to make large investments in retrospective conversion of their manually produced catalog records to machine-readable MARC format records. Such conversions are still continuing. It may be another decade before all U.S. libraries have either fully converted or substantially retrospectively converted their catalogs. However, with the wide variety of conversion services and the shared cataloging benefits that such networks as OCLC provide, coupled with the microcomputer and LAN technology now priced at affordable levels, even the smallest library can use some appropriate information technology coupled with an overall institution strategy for delivering computer- and communications-oriented services.

But one must realize that the retrospective conversion of the library's catalog and other key operational records to computer data is only the tip of the iceberg. The library staff must first have a good grounding in computer and communications technologies that are part of the institution's information technology strategy. The most visible way in which these skills can be demonstrated for building an increase in librarians' perceived worth is to actively mount service programs that have a wide public profile with the clients of the library and the institution as a whole. For example, developing a plan to acquire, stage and deploy a LAN facility in which the library achieves institutional connectivity would be a start. Mounting services such as CD-ROM access on the LAN is a high-profile, wide-information service, much the same as the mounting of a key indexing and abstracting service on the institution's mainframe but at lower operational costs. The institution achieves, at the same time, the necessary connectivity and resources to use the LAN for improving individual staff productivity through deployment of appropriate microcomputer and workstation technologies. If the library and its parent institution are not yet connected to the Internet, the library could take the lead in investigating alternatives for such connectivity and recommending the best approach for the organization. This investigation would take several avenues such as interviewing other organizations that are presently connected, contacting the regional network service provider that serves that geographical location and approaching any university or college sites that are connected. The connection communication alternatives, costs and local connection resources together with the necessary frequently asked question (FAQ) documents would provide a basis for a proposal to institution management for an Internet connection.

Another high-profile information service that could be pilot tested and then put into wide-scale implementation in a staged manner is a document imaging program. These programs have been mounted at some institutions such as Carnegie Mellon's Project Mercury in which a digitized electronic document library is a key facility, linked via several of the commercial abstracting and indexing databases to the electronic image of the work. (1) The Illinois Institute of Technology's Kent College of Law and its Library of International Relations in Chicago are another substantial implementation of this technology, which is making these library collections much more widely accessible. Access to heretofore unreached clients through cooperative usage is demonstrated very well by the Chicago–Kent system. Chicago–Kent began its imaging project in early 1991 in cooperation with the Memex Research Institute of the California State University at Chico and The ExLIBRIS Group. A collection of international statistical documents was the first material they put up on optical media via their LAN. [2–5]

There are costs associated with imaging projects just as there are with the more familiar bibliographic record conversion. Saffady (6) gives imaging project cost data based on a 100,000 bound volume library collection, which can serve as a model to costing smaller and less complex collections of printed items. This cost analysis also figures in the step of photocopying the bound volume pages so as to permit them to be sheet fed into the document scanner since it is difficult to use any other means to deal with bound materials without destroying them. Saffady does show that from a cost basis, imaging projects can be under-taken on a practical basis for collections where wide access is desirable. Bear in mind that copyright permissions must be worked out where copyright laws apply to the works to be scanned.

Another example of using information technology in a broad, visible manner is to develop instructional materials that assist the library users in doing library research in their specialties. These are online visually delivered hypertext- or graphics-implemented courseware systems. They can reach a wider audience in a school or university than formal classroom teaching of these same topics since these programs can be made available to the school's computer laboratories, copied for individual students and faculty or accessed via a LAN facility from any point in the institution or via dial access modem connections. The library client has the convenience of being able to access such teaching materials when it is most convenient rather than fitting a formal classroom session into an already heavily structured day that already typically includes time in the computer laboratory. As more and more colleges and universities mandate that students purchase a microcomputer, more and more instruction and interaction will take place in this manner. Besides building lifelong skills for the workplace, these delivery systems are effective and economical for both student and instructor time. As rising costs to educate students continue to lead to tuition increases, students are being forced to work more hours, even with student loan and scholarship programs available. Therefore, it is critical that alternative forms of educational services delivery be used to make each day a more productive one than would be possible without the use of information technologies.

Those of us who have experienced the information technology changes in writing a paper or book, for example, can document how skill building from the initial technique of putting pen to paper progressed to the typewriter, then to the early IBM mainframe text input systems such as the Wylbur text editor and phototypesetting output programs, next to more elaborate document preparation systems on minicomputers and finally to the present, where one typically uses a microcomputer- or workstation-based program for word processing, spelling and grammar checking, automatic table of contents and index creation. Numerous other program features make possible today the creation of fully finished, complex text and image publications at a much lower cost and with less labor. An author's information technology skill building begins with learning to do basic typing on a Qwerty keyboard. Even if one cannot build one's typing speed to that of a professional typist, use of computer word processing as opposed to typewriting or handwriting certainly boosts one's productivity and can even improve one's writing skills. The most marvelous thing about this evolution to our present technology is the ease with which keyboarding errors can be corrected or style changes effected. I can attest to the validity of these observations, even though I am not a speed freak on the keys.

Another way in which libraries can enhance their perceived societal value is by taking a leadership role in assisting our social agencies as they struggle with today's societal problems. Again, the Chicago–Kent cooperative project with Benito Juarez High School involving Mexican-American students is an example of higher education in a specialized field working with the public school system. In this project, the ExLIBRIS Group has implemented the EXTEND program. Under EXTEND, the imaged library of a public or university library is made available to inner city schools and provides jobs and educational opportunities to students. Goals of EXTEND are to:

1. Provide jobs for inner city youth
2. Provide educational opportunities for minorities
3. Extend library services to the inner city schools without duplicating library collections
4. Convert information into image format so it can be available to all subscribers and participants

Students dial into Chicago–Kent's network to access imaged information such as U.S. reports and law journals. Currently, 12 Juarez students are each employed an average of 9 hours per week converting paper documents to image format. Students are provided jobs and computer skills that translate to skills needed in the job market. Additionally, the Hispanic Law Student Association at Chicago–Kent has a mentoring program with students at Juarez. Other organizations also are involved with this innovative program.

IV. SOLVING REAL-WORLD PROBLEMS WITH INFORMATION TECHNOLOGY

The above example of a special program to deliver information services focuses on education and community involvement through collaborative work with community agencies and organizations. It shows that libraries can be significant agencies for societal change. Motivation to become a significant contributing member of society often is lacking in the inner city environment. The library can be a significant motivating factor if it can reach youth, particularly youth who are not receiving motivation and good role models in the home environment, as they are more likely to drop out to street and gang life and into the maelstrom of crime and violence so prevalent today. One way to do this is to bring the computer to these populations through multimedia programs designed to teach and be fun at the same time. Even basic skills such as reading and value building can be sold under the guise of fun and cool experiences when delivered in community centers or youth drop-in and counseling locations. The library should be a key partner in developing these programs.

Another potentially important information technology tool that could be enlisted in efforts to address societal problems is the FreeNet movement. This began with the establishment of the Cleveland FreeNet by Dr. Tom Grundner at Case Western Reserve University in Cleveland, Ohio. There are now dozens of FreeNet-type systems that have been established worldwide by citizen groups and universities. In many cases the local library community is a significant player. Although the FreeNet initially taps the same market area as the typical electronic bulletin boards, bringing the access points and the needed computer communications skills to the now largely underserved population that cannot afford microcomputers, modems and telephone lines could be quite important in bridging the community services communication gap. Obviously, not all youth or adult underserved populations will be motivated to learn basic computer skills, but this could be a path to helping some part of this population. If Nintendo and Sega can capture the hearts and minds of so many children today, it is but a small step to involving these same young people in the world of learning possible via networked computer resources. Arcade game parlors in the shopping malls could be an extension of potential delivery sites to underserved youth.

In this regard, it is critical that the ideal represented in the Carnegie library be preserved, i.e., that the library is a place of recreation and learning that is freely available to all as a community institution. Despite the trend to increasingly charge for many services in the library, society has to find a way to move with the times and provide a wide range of innovative programs to the community served by that library without forcing the walk-in or remotely served user to pay fees for each service rendered. Otherwise, the gap between the information poor and information rich will continue to increase. Call it society's cost of doing business to provide this wider access to services. Finance it through both tax support as we do our other community agencies and through business community support to increase the pool of qualified workers in the community. Librarians need to be creative and seek involvement with other organizations to develop programs that are mutually supportive.

V. THE FUTURE OF AUTOMATED LIBRARY SYSTEMS

The decade of the nineties has brought a mature spectrum of automated library system solutions to libraries of all sizes and types. While these systems still may not perform every library operation and management task to suit every library, the currently offered systems that have been on the market for the last several years are stable and mature enough to provide wide-ranging current and future support to library operations and a sound underpinning to further electronic services delivery. With the aging of specific hardware platforms and the general trend to more open systems that permit mixed vendor environments to be accommodated, library automation vendors are all attempting to offer newer, more communications-oriented solutions. These are usually based on UNIX System V or another flavor of this popular operating system. With current networking of computer resources on a worldwide basis now dependent on the TCP/IP protocol and the software associated with such networks, it is most common to find that the solutions for local institutions will be to support both a TCP/IP-based network and some popular local area network solution such as Novell Netware 3.12 or 4.0.

A. A New Breed of Information Service

The coming period will see an increase in libraries and their parent institutions mounting numerous electronic text and CD-ROM-based resources. With the cost of smaller RISC-based UNIX server platforms now under $20,000, it is entirely possible for libraries to consider operating their own Internet-accessible servers for their electronic collections. Gopher and/or World-Wide Web server software for UNIX systems rapidly is becoming a common adjunct to the typical automated library system in academic libraries. Although there are limitations to using the technique of Hypertext, the provision of resource guides and data particular to a specific library could be handled using WWW servers. Larger libraries may find that a networked collection of UNIX-based servers will be the way to mount their online catalogs and collection management systems and create links to numerous Internet-accessible online catalogs, Gopher and WWW resources. Increasingly, it may be expected that due to cost considerations CD-ROM as a medium for large databases will be more and more popular than host-based search systems. Writable optical media is getting cheaper and faster as well. Staging CD-ROMs to network server drives for increased performance in a large network is now possible as typically these RISC-based UNIX systems can use 8-GB hard disks. The emerging new SCSI-3 standard calls for 8.4-GB media support. Thus, both RISC and Intel architecture systems will be capable of handling vastly larger databases at increasingly competitive costs. Here is where the real benefit to client/server architecture will make mainframe-hosted systems obsolete for all but possibly a few very large research libraries, where mainframes will act as large network servers and back-up devices for client/server solutions. Even very large libraries will turn to these lower cost platforms for providing some client/server applications such as Gopher and WWW.

Another large area for libraries is developing resources in imaging and multimedia. The living archive can have imaged documents, photographs and perhaps even some full motion video accompanied by appropriate sound bites. While compression techniques have developed to the point of being able to implement these applications, there is still a hurdle for storing numerous minutes of full-motion video on these network systems. The near-term future could change this and thus make possible wider incorporation of full-motion video in electronic information collections. The University of Minnesota Libraries have mounted such a project to develop such an archival system in its Social Welfare History Archive. It is called Project Enlighten.

With cellular telephones and cellular modems, our connectivity options are considerably greater if we are willing to pay the usage rates for these services. Similarly, integrated services digital network (ISDN) connections into businesses and even the home are being pushed by the regional Bell operating companies. ISDN brings video and sound that is digitally based on wide bandwidth into the user's desktop computer equipped with an ISDN connection. Cable companies are also vying for home and office connectivity by deploying fiber optic links that will have added bandwidth to carry more than the traditional cable TV channels. Hooking up to services such as CompuServe, the World or America Online via your cable system provider will be another alternative in a short time.

Numerous library automation vendors are now offering electronic data interchange support with some of the major publication vendors such as Faxon. However, there needs to be much more done to facilitate reliance on total electronic operations for ordering, claiming and invoicing to save libraries further processing costs. Our library users want to have the same speed of service with the same efficiency in handling their questions; their materials acquisition suggestions; and their charging, discharging and renewing of items that they can receive when making hotel reservations, reserving cable pay-per-view TV programs, or booking airline travel.

Some vendors such as Inmagic, Inc., have recently announced enhancements to their products which facilitate storage and retrieval of imaged data in addition to the traditional machine readable ASCII coded data. This will be a mandatory enhancement to automated library systems in the future as libraries increasingly seek to develop remote access to collection resources that require imaged text, photographs or drawings.

Richard M. Dougherty has noted how Harlan Cleveland used the "Twilight of Hierarchy" to convey a sense of the fundamental changes that are reshaping contemporary organizations. (7,8) Dougherty addresses the players and the problems or obstacles to be surmounted in developing new information technology–based systems and services. The global library is being shaped as we speak. Will each of us join in to assure our contribution to this new library future?

B. The Yellow Brick Road to Information

Universities and national libraries, some of whom have existed for more than 400 years, are examples of enduring organizations. Today's equivalent in electronic terms is the melding together of some 20,000 regional networks into the worldwide Internet. Initiatives on the part of the U.S. government and parallel programs in many other countries through their national telecommunications organizations will keep increasing the capacity and clientele connected to the "information superhighway." This is likely to continue to grow for at least the initial decades of the 21st century. In January, 1994, U.S. Vice President Albert Gore became the first elected official in this post to participate in a global electronic conference. This conference was held on CompuServe and involved 900 CompuServe users, who were granted free online time as a public service. The future will bring more electronic communication participation by elected officials at all governmental levels.

The FreeNet movement earlier, in some of its local Public Telecomputing Network affiliate systems, had brought local officials into electronic communication via conferences and electronic mail. More governmental outreach through these systems should be encouraged and will continue to grow as elected officials themselves recognize the importance of and build their computer skills. Usenet has a news group for the White House (alt.dear.whitehouse) in which anyone with Internet access can read and post messages. The Memex Research Institute published its E-Library Program in 1991 which describes its electronic library strategic plan. (9) The previously mentioned Chicago–Kent imaging project is a participant in the Memex E-Library Program.

Hypertext resources are receiving attention as they are a convenient means for the reader to follow particular threads of thought in a text by exploding to lower level hierarchies of explanations or details of a topic or closely related topics. Document markup languages such as those found in the UNIX troff and T_eX programs have been standardized in the Standard Generalized Markup Language (SGML). Hypertext systems have built upon this by being able to read a SGML text file, generate a Hypertext markup and then generate the actual Hypertext database. Rada has described one such system to convert a textbook to Hypertext. (10) This is one example of how further work is making it possible to create more electronic resources that parallel or replace conventional printed works.

While electronic systems may provide a yellow brick road to information, society must ensure that economic means do not result in an "information disadvantaged" societal segment through implementation of cooperative programs with public, school and research libraries.

C. Client/Server Nirvana

Some sage on the Internet likened client/server to teenage sex: everyone talks about it and wants to do it but in actuality few are really doing it. Industry is now in the early stages of implementing the first generation of systems using client/server architecture. Computer systems designers have struggled for years to make application programs more easily used and understood. Cryptic command line interfaces still are present, primarily at the operating system level and certainly in such control files as the .ini files associated with Microsoft Windows. Many UNIX systems, known for their terse commands that pack their power into piping results from one command to another or redirecting input or output, have become easier for the nonprogrammer to use due to adoption of graphical user interfaces such as Motif. Motif and other graphical user interfaces hide the UNIX shell program and provide a point and click manner of performing typical system operations. Microsoft's Windows 3.1 has put an affordable multitasking graphical environment on millions of Intel chip–based desktop computers. Windows for Workgroups v.3.11 has brought peer networking to many users who do not need dedicated server-based networks such as Novell or Banyan Vines. Competing peer networks such as ArtiSoft's LanTastic have popularized this form of networking.

• The next version of Windows is now in the beta stage as the project called "Chicago." This version will incorporate MS-DOS kernel support, peer networking, and some 32-bit application services enabling a successor to Windows and Windows for Workgroups which will not require loading MS-DOS. Microsoft Windows NT, which is a client/server implemented system, promises a uniform operating environment across numerous competing microprocessor platforms. Digital's Alpha AXP, the IBM/Apple/Motorola PowerPC 601 and Intel's Pentium and 80486 are some current microprocessors that will run Windows NT.

Chicago went into beta user site testing in January 1994. One of its features includes support for WIN32S, which will allow 32-bit applications to run on Chicago and Windows NT while still being able to run on Windows 3.1, which is a 16-bit environment. A new graphical user interface incorporates features of the Mac, OS/2 and X-Windows systems. Standard-mode operation has been dropped so that 80286 processors will not be able to run Chicago. WIN32 programs will be able to preemptively multitask. This means that a task can interrupt a lower priority task instead of waiting for the lower priority task to finish. Peer networking support and improved integration with Novell Netware, using Microsoft's Netware redirector and direct IPX protocol support are strong features. Finally, a plug-and-play BIOS will support automatic installation and configuration of new ISA and EISA cards. IBM will likely cooperate in adding plug-and-play for Microchannel architecture cards under Windows. Notebook/laptop systems will automatically reconfigure themselves when removed from their desktop docking stations.

The only serious competitor to Microsoft's vision of the desktop is IBM's OS/2, which is a native-mode 32-bit multitasking system. It will run Windows and MS-DOS programs in addition to OS/2-specific software. Recently, in an attempt to get wider market share, IBM introduced a special version of this system designed to appeal to Windows users. It uses the present Windows system instead of the original IBM Windows emulation. It provides native OS/2 application and MS-DOS services support. IBM has a strong contender for the desktop. However, the main market for OS/2 is to organizations that are developing their own custom client/server applications and in Token Ring network servers running IBM's networking systems. OS/2 is attractive in these settings as it has powerful features for connecting IBM mainframe server programs with desktop clients. Data storage from DB2/2, Oracle 7 or similar systems—with communications support from Communications Manager/2, REMOTE OS or TalkThru—make client/server applications development and operation easier. Even transaction processing from CICS or IMS Client/Server/2 V2 can be used in these implementations.

Another development that will ultimately strengthen software efforts is the move to object-oriented techniques. Microsoft Windows provided object linking and embedding (OLE) and version 2 of this capability is one form of interconnecting data in a dynamic and shared manner among several applications. These features will enhance many applications, particularly those incorporating differing types of data such as text, graphics as bitmapped images and digitized sound. However, the biggest push to the end of the decade will be incorporating object-oriented systems into the foundation of the emerging operating systems. Future application development will depend on these techniques. Object orientation will allow more reuse of program code, lessen its hardware dependence, and make it possible to enhance and evolve software in a more reliable and more bug-free manner. Greater portability of code across hardware platforms will result. The goal is zero-defect programming code that can be reused across numerous applications. One of the significant factors in object development is the alliance between NeXT and SunSoft, which will marry Sun's object technology to NeXT's NeXTStep application environment. NeXT's OpenStep application layer and Interface Builder will become standard features in Sun's Solaris. NeXT will get low-level object development code to incorporate into NeXTStep.

We can expect that the rest of the nineties will bring further consolidations within the computing field. There will be fewer but larger corporate competitors serving libraries, just as there will be fewer but larger computer manufacturers. The surviving companies will be those with large installed customer bases and that can position new systems most rapidly on "rightsized" platforms with escalating functionality. Systems based on server networks using Windows or OS/2 software are going to be the newer architecture applications incorporating new graphical user interfaces. UNIX-based systems also have an edge in client/server applications as strong object development tools and standards such as X-Windows make this an attractive system basis. Posix compliancy among both UNIX vendors and proprietary systems will promote software portability and support of multiple software versions.

All of this progress still will not bring nirvana. Libraries will be required to invest in continually evolving technologies and the personnel infrastructures necessary to their effective operation and utilization. However, while these technologies are increasingly complex in themselves, their incorporation into commercial products should simplify the training and support needs across computing platforms for the long term.

VI. CONCLUSION

This work has provided a historical background to present library uses of information technology and has introduced current library automation systems from microcomputer to mainframe platforms. It has attempted to explain some of the most recent developments and trends shaping library use of these computer- and communication-based systems. The scope of computer applications designed to improve library operations and services continues to broaden. Now, the reader is encouraged to keep actively monitoring systems offered on the market, information technology developments on the wider scene, and tools and technologies appropriate for one's own library services. The yellow brick road of the Internet, current journals and conferences can provide much of this continuing education.

REFERENCES

1. Arms, W. et al. The Design of the Mercury Electronic Library. *EDUCOM Review* *27*(6): 38-41 (1992).
2. *LIR Diplomat*, a Bi-annual newsletter published by the Library of International Relations at Chicago-Kent College of Law, Illinois Institute of Technology. Inaugural issue, spring 1993, p. 2.
3. Bulkeley, William M. Information Age: Libraries Shift from Books to Computers. *Wall Street Journal*, Monday, February 8, 1993.
4. Piatt, Joseph M. Private communication, October 29, 1993.
5. Voges, Mickie A. Private communication, October 29, 1993.
6. Saffady, William. Electronic Document Imaging for Library Applications: An Analysis of Selected Implementation Issues. *Library Computer Systems and Equipment Review 15*(1): 3-61 (January - June, 1993).
7. Dougherty, Richard M. "Nudging a Dinosaur in Order to Avoid Library Extinction." In: *Libraries and Electronic Publishing: Promises and Challenges for the 90's*. Edited by Ahmed H. Helal and Joachim W. Weiss. (14th International Essen Symposium, 14 October - 17 October, 1991. Publications of the Essen University Library No. 14.) Essen: Universitatsbibliothek Essen, 1992, pp. 18-29.
8. Cleveland, Harlan. "Twilight of Hierarchy: Speculations on the Global Information Society." In: *Information Technologies and Social Transformation*. Edited by Bruse R. Guile. Washington, D.C.: National Academy Press, 1985, p. 61.
9. Butler, Brett. The Electronic Library Program: Developing networked Electronic Library Collections. *Library HiTech 9*(2): 21-30 (1991).
10. Rada, Roy. Converting a Textbook to Hypertext. *ACM Transactions on Information Systems 10*(3): 294-315 (July, 1992).

INDEX